INSIGHT GUIDES

GUATEMALA, BELIZE & THE YUCATÁN

Walking Eye App

YOUR FREE DESTINATION CONTENT AND EBOOK AVAILABLE THROUGH THE WALKING EYE APP

Your guide now includes a free eBook and destination content for your chosen destination, all for the same great price as before. Simply download the Walking Eye App from the App Store or Google Play to access your free eBook and destination content.

HOW THE WALKING EYE APP WORKS

Through the Walking Eye App, you can purchase a range of eBooks and destination content. However, when you buy this book, you can download the corresponding eBook and destination content for free. Just see below in the grey panels where to find your free content and then scan the QR code at the bottom of this page.

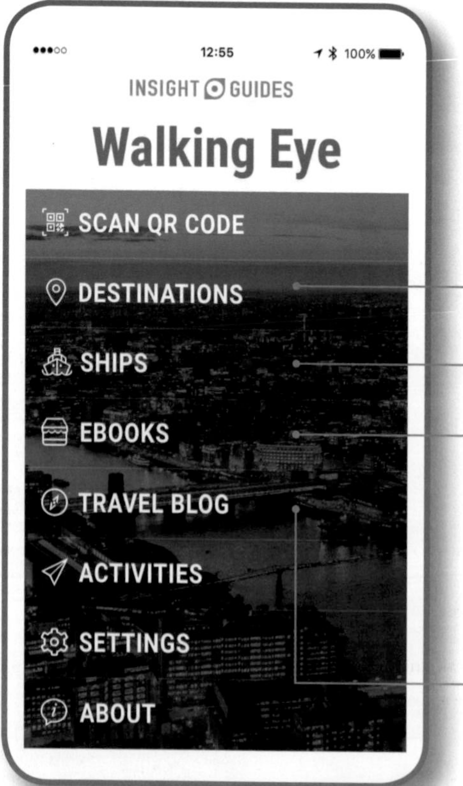

Destinations: Download your corresponding essential destination content from here, featuring recommended sights and attractions, restaurants, hotels and an A–Z of practical information, all for free. Other destinations are available for purchase.

Ships: Interested in ship reviews? Find independent reviews of river and ocean ships in this section, all available for purchase.

eBooks: You can download your free accompanying digital version of this guide here. You will also find a whole range of other eBooks, all available for purchase.

Free access to travel-related blog articles about different destinations, updated on a daily basis.

THE CAYES
BELIZE
PETEN
THE SOUTH
GUATEMALA
THE WESTERN HIGHLANDS
THE EAST
GUATEMALA CITY
ANTIGUA
THE PACIFIC COAST
MEXICO
HONDURAS
EL SALVADOR
PACIFIC OCEAN
SEA
Golfo de Honduras
Belize City
Turneffe Islands
Belmopan
Dangriga
San Ignacio
Xunantunich
Melchor de Mencos
Tikal
Uaxactún
Carmelita
Flores
Petén
Sayaxché
Dolores
Maya Mountains
San Antonio
Punta Gorda
Tenosique de Pino Suarez
Palenque
Tulija
Teapa
Ocosingo
San Cristóbal de Las Casas
Venustiano Carranza
Comitán de Domínguez
Presa de la Angostura
Paso Hondo
Huixtla
Tapachula
Yaxchilán
Bonampak
Usumacinta
Jatatè
Lacantún
Sa del Lacandón
San Pedro
Modesto Méndez
CA13
Barillas
Huehuetenango
Alta Verapaz
Cobán
Cahabón
Sa de Santa Cruz
Izabal
El Estor
Lago de Izabal
El Golfete
Rio Dulce
Puerto Barrios
Morales
Los Amates
CA9
Quiché
Uspantán
Sa de los Cuchumatanes
San Marcos
Sierra Madre
Vol. Tajumulco 4220
Sta Cruz del Quiché
Totonicapán
Salamá
Baja Verapaz
Rio Hondo
Zacapa
El Progreso
Chiquimula
Malacatán
Quezaltenango
Coatepeque
Sololá
Chimaltenango
Lago de Atitlán
Mazatenango
Antigua Guatemala
Guatemala
Jalapa
Tilapa
Retalhuleu
Suchitepéquez
Amatitlán
3766
CA1
CA2
Champerico
Escuintla
Cuilapa
Santa Rosa
Jutiapa
Chalchuapa
Sipacate
Puerto San José
Ahuachapán
Sta Ana
Metapán
Nueva Ocotepeque
Chalatenango
Copán
Sta Rosa de Copán
Puerto Cortés
San Pedro Sula
La Lima
El Progreso
Ulúa
Tela
La Ceiba
Aguán
Saba
Yoro
Comayagua
Marcala
Tegucigalpa
Danlí
Roatán
Islas de la Bahía
Utila

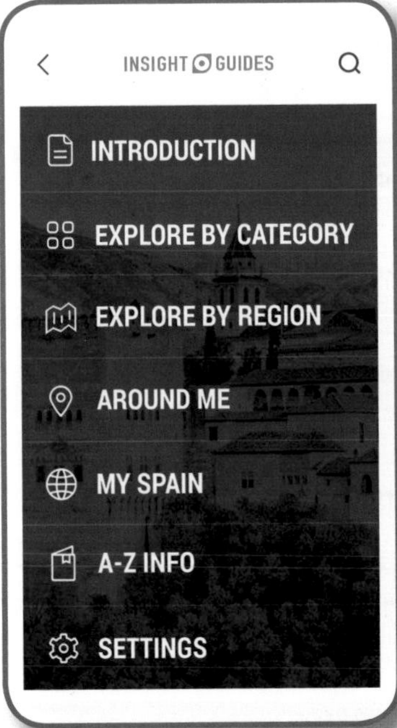

HOW THE DESTINATION CONTENT WORKS

Each destination includes a short introduction, an A–Z of practical information and recommended points of interest, split into 4 different categories:

- Highlights
- Accommodation
- Eating out
- What to do

You can view the location of every point of interest and save it by adding it to your Favourites. In the 'Around Me' section you can view all the points of interest within 5km.

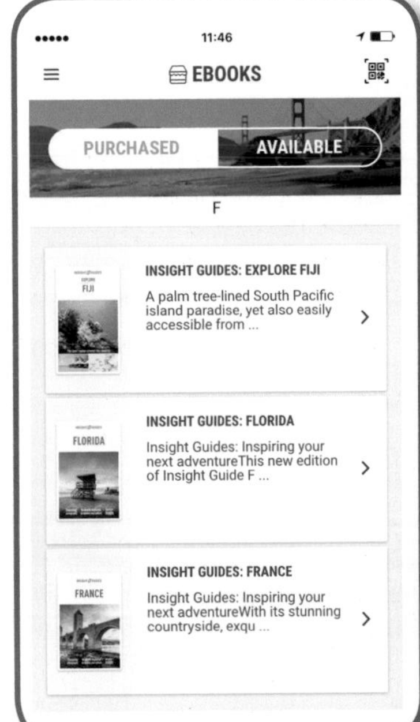

HOW THE EBOOKS WORK

The eBooks are provided in EPUB file format. Please note that you will need an eBook reader installed on your device to open the file. Many devices come with this as standard, but you may still need to install one manually from Google Play.

The eBook content is identical to the content in the printed guide.

HOW TO DOWNLOAD THE WALKING EYE APP

1. Download the Walking Eye App from the App Store or Google Play.
2. Open the app and select the scanning function from the main menu.
3. Scan the QR code on this page – you will then be asked a security question to verify ownership of the book.
4. Once this has been verified, you will see your eBook and destination content in the purchased ebook and destination sections, where you will be able to download them.

Other destination apps and eBooks are available for purchase separately or are free with the purchase of the Insight Guide book.

CONTENTS

Introduction

History & Features

Guatemala

Belize

The Yucatán

Travel Tips

Maps

LEGEND
Insight on
Photo story

THE BEST OF GUATEMALA, BELIZE & THE YUCATÁN: TOP ATTRACTIONS

△ **The Riviera Maya**. Some of the world's finest, softest white-sand beaches provide the setting for Mexico's biggest tourist region. See page 327.

▽ **Chichicastenango Market**. Twice a week, this mountain town holds the region's biggest market. This astonishing bazaar is one of the most vivid, colorful expressions of the Highland Maya way of life. See page 137.

△ **Chichén Itzá**. Declared one of the "New Seven Wonders of the World," this great Maya city is intensely dramatic in style and scale. The Castillo Pyramid is aligned with the sun and stars. See page 320.

△ **Belize's Cultural Mix**. Black Creoles, K'ekchi Maya, German-speaking Mennonites, Garífunas with a mixed Carib and African culture – all get along and give the country a very special feel. See page 188.

△ **Mérida**. Long, white-painted walls and imposing doorways conceal patios full of exuberant tropical plants and flowers in one of the most charming of Mexico's colonial cities. See page 307.

△ **Antigua**. Guatemala's former colonial capital is a gracious city of ornate Baroque churches and rich and colorful traditions. See page 119.

◁ **The Belize Cayes and Reefs**. Miles of lovely sand-and-palm islands line the Belize coast. All around them is a fantastic coral aquarium, in perfect turquoise waters. See page 249.

▽ **Tikal**. Soaring above the jungle canopy, the colossal temple-pyramids of the Maya city seem built to an unearthly scale. See page 170.

▽ **Lake Atitlán**. This exquisite highland lake in a giant caldera (collapsed volcano) is lined by laid-back towns and Maya villages with distinctive customs and shrines. See page 131.

▷ **Cockscomb Basin Wildlife Sanctuary**. One of the best-preserved, most pristine expanses of rainforest in the Americas, Belize's most important reserve is a refuge for jaguars, ocelots, and many species of birds. See page 245.

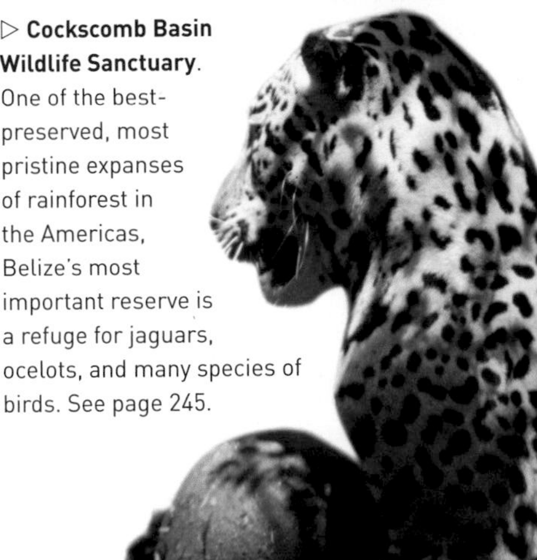

THE BEST OF GUATEMALA, BELIZE & THE YUCATÁN: EDITOR'S CHOICE

Chill out at Ambergris Caye, Belize.

BEST NATURAL WONDERS

Lake Atitlán, Guatemala. An exquisite bowl of blue water in the mountains, ringed by volcanoes. See page 131.

Semuc Champey, Guatemala. One of the most beautiful natural destinations, this series of crystal-clear rock pools and cascades is surrounded by lush forest. See page 158.

Blue Hole, Lighthouse Reef, Belize. One of the most spectacular of many breathtakingly beautiful sights around the Belize reefs, this is a perfectly round hole in the seabed created by a collapsed cavern, which attracts divers from all over the world. See page 254.

Maya Mountains, Belize. When you've had enough of the heat, head to the hills for stunning mountain scenery, a green expanse of pine trees, nature reserves, and waterfalls like Big Rock Falls. See page 241.

The Cozumel Reefs, Yucatán. Marine life abounds in this coral wonderland ranging from small inshore reefs to massive undersea walls and caverns. See page 334.

Sian Ka'an, Yucatán. This vast expanse of forest, mangrove, beach, reef, and silent lagoons provides living space for millions of birds and many rare animals. See page 340.

BEST BEACHES

Ambergris Caye, Belize. Everyone's ideal of a Caribbean island: sand streets, palms, and plenty of hammocks to rent on the beach. See page 250.

Placencia, Belize. A vast stretch of white sands, superb snorkeling in mangrove lagoons, and a village that's the essence of laid-back. See page 245.

Cancún, Yucatán. Every kind of entertainment close to hand, a giant 22km (14-mile) strip of white sand, and turquoise water. See page 327.

Playa del Carmen, Yucatán. The region's hippest beach-party scene, with miles more beach a short walk away. See page 335.

Akumal, Yucatán. Discover the sheer beauty of the curving, palm-lined bays at the "place of the turtles." See page 337.

Tulum, Yucatán. One of the most beautiful tropical beaches you can imagine, with a ruined Maya city above it. See page 338.

Exploring the Sian Ka'an Biosphere Reserve in the Yucatán.

BEST MAYA RUINS

Tikal, Guatemala. Ringed by a wildlife-rich rainforest reserve, this giant city showcases Classic Maya civilization and its extraordinary scale and beauty. See page 168.
Copán, Honduras. Just across the border from Guatemala, Copán's massive sculptures of its kings have a uniquely rich, elaborate style. See page 164.
Caracol, Belize. A colossal Maya city, once the pivotal power during the Classic Maya era, whose crowning architectural achievement is its huge Caana (Sky Palace). See page 242.
Uxmal, Yucatán. The city with the most refined of all Maya architecture, often startlingly modern in its geometry. See page 315.
Calakmul, Yucatán. Once the largest of all the Maya cities, and only extensively excavated in the last 20 years. See page 347.
Palenque, Mexico. The grace and refinement of the temples and palaces at this wonderful site are breathtaking. See page 352.

BEST COLONIAL TOWNS

Antigua, Guatemala. A serene city of churches and colorful fiestas, ringed by three giant volcanoes. See page 119.
Mérida, Yucatán. Yucatán's historic capital maintains a languid charm and unflappable tranquility. See page 307.
San Cristóbal de las Casas, Chiapas. Maya and Spanish traditions are inextricably intertwined in the fascinating capital of the Chiapas Highlands, together with a touch of modern bohemia. See page 355.
Campeche, Yucatán. Its historic centre is wonderfully atmospheric and a Unesco World Heritage Site. See page 349.

The ruins of Copán.

Colored sawdust street carpets are part of the celebrations surrounding Semana Santa (Holy Week).

BEST FIESTAS

Holy Week, Antigua, Guatemala. Several days of spectacular processions through streets carpeted with flowers and intricate patterns of colored sawdust (Mar/Apr).
All Saints' Day, Todos Santos Cucumatán, Guatemala. Crazy, alcohol-fueled horse races and spectacular dances (Nov 1–2).
St George's Caye Day (Sept 10) and Independence Day (Sept 21), Belize. Two celebrations not far apart, so the whole of Belize keeps the party mood going throughout, with loads of Soca, Punta, and other music.
Garífuna Settlement Day, Dangriga, Belize. Masked "John Canoe" dancers go from door to door in a festival that typifies Belize's remarkable ethnic mix (Nov 19).
Carnaval, Yucatán. Mérida, Campeche, and other towns stage their own fun equivalents of the Rio carnival (late Jan–Feb).
Day of the Dead, Yucatán. Families build colorful altars to evoke their dead relatives and celebrate their ongoing contact with the living (Nov 1, but festivities run Oct 31–Nov 2).

Pyramid of Kukulcán, Chichén Itzá, Yucatán.

Market in Chajul in the Ixil region, Guatemala.

Lago de Petén Itzá, Guatemala.

Temple I, Tikal, Guatemala.

THE MAYA WORLD

The magnificent architecture and cultural brilliance of the ancient Maya are attracting a growing tide of visitors.

Textile shop worker, Antigua.

Three thousand years ago, the early Maya were already well established in the region, settling in numbers in the Mirador Basin, as well as along the Pacific coast between Mexico and El Salvador. They concentrated on farming, developing intensive agriculture techniques, and made rudimentary pottery. The first stone civic and religious buildings were erected around 750 BC in the heart of the region at Nakbé, close to the modern borders where Guatemala, Mexico, and Belize meet today.

Gradually these settlements expanded and flourished, and formed a loosely connected network of city-states centered around groups of awesome temple-pyramids, decorated with fine murals and carved stelae. The ruins at Chichén Itzá, Uxmal, Palenque, Copán, Tikal, Calakmul, and El Mirador are some of the most impressive archeological remains in the Americas.

Guatemalan textiles.

MAYA CIVILIZATION

The Maya were the masters, or rather the worshipers, of time. Every day and every daily routine, from the birth of a child to the planting of a crop, had its sacred procedure. Even royal marriages and wars would be planned around propitious dates in the calendar, when the appropriate deity was in ascendance in the heavens.

And then suddenly, sometime around AD 900, the whole Maya civilization collapsed, almost a chain reaction that saw every major city deserted throughout the region. Magnificent temples and palaces were desecrated or were abandoned to the encroaching jungle. The priestly hierarchy fell from grace and the people dispersed. Theories explaining this tragic end are still being offered: drought, invasion, or epidemic disease. Recent studies indicate that over-exploitation of land created an environmental collapse, a theory that has been backed up by strong evidence at Copán in Honduras, one of the best studied of all the Maya sites.

One fallacy should be exposed, however. The Maya as a people did not disappear. More than 6 million still live in Guatemala alone. They are still spread over a similar territory as during the peak of their culture, and many still maintain the same beliefs and traditions as their ancestors. Others, however, have become assimilated into modern society. The Spanish Conquest and subsequent historical upheavals have decimated their numbers and hounded many more into cultural submission.

Market day in Chajul, Ixil region.

The terror returned between the late 1960s and the 1980s in Guatemala, with a vicious civil war between the state and guerrilla armies – one of the bloodiest periods of the region's history. Many thousands of Maya villagers died, and human rights investigators are still working to establish the truth.

PEOPLE AND CULTURES

Latino (ladino) culture dominates the Maya region, and competes with the US for cultural hegemony. Influence from the rest of the Latin world is very evident, especially its music. You will be lambasted with rhythms from all over the continent in the buses, bars, and clubs as merengue tunes from the Dominican Republic, salsa from Colombia, reggaetón from Puerto Rico, and Hispanic hip-hop from California add lyrical joy, sorrow, and social comment to everyday life.

The region's elite is largely of white, European origin and concentrated within a select group of families. Sometimes called *criollos*, this oligarchy retains ties with Spain, but also increasingly with Miami and the US's Latino diaspora.

Happy days in the Yucatán.

Indigenous Maya culture is much less flamboyant, and in traditional villages dancing is something that is reserved for fiestas. The musical soundtrack is above all the hauntingly hypnotic melodies of the xylophone-like marimba.

The third important cultural leverage is from the Caribbean, and in most of the Central American coastal towns the offshore influence is very evident. In Belize thunderous reggae bass lines direct from Jamaica shake the dancehall, while the inimitably reflective wit and harmonies of Trinidadian calypso fill the airwaves.

In southern Belize and on the Caribbean coast of Guatemala, there are several Garífuna communities. The incredible story of the Garífuna, the Afrocaribs who trace their origins back to shipwrecked slave boats, intermarriage with Carib island Indians, wars with Britain, and exile in Roatán and the journey to the Central American mainland, is told on page 247.

There are also small communities of Mennonites, whose fascinating culture originated in the Netherlands in the 16th century. The most significant groups can be found in Belize, where in the past 50 years they have made a tremendous contribution to the agricultural sector.

Climbing El Castillo at Lamanai, Belize.

Member of the Cofradía de San Gaspar, from Chajul in Guatemala's Ixil region.

THE REGION TODAY

The Maya definitely did not disappear; millions live today throughout Central America, in Guatemala, Belize, Mexico, Honduras, and El Salvador.

There's still no definitive explanation for the breakdown of the Classic Maya civilization, roughly between AD 800 and 900. It now seems that it was not caused by cataclysmic natural forces: there was no earthquake, flood, or volcanic eruption that devastated the region. The latest evidence now suggests that a prolonged drought caused harvest failures, almost certainly due to man-made environmental over-exploitation. In turn, widespread hunger may have brought about a class-based uprising against the ruling elite. Some academics even hypothesize that the failure of calendar-based prophesies could have triggered revolt. Whatever the reasons, all the cities in the heartland of the Maya world were all but deserted by AD 909. But the Maya did not disappear.

MAYA AND *LADINOS*

There are around 7 million Maya spread across Guatemala, Mexico, Belize, and Honduras today – about half of the region's total population. These are the survivors, the descendants of the temple builders, the astronomers, the mathematicians, the architects, artists, and artisans, the farmers and soldiers.

As in ancient times, the modern Maya are a far from homogeneous race – they speak some 30 different languages, and worship at Catholic, Protestant, and Evangelical churches. Yet many still also continue Maya religious practices forged over thousands of years, and blend pagan and Western faiths: prayer keepers use the Tzolkin 260-day calendar while celebrating Christianity's holy days. After centuries of cultural attack, ridicule, and humiliation at the hands of the state, this unique fusion of Western and indigenous faiths prevails in most indigenous communities and permeates many more mixed-race minds.

Friendly local in Nebaj, Ixil region.

The other half of the population are *mestizo* (of mixed Maya and European blood), though *mestizo* is a term that you will rarely hear in Central America. In Guatemala and the other Central American states those of mixed blood are usually called *ladinos*. Complicating matters somewhat, a *ladino* is, strictly speaking, someone who is identifiably "Western" in outlook, someone who speaks Spanish, someone who sees themselves as Latin American rather than Native American. There are also *ladinos* who are pure-blood Maya but no longer speak a Mayan language or dress in indigenous style. Generally, most *ladinos* have much more Maya than Spanish blood in their veins, though there are a few *ladinos* who are of pure European ancestry. The ruling elites of the majority of Latin American countries tend to be of European origin.

Maya and *ladinos* may account for 95 percent of the region's inhabitants, but there are other ethnic groups, most obviously in polyglot Belize, a veritable Central American and Caribbean melting pot of peoples, cultures, and tongues.

BELIZE: A COMPLEX ETHNIC MOSAIC

English-speaking Creoles (blacks and mixed black-white) form around a third of Belize's tiny 366,000 population, living mainly in Belize City and the towns. Culturally most Creoles feel much closer to Jamaica and the islands of the British West Indies than the rest of Latin America and listen to reggae, soca, punta, and other Caribbean rhythms. The African-American influence has also grown noticeably: musically, hip-hop and R&B are becoming much more prevalent, and on the sports fields basketball is now more widely played than cricket.

Market day in Chajul, Guatemalan highlands.

The other black Belizeans are the Garífuna (see page 247), a people with an extremely rich history that they trace back to Africa, two shipwrecked slave boats, and the Caribbean islands of St Vincent and Roatán. The Garífuna are sometimes called Black Caribs – ethnically quite accurate as the Garífuna are also descendants of Africans and Carib indians – though the people themselves now prefer the name Garífuna. There are some 22,000 Belizean Garífuna, mainly around Dangriga and in the southern Toledo district, though many more live in Honduras (and the United States). There are also a few Garífuna villages in Nicaragua and Guatemala.

Mestizos now form just over 50 percent of Belize's population, a figure that has increased markedly in the past few decades. Thousands of Central Americans have migrated to Belize from wars elsewhere in Central America and joined an established number of *mestizos*. Most are farmers, and live predominantly in the north of the country and Cayo district. Similarly, a few thousand Q' eqchi' Guatemalan Maya have fled from the civil wars of their homeland to settle in southern Belize close to an established Mopán Maya population. In northern Belize, around Orange Tree Walk, there are a few thousand Yucatec Maya, also found in San Antonio Cayo district; in Botes there are perhaps a few hundred remaining Icaiché Maya. In total, there are around 40,000 Maya in Belize who are becoming integrated into modern life, with many working in the booming tourism industry. Completing the complex Belizean ethnic mosaic are small numbers of Mennonites (see page 197) who arrived there from Mexico in 1958, as well as more recently arrived North Americans, Europeans, Indians (from the Subcontinent), Chinese, and Middle Eastern immigrants.

GUATEMALA'S MANY MAYA GROUPS

Guatemala is far more homogeneous: it is 99.8 percent Maya and *ladino*. There are just 5,000

WAR REFUGEES

The population of Belize was swollen in the 1980s by refugees fleeing from devastating civil wars in neighboring countries, particularly from El Salvador. Although El Salvador has only about 7 million inhabitants, this is over 20 times the number of Belize's population, and the task of absorbing numerous distressed refugees placed considerable pressure on Belize's infrastructure. El Salvador's tragic civil war, which lasted throughout the 1980s, resulted in thousands dead and tens of thousands exiled throughout Central America. Some 4,000 settled in Belize, many becoming squatters and small landowners around Belmopan and other towns.

Garífuna, a tiny number of Creoles, a few thousand European and North American immigrants, and maybe 1,000 Chinese (many of whom live in the eastern highlands). There are also a few dozen indigenous (but non-Maya) Americans called the Xinca. It is the sheer quantity of different Maya groups, however, that gives the country its special character: some 23 languages are spoken, as well as many more dialects.

The Maya mainly live in the western highlands of Guatemala, between the Mexican border and the capital. In these highlands they form some 80 percent of the population, and it is here that Maya customs and traditions remain strongest and continue to defy mainstream Latin American and North American cultural influence. The K'i che' Maya are the most numerous (more than 1 million), the descendants of the warrior Tecún Umán, who was defeated in 1535 by Pedro de Alvarado the conquistador, close to the modern-day town of Quezaltenango. The K'i che' have adapted relatively well to life in modern Guatemala and have a reputation as skillful entrepreneurs and traders. Rigoberta Menchú, the 1992 Nobel Peace Prize winner *(see page* 85*)*, is from a K'i che' family.

West and north of Quezaltenango is Mam Maya country, encompassing some of the highest terrain in the country in the Sierra Madre and Cuchumatanes mountains. The main Mam town is Huehuetenango, and the ancient Mam capital of Zacaleu just outside. Todos Santos Cuchumatán, famous for its horse race and fiesta, is one of the best places to glimpse a traditional Mam village: it now attracts a steady stream of Western travelers. The other most numerous Guatemalan Maya groups are the Kaqchikel, who live between Antigua and Lago de Atitlán; and the Q' eqchi', who live outside the western highlands in a swathe of territory that includes the north coast of Lago de Izabal, much of Alta Verapaz, and southern Petén.

THE MAYA IN MEXICO

Most of Mexico's 1.5 million or so Maya live in the southeastern state of Chiapas and in the Yucatán Peninsula. The Chiapaneco and Yucateco Maya form two distinct communities, each with their own languages and traditions. The vast majority of Chiapas Maya are highlanders, with customs that are very similar to those in Guatemala just over the border (indeed the state was part of Guatemala until the early 19th century). Their rugged, mountainous homeland, with peaks reaching over 3,200 meters (10,500ft), has always been isolated from the rest of Mexico, allowing traditions to survive, particularly around the town of San Cristóbal de las Casas. This is the poorest corner of Mexico, with the highest illiteracy and birth (and also child mortality) rates in the region.

Many villages function at the barest subsistence level: one third of homes do not have running water, and many people do not speak Spanish. The two main tribes here are the Tzeltal, with around 385,000 speakers, and the Tzotzil (405,000); there are also substantial numbers of Ch'ol (220,000) and Zoque (85,000). Over 50 dialects are spoken. Tzeltal men do not generally wear traditional costume but most women still don huipiles. The Tzeltal heartland is northeast and southeast of San Cristóbal de las Casas,

Drumming to the Garífuna punta rock in Dangriga, Belize.

December 21, 2012 marked the end of a Great Cycle (5,125 years) in the Maya Long Count calendar. It was widely believed that it would mark the end of the world – a prophecy that thankfully didn't come true.

though many have now migrated to the lowlands near the Usumacinta River in search of land to farm. Tzotzil Maya primarily live in villages west of San Cristóbal de las Casas, including the deeply traditional Chamula and Zinacantan. They also suffer from a desperate shortage of land, forcing many to turn to handicraft making (you are sure to encounter them selling their wares in the main tourism centers).

Though the Yucatán Peninsula forms the epicenter of the Mexican tourist industry today, as recently as the 1960s it lacked a decent road

Sololá, Guatemala.

connection with the rest of the country, allowing Yucatec customs to endure. Cancún and the so-called Costa Maya now attract all the headlines and tourists, but Yucatec Maya people and culture did not die out with the ruined cities but are spread across the peninsula, and live in settlements close to those of their ancestors (such as Chichén Itzá and Uxmal). As the Yucatán climate is perennially hot, Yucatec women favour long, white, flowing blouses that hang loose over the body, usually embellished with colorful embroidery of flower motifs around the neck. Men do not wear traditional dress. Finally, the traditions and dress of the jungle-dwelling Lacandón Maya are probably closest to that of their ancient ancestors, due to their relative isolation in the Lacandón rainforest of Mexico. You will often see the men around sites like Palenque in knee-length white cotton tunics.

SPANISH REPRESSION AND DISCRIMINATION

It is impossible to analyze the modern Maya world without a brief examination of the historical background of the region. In a nutshell, the arrival of the Spanish was a catastrophe for the Maya. Not only were they outgunned and outmaneuvered by Cortés, Alvarado, and company, but the Spanish also brought a host of diseases to which the Maya had no resistance – around 90 percent of the original population was wiped out in a few decades. The other critical factor was that, at the time of the Spanish arrival, the Maya were divided into disparate, warring tribes; a situation which the Spanish cunningly exploited, forming a series of alliances in order to defeat hostile opponents.

When the governments of Spain and Central America sought to celebrate the 500-year anniversary of Columbus's "discovery" of the Americas, indigenous groups throughout the continent were quick to assert that they had nothing to celebrate, and there were widespread protests. Quezaltenango hosted an alternative quincentenary conference dedicated to the world's indigenous people, which was attended by thousands from all over the globe. There were significant demonstrations in Guatemala City and Sololá. To many onlookers it looked like the beginning of a new Maya activism, encouraged by the success of Rigoberta Menchú after the very dark years of the Central American civil wars had all but stifled democratic opposition.

The inequalities of life in the Maya region are sharply divided on race lines. The statistics make grim reading and are comparable to those of South Africa during the apartheid years. There is a 13-year gap between indigenous and non-indigenous people in terms of life expectancy (the country's average life span is 72). By the Guatemalan government's own estimates, 78 percent of Maya live in poverty and 72 percent are illiterate. In Mexican Chiapas and Yucatán the figures are a little better, but way below the national averages.

Land reform is another very significant issue. In both Mexico and Guatemala, much of the best agricultural land is controlled by a handful of

Bloodletting dates back to the days of the ancient Maya rulers: the king would draw blood from his genitals and other body parts, which was soaked up by bark paper and then ritually burned.

wealthy families and more and more marginal plots are being farmed by desperate *campesinos*, with severe environmental repercussions. Thousands of Maya from remote communities (many barely able to speak Spanish) flee north to the US in search of work. Even in sparsely populated, land-rich Belize there have been angry conflicts between the government and Maya over state-backed logging schemes in the Toledo district.

WINNING CONCESSIONS

Against the odds, and despite continuing discrimination, there are a number of indigenous groups fighting hard and winning concessions for Maya people throughout the region. It is in Guatemala that this is most noticeable. The Indigenous Rights Accord was finally passed in 1995; hundreds of schools have been established so that Maya children can study in their own language, and people again feel free to protest publicly without fear of intimidation.

In Mexico, the Zapatista rebellion has brought the discrimination, racism, and land conflicts present in the troubled state of Chiapas into the public eye, onto television screens and the front pages of major newspapers all over the globe.

POLITICAL APATHY

One of the biggest problems in the region is political apathy and a lack of voter participation; most Maya still feel that voting is something *ladinos* do. Despite the commendable efforts of groups such as the Rigoberta Menchú Foundation to register the indigenous electorate, turnout remains low in Maya areas.

The insular nature of Maya society is one of the main reasons for this lack of political appetite. For hundreds of years, traditions

A watchful local girl in Chichicastenango.

THE COFRADÍAS, OR RELIGIOUS BROTHERHOODS

If you visit Chichicastenango or Sololá on a Sunday morning, look out for a procession of serious, silver emblem-bearing men dressed in their finest *traje* heading for and from Mass. They may be accompanied by musicians and fireworks. The men are *cofrades*, members of a *cofradía* (religious brotherhood), dedicated to a Christian saint. Most Maya towns have a number of *cofradías*. It is a great honor to be a *cofrade*, a social status given only to respected male members of the community, and to be elected as leader is a great honor. Membership involves considerable financial sacrifice, as *cofrades* are expected to contribute significantly toward the village celebrations and annual fiesta arrangements, including the provision of costumes and alcohol. The image of the saint must also be maintained. Outwardly, the *cofradías* may seem integrated within the Catholic Church, but they also perform a crucial function in maintaining ancient Maya religious beliefs – keeping the Tzolkin calendar, venerating Maya "idol saints" and worshiping Tiox Mundo, the earth god. For centuries the Catholic hierarchy accepted these practices, but from the 1950s the Catholic Action movement and Evangelical denominations began to forbid "pagan" worship and upset age-old community traditions. Today many young men choose not to enter *cofradías* because of their Evangelical faith or for financial reasons. In Chiapas the word *cargo* is usually used instead of *cofradía*.

have been maintained in Maya communities by excluding outsiders from village affairs. The power structure in indigenous communities is controlled by the village elders, the *alcalde* (mayor), *cofradías* (religious brotherhoods), *aj q' ijab* (prayer keepers), shamans, teachers, and healers. In larger settlements, the state may have more of an influence. In some towns with large mixed populations (such as Chichicastenango and Sololá) there are two separate municipal councils, one for *ladinos* and another for Maya.

The shrine of Maximón in San Andrés Xecul.

TRADITIONAL JUSTICE

Maya cultural traditions have also been perpetuated through *costumbres,* customs that include a legal system which has survived in rural areas where the state's influence is minimal. In isolated communities, justice is often dispensed according to restitution (confession and compensation) rather than punishment for minor crimes. The inertia and endemic corruption of the state legal system in Mexico and Guatemala, the expense, time, and travel involved, and the fact that court business is conducted in Spanish further discourage the Maya from attempting to use conventional legal procedures. This lack of confidence in the courts is prevalent throughout the Maya world and is a contributory factor in the wave of public lynchings of suspected criminals, in both indigenous and *ladino* areas. Many innocent people have died.

On a more esoteric level, virtually all villages will have *costumbristas,* keepers of Maya customs, including shamans, day keepers and healers. Shamans are specialist practitioners who narrate between the physical and spiritual worlds utilizing crystals, sacrifices, incense, and sometimes taking advantage of natural psychedelics including mushrooms, the white water-lily flower, herbs, and alcohol to achieve a trance-like vision state. This vision quest has been a feature of Maya spirituality since ancient times, and the most famous images are depicted on the stone carvings of Yaxchilán that can now be found in the British Museum in London. On a Yaxchilán door lintel, Lady Xoc practices bloodletting by gruesomely pulling a thorny rope through her tongue, no doubt after consuming copious quantities of hallucinogens. This bloody ritual is guaranteed to stimulate trippy visions in abundance.

DAY KEEPERS

The role of the day keeper or calendar priest *(aj q' ijab)* is to ensure that the Tzolkin 260-day and 365-day solar calender (Haab) are observed correctly. As a *costumbrista* he may combine this with shamanic duties and some fortune-telling. All over the Maya world, especially in the Chiapas and Guatemala highlands, you see shrines on hilltops (such as Pascual Abaj, see page 138), the stone images blackened by candle smoke, the earth littered with incense wrappers, flowers, *aguardiente* bottles, and perhaps feathers from a chicken sacrifice.

At all the main ruins throughout the highlands (including Iximché, K'umarcaah, El Baúl, and Zaculeu) day keepers visit on important dates in the calendar to make an offering, pray to Tiox Mundo and the day lords and perhaps chant the sacred text of the *Popol Vuh*. The most important town in the Maya region for the training of shamans, day keepers, and Maya priests is Momostenango (see page 143), and every Guaxaquib Batz (Maya New Year) hundreds of *costumbristas* descend on Momostenango to celebrate, pray, and burn offerings.

The brightly colored cemetery at Chichicastenango.

The coffee harvest at Las Nubes plantation in Guatemala, 1875.

DECISIVE DATES

THE PRE-HISPANIC ERA

c.10,000 BC
Earliest animal remains: mammoth bones found at Loltún in Yucatán.

c.6000–2000 BC
Early settlers farm maize and beans, make pottery, and probably speak a Proto-Maya language.

c.2000 BC
First evidence of fixed Maya settlements at Nakbé, Cuello, Loltún, Mani, and along the Pacific coast at Ocos.

700 BC
Evidence of large-scale settlement at Kaminaljuyú in Guatemala.

500 BC
Period of first monumental buildings at sites such as Tikal. Influence of the Olmec culture.

300 BC
Izapa-style pottery, and the first hieroglyphs. Nakbé thought to be at its height. Huge temple-building projects commence at El Mirador.

Temple I, Tikal, Guatemala.

Mayan Classic-period censer of a deity holding a human head, Museo Tikal, Guatemala.

100 BC
El Mirador established as the first Maya "superpower"; 70-meter (230ft) temples are completed and fabulous murals of San Bartolo painted.

c. AD 1
Emergence of Teotihuacán in Mexico.

AD 150
Collapse of Preclassic cities, including El Mirador, probably due to environmental breakdown.

250–450
Maya region and much of Mexico influenced, or even dominated, by Teotihuacán.

300
Start of Classic period. First stelae found with exact date in central region: Stela 29 at Tikal, dated AD 292.

426
Yax K'uk Mo' (probably from Teotihuacán) founds dynasty at Copán.

550–695
Rival "superpowers" Tikal and Calakmul fight for dominance in the central region. In AD 695 Tikal avenges a bitter earlier defeat by overrunning Calakmul, and the city never recovers its former glory.

700–800
Peak of Maya Classic period, all through the region: sites such as Uxmal, Kabah, and Chichén Itzá at their height in Yucatán, Palenque in Chiapas. Population in central region reaches an estimated 10 million by 750. Bonampak murals are painted around AD 790 but the site is abandoned soon afterwards.

800–900
Decline of Classic Maya sites, possibly due to overpopulation and drought leading to environmental collapse. The last recorded inscription at Palenque is from AD 799; at Tikal it is AD 869.

1000
Postclassic period, with the emergence of fortified sites in Yucatán region and several competing groups in Guatemala.

1250
The fall of Chichén Itzá and emergence of Mayapán as center of influence in Yucatán. In Guatemala the K'i che', Kaqchikel, and Mam tribes dominate region. Tulum, on eastern seaboard of Yucatán, emerges as important trading center.

Pedro de Alvarado, Spanish conquistador.

1440
Decline of Mayapán, and breakup of Maya groups in Yucatán into small areas of influence.

THE SPANISH CONQUEST

1512
Shipwreck leaves first two Spaniards, Gonzalo Guerrero and Jerónimo de Aguilar, among the Maya of Yucatán. The family Guerrero forms with his Maya wife is the beginning of the mixed race or *mestizaje* of Mexico.

1519
Hernán Cortés arrives on island of Cozumel off Yucatán at the start of the discovery and conquest of Mexico; the first Mass held in the American continent.

1523
Spanish exploration and conquest of Guatemala under Pedro de Alvarado, who defeats the K'i che'.

THE COLONIAL ERA

1527
First Spanish capital of Guatemala founded. Francisco de Montejo begins his conquest of Yucatán.

1541
Pedro de Alvarado dies. Capital of Guatemala is moved to Antigua.

1542
Foundation of Mérida, which becomes the Spanish capital of Yucatán.

1540s
Franciscan friars set out to bring Christianity to Maya. In Yucatán, Bishop Diego de Landa publishes *Relación de las cosas de Yucatán*, an invaluable insight into Maya way of life. But he also persecutes the Maya, and in 1562 organizes huge burning of Maya manuscripts and sculptures.

1576
Report to Spanish crown on ruins of Copán drawn up by Diego García de Palacio.

1600s
First "Baymen" begin to settle near mouth of Belize River and to exploit forests of the region and trade in logwood for dyes.

1638–40
Maya rebellion drives Spanish out of Belize.

1697
Last Maya stronghold in Guatemala falls with conquest of the Itzá on a Lake Petén Itzá island.

1739
First of the Maya manuscripts rediscovered in Vienna and taken to the German city of Dresden, to become known as the Dresden Codex.

1746
Father Antonio de Solis is first European to discover the site of Palenque in Chiapas, Mexico.

1765
A set of regulations, "Burnaby's Code," drawn up as first constitution for what became British Honduras (Belize).

1786
Spanish captain Antonio del Río explores Palenque for Spanish king. When his report is published in English in 1822, with engravings by J.F. de Waldeck, it creates immense interest. Waldeck and others are convinced that the Maya civilization must have come from Europe.

Cortés and Montezuma II at Tenochtitlán, 1519.

INDEPENDENCE MOVEMENTS

1798

The Battle of St George's Caye between British and Spanish naval forces. Defeat of Spanish fleet firmly establishes British rule of Belize region.

1821

Mexico and Central America win independence from Spain. Guatemala, Honduras, Nicaragua, and El Salvador form Central American federation. Yucatán and Chiapas also join federation, but join Mexico in 1823. Garífuna establish first settlement in Dangriga, Belize.

1841

Incidents of Travel in Central America, Chiapas and Yucatán by the explorer John Stephens, illustrated by Frederick Catherwood, begins the era of scientific investigation of the great Maya sites. Maya of Yucatán declare independence from Mexico. A republic is declared, which lasts until 1848.

1847

Guatemala becomes independent republic. War of the Castes erupts in Yucatán, a Maya revolt that simmers for more than 50 years.

Harvesting bananas on a United Fruit Company plantation.

1857

The *Popol Vuh*, the sacred book of the K'i che' Maya, is published in a French translation.

1859

Convention between the UK and Guatemala recognizes the boundaries of British Honduras, but these are subsequently disputed by Guatemala.

1862

British Honduras becomes official British colony.

THE MODERN ERA

1880s

Englishman Alfred Maudslay begins first modern scientific exploration of Maya sites.

1893

Mexico renounces its longstanding claim to territory of British Honduras and signs a peace treaty. Guatemala still claims sovereignty.

1910

Mexican revolution led by Francisco Madero against Porfirio Díaz.

1923

Yucatán governed by revolutionary socialists.

1924

Yucatán's Socialist leader, Governor Felipe Carrillo Puerto, assassinated during a failed military revolt.

1931

Dictator Jorge Ubico president in Guatemala: banana boom led by United Fruit Company. Belize City destroyed by hurricane.

1937

Mexican president Lázaro Cárdenas orders massive land redistribution in Yucatán.

1944–54

Progressive nationalist governments in Guatemala under presidents Arévalo and Jácobo Arbenz. Land reform and attempts to curb power of US-owned banana companies.

1949

A railroad track provides the first overland route linking Mérida to Mexico City.

1954

Che Guevara arrives in Guatemala City, which is a mecca for leftist revolutionaries, many inspired by the Socialist government of Arbenz. A CIA-backed coup in Guatemala leads to overthrow of Arbenz, start of military rule, and civil war.

1970s

A period of prosperity commences for Yucatán as oil is discovered off the Campeche coast, and Cancún is developed for mass tourism.

1973

British Honduras is renamed Belize.

1976

Earthquake in Guatemala leaves 23,000 dead.

1981

Belize gains independence from the UK.

1982

Guatemalan guerrillas form Guatemalan National Revolutionary Unity (URNG). Dictator Ríos Montt intensifies

Holidaying in Belize.

war in countryside: thousands of Maya are killed.

1986
Guatemala returns to civilian government with election of Christian Democrat Vinicio Cerezo.

1991
Guatemala recognizes self-determination of the people of Belize in return for Caribbean coastal waters.

1992
Rigoberta Menchú is awarded the Nobel Prize for Peace.

1994
On January 1, Mexico joins North American Free Trade Agreement with the US and Canada. The same day, Lacandón Maya Indians and the Zapatista National Liberation Army rebel in Chiapas.

1996
Final peace accords signed in Guatemala end more than 30 years of civil war in which about 200,000, mostly Maya, were killed or disappeared.

1998
Hurricane Mitch sweeps Central America.

2000
Mérida celebrates a year as the "Continental Capital of Culture."

2004
Military numbers and budget cut in Guatemala; CAFTA trade agreement approved.

2005
Hurricane Wilma wreaks havoc in Mexico's Yucatán Peninsula; several people are killed.

2008
The social democrat Álvaro Colom is installed as president of Guatemala. Dean Barrow of the UDP is sworn in as Belize's first black prime minister.

2010
Tourist arrivals reach a million per year in Belize, as the country successfully projects itself as an eco-tourism destination.

2011
Mexico's party of the establishment, the PRI, regains control of Mérida.

2012
Ex-military officer Otto Pérez begins Guatemalan presidency with mandate to tackle crime. Festivities held across the Maya world to mark the end of a Great Cycle in the Maya calendar on December 21.

2015
Former comedian Jimmy Morales wins presidential election in Guatemala on promises to tackle corruption.

2016
Guatemala deploys troops along its disputed border with Belize after a Guatemalan teenager is killed.

2017
President Morales expels the head of the UN anti-corruption mission after he backs Guatemalan prosecutors accusing the president of funding irregularities in the 2015 election campaign.

Dean Barrow, winner of Belize's 2008 and 2012 general elections.

Chichén Itzá ruins.

MAYA ROOTS

Human settlement of the Maya region dates back thousands of years, with their cultural origins linked to the mysterious civilization of the Olmecs.

The Maya people settled what are today five different countries in Central America: the Yucatán Peninsula in Mexico, Guatemala, Belize, and parts of Honduras and El Salvador. In total, the Maya occupied territory of more than 300,000 sq km (115,850 sq miles), in very varied natural surroundings. These included the highlands of Guatemala, the dense jungles of Petén, Belize, and Chiapas, and the flat limestone peninsula of the Yucatán. The Maya groups adapted to survive in these varied environments, but shared common beliefs, social structures, languages, and an architecture that clearly define them.

ARCHEOLOGICAL REMAINS

Hunter gatherers are first thought to have arrived in the region around 10,000 BC, and spears and tools dating from 9000 BC have been unearthed in the Guatemalan highlands. By 2000 BC villages were beginning to be established along the Pacific coast. These Pacific coast people seem to have lived primarily on shellfish, fish, and iguanas. Meanwhile, up in the Petén, evidence has recently emerged that villages were in place here by around 1700 BC, and by 1100 BC the first rudimentary ceremonial structures were being built at Nakbé, and the first temples by 750 BC. Gradually more and more Preclassic settlements began to flourish in the northern Petén, above all the giant city of El Mirador. The hub of the first empire in the Americas, El Mirador grew to obtain superpower status by the time of Christ, when its population approached 100,000 – its center crowned by a triadic temple complex that reached over 70 meters (230ft). Outside the northern Petén most Maya still lived as farmers, cultivating maize and other vegetables, living in small family units.

Ceramic recovered from excavations at Tikal, in Museo Tikal, Guatemala.

These ordinary Maya were governed by an elite who enjoyed religious and military power, and who passed the power on in dynasties. They increasingly celebrated that power in vast ceremonial buildings, and in inscriptions and stelae (carved stone monuments) which recalled their deeds as well as depicting their gods. By AD 250–300, what is known as the Classic period of Maya civilization began. This lasted until approximately AD 900, and is the period when most of the great Maya centers were built.

One of the most important early centers was at Kaminaljuyú, close to the modern Guatemala

City. Here, local obsidian was worked into tools and traded all over Maya territory. More than 400 ceremonial mounds have been located at Kaminaljuyú, though these have mostly been lost to urban sprawl.

Tikal (see page 170), the second great city to emerge in Petén, is one of the few Maya centers to have been fully excavated, giving a good idea of how a settlement might have looked some 1,200 years ago. Archeologists estimate a population of perhaps 80,000 in the peak of the Classic period grouped around an imposing ceremonial core of palaces, courtyards, and pyramids, with broad causeways connecting the center to other parts of the city. The temple-pyramids were built on a base of earth and rubble and covered with limestone blocks. At the summit of these pyramids were narrow rooms decorated with plaster and vividly painted with murals, probably reserved for sacred rituals. The whole construction is topped off with a further extension – a roof comb of stone that adds height and solemnity, and was usually covered in brightly painted stucco reliefs.

Replica of the Rosalila Temple in Museo de Escultura, Copán.

THE MAYA CALENDAR

The observation of the heavens, and the calculation of time based on the movement of the stars, the sun, and the moon, was of the utmost importance to the Maya. Many great Maya sites, such as Chichén Itzá, had observatories from where the experts could calculate the calendar, and they proved to be extremely accurate.

Over the centuries, the Maya developed three different calendar systems. The first one consisted of 20 named days, which interlocked like a cogwheel with the numbers 1 to 13, giving a total cycle of 260 days. In some of the more remote Maya villages in Guatemala, this calendar is still remembered, and some elders still tell the meaning and portents of each day. Alongside this system was one more closely based on the sun's movement. In this calendar, there were 18 months – again, each one 20 days long. Then at the end of the year came five days to complete the solar cycle (the extra quarter-day of the annual solar cycle was ignored). These five days were regarded with dread, and only the knowledge and skill of the priests could guarantee that the yearly round would continue as normal. These two calendar systems, one based on 260 days, the other on 365, came back to their starting point every 18,980 days, or 52 years.

In addition an early calendar system, known as the Long Count, was used for historical monuments (though it was little used after AD 250); see box on page 42.

STONE STELAE

In the courtyards in front of the palaces, the Maya placed stelae or free-standing stone columns on which the figure of the ruler who put up the building is shown, with elaborate dating and details of his dynastic position inscribed in hieroglyphic writing.

The other main ceremonial centers, such as Palenque (see page 352), Calakmul, Piedras Negras, Yaxchilán, Copán, Yaxhá, Uxmal, and part of Chichén Itzá were also built during the Classic period. These sites show not only the complexity of the religious beliefs of their inhabitants, but also their fascination with astronomy and time, the strong hierarchy in their society, and their sense of history as reflected in the written inscriptions on the many stelae erected.

View from Temple V, Tikal, Guatemala.

CLASSIC MAYA ARCHITECTURE

The architecture of the Classic period is one of the greatest glories of the Maya. They used earlier ceremonial mounds to construct tall and graceful pyramids, topped off with rooms using the corbel arch. The Maya built intricate observatories such as the one at Chichén Itzá to carry out their studies of the stars, the sun and moon and Venus, on which they based their calendar. Platforms and temples for religious ceremonies were aligned with the movements of the sun and moon. Paved roads or *sacbeob* linked ceremonial centers. And most of the ceremonial sites also had a court for the famous ball game, with stone hoops for the ball to pass through. The ball game itself was a battle between cosmic opposites: sun and moon, night and day, the life-giving gods versus those of the underworld. It has often been said that the losing team was sacrificed after these games, but some archeologists dispute this.

WAR AND SACRIFICE

Although for many years the idea prevailed that the Maya were a peaceful people, interested only in science and art, we now know they were just as warlike as any of the other civilizations of Mesoamerica. In the ever-changing power politics of the time the elite cities formed a network of alliances with minor settlements, contested trade routes, and fought for hegemony in outright warfare, such as Tikal's famous defeat at the hands of Calakmul and Caracol in the battle of 562. Warfare was essential for the capture of prisoners, as the Maya used human sacrifice as a guarantee of cosmic order, to help ensure that nature did not destroy mankind. These sacrifices were used to mark important dates in the Maya

THE MAYA CODICES

In the 16th century, hundreds of these sacred manuscripts were in existence. Today, only four Maya codices have survived.

Detail from the Dresden Codex, kept at the Saxon State Library in Dresden, Germany.

The Maya not only engraved monuments with hieroglyphs depicting their gods and their history; they also wrote and drew about their beliefs on long strips of tree bark or animal hides. These were then folded like a screen to form books or codices. When the Spaniards arrived in the 16th century, hundreds of these sacred books were in existence. Bishop Diego de Landa in Yucatán had an important collection of them, but in 1562 he decided they were all heretical, and so organized a huge burning of his collection of manuscripts.

Because of this and other accidents or deliberate acts of destruction, only four of the ancient Maya codices have survived to our day. Three of them are known after the cities where they can be found: Dresden, Madrid, and Paris. The fourth, which came to light in the 1970s, is named the Grolier Codex after the association of bibliophiles who helped identify it; this is the only one still in Mexico.

These books are thought to have been owned originally by Maya priests, who consulted them to make sure that the proper rituals were carried out on different days of the cycle. These sacred books told the priest which god was to be worshiped when, and what kind of sacrifice or offering was to be made. In this way, the Maya knew when to plant their maize, when it was propitious to go hunting, and when to start out on a new venture.

The Dresden Codex is thought to have arrived in Europe during the reign of Carlos V, that is, early on in the conquest of Mexico. It is a single piece of bark more than 3 meters (10ft) long, covered in white plaster with black, red, and yellow pictures and writing. These show a series of seated gods, human beings, animals, and fish. The celebrated British Mayanist Eric Thompson argued that there were 13 chapters in the codex, showing different calendars, the movements of Venus, a torrent of rain, and other calculations. You can see a copy of this codex in Guatemala City's Museo Popol Vuh.

Almost twice as long as the Dresden Codex, the Madrid Codex has 56 pages, but the drawing and writing are less precise. It also concentrates on key rituals (such as hunting, beekeeping, and trade) and has a section on the rites to be observed during the key period of five days when one year was at its close. Today this codex can be found in the Museo de América in Madrid.

The Paris Codex is especially interesting for its astronomical data. It shows the gods who govern each *katun* or period of 20 years that was important to the Maya.

Located in the National Library of Anthropology and History in Mexico City, the Grolier Codex is not on public display because many experts question its authenticity. Like the Dresden Codex, it is concerned above all with the movements of the planet Venus, which was considered a dangerous influence.

The codices are remarkable works of art. They show a great ability to combine writing with skillfully depicted figures of deities, animals, and other creatures of this world and the complicated pantheon of their deities. Looking at them, it is hard to suppress a strangely pleasing sense of satisfaction that these few remaining examples of a vast and complex library of signs can still resist almost all attempts to decipher them, centuries after they were conceived.

The Maya carefully monitored the movements of Venus as it was linked with success in war. Many stelae record its appearance prompting the decision to attack.

calendar and to glorify victories in battle, with prisoners ritually killed (by decapitation or by the removal of their hearts) to appease the Maya gods and mark the accession of a new ruler.

RELIGION AND RITUAL

Maya rulers were also religious leaders, governing over the masses along with shamans and priests, who were experts on calendrics and ritual. In the tomb of one of these leaders, Pakal at Palenque, he is carrying a jade sphere in one hand and a dart in the other, representing the powers of heaven and earth. On the lid of his sarcophagus is a sculpture of a dragon in the form of a cross. This is the dragon Itzamna, the most powerful god in the Maya pantheon; dozens of other gods were associated with everything from planting corn to sex. Religious ritual was primarily concerned with honoring the correct god on the correct day of the calendar. Preceding an important event, the Maya priests and rulers would fast and remain abstinent. Then a ceremony would take place involving bloodletting (by pricking the tongue, ears, and genitals), the participants under the influence of alcohol and hallucinogenic mushrooms.

A CULTURE IN DECLINE

By the 9th century of our era, there were signs that Maya culture was in decline. Most experts now concur that a long drought was the primary factor, perhaps brought on by forest clearance and overpopulation.

Whatever the reason for this decline, the large centers in Guatemala and Chiapas were abandoned. Other archeologists argue that there was no sudden collapse, but that the hub of Maya culture moved to the northern lowlands of the Yucatán, to the Puuc region, and above all to the great center of Chichén Itzá.

Over a lengthy period of time, an immense and elaborate ceremonial center was built on this site in the north of the Yucatán Peninsula. At its heart was the sacred *cenote* or pool, which was a place of pilgrimage for people throughout the region. Thousands of votive offerings, as well as the remains of human sacrifice, have been discovered in the mud at the bottom of this pool.

Chichén Itzá itself is a hybrid of styles and influences, which suggests that the Maya came into contact with, or had been conquered by, groups from farther north in Mexico. The Toltecs brought in the worship of Kukulcán, a feathered serpent worshiped in other Mexican cultures as Quetzalcoatl. The most important building at Chichén Itzá, the so-called Castillo, is a temple built in his

Looking over the Great Plaza at Copán, Honduras.

PEON POWER

Maya society was highly structured, with strict divisions between the classes. Most numerous were the *peones*, at the bottom of the scale, whose primary role was to work the land intensively to provide food for the community. In addition, they performed regular military service duties. But their most lasting contribution was to provide the labor needed to construct the temples found in the center of every Maya city. These great structures were achieved by human power alone, without the use of wagons or wheelbarrows – the Maya did not have the wheel – and without the aid of any draft animals such as horses, mules, or oxen.

honor, which is clearly in the style of the Toltec Maya. At some point in the 13th century, however, Chichén Itzá was also abandoned, as power shifted at the start of the Postclassic era.

DEFENSIVE STRONGHOLDS

The center of Postclassic Yucatán was Mayapán, a walled city in the west of the Yucatán Peninsula. As many as 12,000 people are thought to have lived in this important trading city, which covered more than 5 sq km (2 sq miles) of land and where up to 2,000 dwellings have been discovered. Although the Itzá did build temples and various other ceremonial buildings, they had lost many of the skills of the Classic Maya. Mayapán appears to have been the defensive redoubt of a warlike group of people who exacted tribute from neighboring tribes.

Another center built during this last phase of the Classic Maya culture was the breathtaking site of Tulum, on the Caribbean coast of the Yucatán Peninsula (see page 338). This too was a defensive stronghold, surrounded by walls on three sides and the ocean on the fourth. Its buildings, paintings, and inscriptions show it to have been a mixture of styles and influences. Its isolated position means that it may have survived into the Spanish era.

In 1441, Mayapán was overrun by its enemies. Mayapán was the last of the major Maya centers; when the Spaniards arrived 150 years later they found the sites deserted, and the Maya of Mexico living in small, dispersed groups.

WARRING LOCAL FACTIONS

The Maya in the Guatemalan highlands underwent a similar fate. Toltecs arrived in the region from farther north in the 13th century. They appear to have overcome the local indigenous Maya, and formed several local empires. The most powerful of these were the K'i che', whose capital was K'umarkaaj. Other groups included the Kaqchikel and the Mam, but these last two were conquered by the Ki che' in the 15th century. But when Quicab, the powerful leader of the K'i che', died in 1475, the other Guatemalan Maya tribes broke away from their rule. As in Mexico, when the Spaniards arrived they found the local tribes at war with each other, and were quick to exploit this enmity to their own advantage.

The Classic Maya held deep religious beliefs. They thought that the gods found their purpose in the creation of mankind, who repaid them for their existence by showing fidelity to them and the rituals the gods demanded. They carved

One of the ruins at Tulum, south of Cozumel in the Yucatán.

stylized representations of their gods on temples and stelae, and wrote about them in the codices (see page 38). They conceived of the world as flat and square (some paintings and codices suggest it was seen as the back of a huge crocodile floating in a pond full of waterlilies), and among their most important gods were the four Bacab who occupied each corner. They were each identified with a color (white for north, yellow for south, red for east, and black for west) and between them held up the heavens, where the other gods lived.

The exact number and attributes of these gods are difficult to ascertain. It seems that each of them had four different aspects, corresponding to the colors of each corner of the world. Then too, they all seem to have had a counterpart of the opposite sex, reflecting the dualism that underlies much of Maya thought. To complicate matters still further, it is thought that the Maya gods had a double in the layers of the dark underworld where, like the sun, all the gods had to pass in order to be reborn.

Mayan God of Fire, National Museum of Anthropology, Mexico.

HEAVENLY HIERARCHY

There were 13 layers in the Maya heaven. In the topmost layer lived Itzamna, the "celestial dragon" or serpent, the male figure who was the god of creation, of agriculture, writing, and the all-important calendar. Itzamna was also identified with the sun, with maize and semen, and with blood. His companion was Ixchel (Rainbow Lady), who was also identified with the moon. All the other gods in the Maya pantheon were the offspring of these two.

Each of the 13 layers was identified with a particular god, among whom were the north star god, the maize god, and the young moon goddess. The benevolent rain gods, or Chacs, were also to be found at the four corners of the earth, together with the Bacabs.

RHYTHM AND RITUAL

Each day had its appropriate ritual according to its place in the 260-day calendar. The most important rites seem to have taken place during the five-day period at the end of one year and the beginning of the next. For the Maya, the cosmos was in constant movement, and only by fulfilling the rituals could they be assured that not only would the land be fertile, but that the sun and moon would continue their course through the heavens.

READING THE MAYA

The Maya ceremonial centers contained many examples of their writing. These beautifully chiseled small pictures or glyphs accompanied the sculptures on temple lintels, and were included in the decoration of the many stelae (stone columns) that were characteristically placed in rows in front of the main buildings.

The meaning of these glyphs was lost by the time the Spanish entered the Maya territory in the 16th century. Attempts to decipher them have been one of the most exciting adventures in Maya studies, and have only recently been truly successful.

The first to try to understand Maya writing was the redoubtable Bishop Diego de Landa, the Franciscan who was in charge of bringing Christianity to the Yucatán in the middle of the 16th century. While on the one hand he was the man responsible for burning most of the Maya manuscripts which he considered heretical, on the other he was genuinely interested in the culture and language of the Maya among whom he lived. He learned their language, and compiled the first dictionary of Mayan and Spanish. He also suggested that the writing in the ancient Maya manuscripts might be closely related to what the Maya around him were speaking.

Francisco de Montejo, founder of Mérida.

Attempts to read ancient Mayan language after him were often hampered by racism and far-fetched notions of antiquity. In the 18th and 19th centuries, there were several attempts to demonstrate that the Mayan language must be derived from an Indo-European one that had somehow been taken across the Atlantic. Just as there have been many fantastic theories to explain the extraordinary buildings of the Maya sites – including visits from outer space – so it was a long time before researchers into Maya writing were free of similarly distorted views that the ancient peoples of Mexico and Guatemala were not capable of producing such an elaborate system unaided.

Toward the end of the 19th century, though, attempts were made in earnest to decipher the Maya inscriptions. The rediscovery of Maya sites by John Lloyd Stephens and in particular the marvelous engravings of buildings and stelae by his companion Frederick Catherwood in the late 1840s paved the way. But it was a French

⊙ THE MAYA LONG COUNT CALENDAR

In addition to their two intermeshing calendars, which completed their full cycle every 52 years, at some point the Maya also developed a system designed for calculating longer historical dates and distinguishing the 52-year cycles from one another. Confusingly, this seems to have been based on a year made up of 360 rather than 365 days, known as a *tun*. The system, called the Long Count, came into use during the Classic Maya period, and is based on the great cycle of 13 *baktuns* – a period of 1,872,000 days, or 5,125 years.

Many of the Maya monuments have the date of their construction written in this Long Count in hieroglyphs. Most archeologists have followed the idea of the British Maya expert Sir Eric Thompson that these dates of the Long Count began from a fixed date far in the past when the Maya thought the world had begun. Thompson calculated that this must have been on August 11, 3114 BC, which in the Maya script was 4 Ahau 8 Cumku. The date written on Classic Maya monuments is meant to show how many days had elapsed between 4 Ahau 8 Cumku and the moment the stela or temple was built.

The last cycle ended on December 21, 2012. Doomsayers and New Agers claimed it would mark the end of the world, though for the Maya it simply meant the end of one great cycle and the beginning of another.

priest, Charles-André Brasseur de Bourbourg, who made the first important breakthrough in reading Maya scripts when he discovered a manuscript of Bishop Diego de Landa's work in a Madrid library.

> *The Maya had no metal tools – they were ignorant of iron and bronze – yet they produced a mass of finely worked gold objects, jade carvings, and pottery.*

CALENDARS AND COUNTING SYSTEMS

This manuscript helped de Bourbourg to decipher some of the Maya calendar, and to work out Maya numerals, based on a dot for the numbers one to four, a bar for the number five, and an adapted conch shell for the all-important zero. However, he too was convinced that the Maya had not developed these ideas all alone – his pet theory was that their writing "proved" they were the lost civilization of Atlantis.

Dominican missionaries baptize the Maya, as part of the Spaniards' campaign to win Maya hearts as well as their lands.

Englishman Alfred P. Maudslay made further forays into Maya territory at the end of the 19th century, and brought back plaster casts and accurate drawings of the hieroglyphs. These were studied by perhaps the most influential of all the Mayanists, Eric Thompson. His great contribution was in working out the extraordinarily complex calendar systems employed by the Classic Maya. At the same time, he was dismissive of the idea that many of the hieroglyphs could be related to other things, and might be phonetic rather than just pictures – that they might represent the sounds of the Mayan language as it was spoken and not just be commonly recognized pictorial shorthand.

SYMBOLS AS SOUNDS

The counter-argument – that the inscriptions on Maya buildings could be read and pronounced in a similar way to other early languages – was put forward in the late 1940s by Russian scholars Tatiana Prouskouriakoff and Yuri Knosorov. They reinterpreted Bishop de Landa's observations, and offered a method to understand the grammar and phonetic construction of the language.

It was the Russians' approach which has proved more fruitful, and in subsequent years it was revealed that the inscriptions, rather than being wholly concerned with astronomy or religion, were a description of the history of the royal families who were commemorated in the buildings.

It is now plain that many of the glyphs found on Maya monuments represent phonetic syllables. One example is the word for *cacao* (chocolate), which was of great symbolic importance for the Maya.

THE SPANISH ERA

The first Spanish expedition to land in the Maya world was led by Francisco Hernández de Córdoba in 1517. Hernán Cortés followed two years later. He landed on the island of Cozumel, where the first Christian Mass was said on the American continent.

Pedro de Alvarado (1485–1541), scourge of the Maya in Guatemala.

One of Cortés's lieutenants, Francisco de Montejo, returned to the Yucatán in 1527 to extend Spanish rule to the Maya living there. At first he was unsuccessful, both on the Caribbean coast near Campeche and on the Atlantic side. It was Montejo's son and nephew who in 1540 began a second conquest of the Yucatán, and this time the Spaniards succeeded in establishing their rule. In 1542 they founded the city of Mérida, and as in Mexico City, built the new cathedral directly on top of the ruins of a Maya temple.

SYSTEMATIC REPRESSION

From their base in newly established towns, the Spaniards spread their control in several ways. They defeated and killed the leaders of the Maya. They took their lands, and forced the Maya to work for them. They imposed their own system of local government and set up their own authorities. They forbade the native religions, and brought in Franciscan friars to spread the Christian message throughout the peninsula. The Europeans also carried with them diseases such as measles and smallpox to which the Maya had no resistance, leading to more deaths and greater demoralization. Even so, the Maya of Yucatán and Chiapas never accepted Spanish rule entirely, and rose against it on many occasions.

LEGENDARY FEROCITY

The Spanish conquest of the Maya in Guatemala was entrusted to Pedro de Alvarado. He achieved it with a ferocity that became legendary. In 1523, he and some 800 men defeated the main army of the K'i che' and slew their leader, Tecún Umán. Alvarado then advanced on the K'i che' capital, K'umarkaaj, and burned it down. He was equally ruthless with the Kaqchikel, and set about conquering the many mountain tribes. In 1527, Alvarado founded the first Spanish capital of Guatemala at Santiago de los Caballeros, close to the modern-day city of Antigua.

Resistance to Alvarado's rule continued through the 1530s, especially in the highlands of Verapaz, where in the end it was Christian missionaries led by Fray Bartolomé de las Casas who managed to get the Maya to accept Christianity and Spanish rule. By the time of Alvarado's death in 1541, almost the entire Maya population of Guatemala was under Spanish control. As in Mexico, however, this did not mean a complete end to resistance, and it was more than a century and a half later, in 1697, that the last descendants of the independent Maya kingdoms, who lived in Tayasal, an island on Lake Petén Itzá in northern Guatemala, were finally subdued.

LIFE UNDER SPANISH RULE

By the mid-16th century, the original Spanish conquistadors had died, and Spanish rule was directed more impersonally from Spain and from the capital of the viceroyalty in Mexico City. The Yucatán and Guatemala (from where Honduras and Chiapas were governed) were far from these centers, and this distance on the one hand led to greater abuses, but on the other protected the Maya way of life, as it was never entirely dominated by the newcomers.

Among the first measures taken by the Spanish administration was the concentration of the native population in villages and towns, known as *reducciones*. Each of these was laid out in the Spanish style, with a central square where the Catholic church and the town hall or *ayuntamiento* were situated. The local population was brought into these new villages for several reasons. It was easier for the Spaniards to control them, and to make sure they paid their taxes. They were on hand for the communal work demanded of them, while at the same time it facilitated the missionaries' work of evangelization. In this way, the Maya were forced to become part of Spanish colonial society – which, in a very racist way, always regarded them as the lowest element in that society.

As the Spaniards developed agriculture and their estates or *haciendas* extended throughout the region, they also forced the Maya to work there – and in Guatemala, for example, began the wholesale transfer of laborers from the highlands down to the plantations on the Pacific coast.

SKILLFUL ADAPTATION

Although some Maya were given posts of minor authority in the new Spanish villages, there was little chance of them wielding any real power. Instead, they continued their traditional practices and communal organization in parallel with the Spanish system.

Authority in the more remote villages continued to be held by the *principales* or village elders. Communal efforts were organized among Maya *cofradías* or brotherhoods, who used their role as keepers of the local saints to run self-help schemes, joint work on the *milpas* (maize fields), or even land transfers among villagers. Together with this, the colonial Maya were skillful at adapting the Christian religion to their own beliefs, continuing to worship the old gods in the guise of the Christian pantheon.

BOURBON INFLUENCE

For more than two centuries after the Spanish Conquest, these efforts and the isolation of much of the Maya world from the centers of Spanish interest helped to protect the Maya from the worst ravages found elsewhere in the empire. The Maya's position worsened considerably during the second half of the 18th century, however, when the Bourbon monarchy in Spain attempted to regain effective control of its rebellious colonies. The provinces were subdivided and reorganized into *intendencias* and *partidos,* and indigenous officials were removed from office and replaced by Spaniards or *criollos.*

At the same time, an effort was made to redistribute land and to make the *haciendas* more productive. The profitable new crops of sisal,

A 16th-century lithograph of Pedro de Alvarado attacking the Kaqchikel in Guatemala.

tobacco, sugar cane, and cotton demanded more land, which was seized from communal Maya holdings. Increasingly, the Maya were employed as laborers on these estates, often in conditions of near-slavery.

When the struggle for independence began in Spanish America during the first decades of the 19th century, the Maya were still regarded as the lowest sector of society. Their customs and beliefs were largely ignored, if not despised. By this time they had very little idea of their ancestors' glorious achievements, and yet many elements of their distinctive culture – language, dress, social habits, and structures – had managed to survive against the odds.

UNCOVERING THE MAYA PAST

The Maya region is currently perhaps the globe's hottest archeological area, and a series of recent discoveries has led to a total rethink about the early Maya.

Dr Richard Hansen and his team at El Mirador have rewritten Preclassic history, proving that the great city of the Kaan dynasty was a superpower of its day, controlling vast swathes of the Petén, flourishing alongside and ultimately overpowering the Olmecs. A stunning stucco panel at Mirador of the fabled hero twins, created around 200 BC, has proved a pivotal link between the Preclassic Maya and the Popul Vuh, the Maya creation myth. Other discoveries include a ball court dating back to 500 BC unearthed at Nakbé and even a complete "lost city" – Wakná, located near El Mirador. Academics are now able to read Maya glyphs far more accurately, revealing the names of the rulers, their family lineages, and the key political alliances of the era. It is now clear that bloodletting and human sacrifice were pivotal to the Maya religion, governing ceremonies and used in all aspects of life, from planning agriculture to warfare.

The magnificent carved stelae at Copán in Honduras are considered the finest in the Maya world. Stelae A, above, can now be seen in the Museo de Escultura at Copán.

A reproduction of the colorful Rosalila Temple, found under Temple 16 at Copán. This true-scale replica is in the Museo de Escultura, Copán.

ARCHEOLOGISTS VERSUS LOOTERS

Today the texts written on tombs' interior walls help unlock Maya secrets, yet these texts are all too often destroyed by looters foraging for artifacts for the lucrative, illegal pre-Columbian art trade. Regional governments and archeologists are racing against time to find and protect important undiscovered sites. Today, scientists are turning to airborne sensors operated from aircraft and satellites. Landsat, a satellite that delineates natural and large, man-made features, helped uncover the astonishing murals at San Bartolo, Guatemala, and Wakná deep in the Petén forest.

A huge cache of finely worked jade pieces was found at Altun Há, a major Maya site in northern Belize.

The vivid 19th-century drawings of Maya ruins by Frederick Catherwood captured the world's imagination.

Archeological Expeditions

The birth of modern Maya archeology traces its popular origin to the epic expeditions, between 1839 and 1842, of adventurers John L. Stephens and Frederick Catherwood. Their discovery of immense ruined cities among the tropical jungles of Mesoamerica caught the imagination of the academic world.

Catherwood's beautiful lithographs of the ruins of Chichén Itzá, Uxmal, Palenque, and Copán were widely published in Europe and North America. The intrepid explorers' tales of discovery were hailed as the greatest of the century.

Some 80 years later, archeologists such as Thompson, Morley, Tozzer, Joyce, and Maler led expeditions to the jungles of Central America to try to unlock the mystery of the Maya civilization.

But it was only in the 1970s, with the help of modern technology, that archeologists began to decipher more than dates and numerals. Today, archeologists concentrating on minor sites, such as La Blanca in Guatemala, have revealed convincing evidence that suggests the late Classic Maya rulers may have suffered a revolt at the hands of their own people, possibly due to failing harvests and drought, as the masses lost faith in the divine influence of their rulers.

Detail on Stela 32 from the Tikal ruins, held in Museo Tikal near the ruins in Petén, Guatemala.

The natural blanket of the jungle helped to preserve the Tikal ruins for the first explorers.

Stela P stands in front of Temple 16 at Copán and was constructed when the Rosalila Temple (now underneath Temple 16) was still being used.

Although vegetarians will find their diet somewhat restricted if traveling outside tourist areas, a huge array of fruit and vegetables can be found at markets.

REGIONAL CUISINE

Corn-based *tortillas* and *tamales*, rice 'n' beans, tropical fruits, nuclear-strength *aguardiente*, and fresh seafood are the specialties of the region.

In Maya mythology, the gods created man from maize, after earlier unsuccessful attempts with clay and wood. Even today, corn retains a semi-sacred status throughout the Maya region for many indigenous people, and is certainly regarded as more than just another staple crop. In the more traditional Maya areas, it is considered morally wrong to throw away uneaten corn, and children are taught to finish every last scrap on their plates.

THE FIRST FOODS

Some 10,000 years ago, hunter gatherers began successfully to domesticate corn – a seminal development that enabled the first Americans to settle and farm, and much later enabled the Maya civilization to flourish. The Preclassic and Classic Maya diet was very similar to their modern range of foodstuffs, with corn *(maíz)*, beans *(frijoles)*, squash *(calabaza)*, and chili eaten most mealtimes.

Corn or maize is most often eaten in the form of a *tortilla*, a thin, circular pancake made from corn dough, either shaped by hand (in Guatemala) or by a machine press (the usual method in Mexico) and then toasted on a metal tray *(comal)* over a fire. In rural Guatemala, the first noise of the day (along with the inevitable rooster) is the pat-pat sound of the making and shaping of *tortillas* by the village women, long before the sun has risen.

Tortillas are eaten as an accompaniment to virtually every meal in Guatemala. They are best served while still warm – often wrapped inside a cotton cloth. Fresh, warm *tortillas* are delicious, often combining a wonderful smoky flavor from the wood fire and a dense but pliable texture. If you are served tough, dry *tortillas*, send them back, just as Guatemalans do.

In Mexico, the *tortilla* is also used as the basis of a number of delicious dishes that are now familiar all over the world. *Enchiladas* are *tortillas* stuffed with mince or cheese; *quesadillas* are *tortillas* covered with melted cheese; *tacos* are fried, filled *tortillas*, and *tostadas* are crispy, deep-fried *tortillas* served with salad. Other variants include *flautas*, *chimichangas*, and *tlacoyos*.

Tequila-flamed shrimp stacks in Belize.

Tortillas aside, the other way maize is consumed is in the form of a *tamal*: maize dough stuffed with a little meat or a sweet filling and steamed in a corn husk or a banana leaf. In Guatemala, a mini *tamal (chuchito)* is a popular street snack and considerably more traditional than other fast foods; it is known that *tamales* were prepared and cooked in an almost identical fashion by the ancient Maya. In Belize, eating habits are more divided on ethnic lines, with *ladinos* and Maya eating tortillas, *tamales*, and *tacos*, while Creoles prefer beans cooked with rice, seasoning, and coconut oil – a dish they call "rice 'n' beans" – or served separately with meat, fish or seafood.

In fact, after maize, beans *(frijoles)* are the second fundamental ingredient in the regional diet, and were also cultivated by the ancient Maya. They are the most important protein source for the vast majority of people, for whom meat is a luxury. *Frijoles* are often grown in maize fields as companion plants; the bean plant winds itself around the corn stalk and is harvested a little later in the season.

Salbutes are tortillas loaded with lettuce, red onion, tomato, and lime juice.

Black beans are the most popular variety, but red pinto (literally "painted") beans are also eaten. Black beans are usually served whole *(volteados)* in a little brine, often with some onion or garlic added. Pinto beans are prepared *refritos* (refried). The beans are boiled, then mashed and fried in a pan; sometimes a little cream is added to the bean pulp, and occasionally a little chopped *chorizo* (spicy sausage) is mixed in for flavor. You will find that wherever you are in the Maya world, and whatever time of day it is, mealtimes usually include a portion of *frijoles* – in some shape or form.

> *Tamales are usually cooked by the dozen, so it is common for families to sell a few they have spare – a red lantern outside a home indicates they have fresh tamales for sale.*

VEGETABLES AND FRUIT

Historically, squash *(calabaza)* has always been one of the most frequently cultivated vegetables, and it remains very popular today as it grows well in the cornfield *(milpas)* after the maize and beans have been harvested. Chilies *(see box)* are very popular and used as an accompaniment to most meals.

A great variety of other vegetables is also grown: carrots, peppers, onions, and greens including cabbage, spinach, green beans, and broccoli (which is mainly exported to North America). And the region's extensive microclimates support the cultivation of almost every conceivable variety of fruit.

Bananas are everywhere, but avocados, tomatoes, blueberries, raspberries, apples, oranges, limes, papayas, and mangoes also feature. The creamy pink flesh of the zapote fruit, for example, is amazing. Fruit is often consumed as part of a shake or *licuado*.

PROTEIN ON THE MENU

Historically, turkey, wild pig, and iguana were all eaten, but except in jungle areas, you will find that these days chicken, pork, and beef are the meats specified on most menus, either grilled, fried, or

CHILIES

Native to the region, chilies form an integral part of the diet in the Maya World – over 100 varieties are eaten. Chili is commonly served in a salsa sauce that you will find at every dinner table. In Guatemala this salsa is often just called *picante* (spice) and can be from a bottle or freshly made. In Mexico the art of salsa-making is taken very seriously, and every establishment will produce a bottle or two of homemade salsa; reputations live or die by it. Belizean diners also invariably keep a bottle or two of hot, chili-based sauce on standby. The main Belizean brand is Marie Sharp, which comes in several spice levels (from "Mild" to "Beware"), and is made from a hybrid of Scotch bonnet and Jamaican varieties.

in a stew. Eggs (*huevos*) are very commonly eaten for protein and prepared in many different styles: *rancheros* (fried and served on a tortilla with salsa topping), *a la Mexicana* (scrambled with tomato, onion, and chili), or *motuleños* (fried with refried black beans and topped with cheese).

You will find plentiful fish and seafood served near the coast. Snapper, grouper, barracuda, and shark are all popular, while lobster is on many upmarket restaurant menus, as well as shrimp, crab, and conch; ceviche (raw seafood marinated in lime juice) is a favorite in many areas.

THE TOURIST'S CHOICE

You will find the most varied and sophisticated cuisine in Mexico. In Belize, there's some superb and inexpensive seafood available on the coast and *cayes*, but away from the top hotels, inland menus usually only offer a limited choice. In Guatemala there is a two-tier structure in evidence, which effectively means that the more adventurous traveler must forgo culinary pleasures.

Any establishment that calls itself a "restaurant" has upmarket pretensions; it may sell wine, and the menu is usually reasonably varied

Tray laden with ceviche in Monterrico, Guatemala.

EATING OUT WITHOUT MEAT

Traveling as a vegetarian *(vegetariano)* in the Maya region can be a frustrating experience, and dining out is rarely a real pleasure. But there are worse places in the world to eat a meat-free diet.

In the major towns geared towards tourism, places like Panajachel, San Cristóbal de las Casas and Antigua, plenty of itinerant veggies have trodden the trail before, and waiters and restaurateurs are fairly familiar with the concept. In these places most menus offer plenty of choice. And as foreigners have settled and opened their own restaurants, so you will find good meat-free European, American, Asian, and wholefood dishes offering a change from the sometimes predictable vegetarian options in traditional Central American establishments. Chinese restaurants are also a good option for vegetarian meals. But be careful, as soup may be made with meat stock.

Off the beaten track, the main problem is simply that few locals will understand the principle that some people choose not to eat meat, and no matter how many times you try to tell them, "I don't eat meat" *(No como carne)*, it seems to find its way onto your plate somehow. Seasoned travelers find that explaining it as a religious issue *(es mi religión)*, even if inaccurate, is the simplest and most effective way to get the point across. Luckily, there are always eggs, beans, and *tortillas*, and plenty of nuts and fruit in the market.

and prices a bit higher than in other places that will provide you with a meal. A *comedor*, by contrast, is the local equivalent of an American diner – a basic line-up of popular local dishes, nothing fancy, served up quickly and priced cheaply. There are plenty of fascinating street snacks as well, but hygiene standards can be dubious, so take care. In Guatemala and Honduras popular street snacks include *pupusas* and *baleadas*, which are corn *tortillas* served with dry cheese, refried beans, and chopped salad. In Mexico the humble *taco* is a ubiquitous, if often greasy, stomach-filler that consists of a small *tortilla* folded around a filling. You will also find most of the big American fast-food outlets, plus home-grown equivalents like Pollo Campero, which sells fried chicken.

Bohemia beer, brewed in Mexico.

LIQUID REFRESHMENT

Stick to bottled water, which is cheap and widely available. Many locals drink *refresco* with their lunch or dinner, which is iced water with a little lime, *rosa de jamaica* (hibiscus), orange, or tamarind juice added. It's very refreshing, but check that it has been made with purified water. The usual international brands of fizzy drinks are all readily available; confusingly, however, all are known as *aguas* in Guatemala.

> *In the highlands of Guatemala and Chiapas you'll regularly encounter chicha, a local moonshine that's flavored with a myriad of fruits including cherry, plum, apple, sugar cane, and apricot.*

A little more exciting is a *licuado*, which is a water- or milk-based fresh fruit shake. You will see specialist vendors chopping and blending fruit for *licuados* at markets and bus stations all over the region, except in Belize. Fresh fruit juices *(jugos)* are less commonly available. Orange juice *(jugo de naranja)* is the one most likely to be on offer, often consumed by local people with a raw egg.

In the popular tourist towns you are sure to be able to find good coffee *(café)*, and as the region has superb growing conditions, arabica bean aficionados will encounter many aromatic blends. However, once you venture off the beaten path you must prepare yourself for instant coffee or a watery, banal blend of inferior beans.

Tea *(té)* is quite popular in Belize, thanks to the British influence, but is rarely on offer elsewhere – except camomile tea *(té de manzanilla)*, which is commonly served in Guatemala and Mexico. Cacao beans were used to make a sacred chocolate drink in ancient times, and were so highly prized that they were used as a unit of currency. Today cocoa drinks are rare, but bitter chocolate forms the basis of several *salsas* in Mexican cuisine.

ALCOHOLIC DRINKS

Beer *(cerveza)* is best and cheapest in Mexico, where there are many excellent local and national brands. Lager-style brews include Sol, Bohémia, Victoria, and Dos Equis, and darker beers include Negra Modelo and Bohémia Obscura. In Guatemala the bland Gallo brand is everywhere, though there are also Brahma, Cabro, and the dark Moza. Belizean beer is quite pricey; the Beliken brand is popular, and the company brews four different beers, including a stout.

Rum *(ron)* is the most widely available liquor: look out for the Guatemalan brand Ron Centenario Zacapa, which is one of the world's finest. In Mexico tequila is, of course, the national drink, though artisan-produced *mescal* is gaining in popularity. Any liquor labeled *añejo* (aged) is worth paying a little more for. And if you are feeling brave, try one of the local firewaters, known as *aguardiente* or *chicha*.

Todos Santos Cuchumatán is home to small-scale bakery and weaving co-operatives.

St Herman's Blue Hole National Park, Belize.

OUTDOOR ADVENTURE

Options include trekking in Belizean rainforest, climbing an active volcano in Guatemala, diving on the spectacular coral reef, or white-water rafting down the Río Usumacinta.

With more than 30 volcanoes, 4,000-meter (13,000ft) high mountains, Pacific and Caribbean coastlines, huge swathes of virtually untouched rainforest, subtropical moist forest, vast savannas, wetlands, intriguing limestone cave complexes, and the world's second-largest barrier reef just offshore, the Maya region's wealth of exciting natural settings makes it a paradise for hikers, scuba-divers, cavers, or anyone with a sense of adventure.

Hiking on Volcán Pacaya, Guatemala.

HIGHLAND HIKING

The Maya region offers some of the finest walking – jungle, mountain, and coastal hikes – in the world. In Guatemala the spectacular highland scenery is the main attraction: it is a spellbindingly dramatic landscape of lofty peaks, verdant river valleys, thick pine forests, traditional adobe villages, and huge whitewashed colonial churches. Villages are linked by a web of well-maintained trails, paths, and dirt tracks that the locals use to get to the market or to distant cornfields, making hiking a real pleasure. There are simple accommodations in *hospedajes*, and *comedores* in most of the larger villages serve inexpensive local food.

There are many superb trails through epic Cuchumatán mountain scenery, but two of the best routes are the six-hour hike from Todos Santos Cuchumatán to the equally traditional Mam Maya village of San Juan Atitán and trek up La Torre (3,837 meters/12,589ft), the highest non-volcanic peak in Guatemala.

The countryside around the Ixil Triangle villages of Nebaj, Chajul, and Cotzal is equally rewarding to hike across, with breathtaking, craggy mountaintops, vast, grassy valleys interspersed with farmhouses, cornfields, and fast-flowing streams. If you trek to the village of Acul from Nebaj, you can return via an Italian-Guatemalan *finca*, which sells some of the finest cheese in the country (and also has guest rooms). Contact guides at Trekking Ixil in Nebaj, where daily rates are very reasonable.

Lake Atitlán, a mandatory destination for every visitor to Guatemala, is also world-class trekking country (see page 131). An idyllic network of trails snakes around the steep banks and volcanic slopes of the lake, connecting all the 13 shoreside settlements, past patchwork cornfields and vegetable gardens. Sadly, as there have been incidents of walkers being robbed, it is best to take a local guide with you; Pedro Solis based in Santa Cruz La Laguna is recommended, or there are several agencies in San Pedro La Laguna. If you only want to walk one section of the lake, then the five-hour trail between Santa Cruz La Laguna and San Pedro La Laguna is especially picturesque, as it passes through some of the least populated parts of the lakeshore, the path clinging to the edge of the caldera at times.

WILDLIFE AND RUINS

Moving up from Guatemala, the Maya mountains of Belize offer more spectacular walking.

Climbing up the pyramid Nohoch Mul at Cobá, in the Yucatán.

Here the altitude is lower, and the subtropical vegetation much denser, with thick forests of mahogany and *ceiba* trees, epiphytes, and giant ferns all protected in a series of reserves. These mountain forests offer superb opportunities to see some of the area's magnificent wildlife, including birds of prey, tapirs, and perhaps even a jaguar. The village of Maya Centre is a good place to head for to explore the Cockscomb Basin Wildlife Sanctuary (see page 245). Here there are some short trails, or you can tackle the two-day trek to the summit of Victoria Peak; excellent guides are on hand.

Another fine hiking destination in Belize is the Mountain Pine Ridge and Macal River area, where there are the Río On pools, the Thousand Foot waterfalls and, in the rainforest south of Mountain Pine Ridge, the large Maya ruins of Caracol. A number of agencies offer tours to the area from San Ignacio, or there are several accommodation possibilities, including some luxurious lodges.

Still closer to sea level, the huge forest that straddles the Guatemalan-Mexican border was the cradle where the Maya civilization first flourished. Dozens of ruined cities lie buried in the Maya Biosphere Reserve and bordering forests. The town of Flores in Guatemala has trekking companies that will provide the expertise, guides, and supplies to explore this frontier zone. There are dozens of ruins in the jungle north of Flores, but the ultimate excursion is the five-day return hike to the colossal ruins of El Mirador, through dense rainforest (see page 177).

Hiking opportunities in Mexico are modest by comparison, as much of the terrain is flat and the climate usually too hot for enjoyable hiking. However, the huge Calakmul Reserve represents one intriguing option, where you can experience the jungle and perhaps catch a glimpse of some wildlife. The agency Servidores Turísticos Campamento Yaax´Che de Calakmul offers guided hikes in the reserve (www.ecoturismocalakmul.com) taking you past unrestored Maya temples deep in the jungle, skirting the fringes of the ancient heart of Calakmul which supported a population of around 80,000 in the Classic era.

ACTIVE VOLCANOES

The most spectacular volcano in Guatemala is Volcán Pacaya (see page 117), which has been in a constant state of eruption since 1965, spewing a stream of lava, gases, and rocks into the sky above Guatemala City. Every year many thousands of people climb the 2,550-meter (8,370ft) peak to witness its spectacular pyrogenics. Guided trips to Pacaya are best joined in Antigua. There are several volcanoes near Antigua, which also make popular hikes. Volcán de Acatenango, at 3,975 meters (13,041ft), is one of the most challenging and rewarding, with amazing views down to the Pacific coast on clear days. Allow 5–7 hours for the tough climb to the top.

VOLCANO CLIMBING

There are more than 30 volcanoes in the Maya region, concentrated in Guatemala, where a spectacular chain of peaks rises above the Pacific shore and forms a barrier between the highlands and the coast. You do not need any special equipment to climb Guatemala's volcanoes, just hiking boots and warm layers if you plan to camp out on the summit.

Altitude sickness can occur at heights of more than 3,000 meters (9,8430ft), and you may find exercise a struggle a good deal lower than that, so it is a good idea to postpone any attempt on Tajumulco or Tacaná, which are both above 4,000 meters (13,000ft), until you are sure that you have acclimatized. If you experience symptoms such as headaches, descend immediately.

Volcán de Agua, at 3,763 meters (12,346ft), is the most popular of all the big peaks to climb. It is a fairly straightforward five-hour trek to the summit from the village of Santa María de Jesús, close to Antigua (see page 126). Of the three volcanoes that surround Lake Atitlán, Volcán San Pedro (3,020 meters/9,900ft) is by far the easiest to climb. A guide association in San Pedro will provide you with a local to accompany you to the summit, which is about a five-hour climb. The Atitlán and Tolimán volcanoes (respectively 3,537 meters/11,604ft and 3,158 meters/10,360ft) present a much stiffer challenge. Pick up a guide in either Santiago Atitlán or San Lucas Tolimán.

From Quezaltenango there are numerous other peaks to conquer, the almost perfect cone of Santa María being the most obvious choice. In addition to this, there's the stunningly beautiful crater lake atop the 2,900-meter (9,500ft) high Chicabal. Expeditions to Volcán Tajumulco which, at 4,220 meters (13,846ft), is the highest peak in Central America, also begin in Guatemala's second city. Quetzaltrekkers (Casa Argentina, Diagonal 12, 8–43, Zona 1; tel: 7765 5895; www.quetzaltrekkers.com) is a good trekking company based in Quezaltenango which offers hikes all over the Guatemalan highlands; all profits benefit a street children charity.

The glowing embers of Volcán Pacaya.

MOUNTAIN BIKING

Off-road trails in the Guatemalan highlands and the western districts of Belize are ideal for mountain biking. Antigua is an excellent base – biking specialists there organize trips and rent bikes. OX Expeditions (tel: 4149 4380; www.oxexpeditions.com) and Old Town Outfitters (tel: 7832 4171; www.adventureguatemala.com) will both take you on an escorted tour of the countryside around Antigua or Lago de Atitlán.

Many of the dramatic trails around Antigua and Lake Atitlán skirt volcanoes and run through coffee plantations and cornfields, past hot springs. You can rent bikes in Panajachel in order to explore the hillsides around the beautiful Lake Atitlán (see page 132), and, farther west, Quezaltenango is another good starting point, with its rugged setting among high mountains and volcanoes. You can join guided bike rides or hire cycles here from the specialist agency Adrenalina Tours (tel: 5308 1489; www.adrenalinatours.com) based in Antigua.

In Belize, head for the Mountain Pine Ridge/Macal River area where there is a vast network of isolated forest trails (see page 241). The main town of San Ignacio makes a good base for budget travelers, but if you want more comfort, try a jungle lodge deep inside the reserve. Waterfalls, jagged peaks, and dramatic rivers are also perfect for canoeing and tubing, and a wide range of such activities is available in the area. Mountain bikes can be hired from tour operators in San Ignacio.

Of the dozen extinct volcanoes in the eastern highlands, Volcán de Ipala (1,650 meters/5,413ft) is the one to climb. It is an easy two-hour hike from the village of Aguas Blancas and, as with Chicabal, there's a glorious crater lake at the summit that is ringed by rainforest and is perfect for a refreshing dip.

Belize's barrier-reef reserves were given Unesco World Heritage Site status in 1996, confirming the global importance of the Caribbean reefs and their marine life.

DIVING ON THE REEF

Tracking the entire Caribbean coast of the Maya region, from Puerto Morelos in Mexico south through Belizean waters to the Bay Islands of

Scuba-diving in the cave systems that proliferate throughout the Yucatán Peninsula.

Honduras, is the world's second-longest barrier reef, an aquatic paradise for scuba-divers. Like the Australian Great Barrier Reef, it is not just one continuous barrier or coral wall, though in many places the reef crest stretches for miles just below the surface. Additionally there are hundreds of large and small coral-fringed islands or *cayes*, underwater seamounts and ridges, and four coral atolls.

Starting in the north, there's some good diving around Isla Mujeres and Cancún, and there are several well-established dive schools on both islands. The famous Garrafón Reef (now a marine reserve) off the southern tip of Isla Mujeres, however, is now in poor condition after many years of abuse by snorkelers, boat skippers, divers and day-trippers; it also costs a hefty US$89 to enter. For better sea life in the Isla Mujeres area head for El Farolito, off the nearby Sac Bajo Peninsula, which is also great for snorkeling. If you are in the area between May and September you have the chance to snorkel with whale sharks, which gather off the coast – trips cost around US$125. Whale shark snorkeling trips can also be set up in Isla Holbox. As a result of the sheer numbers of tourists (and dive schools) in the Cancún area, many of the local sites are crowded, yet there's good fish life at Punta Nizuc, to the south of the Zona Hotelera, while offshore Angel Reef is even better.

Cozumel is the next important location, with some world-class diving on rich coral reefs, with deep trenches, coral patches and steep drop-offs. Palancar Reef, which was first popularized by the French underwater explorer and marine biologist Jacques Cousteau, is justly famous throughout the diving world for its incredible coral wall. Other spectacular sites include Columbia Shallows, a dazzling coral garden, and Punta Sur, which offers wonderful coral formations (and also strong currents). There are plenty of dive schools in Cozumel.

Following the coastal path south to Tulum, there are a number of small, less developed beaches, and several dive schools at Puerto Aventuras, Akumal, and Tulum itself. There is some amazing diving and snorkeling in these parts, not just in the sea offshore but also inland in *cenotes* (freshwater pools). South of here, the spectacular Sian Ka'an Biosphere Reserve incorporates the offshore reef within its boundaries, and, although there are no dive schools in this region, snorkeling trips can be organized in nearby Punta Allen, to the north of the reserve. Perhaps the ultimate diving on this stretch of coastline is the underwater jewel of Banco Chinchorro, a remarkably pristine coral atoll about 20km (12.5 miles) off the coast at the southernmost tip of the country, with dozens of shipwrecks to explore and lots of big pelagic fish (see page 342). The gateway to Chinchorro (a biosphere reserve) is the resort of Mahahual, which has numerous dive shops and also some good snorkeling on the reef just offshore. Finally, in the extreme south of this coastline bordering Belize, Xcalak has more superb snorkeling and scuba-diving on the offshore reef, plenty of hotels which will rent gear, and there's a good dive shop too.

In southern Belizean waters there is good diving around most of the *cayes* – Tobacco Reef, Columbus Reef, and South Water Caye particularly – but Glover's Reef, further offshore, is the place that people rave about (see page 256). Designated as a marine reserve, it is a large atoll with some epic wall diving and beautiful snorkeling gardens. The real thrills for most visitors, however, are the close encounters with pelagic sea life, including the enormous, migrating whale sharks in October.

Jet-skiing along Cancún's coast.

BELIZE'S BEST DIVE SPOTS

Belize offers arguably the best diving in the western hemisphere. The sheer number and variety of dive sites is astonishing, the marine environment is well protected, and there are some excellent dive schools.

Lighthouse Reef, one of the atolls, is where you'll find the much-touted Blue Hole, which looks as if it was created by a bomb blast but is actually the result of a collapsed cavern. There are several shipwrecks in the area that have formed artificial reefs, which you can explore, and there's the Half Moon Caye Natural Monument, which in 1982 became the first marine location in Belize to be made into a reserve.

HIGH-ALTITUDE DIVING

Guatemala has a few tiny patches of reef on its Caribbean coast, but most divers head to the southern Belizean reefs (Hunting and Sapodilla *cayes*) on trips that can be organized in Río Dulce or Lívingston. There's also an excellent dive school based on Lago de Atitlán, if you fancy some freshwater, high-altitude diving. It is an amazing experience to surface after an Atitlán dive and look up and see volcanoes.

RAFTING, CANOEING, AND TUBING

The Maya region offers phenomenal white-water rafting all year round. There are at least a dozen exceptional rivers to raft down throughout Guatemala and Belize, with all grades represented from I (easy) to V (very challenging). There are only underground rivers in the Yucatán.

A day trip on Guatemala's Río Naranjo costs from US$95 per person, a three-day expedition down the Río Cahabón around US$300. Perhaps the most remarkable rafting trip in the region is along the Río Usumacinta, which divides Mexico and Guatemala, passing the ruins of Yaxchilán and Bonampak and finishing at Piedras Negras. Contact Maya Expeditions (www.mayaexpeditions.com) in Guatemala City. It is also possible to kayak around the shores of idyllic Lago de Atitlán (there's a kayaking tour company in Santa Cruz La Laguna) and also through the beautiful Río Dulce gorge and its estuaries – where you might spot a manatee.

River tubing at Semuc Champey, Guatemala.

In Belize there is more outstanding rafting, canoeing, and tubing, especially in the Cayo district, and there are plenty of specialist whitewater companies. The Macal River valley is a favorite place for these sports, and more and more people are kayaking, canoeing, and tubing the Sibul and Mopan rivers. In the south there's more fun to be had on South Stann Creek, Placencia Lagoon, and Big Falls.

CAVING

To the ancient Maya, caves were entrances to the underworld – *Xibalba* – the Place of Fright. Recent research indicates that every major Maya settlement was built near a cave, usually a natural one, though in some cases an artificial chamber was hollowed out of the rock. Caves were essential elements in the Maya belief system and, although the ancient Maya never made permanent settlements in caves, every cave so far explored in the region exhibits evidence of a Maya presence long ago. From cave entrances to deep underground, records of ceremonial visits remain in the form of pottery, petroglyphs, carvings, and fire-hearths.

In Belize, visitors can take an amazing journey into the realm of *Xibalba*. Caves Branch Jungle Lodge (www.cavesbranch.com), on the Hummingbird Highway, 21km (13 miles) south of Belmopan, has the best guided caving trips in the Maya world. Ian Anderson's Cave Branch Jungle Lodge, on the bank of the Caves Branch River, midway between the huge St Herman's Cave and the Blue Hole National Park, has a range of accommodations, from dorm rooms to secluded cabaña suites.

In Guatemala the huge Candelaria cave systems, extending for around 80km (50 miles) in length, contain some vast caverns. Confusingly there are at least four separate access points, but the Complejo Cultural de Candelaria near the town of Raxrujá contains the most impressive chambers. There are more remarkable caves near Semuc Champey, including the Lanquín cave, which is best visited at dusk to view the thousands of bats which emerge from the main cavern.

Yucatán is riddled with impressive cave networks. Some of the most impressive are the Río Secreto, a wet and dry cave system which you explore in a wetsuit and by torchlight, clamboring over rocks and swimming part of the way; it is near Xcaret, south of Playa del Carmen. The caves of Loltún, which are well organized for visitors, include rock art and carving dating back to ancient Maya times. Other possibilities include the multiple cave systems around Oxkintok, Balankanché, and Dzitnup.

Some of the best highland hiking in Guatemala is in the mountains north of Huehuetenango, around Todos Santos Cuchumatán, one of the most picturesque and traditional Maya villages in the country.

Cenote Yokdzonot eco-park in the Yucatán is run by Maya women.

WEATHERING THE STORMS

Forces of nature have produced the spectacular landscapes for which Guatemala, Belize, and the Yucatán are so famous.

A satellite image of the swirling path of Hurricane Mitch, which devastated Central America in 1998.

Periodically wracked by volcanic eruptions, earthquakes, and hurricanes, the land of the Maya has been as prone to natural disasters as it has to man-made cataclysms. Indeed, there is a certain symmetry between the history and the geology of the region, its strategic location where the opposing forces of north and south meet, appearing at times to generate this political and environmental upheaval. The forces of nature have often helped to shape the region's history, compelling the relocation of capital cities and ravaging entire populations and economies. Yet the power and fury of these natural cataclysms have also produced the spectacular landscapes for which Guatemala, Belize, and the Yucatán are so famous, while the active Pacaya volcano continues to attract sightseers from around the world.

HURRICANES AND TROPICAL STORMS

The path of destruction left in the wake of hurricane Nate in October 2017 was the latest in a long series of natural disasters that have left their mark on the history of this region. One of the earliest recorded hurricanes was the Great Hurricane of 1780, which struck the eastern Caribbean, killing approximately 20,000 people.

Devastating tropical storms build in the Gulf of Mexico before winging their way through the Central American isthmus. Possibly because of global warming they seem to be increasing in frequency and severity in recent years. Positioned to the west of the hurricane's usual path, Belize has managed to avoid a good many of the Caribbean hurricanes of the past 40 years, but those that have scored a direct hit have been disastrous.

In 1961 Hurricane Hattie leveled Belize City, prompting the building of the modern, planned capital of Belmopan and the relocation of all government offices. Six years earlier, Hurricane Janet completely destroyed the northern town of Sarteneja and in 1931 another powerful hurricane killed around 15 percent of the population. While Honduras and Nicaragua bore the brunt of the havoc wreaked by Hurricane Mitch in 1998, in Guatemala the storm brought heavy rains, causing landslides and flooding, resulting in 260 deaths and tens of thousands made homeless. Yucatán is also periodically blasted by extreme winds – the damage inflicted by 320kph (200mph) Hurricane Dean in 2007 destroyed the resort of Mahahual, though it has since been rebuilt. Fortunately the region escaped largely unscathed from voracious hurricane Irma, which ravished several Caribbean islands in 2017, including Barbuda and Puerto Rico.

TECTONIC ACTIVITY IN GUATEMALA

Beneath the earth's crust, minute movements of continental tectonic plates cause seismic convulsions and volcanic eruptions in a region plagued by the most powerful natural forces that planet Earth can muster. Historically, Guatemala has been on the receiving end of much of the region's seismic activity, located as it is between the Pacific and Caribbean coasts, and with a chain of volcanoes spanning the southwest of the country. The Mesoamerican Pacific coast belongs to the continent's active tectonic field, where the small Cocos Plate is pushed and shoved by the forces of the larger Caribbean Plate to the east.

Just two days after Pedro de Alvarado's widow had been installed as governor of the newly established colonial capital at Ciudad Vieja in 1541, the Agua volcano buried the city under a torrent of mud and water – an event recorded somewhat gleefully in the Maya Annals of the Kaqchikeles. The Spaniards then moved the capital 8km (5 miles) to the north to Antigua, until an earthquake in 1773 forced another move to the Guatemala City site. History repeated itself in 2010 when another Agua mudslide caused nine deaths close to the town of Antigua.

The present capital was virtually flattened by quakes in 1917 and 1918 and again most recently in 1976, when at least 25,000 people were killed and a million left homeless. With its epicenter in Chimaltenango and measuring 7.5 on the Richter Scale, the tremendous reach of this disaster exposed and exacerbated governmental corruption alongside the progressive suffering of the poor. More recently, in June 2017, Guatemala experienced a 6.8 magnitude quake, thankfully causing only material damage in several parts of the country, including Antigua.

UNDER THE VOLCANOES

The Sierra Madre in the southern Mexican state of Chiapas marks the beginning of a long volcanic chain which stretches down along the Pacific coast and into the western highlands of Guatemala. Forming the backbone of the Central American isthmus, this rugged range of mountains and volcanic peaks cuts a swathe through the land of the Maya, dividing it into highlands and tropical lowlands. This central range and the proximity of the two coasts that lie to either side of it contribute to the wide variety of microclimates which occur, each with its own ecological characteristics. The rich volcanic soils, fed by ash spewed out millions of years ago, also proved perfect for growing coffee, the crop which more than any other has shaped Guatemalan history and society since the late 19th century.

GREAT BALLS OF FIRE

Starkly beautiful and at the same time darkly threatening in appearance, many of the 33 volcanoes towering over Guatemala's highlands are either inactive or long dormant. Several remain active, however, in particular Volcán Pacaya, which has been in an almost constant state of eruption since 1965. This activity ranges from minor gaseous emissions and gentle steam eruptions, to explosions so powerful as to hurl "bombs" up to 12km (7.5 miles) into the air. Although such serious outbursts are rare, Pacaya, which looms over the south of Guatemala City, does emit lava flows on a daily basis, and an ashy pall often hangs over the immediate area. Occasionally local villages need to be evacuated, and in 2010 a large eruption closed Guatemala City's airport for a week and blanketed the capital in volcanic ash.

Lava flow on Guatemala's Volcán Pacaya.

The spectacle of erupting Pacaya is most impressive at night, when its brilliant orange plume lights up the sky. Equally breathtaking, if less dramatic, are the views that can be had from the peaks of the country's many dormant volcanoes, which can also be climbed.

Early morning mist at Guatemala's Santiago Atitlán.

Decorated bus on Antigua's colonial streets.

6-B

Procession during the annual festival of Zunil's patron saint Santa Catalina de Alejandría, Guatemala.

The dazzling colors of the church of San Andrés Xecul, near Quezaltenango.

GUATEMALA

A heady combination of colonial architecture, ancient and modern Maya culture, and breathtaking scenery, Guatemala is an intoxicating country to explore.

Market day in Chajul.

An incredibly diverse, beautiful, and complex nation, Guatemala is both the ancient and modern heart of the Maya world. More than 6.5 million Maya live in Guatemala, forming around 40 percent of the country's population, and it is their dynamic, unique cultural tradition that is the nation's most distinctive feature. With the possible exception of Bolivia, Guatemala is the least Latin of all Latin American countries, a land where sophisticated pre-Conquest traditions, language, religion, culture, and dress still endure over 500 years after the Spanish first arrived in the continent.

For such a small country, Guatemala combines a multiplicity of landscapes. Vast tropical forests cover the Petén, in the northern third of the country, a sparsely populated region rich in wildlife and studded with the ruins of dozens of ancient Maya cities. The east of the country has an extreme juxtaposition of geophysical systems: cloud forests, the gorge systems of the Río Dulce, a humid Caribbean coastline, and even a small desert region near Chiquimula.

Detail of a street "carpet" created to celebrate Semana Santa in Antigua.

The southern swathe of the nation is extremely mountainous and crowned by volcanoes. Most Guatemaltecos live in this southern belt between the capital, Guatemala City, and the second city of Quezaltenango, where the fertile land is dusted by ash from sporadic volcanic eruptions. Below these highlands are the black-sand Pacific beaches and vast agribusiness cotton and sugar plantations.

In the beautiful highlands, the rural population is mostly indigenous, and life revolves around the unique community traditions that have evolved since the Conquest. Though most Maya are nominally either Catholic or belong to Evangelical churches, ancient Maya spiritual beliefs are integrated into highland worship and fiesta celebrations. Beans and vegetables are farmed, but above all it is maize that remains the important crop – it also retains a sacred status, since in Maya mythology man was created from corn.

Political and economic power is concentrated in the hands of the *mestizo* population, called *ladinos*. Differences between the two halves of Guatemalan society are sharp. *Ladino* culture is heavily influenced by the rest of Latin America and the USA, consuming tropical musical rhythms from Cuba and Hollywood movies with equal relish. *Ladino* Guatemalans also control the military, which remains a powerful force in Guatemala, with civilian rule only re-established in 1986. A 36-year guerrilla conflict waged by a number of small rebel groups is over, and since the 1996 peace accords political violence has largely disappeared, though rising crime rates threaten social stability. Nevertheless, the outlook is positive, as Guatemala looks forward to a period of building prosperity: the country's GDP growth in 2017 reached 4 percent.

Iguana in the Biotopo Monterrico-Hawaii reserve.

Guatemala has been the center of power in Central America since Preclassic Maya times, when the great trading cities of the region, El Mirador and Kaminaljuyú, first emerged. Tikal later dominated the Classic period. When the Spanish conquistadors arrived from Mexico in 1523 they established their first capital in Guatemala before moving down through the rest of the isthmus. The colonial capital of Antigua was one of the glorious cities of the Americas, ranking alongside Mexico City and Lima as one of the greatest in the continent. Today, Guatemala is the most populous of the seven Central American nations, with a population of around 17 million, and Guatemala City is the region's largest and most important industrial and commercial center.

CLIMATE

The Inguat (tourist board) hyperbole is that Guatemala is the "Land of Eternal Spring." There is actually a lot of truth in this, as much of the country is blessed with an extremely agreeable, almost benign climate – but there are significant exceptions.

The Río Dulce.

The most important climatic consideration in Guatemala at any time of year is the altitude. Broadly, in most of the highlands, including Guatemala City, Antigua, Lago de Atitlán, Cobán, Chichicastenango, and Huehuetenango, the altitude is between 1,300 and 2,100 meters (4,260–6,890ft), and the daytime climate is usually delightful – between 18 and 28°C (64–82°F). Above 2,100 meters (6,890ft) it can get quite chilly at night.

By the coasts, and in the Petén jungle lowlands, the heat can be exhausting, with temperatures regularly above 30°C (86°F) all year round. If you are visiting Tikal in Petén, be prepared for steamy, humid conditions.

There are two seasons in Guatemala. *Invierno* (winter) is between May and October and is the rainy season. The dry season, *verano* (summer), is between November and April. Paradoxically, though, this is the Guatemalan summer and skies are usually clear; the coolest night-time temperatures occur in December and January, with the occasional snowfall and frosts not unheard of at very high altitudes. For most of the country, however, this is the best time of year to visit Guatemala, though by March temperatures are climbing rapidly – and April is the hottest month.

Thursday market in Chichicastenango.

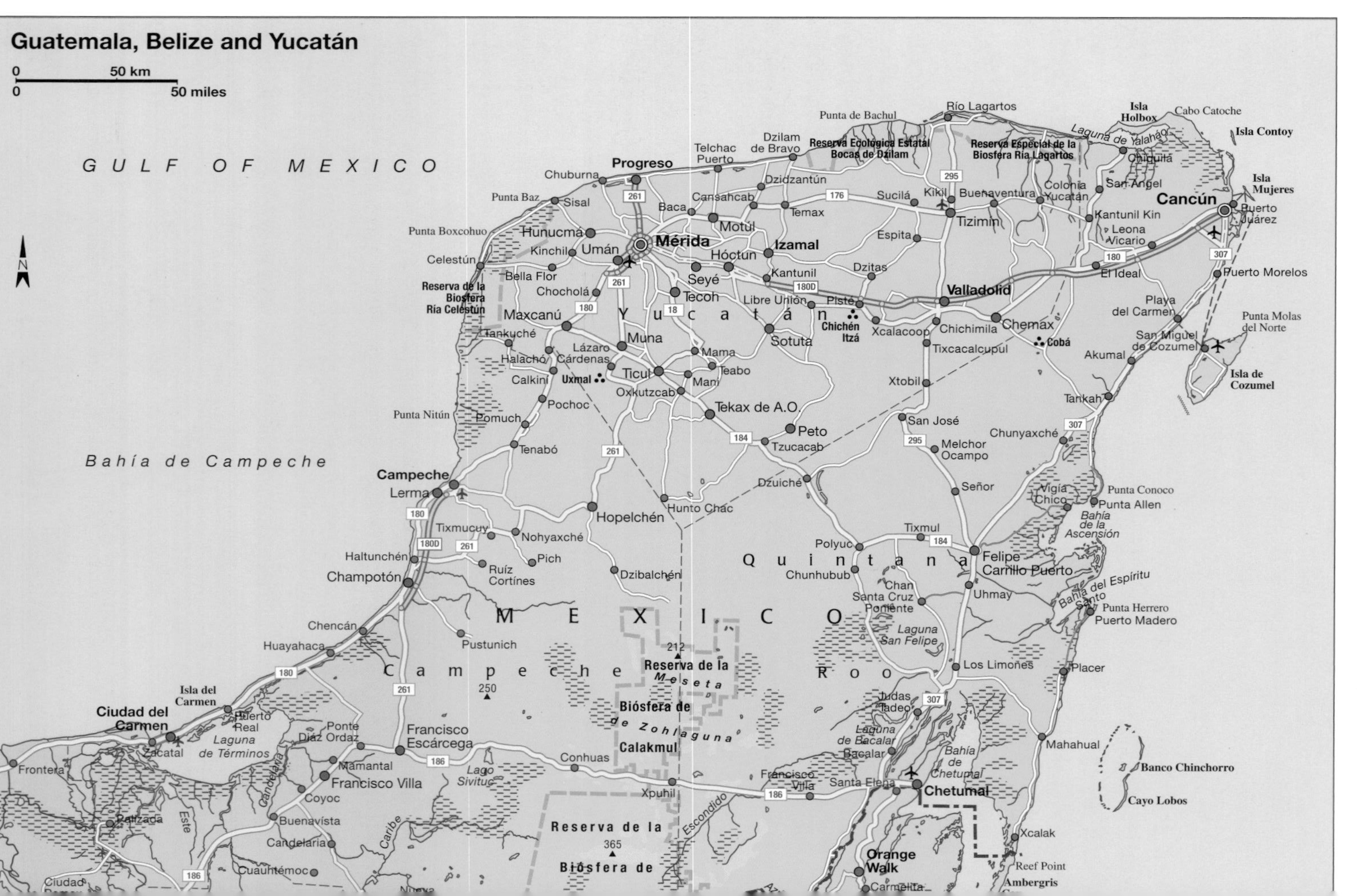
Guatemala, Belize and Yucatán
0 50 km
0 50 miles
N
GULF OF MEXICO
Bahía de Campeche
MEXICO
Yucatán
Quintana Roo
Campeche
Punta de Bachul
Río Lagartos
Isla Holbox
Cabo Catoche
Isla Contoy
Laguna de Yalahao
Chiquilá
Reserva Ecológica Estatal Bocas de Dzilam
Reserva Especial de la Biosfera Ría Lagartos
Dzilam de Bravo
Telchac Puerto
Progreso
Chuburna
Dzidzantún
Isla Mujeres
Puerto Juárez
Cancún
Punta Baz
Sisal
Cansahcab
Sucilá
Kikil
Buenaventura
Colonia Yucatán
San Ángel
Baca
Temax
Tizimín
Kantunil Kin
Leona Vicario
Punta Boxcohuo
Hunucmá
Mérida
Motul
Izamal
Espita
Kinchil
Umán
Hoctún
Celestún
Bella Flor
Seyé
Kantunil
Dzitas
El Ideal
Puerto Morelos
Reserva de la Biosfera Ría Celestún
Chocholá
Tecoh
Libre Unión
Pisté
Valladolid
Playa del Carmen
Maxcanú
Chichén Itzá
Xcalacoop
Chichimila
Chemax
Punta Molas del Norte
Tankuché
Muna
Sotuta
Tixcacalcupul
Cobá
San Miguel de Cozumel
Lázaro Cárdenas
Mama
Akumal
Halachó
Isla de Cozumel
Calkiní
Uxmal
Ticul
Teabo
Maní
Xtobil
Oxkutzcab
Tankah
Pochoc
Tekax de A.O.
Punta Nitún
Pomuch
San José
Peto
Chunyaxché
Tzucacab
Melchor Ocampo
Tenabó
Campeche
Dzuiché
Señor
Punta Conoco
Lerma
Vigía Chico
Punta Allen
Hunto Chac
Hopelchén
Bahía de la Ascensión
Tixmucuy
Nohyaxché
Tixmul
Polyuc
Haltunchén
Pich
Felipe Carrillo Puerto
Champotón
Ruíz Cortínes
Dzibalchén
Chunhubub
Chan Santa Cruz Poniente
Bahía del Espíritu Santo
Uhmay
Punta Herrero
Puerto Madero
Chencán
Pustunich
Laguna San Felipe
212
Huayahaca
Reserva de la Biósfera de Calakmul
Meseta de Zoh Laguna
Los Limones
Placer
250
Isla del Carmen
Judas Tadeo
Ciudad del Carmen
Puerto Real
Laguna de Términos
Ponte Díaz Ordaz
Francisco Escárcega
Laguna de Bacalar
Mahahual
Zacatal
Bacalar
Bahía de Chetumal
Frontera
Mamantal
Conhuas
Banco Chinchorro
Francisco Villa
Lago Sivituc
Francisco Villa
Santa Elena
Chetumal
Candelaria
Xpuhil
Coyoc
Este
Cayo Lobos
Palizada
Buenavista
Caribe
Escondido
Reserva de la Biósfera de
365
Xcalak
Candelaria
Orange Walk
Reef Point
Cuauhtémoc
Ambergris
Ciudad
Carmelita
295
176
261
180
180D
18
307
184
186

Reserva Biósfera Maya
Río Azul
Palenque
Tulijá
Tenosique de Pino Suárez
Biotopo Laguna de Tigre-Río Escondido
San Pedro
Carmelita
Uaxactún
Tikal
BELIZE
Belize
Belize City
Turneffe Islands
SEA
Belmopan
Xunantunich
San Ignacio
Melchor de Mencos
Dangriga
Sa del Lacandón
Parque Nacional Sierra de Lacandón
Yaxchilán
Usumacinta
Bonampak
Ocosingo
San Cristóbal de Las Casas
MEXICO
San Andrés
Flores
Petén
Caracol
Chiquibul Nat. Park
Maya Mountains
Sayaxché
Dolores
Jataté
Roatán
Islas de la Bahía
Utila
Comitán de Domínguez
San Antonio
Punta Gorda
Presa de la Angostura
Lacantún
CA13
Golfo de Honduras
Raxrujá
Modesto Méndez
Barillas
Huehuetenango
GUATEMALA
Alta Verapaz
Puerto Barrios
Puerto Cortés
La Ceiba
Tela
Paso Hondo
Parque Nacional Los Cuchumatanes
Cahabón
Sa de Santa Cruz
Izabal
El Golfete
Río Dulce
El Estor
Lago de Izabal
San Pedro Sula
Sa de los Cuchumatanes
Quiché
Cobán
Morales
La Lima
El Progreso
Aguán
Huehuetenango
Uspantán
Ulúa
San Marcos
Sierra Madre
CA1
Los Amates
CA9
Huixtla
Sta Cruz del Quiché
Salamá
Sierra de las Minas
Yoro
Vol. Tajumulco 4220
San Marcos
Totonicapán
Baja Verapaz
Río Hondo
Zacapa
Zacapa
Malacatán
Totonicapán
El Progreso
Tapachula
Quezaltenango
Sololá
Chimaltenango
Copán
Sta Rosa de Copán
Coatepeque
Sololá
Chimaltenango
Chiquimula
Lago de Atitlán
Mixco
CA2
Jalapa
Chiquimula
HONDURAS
Guatemala
Mazatenango
Antigua Guatemala
Jalapa
Tilapa
Retalhuleu
Retalhuleu
Suchitepéquez
3766
Amatitlán
Comayagua
Nueva Ocotepeque
CA1
Cuilapa
Metapán
Champerico
Escuintla
Jutiapa
Masagua
Santa Rosa
Jutiapa
Escuintla
CA9
Marcala
Tegucigalpa
Chalatenango
Chalchuapa
Sta Ana
Danlí
Sipacate
CA2
EL SALVADOR
Puerto San José
Ahuachapán
PACIFIC OCEAN
San Salvador
Sta Tecla

Staying out of the midday sun in Santiago de Atitlán.

An 1885 engraving of a coffee plantation.

MODERN HISTORY OF GUATEMALA

Dictatorships and bloodshed have plagued Guatemala since independence, but peace and stability seem finally to be taking hold.

Guatemala formally declared itself independent from Spain on September 15, 1821. Almost immediately, however, its territory was taken over by Mexico, which had been the center of the Spanish viceroyalty and was now ruled by an emperor, Agustín Iturbide.

By 1823, the Central American provinces of Guatemala, Honduras, El Salvador, and Nicaragua had broken away from Mexico and formed a united federation based in Guatemala City. The Guatemalan Manuel José Arce became the federation's first president. This arrangement lasted only six years before rebel troops, calling themselves "the allied army for the protection of the law" under General Francisco Morazán from Honduras, took Guatemala City in 1829.

General Justo Rufino Barrios, whose dictatorship from 1873 to 1885 was marked by tyrannical reform.

MORAZÁN AND HIS SUCCESSORS

Morazán was the first in a long line of dictatorial rulers in Guatemala, setting the precedent by declaring himself the head of the federation in 1830. Over the next eight years, Morazán set about reforming Guatemala single-handedly. He abolished the privileges of the Catholic Church, reformed landownership, and encouraged new settlement.

In 1833, Morazán transferred the capital of the Central American Federation to San Salvador. Guatemala itself was governed by Mariano Gálvez, then by Rafael Carrera. Morazán struggled with increasing difficulty to maintain the federation, and in 1838 it was dissolved.

Rafael Carrera was a poor, illiterate, but charismatic leader who led a revolt in the name of Christ and the Catholic Church to overthrow a "godless" government. He was elected the first president of Guatemala in 1839.

From 1839 to 1871, Guatemala was governed by the Conservatives: until 1865 under the *mestizo* Rafael Carrera, and then by Vicente Cerna. Political power was firmly in the hands of a small *mestizo* elite. The majority Maya were excluded almost entirely from the political process, and their lands were taken over by large estates.

Throughout the 19th century, Guatemala was essentially an agricultural country, initially exporting cochineal and indigo for dyes. These were replaced by plantations of cacao and coffee and, around the turn of the 20th century, by the first large-scale banana plantations run by the United Fruit Company of Boston.

GUATEMALA IN THE 20TH CENTURY

A series of weak presidents and military coups characterized the first decades of the 20th century in Guatemala. Then, in 1931, General Jorge Ubico was elected as president; he was to rule until 1944. During his 13 years in power, Ubico managed to improve Guatemala's economic situation and bring about political stability. But individual freedoms were restricted, and he manipulated the constitution, legislative, and legal powers for his own ends. He imposed military discipline throughout Guatemala, so that even the national symphony orchestra played in military uniforms.

> *"In Guatemala there are two presidents, and one of them has a machine gun with which he is always threatening the other." Juan José Arévalo (president from 1945–50)*

Ubico was finally overthrown in 1944, and the reformist Juan José Arévalo was elected president under a new constitution in 1945. Arévalo set in train important changes in education, landownership, and labor laws. These measures brought resistance from the more conservative sectors of Guatemalan society, and there were several attempts to depose him. Despite these plots, Arévalo succeeded in completing his six years in office, and in 1950 handed over to another reform-minded president, Jácobo Arbenz Guzmán. His attempts to break up the huge rural estates through land reform programs and to control the power of the United Fruit Company soon led to protests.

Panzós, a typical thatch-roofed Maya village in the eastern lowlands, during the late 19th century.

The United States branded Arbenz a communist, and in 1954 they backed a coup by Colonel Carlos Castillo Armas and the National Liberation Movement. Faced with an invasion from Honduras led by Castillo, Arbenz was forced to resign on June 27, 1954, paving the way for Castillo Armas to take over.

For the next 30 years, Guatemala was governed by a succession of military rulers. US-supported Colonel Castillo Armas was assassinated in the National Palace in 1957,

The United Fruit Company grew so big in the 1950s, taking over the railroad, radio, telegraph, and electricity companies, it was nicknamed El Pulpo – The Octopus.

and from then on the country was rocked by increasing violence, as trade unions, left-wing guerrillas, and other groups fought against brutal military rule.

including, by the beginning of the 1960s, guerrilla armies.

During the late 1970s and early 1980s the civil war reached its climax. The guerrillas initially scored a number of military victories, but the army hit back using scorched-earth tactics and a murderously successful terror campaign in the highlands.

Several thousand people were killed each year at this time; the vast majority were indigenous Maya peasants who had nothing to do with the struggle.

Early 20th-century church group in Santiago Atitlán, one of the highlands' most traditional villages.

CIVIL WAR

The civil war that rocked Guatemala for more than three decades is widely regarded to have started with the 1954 coup that overthrew Jácobo Arbenz. The Castillo government had built up a "blacklist" of more than 40,000 politicians, trade unionists, grass-roots leaders, and intellectuals whom it regarded as a threat. Many were imprisoned, or forced into exile. The Church, too, was subjected to violence by the armed forces, who resented the clergy for their support of Maya villagers. Between 1978 and 1983, 13 Catholic priests were killed and more than 100 fled the country.

Left-wing groups responded to this military purge by forming a variety of organizations

THE LONG ROAD TO PEACE

In 1982 a military junta toppled the government of Lucas García and, in 1983, General Ríos Montt took control. It was during his period in power that the repression in the countryside reached a peak. Counter-insurgency techniques ruthlessly implemented by the Guatemalan army led to the murder, torture, and displacement of many thousands of peasants in these years, among Guatemala's darkest.

In 1984, the military ruler General Óscar Mejía Víctores ordered the establishment of a new constitution, which led to the election of Guatemala's first civilian president in more than 30 years, Vinicio Cerezo Arévalo, a Christian Democrat.

THE EVANGELISTS

Since the 1970s Protestant and Evangelical sects have won many converts among the Maya population in Guatemala.

Catholicism had been imposed by the Spaniards. In the (almost) five centuries after the Conquest, the Church hierarchy made little effort to reach out to the Maya – there were few attempts to translate the Bible into the indigenous languages, and the liturgy was remote and often inexplicable to the local population. During the turbulent years from the 1950s onwards, the Catholic Church hierarchy largely sided with the armed forces and with repression, and consequently was viewed with increasing suspicion as violence in Guatemalan society increased.

A third of Guatemalans claim adherence to Evangelical Christianity.

In spite of this growing tension, many rural Catholic priests had made efforts to win over Maya communities, supporting development projects and *campesinos'* unions. Unfortunately these activities provoked the suspicions of the military authorities, who labeled the priests as communists and trouble-makers. Paramilitary death squads hunted down and brutally murdered many of these campaigning Catholic priests, to such an extent that by the early 1980s the Catholic Church withdrew altogether from some of the guerrilla-based areas of the highlands, by way of protest and for its own self-preservation. The vacuum thus created by the Catholic Church left many highland Maya wary and fearful of being associated with the guerrilla movement.

Missionaries from the United States adopted a very different approach. They lived in the indigenous communities, and from the start learned the languages and translated the Bible into the local tongues. They also taught converts a way of life that was strict but appealing. They forbade alcohol and openly condemned social behavior they saw as sinful, whereas the Catholic Church had remained aloof on these matters. Significantly, some Evangelists openly voiced their support for the army over the guerrillas, a policy which gained acceptance from those keen to survive further military oppression.

They also attracted many converts because of their promise that by leading a proper Christian life, the faithful would advance in their lives on this earth as well as in the next world. This Evangelical message was extremely seductive for many among the Maya who felt they had been excluded at all levels of society. As a result, by the beginning of the 1980s, the Evangelical churches had become a powerful force in Guatemala. Their position was further reinforced when one of these new converts, General Efraín Ríos Montt, came to power.

Ríos Montt, who had become a born-again Christian in the 1970s when he became a member of the El Verbo Evangelical sect, was the first Protestant president of Guatemala.

Although condemned internationally for the vicious counter-insurgency war that he fought in the Guatemalan countryside, Montt's stern, uncompromising message of bringing law and order to a godless society won him a substantial political following.

This support continued in the 1990s as his Republican Front of Guatemala (FRG) won the 1999 elections. However, the disastrous term of office that followed effectively ended the Montt myth, and his popularity faded. In 2013 he was convicted of genocide and crimes against humanity but the constitutional court suspended the sentence forcing a retrial. Meanwhile, the number of Guatemalan Evangelists, currently approaching 40 percent of the population, continues to grow.

Ríos Montt was ousted in 1982 by his defense minister, Mejía Víctores, who observed that "Guatemala doesn't need more prayers, it needs more executions."

With the return of civilian government in 1986, the attempts to achieve peace began in earnest. The guerrilla organizations realized that they could not overthrow the Guatemalan state by violence. One of the chief problems for these negotiations was the fact that the army considered it had eliminated what it called "subversion," and therefore there was nothing to negotiate. Cerezo moved only cautiously during his four years in office to try to curb the power of the armed forces and to bring the continuing civil war to an end.

Cerezo's successor in 1990 was President Jorge Serrano, who fared even worse. Although talks between the armed forces and the Guatemalan National Revolutionary Unity (URNG) guerrillas began in Mexico City in 1991, very little progress was actually made toward peace. The guerrillas wanted peace accords that would guarantee substantial change in Guatemala. The armed forces were anxious not to be held responsible for the 200,000 deaths that had occurred during the violence. They also wished to avoid any sweeping reforms to the army or the police.

The deteriorating situation within Guatemala led Serrano to attempt to take dictatorial powers in 1993, though he was quickly ousted.

PEACE ACCORDS

Elections were organized for the end of 1995, which gave victory to Álvaro Arzú, a center-right candidate. In March 1996, the guerrilla organization URNG agreed to a ceasefire. This was followed by rapid progress in other areas of the peace negotiations, and on December 29, 1996, an agreement for a firm and lasting peace was signed by the government and the rebels in Guatemala City. The principal parts of the agreement were to carry out an investigation of the human-rights abuses committed during the civil war, a commitment to demilitarize society, and to introduce constitutional changes to safeguard indigenous rights in Guatemala.

Initially, the outlook was positive as the guerrillas handed in their weapons and formed a political party while MINUGUA (the United Nations Mission to Guatemala) arrived to oversee the implementation of the accords. Some reforms of the armed forces were carried out and a new constitution was framed (which promised an inclusive role for indigenous people). A commission was also established to investigate human rights crimes committed during the civil war. Progress proved very slow, however, as the Guatemalan military stalled on key commitments and proved reluctant to relinquish its powerbase.

Memorial in Nebaj to victims of the civil war that raged for three decades from the 1960s.

Army personnel were later implicated in the assassination of Bishop Juan Geradi in 1998, two days after his offices had published a report that blamed the military and civil-defense patrols for 93 percent of civil war deaths. Meanwhile, a referendum rejected a constitutional amendment to legitimize Maya rights.

GUATEMALA TODAY

Rising crime rates and the influence of criminal cartels are two of the most pressing issues facing Guatemala. Mafia-style networks, many with ties to the military, have established Guatemala as a key country for cocaine smuggling and acted with near impunity against a chronically weak judiciary and (perhaps in collusion with) a corruption-riddled police force.

The cult of gang membership in the cities also threatens social stability. Former military dictator Efraín Ríos Montt dominated the political scene for much of the 1980s and 1990s with his FRG Party winning the 1999

Policemen in Antigua.

election led by its candidate Alfonso Portillo, but Portillo's term proved to be disastrous. He and leading members of his cabinet were caught up in a string of corruption scandals, while the security situation deteriorated further. Unsurprisingly, Óscar Berger of the pro-business GANA coalition swept to power in 2003.

By 2005 Guatemala was in a sorry state, and Berger's main task became stabilizing the country. He introduced sweeping reforms to the military, cutting army numbers and curbing their influence. But the resulting power gap was filled by shadowy crime syndicates linked to gangs and drug cartels, many with links to former (and serving) members of the armed forces, as Guatemala became a key transit country for cocaine.

In 2007, Álvaro Colom, a center-left leader, won the presidential elections with a large share of the votes from the Maya population. His deputy, Rafael Espada, a heart surgeon, immediately declared Guatemala as "sick, very sick, in intensive care." Their government faced many challenges – above all tackling criminal syndicates and street gangs. Despite some successes, Guatemalans voted for a change of direction in 2011, favouring the *mano dura* (iron-fist) promised by Otto Pérez, a former director of military intelligence. However, accusations of a remilitarization of society were leveled at his administration as he ordered the army to perform highway patrols and filled his cabinet with ex-military men.

OUTLOOK

Guatemala has many pressing concerns, including endemic corruption, myriad environmental issues, a poor education system (30 percent of adults are illiterate) and some of the highest poverty levels in the hemisphere. Much will depend on the determination of government to address the security question, including dealing with the culture of impunity (fewer than 5 percent of murders result in convictions) and strengthening the justice system.

It must also tackle corruption affecting the highest echelons of power. Indeed, the country's current president, comedian-turned-politician Jimmy Morales, who won the elections in 2015 with the motto "neither corrupt nor thief", is now himself being investigated for the alleged illegal funding of his presidential campaign. To add to his woes, his older brother and own son were arrested on corruption and money-laundering charges in January 2017. As a result, Morales' popularity slumped from 89 to 19 percent.

Morales is also responsible for reigniting a border conflict with Belize that has been simmering for over 150 years. In 2016, the president sent a few thousand-strong troops to the disputed border areas following the death of a Guatemalan teenager who was allegedly attacked and shot by the Belizean patrol – an accusation Belize vigorously denies.

RIGOBERTA MENCHÚ

Rigoberta Menchú, an activist for the rights of the world's indigenous peoples, cuts a controversial figure in Guatemala today.

Globally, the best-known Guatemalan is not the president, a pop star, or even a sporting figure, but the K'i che' Maya peasant turned human rights activist Rigoberta Menchú, who won the 1992 Nobel Peace Prize for her work on behalf of Guatemala's and the world's indigenous peoples. Menchú is a controversial figure in Guatemala, feted by the political left, but also provoking vitriolic polemic from her ideological opponents, who consider her a subversive ex-guerrilla.

Rigoberta Menchú was born in 1959 in Quiché. In the first volume of her autobiography, *I, Rigoberta Menchú*, published in 1983, she describes how the horrific brutality of the Guatemalan civil war affected her family, how her mother, father and brothers were branded guerrilla-sympathizers and killed by the military in their fight to protect the family's farmland. In powerful, unambiguous language, Menchú castigates the inequalities of that ruptured Guatemalan society: the cultural chasm between *ladino* and Maya, the gross disparity of wealth, health education, and opportunity between the country's rich and poor. She also details that she had no formal schooling, how her family had to work in the plantations of the Pacific coast to survive, and her flight to exile in Mexico in 1980.

I, Rigoberta Menchú sold strongly all over the globe, catapulting the author into the international limelight. Menchú became a familiar face at the United Nations in Geneva, tirelessly campaigning for the rights of the Guatemalan Maya and forging connections with other oppressed minorities. This period of her life is recounted in *Crossing Borders (1998)*, the second volume of her autobiography, a less harrowing read. It tackles the controversy over her Nobel Peace Prize award, which split the country on familiar lines as ecstatic supporters celebrated in San Marcos while the president failed to turn up to a rally in the capital, complaining of an earache. The Nobel laureate returned to Guatemala in 1994 as an iconic if contentious figure, but internationally she remained beyond reproach until the publication of David Stoll's biography *Rigoberta Menchú and the Story of All Poor Guatemalans*, in 1998. Stoll's book shook this enshrined reputation, contending that important parts of *I, Rigoberta Menchú* were false: that Menchú had been educated at a convent school and that her family's land dispute was an internecine family quarrel rather than a racially charged indigenous-*ladino* clash. He also alleged a guerrilla past.

Rigoberta Menchú, whose story exposed the inequalities that are still rife in Guatemalan society.

Menchú has since admitted that she received some education at the convent, but remained silent about other allegations. It is fair to say (and Stoll still considers that the Nobel Prize was rightfully awarded) that despite doubts over certain details of Menchú's story, her reputation remains largely intact among her supporters. It is not in dispute that her mother, father, and brothers died at the hands of the military.

Menchú's success bringing global attention to the suffering of the Guatemalan Maya is unquestionable. Her work on behalf of the world's indigenous peoples for the UN has been tireless, and she continues to campaign in Guatemala for political and social justice and on healthcare issues. She has also fought to prosecute armed forces leaders for civil war atrocities. Menchú formally entered politics in 2005, serving as a goodwill ambassador for the peace accords, and went on to contest the 2007 and 2011 presidencies, but only polled 3 percent of the vote in both elections.

Sorting leaves in San Andrés Xecul.

HIGHLAND LIFE

All-important village ties and a rich mélange of cultural influences are revealed in the western highlands' Maya communities on market day and at fiestas.

The majority of Guatemala's nearly 7 million Maya live in small towns and villages in the western highlands (a vast area comprising part of the Sierra Madre mountain range, which rises in Mexico and stretches southeastward to the doorstep of Guatemala City).

As it is traditional for extended families to stay together, married sons are given rooms within the family compound. Young men lead relatively restricted lives under their father's authority, and only those who become traders or make money working in the United States have the option of independence. Few children attend school for the full duration; older girls help their mothers at home and look after younger siblings, whilst the boys accompany their fathers to the fields.

It's estimated that over a million Guatemalans have emigrated to the US, including hundreds of thousands of Maya men (most from the remote villages of the Cuchumatanes).

Village economy is based largely on subsistence agriculture. Most Maya men own a plot of land on which they try to grow enough corn and beans to feed their families. If space allows, cash crops such as carrots, avocados, onions, and squash are also grown and sold at market. However, since many villages were forced to give up their best land to coffee growers in the late 19th century, and as it is customary for fathers to divide their land among their sons, the plots become smaller with each generation, and it is difficult to remain self-sufficient – making migrations to the coast for seasonal work (or even permanently to the US) essential.

Tending the land.

MAYAN RELIGION

Corn has a mystical significance, for besides being the Maya's main subsistence crop, in the *Popol Vuh*, the sacred book of the K'i che' Maya, it is written that the first men were made of corn dough. Black and red corn, as well as the more common yellow and white strains, are indigenous to Guatemala, and the historian Sylvanus Morley has suggested that these four colors were sacred to the ancient Maya because of their association with corn.

Religion is fundamental to the life of the Maya. The majority claim to be Catholics, although many of them practice a unique type of "folk Catholicism," which incorporates traditional beliefs. It was easy for the Maya to adapt to Catholic doctrines taught to them by the Spanish: elaborate ceremonies accompanied by incense had always been a part of religious life, as had the veneration of the cross, an important Maya symbol. Pagan gods simply assumed the identity of Catholic saints and their worship continued as before.

The *cofradía* system (see page 25) was introduced by the Spaniards to promote Catholicism, but soon it also acquired its own syncretic identity. However, although traditional villages like Nebaj, Chichicastenango, and Santiago Atitlán still have up to 10 working *cofradías*, their influence has been in steady decline since the influx of foreign Catholic priests in the 1950s.

Women's dress has changed little since pre-Conquest times, as seen on these women in Nebaj.

THE SHAMAN

Besides worshiping in church, traditionalists also pray at Maya shrines in the mountains. These older rites are the province of the shaman, who acts as an intermediary. He is also called upon to give advice, invoke or revoke curses, foretell the future, cure illness, and officiate at ceremonies asking for rain. He is conversant with the 260-day Maya calendar and chooses propitious days for his ceremonies.

Shamans are particularly numerous amongst the K'i che' Maya of Quezaltenango and Totonicapán, where they hold court in the *cofradías* that contain the figure of Maximón, also known as San Simón. This figure is a seated effigy dressed in European clothes who is rated as having special powers, not only for good, but also evil.

Maya rituals are also well preserved amongst the Q'anjob'al Maya of Huehuetenango, where priests use both the 260-day ritual calendar and the 365-day calendar. The priest's function is to pray for the good of the community and the success of the harvest. Turkeys are sacrificed at relevant times during the year and blood-stained incense and candles are burned at the sacred places. If the rains fail to come, or the crops are ruined by frost, then the Maya priest is blamed; in the past he would have been jailed for not doing his job properly.

The 1990s saw a Maya religion revival movement amongst young Maya intellectuals, who now openly claim to be either followers of the religion or even Maya priests. This is a good example of the growing awareness and pride the younger generation is taking in its cultural heritage. However, this Maya revival (even ex-President Colom claims to have been admitted into the Maya priesthood) has tended to standardize once-disparate Maya traditions, and those of the K'i che' have become recognized as "official."

DISTINCT COSTUMES

The Maya today identify with their villages rather than with their ancestral tribes, although the languages they speak still conform to the pattern of ancient tribal boundaries. Marriages

⊙ DECLINE OF THE COFRADÍA

Each *cofradía* group within a village serves a single Catholic saint, organizing all the required rites and processions. However, in recent years church committees have usurped many traditional *cofradía* functions, such as caring for the church, providing flowers, and officiating at burial ceremonies. Indeed, in many villages there is now considerable friction between the *cofrades* and the parish priest with his modern Catholic Action groups, not least because some *cofradía* ceremonies are accompanied by shamanistic rituals and very heavy drinking. The decline in *cofradía* membership is also due to the high costs involved in organizing a saint's fiesta.

between members of different communities are relatively rare, and village identity is consolidated further by the distinctive clothes worn by the women and some men.

Costumes fall into three categories: everyday dress; more elaborate wear for special occasions; and the ceremonial garments worn by the *cofradías*. Although colors, designs, and the way of wearing particular garments differ from village to village, all women's apparel consists of the same basic articles: a *huipil* (a loose rectangular blouse), a skirt, sash, hair-ribbon, and *tzut* (multi-purpose carrying cloth) or shawl. Each item is hand-woven, either on a simple hip-strap loom or a foot-loom.

MODERN TRENDS

Twenty years ago, it was easy to identify a woman's village by the clothes she was wearing, as not only her *huipil*, but also her belt, *tzut*, and skirt conformed to the colors and designs of her community. Today this is no longer so, as many women are switching from making (or commissioning) village dress to buying the cheaper Totonicapán trade pieces. *Huipiles* woven on foot-looms, or made of commercial cloth with machine embroidery round the neck, are far less expensive than those woven on hip-strap looms with village designs. Brightly striped belts and colorful acrylic shawls also make cheap and cheerful substitutes for traditional sashes and *tzutes*, though the wrap-around skirt is still the style used most, and only in Quezaltenango and the Verapaces have European-style gathered skirts been adopted.

The change from village-specific to generic dress styles began during the civil war in the early 1980s, when thousands fled their villages for the relative safety of large towns. In addition to the cost factor, the anonymity of the Totonicapán textiles gave protection from being identified as possible guerrilla supporters. Now, because more and more young girls leave home to work or study in the large towns, it has become socially acceptable to wear not only trade items of dress, but also the *huipiles* of other communities. These developments are most evident around Guatemala City, Quezaltenango, and Totonicapán.

Despite such changes, traditional costumes are the norm in many villages around Lake Atitlán, in Nebaj and Chajul, and among the Mam-speaking Maya of Huehuetenango, where skirts are still woven on hip-strap looms and very young girls wear full village dress.

ADAPTIVE MEN

Men's traditional costumes have been preserved in only a few villages, most notably in those around Lake Atitlán, and in the mountains of Huehuetenango. Men have always been more open to change than women, as they leave their communities for longer periods of time to trade in the larger towns, try their fortunes in the US, or serve in the army. Because of continuing

Traditional male dress in Todos Santos Cuchumatán.

NO CHANGE IN DRESS STYLE

Women's clothing today differs little in style from that worn in pre-Conquest times. Although only small fragments of cloth have been found at archeological sites, the carvings, figurines, and pottery that have survived have left us clear pictures of pre-Columbian Maya dress.

Women are depicted wearing elaborate headdresses and knee-length *huipiles* which hang over wrap-around skirts – the type of costume still worn by *cofradía* women today, for example in Santiago Atitlán, Nebaj, and Sololá. In a number of communities, such as Palín, Cobán, Joyabaj, and San Mateo Ixtatán, *huipiles* are worn loose at all times.

discrimination, it is always more advantageous to be taken for a mixed-race *ladino* than indigenous. Men's clothing these days has more in common with Western dress than with ancient Maya loincloths and cloaks.

You can recognize Maya men from Lake Atitlán by their striped trousers decorated with village motifs and held up by sashes; sometimes a length of woolen fabric is wrapped around the hips too. Black split over-trousers are used in Todos Santos and by Sololá officials, whilst the men of San Juan Atitán wear woolen *capixays* that resemble the cassocks used by the Spanish friars. In Santiago Atitlán men embroider their own trousers, copying pictures of birds or Maya hieroglyphs.

Traders at Chichicastenango's market.

Although modern Western clothes may be worn on a day-to-day basis, in some villages older dress styles are retained for *cofradía* use. Examples of this are the elaborate costumes worn by *cofrades* in San Juan Sacatepéquez and Chichicastenango. Items such as split over-trousers, knee breeches, capes, and cloaks stem from 18th- and 19th-century Spanish fashions.

CRAFTS AND MARKETS

Crafts make an important contribution to village economy. Some communities specialize in the manufacture of particular items, which are traded throughout the highlands. Regional specialties include woolen blankets from Momostenango, rope from agave fibers in San Pablo La Laguna and San Juan Cotzal, and *petate* mats made from the reeds growing around Santiago Atitlán. Totonicapán is the center for glazed terracotta bowls and cooking pots, whilst in Chinautla plant containers and ornaments are produced for the Guatemala City market, as well as beautiful clay nativity tableaux.

Craft co-operatives established by foreign aid workers in the highlands have had mixed fortunes, many folding when financial backing ends. But you will find thriving co-ops in Zunil, where the Santa Ana Co-operative is run by a committee of women, and there are two excellent weaving co-ops in San Juan La Laguna, another in San Antonio Palopó, and others in towns such as Chajul, Todos Santos Cuchumatán, and Chichicastenago, where your purchases directly support the weavers.

The main outlet for the sale of craft items is the town or village market. Market day is an important social as well as commercial occasion. Although large towns support daily markets, most villages have one main market per week, which takes place around the central square and surrounding streets.

Traders may journey for many hours to participate in important regional markets such as Tecpán, Sololá, San Francisco El Alto, and Totonicapán. Whereas women carry heavy items on their heads, men carry goods on their backs, supported by a leather strap wrapped around their foreheads.

Saturday market day in Almolonga is dedicated mainly to the sale of vegetables (baskets piled high with radishes and carrots make an impressive sight). The Chichicastenango market has developed primarily into a handicraft market for tourists, where very attractive souvenirs and gifts can be bought from the people who make them.

For a list of Guatemala's public holidays and its most important festivals around the country, see Travel Tips, page 366.

The local economy relies heavily on agriculture.

FESTIVALS

Every town and village has a patron saint, whose feast day is celebrated annually with a three- to five-day fiesta. Traders from all over the country flock to the fiesta locations with their goods, packing the streets round the central square with colorful stalls, and there are fairground rides for children.

"Festival queens" are elected at the start of the festivities and are driven around town on floats. In mixed-race communities, one of the "queens" is a *ladina* (part indigenous, part Spanish descent), the other a Maya girl. The municipality lays on a band and dancing in the town hall, whilst various trade organizations sponsor bands to play in the square. It is not unusual to find three bands playing different tunes within a few meters of each other!

No fiesta can claim to have been a total success unless at least one wealthy individual has

WEAVING SKIRTS

Artisans in the communities of Salcajá and Totonicapán specialize in weaving skirts and shawls with attractive tie-dyed (*jaspé*) patterns, which they sell in the markets. Tie-dyeing is a process in which a given number of yarns are bound at specific intervals so that when they are immersed in the dye solution the tied areas retain their original color. The resulting patterns range from simple checks to more complex tree and doll designs.

In Salcajá much of the work takes place in the streets, as the warp yarns for a series of skirts are often 50 meters (160ft) long and need to be stretched out and aligned before they are put on the loom.

sponsored the presentation of one of the masked dances. These fall into two categories: simple fancy-dress dances (usually presented by *ladinos*), where the participants dress up as various comic characters; and the older, traditional dances which tell the story of the Conquest (La Conquista) and the battles between the Christians and the Infidels (Los Moros). The deer dance (Baile de los Venados) is of pre-Conquest origins and is now performed regularly only in Santa Eulalia, as it requires a large cast and months of training to learn the text. The traditional dances are accompanied by music played on the marimba (a type of xylophone) and the native flute and drum.

Members of a dance troupe, wearing masks and costumes representing the Maya's Spanish conquerors, perform at a festival.

The culmination of every fiesta is the patron saint's procession, in which an image of this saint is accompanied by all the lesser saints, musicians, and masked dancers, and the event is trumpeted by fireworks.

FIRECRACKERS AND *TORITOS*

Fireworks are always an important and integral part of the annual fiesta throughout the highlands. They range from the firecrackers, bombs, and rockets that accompany the saints' processions, to the more sophisticated (and highly dangerous) cane structures in the shape of *toritos* (bullocks), which fit over each dancer and shoot rockets out in all directions.

Recommended to experience are the particularly colorful festivals that take place in Patzún for Corpus Christi (late May or early June), in Chichicastenango around December 21, and in Sololá and Nebaj on August 15. The exceptionally strong *cofradía* involvement gives these fiestas an added dimension.

On November 1 and 2 each year, all Maya communities remember their dead with a traditional celebration. A marimba band usually plays in the cemetery and families picnic by the graves of their relatives. In Santiago Sacatépequez, giant kites are brought to the cemetery. Their launch can be a memorable sight if there's enough wind. The village of Todos Santos Cuchumatán also holds its annual patron saint's festival at this time, which is renowned for its drunken horse race.

Easter is celebrated with large-scale Holy Thursday and Good Friday processions everywhere. In Antigua, beautiful carpets of colored sawdust are created for the chief participants in the processions to walk over, and the youths accompanying the processions dress up as Romans, Jews, and Penitents. Stuffed dummies representing Judas are hung from lampposts and burned on Good Friday. In many Maya communities there are also colorful enactments of the Last Supper inside the village church complex, and Passion plays take place on Good Friday, which culminate in Jesus and the Thieves being crucified.

So, important dates in the Catholic and Maya calendars are marked in visually arresting and varied ways, often with centuries-old symbolism that may have syncretized the Maya and Christian religions. It could be said that some of the same characteristics are echoed year-round in the striking handmade costumes worn by Maya men and women, particularly those of the *cofradía*, which not only reflect the individual identity of each village, but also the wearer's status in the community.

Masks and opulent costumes, decorated with metallic threads, mirrors, and ostrich feathers, are hired for the festival dances from costume houses in San Cristóbal Totonicapán or Chichicastenango.

MEN OF MAIZE

Maize, or Indian corn, has always been a staple of the Maya diet, and its sacred aspect plays an important symbolic role.

Since they first settled in Central America, the Maya have grown maize in much the same way. Toward the end of the dry season, they clear the ground – burning off trees and shrubbery in the jungle areas – and make a field known as the *milpa*. Then they dig a row of simple holes with a stick, and place in them the seeds kept from the previous year's crop. If the rains do not fail, in a few months they can hope to have a fresh yield of maize. Often the planting and harvesting were done by several families in the same village, thereby making the cultivation of maize another element that bound the community together.

After being picked, the ripe kernels are boiled with water and a small amount of white lime, making a paste that is the basis for a dough that can later be steamed and made into *tamales* or shaped into flat cakes which are toasted or grilled to make *tortillas*. Archeological digs have found mortars *(metates)* and pestles *(manos)* for grinding the maize kernels similar to those still used in Guatemalan villages today. Another preparation was the broth known as *atole*, which was often drunk with chili peppers in it as the first meal of the day, or fermented to make an alcoholic drink.

But beyond the use of maize as a food, it also occupies an important symbolic role for the Maya. The *Popol Vuh*, the great epic poem of the Guatemalan Maya, describes how the world was created. At first, the gods made mankind from mud, but this was washed away. Next, they made them of wood, but found that this creation was without life and imagination. The third attempt, in which men were made from flesh, ended when these creatures of flesh and blood turned to evil ways, and were finally wiped out in great rains.

The gods decided that to make proper men, they must fashion them from maize meal, "the making, the modeling of our first mother-father, with yellow corn, white corn alone for the flesh, food alone for the human legs and arms, for our first fathers..."

Not only was mankind made from maize, but several of the classic Maya gods represented maize. The figure known to archeologists as God K from the hieroglyphic codices is thought to represent the dragon who is one of the main gods in the Maya pantheon. This god is associated with semen and seeds in general and is seen as a life-giving principle.

This sacred aspect of maize has survived into the present day. Ceremonies for the fertility of the earth and a successful harvest are still common throughout the Guatemalan highlands in Maya villages. And the religious and ritual importance of the crop has also been brilliantly captured in modern Spanish literature by the Guatemalan writer Miguel Ángel Asturias in his novel *Hombres de Maíz* (Men of Maize). Asturias, who in 1971 became the first Latin American novelist to win the Nobel Prize for Literature, was always concerned with the social conditions of the poor, largely Maya in his native country. In *Men of Maize* he draws on sources such as the *Popol Vuh* or the book of *Chilam-Balam* to paint a complex picture of Maya life, their struggle to fit into the modern world, and their continuing dependency on the bounty of nature: "Yes, the earth was a huge nipple, one enormous breast to which every peasant was fastened, hungry for harvest, for milk with the real taste of woman's milk, the way the maize stalks taste when you chew them young and tender. A miraculous crop, the way they all shot up with the first downpours."

Cooking maize at a street market.

Cormorants on Bird Island, Río Dulce.

GUATEMALAN WILDLIFE

The country's diversity of landscape – from cloud forest to mangrove swamp – provides a habitat for an equally varied range of flora and fauna.

The wide variety of climate and habitat in Guatemala, along with its privileged position on the bridge between North and South America, has resulted in a remarkable degree of biodiversity for such a relatively small nation. Sadly, large areas of formerly rich habitat have been seriously degraded – in some cases effectively destroyed – by human activities. Since the 1950s, however, efforts have been increasing to preserve the most significant ecosystems, with the result that just under 50 protected areas have so far been established and several dozen more are under consideration.

The country can be roughly divided into three regions: a narrow Pacific coastal slope, around 50km (30 miles) wide; the highlands, comprising two principal mountain chains and the high plateaux of central Guatemala; and the huge lowland area in the northeast known as the Petén. There is also a much smaller lowland region stretching inland from the short Caribbean coastline, along the Polochic/Dulce and Motagua river valleys.

Revered by the ancient Maya, who believed the world was supported by the branches of a giant specimen, the ceiba is one of the largest hardwoods in the Americas.

Along with the rest of the Central American isthmus, Guatemala is seismically very vulnerable, forming as it does part of the Pacific "ring of fire." Parallel to the Pacific coast runs a chain of volcanoes, many of them active, which includes the region's highest peak, the Volcán

A caiman in Monterrico.

Tajumulco (4,220 meters/13,700ft). Rainfall varies from 500mm to 5,000mm (20–200 inches) a year. Combined with altitude and other factors, this results in more than a dozen different "life zones," which range from semi-desert and savanna to cloud forests, where precipitation is almost constant.

AMONG THE TREES

The name "Guatemala" is said to be derived from a Nahuatl expression, Quauhtitlan, meaning "between the trees," and, despite deforestation, over a third of the country still fits this description. The jungles of the Petén form part of the largest remaining block of moist tropical forest in Central America.

Such forests comprise the world's richest ecosystem in terms of diversity of flora and fauna. Those of Guatemala, however, which are close to the northernmost limit of tropical jungles, are less densely populated with species than the equatorial forests of South America.

The plant life includes the pine trees and mountain oaks of the highlands, tropical hardwoods such as the *ceiba* (up to 70 meters/230ft high), Guatemala's national tree, and some 500 species of orchid.

The distinctive scarlet macaw sometimes seen in the forested foothills.

AROUND THE MANGROVES

Mangrove swamps, occurring on both coasts, are highly specialized habitats in which the vegetation tolerates alternating fresh and salt water. Dominated by the red mangrove (rhizophora), they provide a vital breeding ground for fish and crustaceans and are often home to nesting colonies of birds such as egrets, herons, storks, ducks, and kingfishers. The endangered, elusive West Indian manatee, as well as crocodiles, iguanas, and otters, are among the creatures that can be seen in mangrove swamps such as in the **Biotopo Chacón Machaca**, on the north bank of the Río Dulce (see page 162).

Also on the Caribbean coast is the coastal reserve of **Biotopo Punta de Manabique**. Among its attractions are a swamp featuring a rare type of palm, known as *confra*, and beaches on which sea turtles lay their eggs. Turtle eggs are considered by some Central Americans to be an aphrodisiac and so they are often stolen, adding to the problems facing this endangered species.

GIANT RESERVE

In 1989, a government decree set aside the entire area north of 17° 10' N as the **Maya Biosphere Reserve**. This huge tract of the department of Petén, totaling around 1 million hectares (2.5 million acres) – or nearly 2 million hectares (5 million acres) if you include its severely degraded outer "buffer zone" – includes seven other protected areas within its boundaries. It covers 15 percent of the national territory and borders two other significant reserves, in Belize and Mexico. Sadly this protected status has not been able to stop widespread forest clearance by loggers and settlers, particularly in the west of the reserve, where loggers, campesinos, and ranchers have cleared vast tracts of land.

BIOSPHERE WILDLIFE

The Maya Biosphere Reserve is home to some of Guatemala's most spectacular animal species, including flamboyant parrots, parakeets, and toucans, as well as the region's largest mammal, Baird's tapir. This giant, weighing 150–400kg (330–880lb) and a distant relative of the rhinoceros, has a snout that looks like a small trunk.

> *The long-tailed howler monkey is so called due to the deep roar emitted by the male, which has enlarged vocal cords.*

A variety of wild boar called a peccary rummages for scraps on the forest floor, while other animals commonly found here include porcupines, opossums, and armadillos. Spider and deafening howler monkeys (the latter known locally as *zaraguates*) are regularly seen, often around Maya ruins where patches of rainforest remain – you are almost guaranteed to hear them at Tikal and Yaxhá.

Wild cats are found in Petén and other tropical forest reserves, though are rarely seen. Your best chance of seeing a jaguar (called a *tigre* in Guatemala) is in the Mirador Basin, though they are occasionally spotted in the very early morning at Tikal on the access road to the ruins. The much smaller ocelot and margay, as well as the puma, are also present across the Petén. Finally, the exotic-looking jaguarundi, the smallest and commonest of the wild cats, is perhaps the easiest to see as it is a daytime hunter.

There are more than 300 species of bird in the Tikal National Park alone, and this covers less than 6 percent of the total area of the biosphere reserve. They range from various tiny hummingbirds to the raucous and spectacular scarlet macaw. One rare but well-known bird found only in this region is the brightly plumaged ocellated turkey.

A less appealing discovery is the fearsome fer-de-lance, one of Latin America's most poisonous snakes, which inhabits the forest floor.

Iguanas at the Biotopo Monterrico-Hawaii reserve.

TIPS FOR BIRDWATCHERS

Visitors from temperate zones are often overwhelmed by the sheer variety of birds in a tropical woodland. For the novice, here are some tips worth following:

Birds are sensitive to air temperature, and the best time of day for observing any bird activity is the early morning, when it is cooler.

At times it may seem as if nothing is moving, then the arrival of a mixed feeding flock of small birds suddenly places huge demands on your identification skills. At such times, take notes rather than looking up details of each bird, which may cause you to miss several others.

Bear in mind that fruiting trees and columns of ants often attract a large number of birds. Stay close to one or the other for a while; this may prove to be more productive than moving around.

Make sure to wear long trousers and long-sleeved shirts to deter insects, and use plentiful amounts of insect-repellent cream.

Footwear is an important consideration. Sturdy boots with adequate ankle support, or rubber wellies, are highly recommended – and always watch where you step.

If you come across a snake, it will usually slither away unless you inadvertently corner it or step on it.

FRESHWATER WETLANDS

In the rainy season (May–November), the flooded Río Escondido forms the largest area of freshwater wetlands in Central America, a type of ecosystem that has almost vanished from the region as a result of drainage and land reclamation for farming.

In the northern part of the biosphere lies the **Biotopo El Zotz**, which takes its name from the Maya word for a bat. The fruit bats that live here provide a wonderful spectacle each evening as they emerge in their thousands from caves in the central part of this heavily wooded area.

A well-camouflaged butterfly.

CLOUD FOREST

South of the Petén lies the mountain chain of **Sierra de las Minas**, which is known for its high degree of endemism. This is the home of many threatened birds, including Guatemala's national bird, the quetzal, and is the only place in Guatemala where the harpy eagle (one of the world's largest birds of prey) has been seen in recent years. Jaguar and deer are also found here, the latter often a victim of the former.

With peaks more than 3,000 meters (9,000ft) above sea level, the biosphere reserve contains within its boundaries the largest remaining area of cloud forest in the country. This is a highly localized type of habitat, dependent on plentiful moisture throughout the year.

Guatemala is home to many beautiful, colorful butterflies, including the stunning blue morpho. Look out for the butterflies' huge caterpillars.

ECO-TOURISM

You will find organizations throughout the nation set up to help travelers explore Guatemala's outstanding natural environment. Eco-group Defensores de la Naturaleza (www.defensores.org.gt) combines conservation with sustainable tourism in the Sierra de las Minas and the Bocas del Polochic reserves (see page 162) and also manages the vast Sierra de Lacandón national park in Petén. ProPetén (www.propeten.org) is a conservation organization that runs projects in the Maya Biosphere Reserve including Las Guacamayas, a biological station near Waka' (El Perú) ruins. Here there's a great jungle lodge where you have a chance of seeing scarlet macaws and crocodiles. Based in the town of Cobán, Proyecto Eco-Quetzal concentrates on ecotourism projects in the Verapaces where visitors can stay with Q'eqchi' Maya villagers, including one community in a cloud forest where quetzal birds are common and another on an idyllic turquoise river home to profuse tropical birds.

For more information about voluntary work, contact Arcas (www.arcasguatemala.com), which runs a sea turtle project on the Pacific coast and an animal rescue center in Petén.

A TASTE OF THE WILDLIFE

For those unable to make the trip to the Petén, or to the mountains and valleys of eastern Guatemala, a visit to the **San Buenaventura de Atitlán** reserve (www.atitlanreserva.com) near Panajachel may be a good way to get a sense of the variety of flora and fauna in the country.

The reserve contains a butterfly farm, where 25 different species can be seen, along with 50 kinds of orchid. Various native plants, including fruit trees, have been planted to attract birds, which can be observed from a series of walkways, rope bridges, ziplines, and elevated platforms.

A RESPLENDENT BIRD

Spectacularly beautiful but rarely seen, the resplendent quetzal is a strong contender for the title of most magnificent tropical bird.

A member of the colorful trogon family, the resplendent quetzal is Guatemala's national bird. It has lent its name to the country's second city (Quezaltenango) and the Guatemalan currency, which bears a striking portrait of a male quetzal in flight, its tail streaming behind.

This rare creature is found only in undisturbed cloud forest at around 1,500–3,000 meters (5,000–10,000ft). It can be found virtually anywhere in Central America, from southern Mexico to western Panama, but habitat destruction has placed it high on the list of endangered species.

The adult male quetzal is bright, iridescent green with red underparts and an extraordinary tail, which can reach more than half a meter (2ft) in length. Its striking feathers were highly prized by the pre-Columbian peoples of Mesoamerica, who used them in the headdresses of their priests and rulers, and even in warfare. The Mexica (Aztecs) called the bird a *quetzal-tototl* and toward the end of a battle would sometimes name a *quetzal-owl* warrior, a practice which (until the arrival of the Spanish) was believed to guarantee victory. The birds' feathers were woven onto a frame and they completely concealed the warrior inside.

This warlike aspect also featured in the mythology of the Maya. The *nahual*, or spirit guide, of the great Maya leader Tecún Umán was a quetzal which fought on after his death at the hands of the Spaniards. According to the Maya, the red belly-plumage of the bird was the result of its having been dipped in the blood of slain warriors after the battle of Xela (Quezaltenango).

The steep reduction in the quetzals' numbers today is a reflection of the specialized nature of their dietary and habitat requirements. Although they will eat various kinds of fruit and insects – and even small lizards – their movements are closely tied to the presence of the wild avocado, whose fruit is a major part of their diet. They nest in tree-trunk hollows, but – unlike woodpeckers and parrots, for example – their bills are too weak to carve out holes, unless the tree is thoroughly rotten. They therefore often depend on nesting holes already carved by other birds.

Their breeding period is March–June, with a peak in April–May, which is the best time to look for them. Under normal circumstances quetzals spend most of their time in the upper branches of trees and are thus easily missed. Their plaintive, cooing call is unlikely to be noticed, except by the trained ear. In the breeding season, however, they are obliged to move around in lower branches because of the location of their nest sites, some 3–5 meters (10–16ft) above ground. Sometimes it is possible to detect their presence by the sight of tail plumes emerging from a hole in a tree trunk. The best time of day to look for them, as with most tropical birds, is in the early hours of the morning, when they are at their most active. However, they are also reported to feed in the early evening.

A pair of quetzals show off their magnificent plumage.

One of the key sites in Guatemala for quetzals is the Biotopo Mario Dary Rivera in Baja Verapaz. Located on the road to Cobán, this 1,000-hectare (2,500-acre) reserve reaches an altitude of 2,300 meters (7,500ft) and was established specifically to conserve quetzals and their cloud-forest habitat. It consists of two sections, of which the upper one is accessible only with permission, and is one of the best-preserved areas of cloud forest in the country.

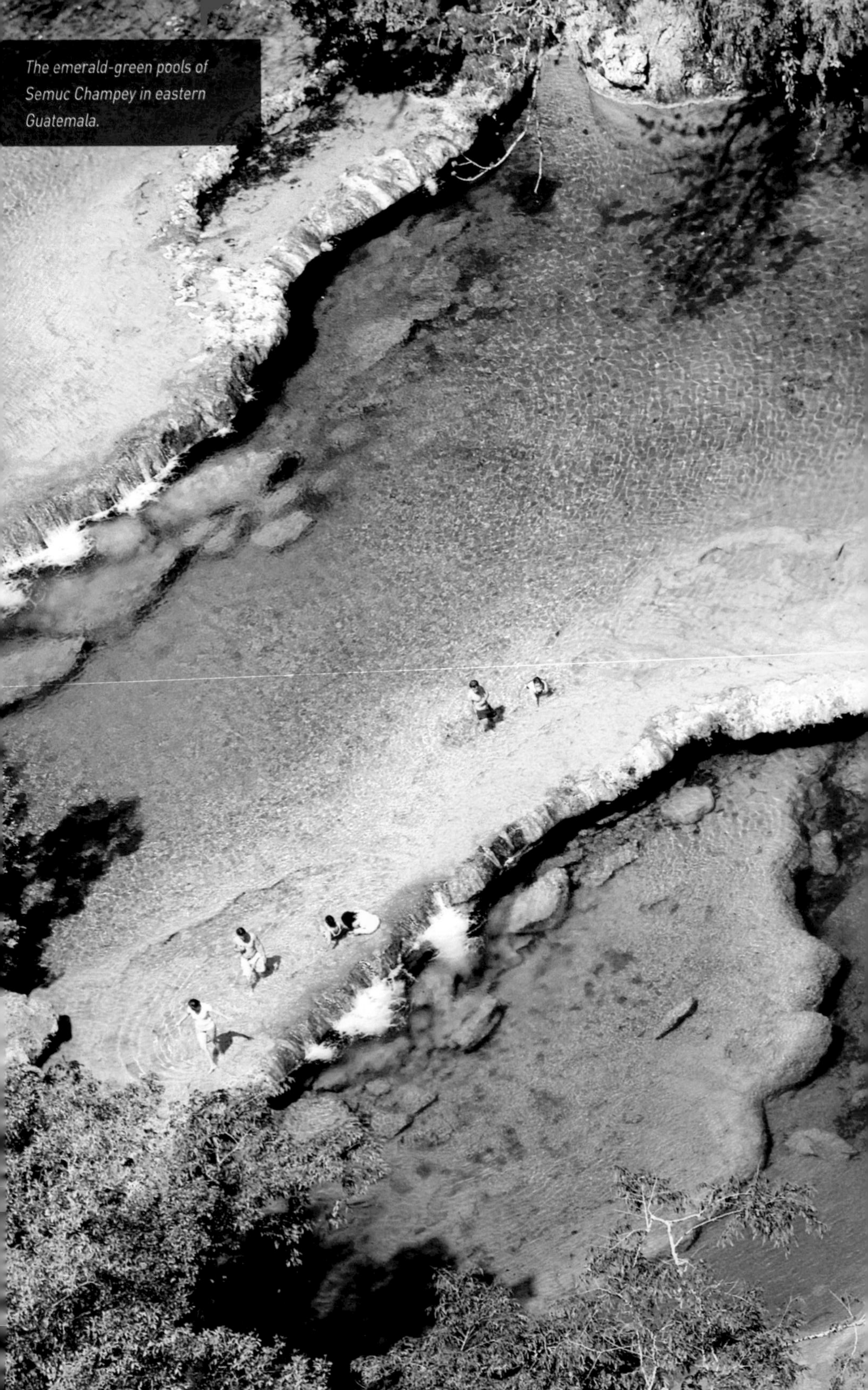

The emerald-green pools of Semuc Champey in eastern Guatemala.

Temple I at the Tikal ruins in Petén.

Working in the fields bordering Lake Atitlán.

Stela N at Copán's ruins.

GUATEMALA PLACES

A detailed guide to the entire country, with principal sites clearly cross-referenced by number to the maps.

Lago de Petén Itzá.

With a multitude of ancient Maya sites to explore, an extravagant colonial architectural legacy to enjoy, and spectacular natural sights, Guatemala is unsurprisingly many people's favorite country in Latin America.

For such a small country there are an astounding number of wonders. The western highlands are breathtakingly beautiful – an inspirational landscape of steep hillsides, sleepy adobe-walled villages, and whitewashed churches. The vast forest reserves of the northern lowlands once contained dozens of thriving Maya city-states. The grace and colonial splendor of the former capital, Antigua, make it the country's most beautiful city.

We begin in the capital, Guatemala City, the largest city in Central America. "Guate", as it is known throughout the country, is in many ways a typical Latin American capital, with the nation's most affluent suburbs and, conversely, the worst poverty and pollution. It is not an especially attractive city, though there are excellent museums and some interesting modern and historic buildings, but it is probably best to make your base in Antigua, less than an hour away.

Hand-weaving in the Highlands.

Antigua, the former capital, is everything that Guate is not: compact, relaxed, and visually stunning. It's a supremely rewarding place to spend a few days; exploring the great ruined Baroque churches, wandering the cobbled streets and enjoying some of the fantastic courtyard cafés and restaurants. Antigua is also a great base for a number of excellent excursions into the surrounding countryside. There are four volcanoes to climb, including Volcán Pacaya, one of the most active in Central America; the shrine of the wicked saint Maximón at San Andrés Itzapa, coffee plantations, and textile markets.

Antigua sits on the cusp of the western highlands, an intoxicatingly beautiful world where most of Guatemala's Maya live, and which is many people's favorite part of the entire country. The volcanic scenery is magnificent, crowned by the awesome beauty of Lago de Atitlán, with its lakeside resort, Panajachel, and 15 other Maya villages to visit. The color and sheer spectacle of Chichicastenango's twice-weekly market is another amazing sight – this is one of the best places to purchase traditional Guatemalan

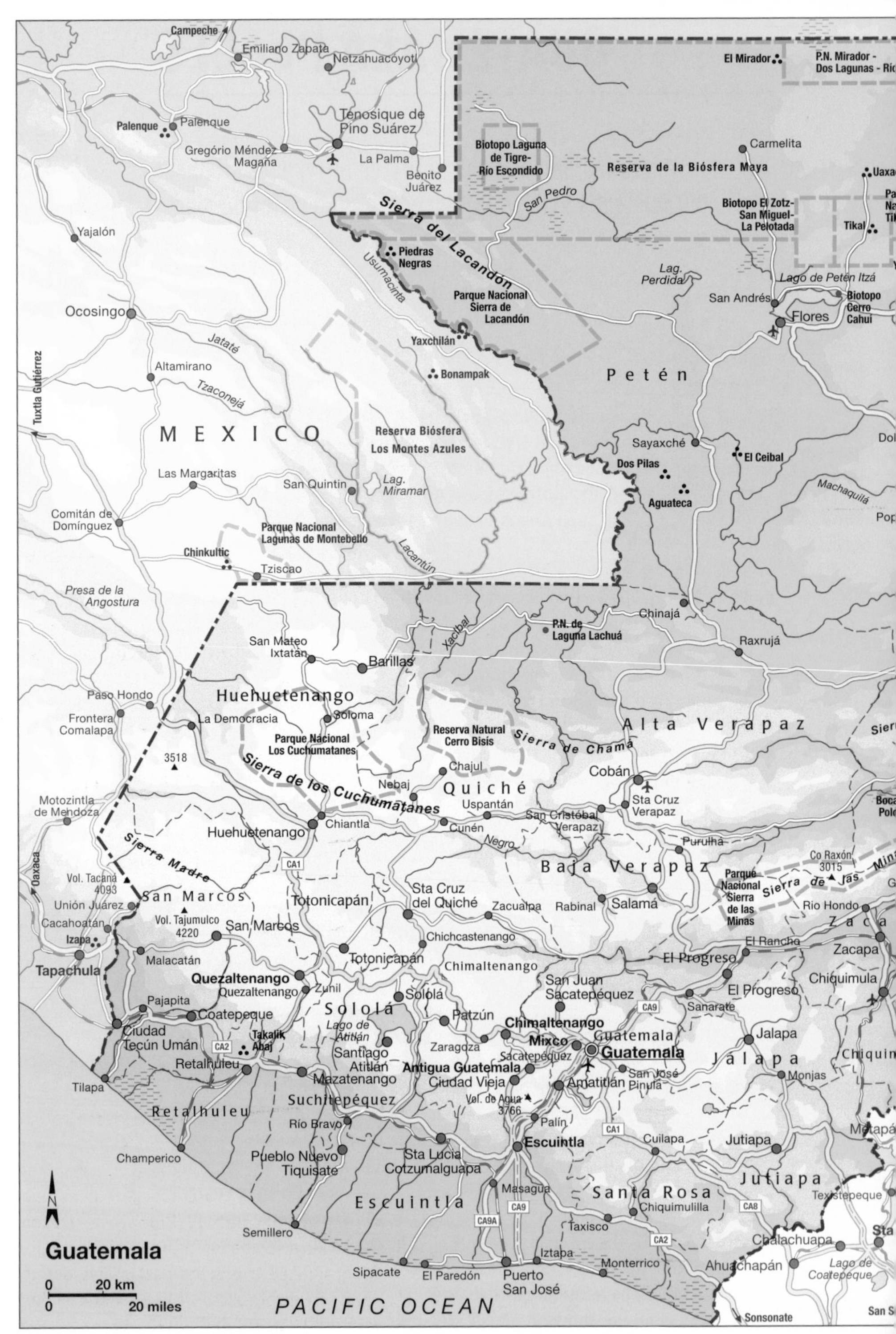
Campeche
Emiliano Zapata
Netzahuacoyotl
El Mirador
P.N. Mirador - Dos Lagunas - Río
Palenque
Palenque
Tenosique de Pino Suárez
Gregório Méndez Magaña
La Palma
Benito Juárez
Biotopo Laguna de Tigre-Río Escondido
Carmelita
Reserva de la Biósfera Maya
Uaxa
San Pedro
Biotopo El Zotz-San Miguel-La Pelotada
Tikal
Yajalón
Sierra del Lacandón
Piedras Negras
Usumacinta
Lag. Perdida
Lago de Petén Itzá
Parque Nacional Sierra de Lacandón
San Andrés
Biotopo Cerro Cahui
Flores
Ocosingo
Jataté
Yaxchilán
Bonampak
Altamirano
Tzaconejá
Petén
Tuxtla Gutiérrez
MEXICO
Reserva Biósfera Los Montes Azules
Sayaxché
El Ceibal
Dos Pilas
Aguateca
Machaquilá
Las Margaritas
San Quintín
Lag. Miramar
Comitán de Domínguez
Parque Nacional Lagunas de Montebello
Lacantún
Chinkultic
Tziscao
Presa de la Angostura
Chinajá
Xacbal
P.N. de Laguna Lachuá
Raxrujá
San Mateo Ixtatán
Barillas
Huehuetenango
Paso Hondo
Frontera Comalapa
La Democracia
Soloma
Parque Nacional Los Cuchumatanes
Reserva Natural Cerro Bisis
Sierra de Chamá
Alta Verapaz
3518
Sierra de los Cuchumatanes
Chajul
Nebaj
Quiché
Cobán
Sta Cruz Verapaz
Uspantán
San Cristóbal Verapaz
Motozintla de Mendoza
Chiantla
Huehuetenango
Cunén
Negro
Purulhá
Sierra Madre
CA1
Baja Verapaz
Co Raxón 3015
Oaxaca
Vol. Tacaná 4093
Parque Nacional Sierra de las Minas
Sierra de las Minas
San Marcos
Totonicapán
Sta Cruz del Quiché
Zacualpa
Rabinal
Salamá
Unión Juárez
Río Hondo
Cacahoatán
Vol. Tajumulco 4220
San Marcos
Chichcastenango
Izapa
El Rancho
Zacapa
Tapachula
Malacatán
Totonicapán
Chimaltenango
El Progreso
Quezaltenango
Quezaltenango
Zunil
San Juan Sacatepéquez
Chiquimula
Pajapita
Sololá
El Progreso
Coatepeque
Sololá
Sanarate
CA9
Lago de Atitlán
Patzún
Chimaltenango
Ciudad Tecún Umán
Takalik Abaj
Santiago Atitlán
Zaragoza
Mixco
Guatemala
Guatemala
Jalapa
CA2
Sacatepéquez
Jalapa
Retalhuleu
Antigua Guatemala
San José Pinula
Chiquimula
Tilapa
Mazatenango
Ciudad Vieja
Amatitlán
Monjas
Suchitepéquez
Vol. de Agua 3766
Retalhuleu
Río Bravo
Palín
CA1
Metapán
Champerico
Escuintla
Cuilapa
Jutiapa
Pueblo Nuevo Tiquisate
Sta Lucía Cotzumalguapa
Jutiapa
Masagua
Escuintla
Santa Rosa
Texistepeque
CA9
CA8
CA9A
Chiquimulilla
Semillero
Taxisco
CA2
Chalchuapa
Guatemala
Iztapa
Monterrico
Ahuachapán
Lago de Coatepeque
Sipacate
El Paredón
Puerto San José
0 20 km
0 20 miles
PACIFIC OCEAN
Sonsonate

textiles, crafts, and souvenirs. There are more fascinating villages around the second city of Quezaltenango to the west. The nearby market towns are especially interesting, and include Zunil, where there is another shrine to Maximón and the heavenly hot springs of Fuentes Georginas. San Francisco El Alto hosts possibly the largest market in Central America every Friday.

Below the highlands, the Pacific beaches are not Guatemala's best attraction, but the small resorts of Monterrico and El Paredón (home to a fine new surf lodge) are worth a visit. Heading east of the capital, there are hot springs, waterfalls, and a Spanish-built fortress to see around peaceful Lago de Izabal and the momentous Río Dulce gorge. Right on the Caribbean coast, the Garífuna village of Lívingston is home to Guatemala's only black population, and the cuisine and music (reggae and punta rock) make a fascinating cultural diversion from the rest of the country. There's the alpine scenery and cave systems of the Verapaces around Cobán, a town that is fast establishing itself as Guatemala's top ecotourism destination. Not far from Cobán are the exquisite pools of Semuc Champey, the turquoise lake of Laguna Lachuá, and the Quetzal Reserve – where there are significant numbers of this beautiful national bird.

In the far north of Guatemala, the magnificent jungles and savannas of Petén comprise nearly one-third of the national landmass. This region was once the very heart of the Classic Maya civilization, led by the city-states of El Mirador, Tikal, and Yaxhá. The delicate ecosystem is home to a plethora of exotic animals, including jaguar, tapir, toucans, and monkeys.

At the magnificent ruins of Tikal you have every chance of seeing wildlife as well as the superb monumental architecture and carved stelae. There are hotels at the ruins, or alternatively stay at the pleasant island town of Flores or El Remate, another village on the great Lago de Petén Itzá. Dozens more Maya cities lie in the Petén's jungles; an organized trip is the best way to see the more rewmote sites of El Mirador, Nakbé, Piedras Negras, and Aguateca.

Guatemala City.

GUATEMALA CITY

Guatemala's capital has an undeniable energy, some good museums, and quirky attractions, even if it is not the most graceful city.

It is the political and administrative hub of the country, but many travelers prefer to make their base in the more charming and tranquil Antigua.

An urban vortex of humanity and traffic, Guatemala City, colloquially known as "Guate," is in most respects everything that the rest of the country is not. Plagued by pollution, many of the crumbling streets of the central zone are run down, but steadily parts of the historic centre are being revitalized by pedestrianization, renovation, and improved transportation links. In the richer suburbs in the south of the city, the atmosphere is very different, but even here the bougainvillea flowers draped over middle-class homes are intertwined with razor wire, put up to deter intruders.

Nevertheless, if you want to get a real flavor of the complexities (and inequalities) of the country, then a day or two in "Guate" is essential. Stroll pretty La Sexta avenue (Paseo de la Sexta, also known as la Calle de los Abuelos) in the historic centre and take a coffee, and mingle with the Guatemalan elite in the Zona Viva. There are several excellent museums and a cosmopolitan plethora of restaurants, bars, and clubs. The climate – as the city is at 1,500 meters (4,900ft) – is also benign, and never gets oppressively hot.

ORIGINS AND DEVELOPMENT

Guatemala City ❶ is actually the country's fourth capital city, only established after a series of catastrophic earthquakes and mudslides all but destroyed nearby Antigua in 1773. Yet the new capital was built close to the ruins of Kaminaljuyú, which 2,000 years ago was the most important highland Maya city.

Today, the plazas and temples of **Kaminaljuyú** have been all but swallowed by Guatemala City's suburbs, and the architectural remains in Zona 7, 3km (2 miles) from the center of town, give no

Main Attractions

- Palacio Nacional
- Catedral
- Casa Mima
- Teatro Nacional
- Museo Ixchel del Traje Indígena
- Museo Popol Vuh de Arqueología
- Museo Nacional de Arqueología y Etnología
- Kaminaljuyú
- Volcán de Pacaya

Maps on pages 112, 116

The Centro Cívico.

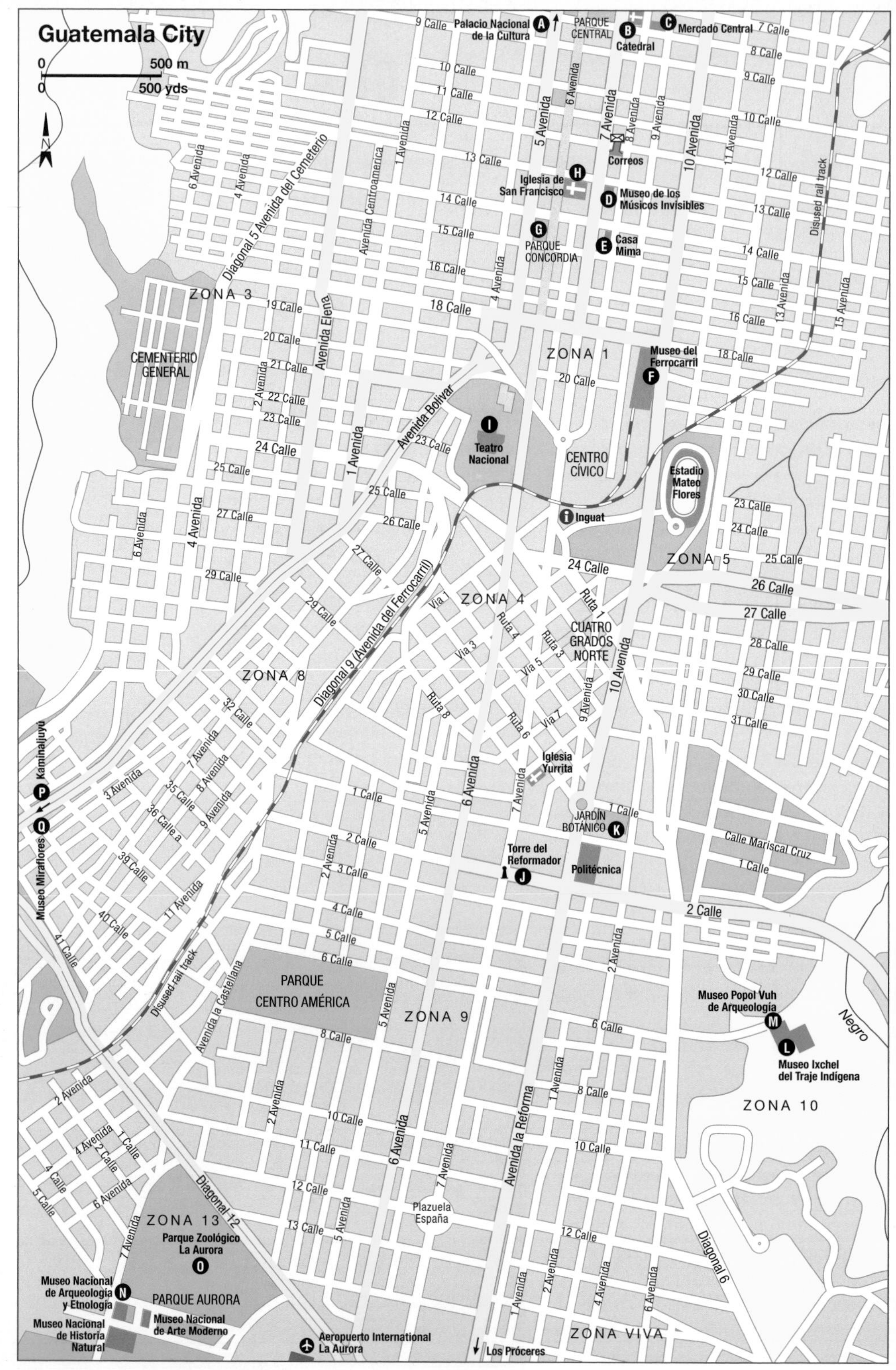
Guatemala City
0 500 m
0 500 yds
Palacio Nacional de la Cultura
PARQUE CENTRAL
Catedral
Mercado Central
Correos
Iglesia de San Francisco
Museo de los Músicos Invisibles
PARQUE CONCORDIA
Casa Mima
ZONA 3
ZONA 1
CEMENTERIO GENERAL
Museo del Ferrocarril
Teatro Nacional
CENTRO CÍVICO
Estadio Mateo Flores
Inguat
ZONA 5
ZONA 4
CUATRO GRADOS NORTE
ZONA 8
Iglesia Yurrita
JARDÍN BOTÁNICO
Torre del Reformador
Politécnica
Kaminaljuyú
Museo Miraflores
PARQUE CENTRO AMÉRICA
ZONA 9
Museo Popol Vuh de Arqueología
Museo Ixchel del Traje Indígena
ZONA 10
Plazuela España
ZONA 13
Parque Zoológico La Aurora
Museo Nacional de Arqueología y Etnología
PARQUE AURORA
Museo Nacional de Historia Natural
Museo Nacional de Arte Moderno
Aeropuerto International La Aurora
Los Próceres
ZONA VIVA
Diagonal 5 Avenida del Cementerio
Avenida Elena
Avenida Centroamerica
Avenida Bolivar
Diagonal 9 (Avenida del Ferrocarril)
Disused rail track
Avenida la Castellana
Avenida la Reforma
Diagonal 12
Diagonal 6
Calle Mariscal Cruz
Negro

impression of the Maya city's size (around 50,000 inhabitants) and its position as a pivotal trade center for the transportation of obsidian and quetzal feathers.

The new capital did not develop quickly at first, but following the 1902 earthquake that decimated the rival city of Quezaltenango, Guatemala City grew rapidly and uncontrollably as waves of migrants arrived in the capital. Many were landless *campesinos* (land workers), who were forced to settle in totally inappropriate *barrio* shantytowns, situated tight against railroad tracks and highways and on the fringes of the ravines that surround the north of the city.

Guatemala City, in common with most capitals in the developing world, faces many problems, yet in recent years there have been sure signs of regeneration. The city now boasts a modern bus transportation system, the Transmetro (www.muniguate.com/muni/transmetro), which is efficient, secure, and the fastest way to get around. New life has been breathed into the heart of the city, Zona 1, as restaurants and bohemian bars have opened in colonial buildings. That said, crime, pollution, and urban decay remain pressing issues, and much work needs to be done before Guate becomes a really rewarding place to visit.

GETTING YOUR BEARINGS

Fortunately, almost everything of interest is in five zones: Zona 1 in the north of the city, Zona 4 in the center, and Zonas 9, 10, and 13 in the south. In common with most Latin American capitals, Guatemala City is organized according to the Spanish grid system: all *calles* run east to west and all *avenidas* north to south. The Parque Central in the heart of Zona 1 is the most important landmark. Other landmarks include the Centro Cívico bureaucratic buildings and the Torre del Reformador, a Guatemalan copy of the Eiffel Tower, in Zona 9.

To find an address, first find the *zona*, followed by the street, and then the number. If you are given the address "10 C, 12–15, Zona 9", first look for Zona 9, then the street (10 Calle), then the number (12–15); 12 means the street is between 12 and 13 avenidas, and 15 is the number of the house.

ZONA 1

The Parque Central is considered both the heart of the city and the nation; indeed, all distances are measured from here. It is surrounded by some of the most historic and prestigious edifices in the country. On Sundays, when it is occupied by a huge indigenous textiles market, this plaza really comes to life.

Presiding over the Parque, on the northern side, is the monumental bulk of the **Palacio Nacional de la Cultura** Ⓐ (daily 9.30am–4pm; http://mcd.gob.gt/palacio-nacional-de-la-cultura), built by the architect Rafael Pérez de León during the Ubico dictatorship between 1939 and 1943. The Palacio contained the presidential offices until 1998; you can take a guided tour (in English and Spanish; tel: 5971-5593; palacionacionalgt@gmail.com). The sober grey-green stone exterior belies an eclectically decorative interior

> **Tip**
>
> Guatemala City presents security concerns for travelers, and you should always take basic precautions to minimize the risk of being robbed: keep your valuables (including cell phones) out of sight. Though Zona 1 looks run down, it is considered safe to explore during daylight hours and in the early evening. The Zona Viva (in Zona 10) is a lively upmarket area, and the sheer number of cafés and restaurants here make it fine to explore on foot, except perhaps very late at night. The Transmetro bus network is a safe, fast way to get around the city, but after 8pm or so stick to taxis – Amarillo (tel: 2470 1515; www.amarilloexpress.com) is a reliable company with metered cabs.

Palacio Nacional.

The Guatemalan flag flying in Zona 4.

of Moorish and neoclassical influences. Giant stairwell murals by Alfredo Gálvez Suárez depict an idealized history of Guatemala, and in the reception hall on the first floor a massive chandelier groans under the weight of crystal and four bronze quetzals. In the banqueting hall are stained-glass windows by Julio Urruela Vásquez and Roberto González Goyri. Don't miss the two attractive Mudéjar (Moorish) inner courtyards planted with palm trees on the ground floor.

Dominating the east side of the Parque Central is the city **Catedral** B (daily 7am–noon, 3–7pm; free; http://catedralbicentenaria.org), constructed in a mixture of Baroque and neoclassical styles between 1782 and 1809, though its blue-tiled dome and towers were added later, in 1868. It does not rank amongst Guatemala's most impressive churches, but its sturdy construction has at least survived two earthquakes. The somewhat austere interior contains three naves and 16 altars, some painted in gold leaf. Its small museum contains religious art (Tue–Fri 9am–1pm, 2–5pm, Sat until 4pm).

Iglesia de San Francisco.

Around the corner from the Catedral on 8 Calle is the **Mercado Central** C, in an inauspicious triple-deck sunken concrete block. Though it does not look especially inviting, this is quite a good place to shop for textiles, leather goods, basketry, and other handicrafts. If you are feeling adventurous, there's a huge number of foodstalls on the middle floor serving up a range of *caldos* (stews) and snacks.

Heading south from the Mercado, the **Correos** (post office), on 12 Calle and 7 Avenida, is the next place of interest. Its great arch spans 12 Calle and the whole building is painted salmon pink. Continuing south along 7 Avenida you soon reach **Museo de los Músicos Invisibles** D (Mon–Fri 9am–5pm), a quirky museum devoted to the "invisible musician" which has an incredible collection of automated antique musical instruments – including organs, jukeboxes, and Art Deco radios – all in working order, and demonstrated as part of the tour. A block south of here on 8 Avenida is **Casa Mima** E (Mon–Sat 10am–5pm; www.casamima.org), a fine 19th-century town house that has been beautifully restored and contains some fine period furniture and furnishings. Six blocks from here, at 18 Calle and 9 Avenida, Guatemala City's former train station has been converted into the excellent **Museo del Ferrocarril** F (Tue–Fri 9am–4pm, Sat–Sun 10am–4pm; http://museofegua.com), devoted to the history of Guatemalan railroads. There are several superb old steam engines, plus a small collection of classic cars and train paraphernalia.

If you head west of here you can return to the Parque Central via pedestrianized Sexta Avenida (6 Av), a delight to stroll as it takes you past fine 19th-century and Art Nouveau buildings and cafés. You will pass the **Parque Concordia** G, a small green oasis with a good percentage of Zona 1's very few trees. This little city park is popular with preachers, *limpiabotas* (shoeshine boys), street performers, quack medicine sellers, and amateur philosophers.

Next up, close to the castle-like Police Headquarters, is the **Iglesia de San Francisco** H. The church was built in 1780 in an Italianate neoclassical style, and the mortar used to construct it consisted of milk, cane syrup, and egg white. There is a terrific collection of paintings of martyrs, and the relics include the sacred heart of Trujillo. A small but worthwhile museum inside the church houses the belongings of Fray Francisco Vásquez, a Franciscan friar. From here the Parque Central is just a five-minute walk away, to the north.

THE CENTRO CÍVICO – ZONA 4

Bridging the divide between the old quarter of Zona 1 and the richer, leafy environs of Zonas 9 and 10 is the cluster of concrete buildings known as the Centro Cívico. Here you will find **Inguat** (www.inguat.gob.gt), the tourist board HQ, housed in a large block on 7 Avenida, near the railroad tracks.

The **Teatro Nacional** I, part of the Centro Cultural Miguel Ángel Asturias (www.ccmaa.gob.gt), is also in this zone, set superbly above the traffic on the remains of the old Spanish fortress of San José – the ancient ramparts are still evident. The views over the city and of the surrounding mountains, including Volcán de Pacaya, are excellent. The Teatro Nacional was completed in 1978 to a radical design that has a distinctly nautical flavor, painted blue and white, with porthole windows, reminiscent of an ocean liner. A Greek-style outdoor theater, a small chamber-music auditorium, and a small armament museum complete the complex (Mon–Fri 9am–5pm and for performances).

In the south of Zona 4, the neo-Gothic **Iglesia Yurrita** (Nuestra Señora de las Angustias) on Ruta 6 is a startling sight (note the leaning spire, damaged in the 1976 earthquake).

ZONAS 9 AND 10

These two wealthy *zonas* are bisected by Avenida la Reforma, an attractive tree-lined boulevard. Zona 9, to the west, is the less exclusive of the two, with a mixed combination of businesses, mid-range restaurants, and hotels. The one landmark in this part of the city is the **Torre del Reformador** J, a small-scale imitation of the Eiffel Tower in Paris, erected in 1935 in honor of Guatemala's liberal reformer, President Rufino Barrios (1873–85). At the southern end of the boulevard is the Parque El Obelisco, named after the huge obelisk commemorating Guatemalan independence.

On the opposite side of Avenida la Reforma, in Zona 10, there is much more of interest. This is the natural abode of Guatemala's wealthy elite, with a good proportion of all the city's luxurious hotels, restaurants, and nightlife. At the **Jardín Botánico** K (Botanical Garden; http://sitios.usac.edu.gt/jardinbotanico), just off the Avenida la Reforma on Calle Mariscal Cruz, there's a diverse range of nearly 1,000

Cashew fruits are among the many exotic fruits, vegetables, and flowers sold at the Mercado Central.

The Catedral on Parque Central.

Taking a break at the Museo del Ferrocarril, a museum devoted to the history of Guatemalan railroads.

species of Guatemalan plant life, and a small museum with some stuffed birds, including a quetzal (Mon–Fri 8.30am–3pm).

TOP MUSEUMS

Perhaps the two biggest attractions in the city are the twin museums inside the verdant grounds of the Universidad Francisco Marroquín, down 6 Calle Final in the valley of the Río Negro. **Museo Ixchel del Traje Indígena** Ⓛ, superbly set in a dramatic Maya-esque structure, is dedicated to Maya culture, especially textiles. All the exhibits are clearly presented and explained in English as well as Spanish; it also has a good gift shop selling some unusual textiles (Mon–Fri 9am–5pm, Sat 9am–1pm; https://museoixchel.org).

The **Museo Popol Vuh de Arqueología** Ⓜ, adjacent to the Ixchel, is another private museum with a small range of top-quality archeological artifacts arranged into pre-Classic, Maya Classic, post-Classic and Colonial rooms. Highlights include a replica of the Dresden Codex and some stunning funerary urns (Mon–Fri 9am–5pm, Sat 9am–1pm; http://popolvuh.ufm.edu).

There are also a couple of museums worth a visit in Zona 13, just to the south (all Tue–Fri 9am–4pm, Sat–Sun 9am–noon, 1.30–4pm). By far the most impressive is the **Museo Nacional de Arqueología y Etnología** Ⓝ (http://mcd.gob.gt/museo-nacional-de-arqueologia-y-etnologia), in the Parque Aurora, which has some spectacular Maya art, costumes, masks, and jade artifacts. Spend an hour or two at the **Parque Zoológico La Aurora** Ⓞ close by, where there is plenty of endemic wildlife, and even elephants, tigers, leopards, and lions, all looking quite healthy (Tue–Sun 9am–4pm; http://www.aurorazoo.org.gt).

The whole area is expected to be transformed when the new **Museo Maya de América** (MUMA; http://museomayadeamerica.org) opens on the site of the former Mercado de Artesania. Designed by Harry Gugger Studio from Basel, Switzerland, it is a modern take on Mayan temple architecture and it is hoped to trigger

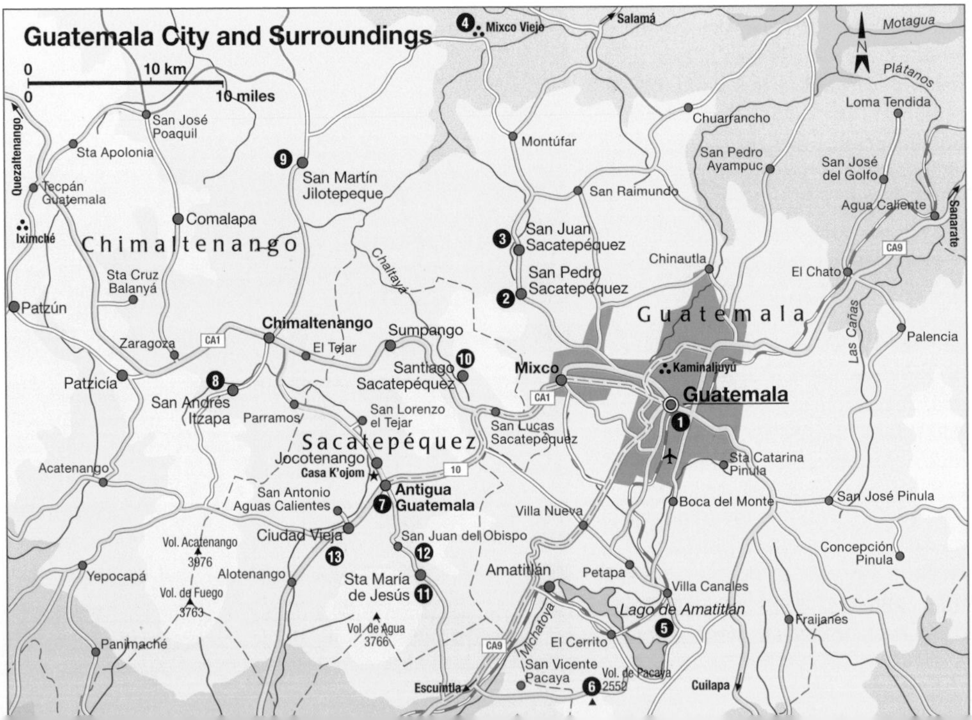

Guatemala City and Surroundings

0 10 km
0 10 miles

Chimaltenango · Sacatepéquez · Guatemala · Guatemala · Mixco · Antigua Guatemala · Chimaltenango · Lago de Amatitlán · Kaminaljuyú · Mixco Viejo · Iximché · San Juan Sacatepéquez · San Pedro Sacatepéquez · San Martín Jilotepeque · Sumpango · Santiago Sacatepéquez · San Lucas Sacatepéquez · Jocotenango · Casa K'ojom · Ciudad Vieja · San Juan del Obispo · Sta María de Jesús · Amatitlán · Villa Nueva · Petapa · Villa Canales · Sta Catarina Pinula · Boca del Monte · San José Pinula · Concepción Pinula · Fraijanes · El Cerrito · San Vicente Pacaya · Vol. de Pacaya 2552 · Vol. de Agua 3766 · Vol. de Fuego 3763 · Vol. Acatenango 3976 · Escuintla · Cuilapa · Salamá · Motagua · Plátanos · Sanarate · Palencia · El Chato · Chinautla · Agua Caliente · San José del Golfo · Loma Tendida · San Pedro Ayampuc · Chuarrancho · Montúfar · San Raimundo · Comalapa · San José Poaquil · Sta Apolonia · Tecpán Guatemala · Patzún · Sta Cruz Balanyá · Zaragoza · Patzicía · San Andrés Itzapa · Parramos · El Tejar · San Lorenzo el Tejar · San Antonio Aguas Calientes · Acatenango · Yepocapá · Alotenango · Panimaché · Quezaltenango · Chaltaya · Las Cañas · Michatoya · CA1 · CA9 · 10

a "Guggenheim Bilbao effect" and bring swathes of new visitors to the capital. The building will house both the national Maya collection and the private collection of the Ruta Maya Foundation, and will also incorporate the collections of the Museo de Historia Natural, Museo de Arte Moderno and Museo del Niño.

AROUND GUATEMALA CITY

Heading northwest of the capital, along Calle de San Juan Sacatepéquez, you pass close to the ruins of **Kaminaljuyú** ❶, once one of the most important cities of the Maya world, and believed to be one of the very first centers where writing developed. It is now reduced to an inauspicious collection of grassy mounds, but you can get an idea of its former splendor in the nearby **Museo Miraflores** Ⓠ on Calzada Roosevelt (Tue–Sun 9am–7pm, www.museomiraflores.org.gt), a 10-minute walk south of the ruins. This modern museum has exhibits such as stone sculptures and ceramics, jade jewelry, and also a permanent exhibition of Guatemalan textiles.

Continuing farther out of the city, you pass through the Maya villages of **San Pedro Sacatepéquez** ❷ and **San Juan Sacatepéquez** ❸, both sharing a prestigious weaving tradition and the same market day – Friday – when they come alive, particularly the larger San Juan, where the women wear striking *huipiles*. Some 28km (17.5 miles) from San Juan Sacatepéquez are the ruins of **Mixco Viejo** ❹, the former capital of the Pokoman Maya. The site, comprising nine temples and two ball courts, has been well restored, forming a dramatic setting on flat-topped ridges surrounded by steep ravines (daily 8am–4pm; http://mcd.gob.gt/mixco-viejo-chuaw-nima-abaj).

About 30km (18.5 miles) to the south of Guatemala City, following the Carretera del Pacífico, is one of the most beautiful lakes in Guatemala, **Lago de Amatitlán** ❺. Unfortunately, its waters have been polluted for years and are not safe for swimming.

High above the lake is **Volcán de Pacaya** ❻ (www.volcanpacaya.info; daily 7am–5pm), one of the most active volcanoes in Central America, which has been in a state of almost constant eruption since 1965. Pacaya is an astonishing sight, especially at night when the finest sound and light show in Guatemala can paint the sky orange with great plumes of lava and gas. There are two trails to climb the volcano: La Corona, in Concepción El Cedro, and through the visitors center in San Francisco de Sales. All visitors need to register at the entrance of the park; to camp here you will need a special permit from the park's authorities, to be requested 48 hours in advance.

Tour agencies in Antigua or Guatemala City can arrange transportation and a guide for the volcano hike, which is about a one-hour climb. (see page 374, for contact details).

Tip

The Museo Ixchel has a superb collection of *huipiles* complete with explanations about the weaving process and the importance of Maya symbolism in the colorful patterns and designs.

The active Volcán de Pacaya.

Elaborate sawdust carpets and procession celebrating Semana Santa.

ANTIGUA

The colonial charm of this tranquil city and its setting amid forest-clad volcanic peaks make it one of the most popular tourist destinations in Guatemala.

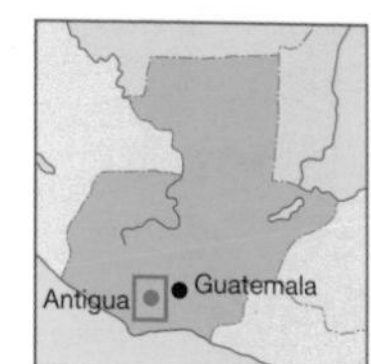

Serene, civilized **Antigua Guatemala ❼**, the former capital, is the most beautiful city in the entire Maya region. The attractions are outstanding. Primarily, there is the vast legacy of stunning colonial architecture. The city's compact size (population around 45,000) is another factor – walking the almost traffic-free cobbled streets is a pleasure, and the pace of life is easy-going. The city's inhabitants, Antigüeños, are an outward-looking and cultured bunch, well used to playing host to visitors from overseas. Enhancing the cosmopolitan atmosphere, hundreds of people from all over the world have been seduced by Antigua's charm and the temperate climate and settled in the city to run European and North American-style restaurants, cafés, and bars.

The setting is also spectacular, in a beautiful, broad highland valley where the hills are thick with pine trees and even cloud forest on the upper slopes, interspersed with coffee plantations and small *milpas* (cornfields). Higher above the tree line and enveloping the city are three giant cones: Volcán de Agua, which destroyed the first Guatemalan capital; Volcán de Fuego, active and smoking plumes of gas; and slumbering Volcán Acatenango, the largest but least threatening of the trio.

EARTHQUAKE THREAT

Few cities anywhere in the world can claim such a cataclysmic history, founded on disaster and punctuated by periods of glory and seismic destruction. Antigua was actually the third capital of Guatemala. The Spanish first settled close to the modern town of Tecpán, near the ruins of their allies, the Kaqchikel Maya, at Iximché, but quickly moved to set up a permanent capital near the town of Ciudad Vieja in 1527. Disaster soon struck here, though, and after torrential rain,

Main Attractions

Maps on pages 116, 120, 124

Shoeshiners by Parque Central.

Participant in the costumed procession marking Semana Santa.

a massive mudslide from nearby Volcán de Agua destroyed the settlement and killed the widow of Alvarado the conquistador. The site chosen for the third capital, in the Panchoy valley just 5km (3 miles) away, is where Antigua stands today.

The city we know today as Antigua, originally called Santiago de los Caballeros de Guatemala, grew steadily after it was founded in 1543 to become the most important city in the Americas between Mexico City and Lima. Prestigious political and municipal buildings were constructed and a wave of religious orders moved in and added churches, monasteries, convents, and schools. Bishops and wealthy merchants commissioned imposing palaces. A printing press, only the third in the Americas, was installed in 1660. A university was established in 1681. Yet the entire colony was underpinned by a complex apartheid system that divided the population into rigid social classes: Spanish-born whites, Guatemalan-born whites, *mestizos*, mulattos, African-born slaves, and Maya at the bottom of the heap.

Santiago expanded further following the 1717 earthquake, which demolished many weaker buildings and necessitated the strengthening of those remaining. Many of Antigua's colonial structures date from this period, built in a uniquely "squat Baroque" style with colossal walls in an attempt to resist future seismic activity.

The city prospered again until 1773, its population growing to around 75,000, when a six-month long series of tremors all but crippled the capital. Damage and disease epidemics forced the government out of the city, and the king of Spain ordered it to be evacuated in favor of a new capital (Guatemala City) some 45km (28 miles) away in the valley of Ermita.

Antigua was never completely abandoned, and the fertile hillsides around the old capital proved perfect for the production of cochineal dye and coffee. Wealthy enthusiasts renovated colonial mansions, and

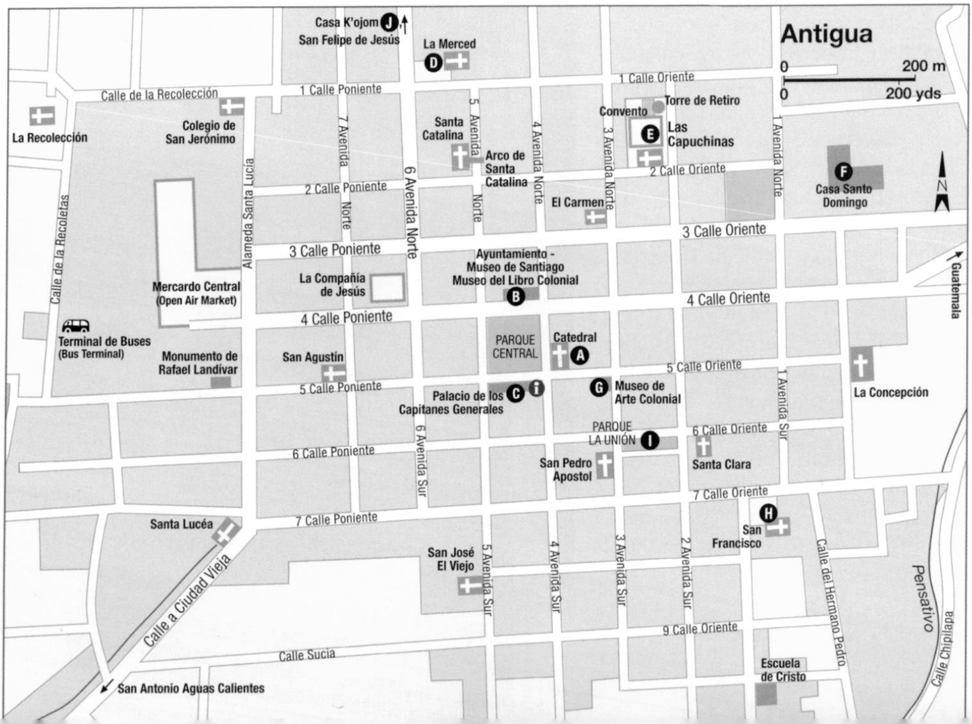

Antigua
0 200 m
0 200 yds
Casa K'ojom J
San Felipe de Jesús
La Merced D
La Recolección
Colegio de San Jerónimo
Santa Catalina
Arco de Santa Catalina
Convento
Torre de Retiro
Las Capuchinas E
El Carmen
Casa Santo Domingo F
Mercardo Central (Open Air Market)
La Compañía de Jesús
Ayuntamiento - Museo de Santiago Museo del Libro Colonial B
Terminal de Buses (Bus Terminal)
Monumento de Rafael Landívar
San Agustín
PARQUE CENTRAL
Catedral A
Palacio de los Capitanes Generales C
Museo de Arte Colonial G
PARQUE LA UNIÓN I
San Pedro Apostol
Santa Clara
La Concepción
Santa Lucéa
San Francisco H
San José El Viejo
Escuela de Cristo
San Antonio Aguas Calientes
Guatemala
Calle de la Recolección
1 Calle Poniente
2 Calle Poniente
3 Calle Poniente
4 Calle Poniente
5 Calle Poniente
6 Calle Poniente
7 Calle Poniente
Calle Sucia
1 Calle Oriente
2 Calle Oriente
3 Calle Oriente
4 Calle Oriente
5 Calle Oriente
6 Calle Oriente
7 Calle Oriente
9 Calle Oriente
Calle de la Recoletas
Alameda Santa Lucía
7 Avenida Norte
6 Avenida Norte
5 Avenida Norte
4 Avenida Norte
3 Avenida Norte
1 Avenida Norte
6 Avenida Sur
5 Avenida Sur
4 Avenida Sur
3 Avenida Sur
2 Avenida Sur
1 Avenida Sur
Calle a Ciudad Vieja
Calle del Hermano Pedro
Pensativo
Calle Chipilapa

middle-class Guatemalans again repopulated the city. Today, Antigua is one of the most international cities in the Americas and the most prosperous place in Guatemala. It is estimated that at least 80 percent of its economy is dependent on the booming tourist trade and language-school industry.

THE PARQUE CENTRAL

The heart of Antigua is the **Parque Central**, the delightful main square, popular night and day with locals and visitors who come to soak up the atmosphere. The *parque* is bounded on all four sides by imposing, graceful colonial buildings that represented the epicenter of the Spanish empire in Central America for more than 200 years, now occupied by local government offices and museums. Note the risqué fountain (where topless mermaids spurt water from their nipples) in the centre of the square.

The **Catedral** Ⓐ, on the east of the square, dates from 1669, though it was built above the ruins of an earlier building that dated back to 1543. The Catedral survived the 1717 earthquake, but was all but reduced to rubble after the 1773 tremors. What is left today is only about a third of the original building, which had a 21-meter (69ft) dome, twin belltowers, three naves, eight domed bays, and measured almost 100 meters (330ft) in length. Inside, the Catedral sparkled in a riot of tortoiseshell, marble, and bronze. Now the building is much more perfunctory, with most of the original in ruins to the rear and the interior relatively bare. Below the Catedral are several crypts and the remains of the Royal Chapel, and supposedly the remains of many historic figures, including Pedro de Alvarado, Francisco Marroquín, and Bernal Díaz de Castillo.

Situated on the north side of the square is the **Ayuntamiento** Ⓑ, the city's municipal offices, with its twin-deck facade of solid stone arches built in a Tuscan style. This has hardly changed in appearance since it was

Fountain of the Sirens outside the Catedral.

ANTIGUA'S CHURCHES

Antigua's numerous churches are, to many visitors, the most dazzling jewels in this colonialized city's crown.

Antigua's churches are characterized by a unique "squat Baroque" architectural style, with immensely thick walls, supported by colossal foundations and giant buttresses, which were developed in a futile effort to resist the perpetual tremors that have plagued the city since it was founded in 1543.

The fledgling capital was all but destroyed by a series of earthquakes between 1585 and 1586. More tremors shook the city in 1607, 1651, 1681, 1684, 1689, 1702, 1717, 1751, and 1765 before the final ruinous quake of 1773 precipitated the evacuation of Antigua and the establishment of the new capital, Guatemala City. Immediately before the 1773 earthquake, Antigua had been a thriving city of some 75,000 inhabitants.

The spectacular facade of La Merced.

Ironically, the destruction of 1773 saved the city: the abandonment protected it from the ravages of industrialization, shoddy construction, and the inevitable population boom, which have tainted all other Latin American capitals.

Structurally, 21st-century Antigua is almost entirely an 18th-century city. A few earlier details have survived, but the dominant style is Iberian-American Baroque, a supremely pictorial, decorative, and flamboyant style that's expressed on virtually all Antigua's church facades. It's also called Churrigueresque, and not to everyone's taste. The Maudslays, who wrote *A Glimpse at Guatemala*, based on visits in the late 1890s, the height of the Victorian Gothic revival, considered it vulgar, garish, and ostentatious. But at its best, as witnessed at the restored La Merced, or at Santa Cruz, the depth, fluidity, and theatrical nature of Antiguan Baroque is astounding – undeniably grandiose, with dreamy facades embellished with astonishing detail.

These remarkable facades were created by applying layers of plaster over the exterior masonry, a technique called *ataurique*. The masonry itself was a humble mix of tamped earth and brick, which was always given a lime-based plaster finish. Little stone has ever been used in Antigua – the local basalt rock is extremely hard to quarry and shape.

The sheer number of ecclesiastical buildings in Antigua is amazing: there are over 30 within a few blocks of the Parque Central. By the mid-17th century, all the main denominations and many more minor ones were established in the city. The religious orders were possibly the greatest power in Central America: free from taxation and granted huge swathes of the most productive land where sugar, tobacco, wheat, and, most lucratively, cochineal and indigo were farmed.

The orders were also allocated vast numbers of Maya labourers to work in the fields and construct the grand edifices of the capital. These laborers managed to implant indigenous imagery onto some of the great church facades: corn cobs (sacred to the Maya) at La Merced and the white water-lily (a hallucinogenic used in sacred rituals) at San Francisco.

built in 1740, surviving both the 1773 and 1976 earthquakes.

The Ayuntamiento houses two museums, the **Museo de Santiago** (also known as the Museo de Armas), where there is a collection of colonial art and artifacts, as well as some traditional weapons dating back to the days of the Conquest, including Alvarado's sword and Maya clubs. Next door is the small **Museo del Libro Antiguo**, dedicated to publishing, where there is a replica of the first printing press in Central America, and a collection of colonial books (both museums Tue–Fri 9am–4pm, Sat–Sun 9am–noon, 2–4pm).

Facing the Ayuntamiento on the other side of the *parque* is the **Palacio de los Capitanes Generales** ©, occupying the whole of its southern side, again built over an earlier civic construction. The two-story colonnade building dates from 1761 and originally extended back to cover the whole block behind. The building survived the 1773 quake, but was cannibalized to provide building material for the new capital in Guatemala City. The site was the nucleus of power in Central America for over two centuries, the home of the colonial rulers and also the Courts of Justice, the Mint, a prison, and barracks. Following a vast refurbishment the palacio now houses the **Centro Cultural del Real Palacio de la Antigua Guatemala** (http://centroculturalrealpalacio.org.gt).

The west side of the square has much less historical interest; its polyglot occupants currently include several stores, Café Condesa (www.cafecondesa.com.gt), an Evangelical church and a good bookstore.

NORTH OF THE PLAZA

From the plaza, heading up 5 Avenida Norte, you will immediately notice the Arco de Santa Catalina – one of the great Antiguan landmarks. The arch was built in 1693 to connect the convent of Santa Catalina to orchards and gardens on the other side of the street so that the nuns could cross the street

Tip

Antigua's most important festival is Holy Week, when costumed processions parade through the central streets, which are carpeted with colorfully dyed sawdust laid out in patterns. It is virtually impossible to find a hotel in town at this time, so consider staying in Guatemala City or even Lago de Atitlán.

The Arco de Santa Catalina.

Tip

You can get an excellent bird's-eye view of the city from the nearby Cerro de la Cruz hill. It was a robbery hotspot for many years, but security is now provided and consequently it is considered safe. Contact the tourist police (see page 365) and they'll run you up here and back.

without fear of contamination by the outside world. The arch was later restored in the 19th century. Continuing up 5 Avenida, you soon reach a small plaza at the junction with 1 Calle Poniente, and the church of **La Merced D**, whose "wedding cake" facade is the finest in all Antigua, recently restored and painted a fantastic shade of yellow with white detail. Inside, at the end of the south nave is the figure of Jesus Nazarene, sculpted by Alonso de la Paz in 1650, and in the ruins of the adjacent cloisters a fountain that is said to be the largest in Central America.

Perhaps the most evocative of all Antigua's ruins, **Las Capuchinas E**, also lie in the north of the city at 2 Avenida Norte and 2 Calle Oriente, set in beautiful gardens (daily 9am–5pm). The Capuchin order was an extremely severe splinter group of the Franciscans: nuns were permitted no contact at all with the outside world. The unique (and intriguing) feature at Las Capuchinas is the Torre de Retiro (Tower of Retreat), a circular courtyard of 18 tiny cells thought to have been a retreat cloister for nuns. Don't miss the fine museum, which has some impressive religious art and ecclesiastical artifacts.

One block to the south and two to the east on 3 Calle Oriente is **Casa Santo Domingo F** (Mon–Sat 9am–6pm, Sun 11.15am–6pm; www.casasantodomingo.com.gt), once a monastery, now a luxury hotel and cultural center. The site given to the Dominicans in 1541 was the largest occupied by any religious body, and the monastery grew to become the wealthiest order in the city. It also started up a college for the study of theology, philosophy, art, Latin, and Mayan language, which in 1676 was established as the University of San Carlos. Santo Domingo was reduced to rubble in 1773, but a superb restoration has transformed much of the site, and several rooms have been converted into small museums (your ticket provides entrance to all).

The Museo Colonial has religious treasures from the Spanish era,

The Good Friday procession.

including some stunning golden crowns and chalices. Inside the Museo Arqueológico are Maya ceramics, funerary urns, and incense burners, while the Museo Arte de Precolombino y Vidrio Moderno has exhibits of Maya artifacts and ceramics alongside contemporary glassworks. You can also tour some fascinating crypts, an art exhibition space, artisans' workshops, and a re-creation of an early pharmacy.

SOUTH AND EAST OF THE PLAZA

Just off the *parque*, at 5 Calle Oriente is the **Museo de Arte Colonial** G (Tue–Fri 9am–4pm, Sat–Sun 9am–noon, 2–4pm; Sun free), sited in the old premises of the University of San Carlos, which has now moved to Guatemala City. The university only occupied this site for 10 years, between 1763 and 1773, but the building did survive the earthquake of that year, leaving its Moorish-style patio intact. The museum is arguably less interesting than the building, but there are paintings of the Life of St Francis of Assisi by Villalpando and Christ's Passion by Tomás de Merlo.

The **Iglesia de San Francisco** H, situated around the corner on 1 Avenida Sur, is another mighty church. It is most noticeable for the tomb and shrine of Hermano Pedro de Betancourt, a teacher-friar who tirelessly cared for the sick, street children, and the poor and established hospitals and convalescent homes. Pope John Paul II made the friar Central America's first saint in 2002. Today hundreds of Guatemalans visit his shrine to ask for his help, and he is credited with many miracles. Don't miss the extensive ruins (daily 9am–5pm) and small museum located behind the church.

To get back to the *parque* from here, return by the **Parque la Unión** I, a small plaza where indigenous women from all over the highlands gather to sell and weave textiles. At the east end of the plaza there's a large *pila* (wash house) still in use, and Santa Clara, the site of a church and a

Iglesia de San Francisco.

Creating crochet in a textile shop.

convent which was founded in 1699 by nuns from Puebla, in Mexico, becoming popular with ladies who desired a little extra comfort after taking their vows. Facing Santa Clara across the plaza is San Pedro Apóstol, which was built as a hospital and church.

TO THE WEST OF THE PLAZA

Leaving the Parque Central down 4 Calle Poniente, you pass the remains of the Convento de La Compañía de Jesús on the corner of 6 Avenida Norte, which currently houses a cultural center. At the end of the road is the busiest, most "Guatemalan" part of town, where you'll find the main *mercado* (daily), the *terminal de buses*, and a row of stores. This is the noisiest part of town, the air thick with diesel fumes, the streets packed with villagers from the surrounding region.

AROUND ANTIGUA

There are some fascinating sights in the stunning countryside of pine trees, coffee bushes, and volcanoes around Antigua, and many interesting villages, both indigenous and *ladino*. It is best to explore the area as a series of day and half-day trips, using Antigua as your base. To the north of Antigua, on the road to Chimaltenango, you pass through the village of Jocotenango, almost a suburb of Antigua, where you will find the impressive Centro La Azotea (Mon–Fri 8.30am–4.30pm, Sat 8.30am–2pm). One half of this center contains a museum, the **Casa K'ojom** ❶ (House of Music; http://kojom.org), which has an incredible wealth of musical recordings, instruments, and information about Maya musical traditions. Next door is an organic coffee *finca*, which has guided tours of the plantation.

⊙ CLIMBING THE VOLCANOES

The three spectacular volcanic peaks near Antigua – Volcán de Agua, Volcán de Fuego, and Volcán Acatenango – can all be climbed, offering unrivaled views of the surrounding landscape.

The easiest of the three is Volcán de Agua (3,766 meters/12,346ft). You start from Santa María de Jesús, heading uphill from the plaza, past the cemetery and out of the village, up a well-marked path that crosses a road, which goes most of the way to the top. At the summit there is a shelter (often full overnight) and a small chapel, but it gets bitterly cold at night. In total, the walk takes most people 4–6 hours up and 2–4 hours down.

The adjacent Fuego (3,763 meters/12,346ft) and Acatenango (3,976 meters/13,045ft) volcanoes are a much more serious challenge altogether, and Fuego should only be attempted if you are an experienced hiker and conditions are favorable (it is highly active). The climb for both starts from the village of Soledad, southwest of Ciudad Vieja; it takes a full day to ascend Acatenango, and Fuego is at least a 12-hour hike.

For all three walks, you need to wear warm clothing, and proper climbing boots are highly recommended. Adventure sports agencies in Antigua offer guided hikes (see page 368).

Volcán de Agua and the San Hermano Pedro church.

Regular minibuses leave Antigua's 4 Calle Oriente for the Centro La Azotea.

Heading north from Jocotenango, the next place of interest, down a dirt road before you reach the Interamericana Highway, is **San Andrés Itzapa 8**, where there is a Tuesday market, but also a shrine to the pagan saint of Maximón (see page 129). This Maximón (or San Simón) is particularly interesting because he attracts a primarily *ladino* clientele, especially prostitutes. It is customary to light a candle or two in Maximón's chapel to ask for good fortune, but if you want to take things further, pay one of the cigar-smoking women attendants for a *limpía* (soul cleansing), which involves you both drinking *aguardiente* liquor and getting thrashed by a bundle of herbs. Maximón's abode is open daily, 6am–6pm.

North of the Interamericana there are three more villages worth a visit. **San Martín Jilotepeque 9** is a pleasant place with an excellent Sunday market, with beautiful local *huipiles* and good-value weavings for sale. At Comalapa to the west, there is a long-established tradition of *primitiva* (folk art) painting, with plenty of artwork on sale locally and also the spectacular crumbling Baroque facade of the village church. Market day is on Tuesday in Comalapa. Heading in the other direction toward Guatemala City along the Interamericana highway, the village of **Santiago Sacatepéquez 10** is famous throughout Guatemala for its giant kites, constructed by the villagers every year to be flown on the Day of the Dead (November 1). The kites, which can be up to 7 meters (23ft) in diameter, are flown in a symbolic act to release the souls of the dead. At other times of the year there's much less going on, but there is a market (Tue and Fri) and a museum full of pottery and figurines.

To the south of Antigua there are four villages of interest. Set on the northern shoulder of the Volcán de Agua, **Santa María de Jesús 11** is the most traditional Maya village in the vicinity. It is a scruffy place, but the base camp for hikers should you

Selling strawberries at Antigua's daily market.

See Antigua on horseback.

want to climb Agua. The trail is easily followed and takes around five hours to the summit. Just below Santa María is the little village of **San Juan del Obispo** ⓬ where there's a huge restored colonial palace, the Palacio de Francisco Marroquín (daily 9am–noon, 2–4pm; donation), where the stunning interior is filled with fine art and wonderful furniture. Marroquín is credited with introducing Christianity to Guatemala, and is seen as something of a father of the nation because of his benevolent behavior toward the Maya.

Learning some basic Spanish will add to your interactions with local communities.

On the northwest flank of the Agua volcano is the village of **Ciudad Vieja** ⓭, site of the second Guatemalan capital, which was devastated by a vast mudflow in 1541, killing Alvarado's widow, Doña Beatriz de la Cueva, who had been made ruler of Central America for all of two days. There's little to see in the village now except a fine church that dates from the 19th century, and nothing left of the former capital, whose center was actually 2km (1.2 miles) to the west.

Textile enthusiasts may want to head for **San Antonio Aguas Calientes**, just 2km (1.2 miles) from Cuidad Vieja, which is the premier weaving center in the Antigua area. The sprawling village is mainly Maya, and is the base for a number of different collectives and stores selling textiles from all over the country, some of which also give weaving lessons. The local *huipil* design combines elaborate floral and geometric patterns on a predominantly red background.

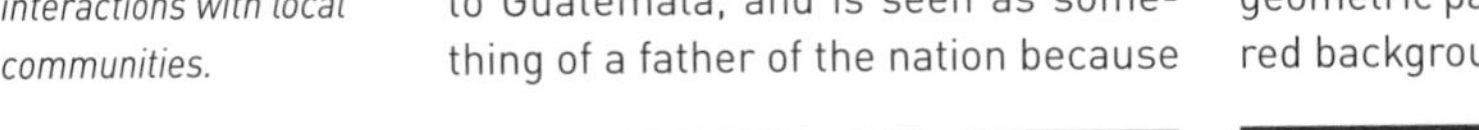

STUDYING SPANISH

Antigua has over 50 language schools, catering for all levels. It is a great place to learn Spanish, with highly affordable rates. There are also schools in Quetzaltenango, Petén, and around Lago de Atitlán.

The schools below charge US$170–310 per week for 20 hours of private lessons and full family-based lodging and meals.

Antigüeña Spanish Academy, 1 C Pte 10; tel: 7832 7241; www.spanishacademyantiguena.com

Centro Lingüístico Maya, 5a C Pte 20; tel: 7832 0656; www.clmaya.com

Ixchel Spanish School, 9a C Oriente 5; tel: 7832 3440; www.ixchelschool.com

Ixquic, 7a Av Norte 74a; tel: 7832 2402; www.ixquic.edu.gt

Probigua, 6A Av Norte 41B; tel: 7832 2998; www.probigua.org

San José El Viejo, 5 Av Sur 34; tel: 7832 3028; www.sanjoseelviejo.com

THE MAXIMÓN CULT

The object of the pagan-Maya cult of Maximón or San Simón is the most highly venerated deity in the Guatemalan highlands.

The cult of Maximón is the most enigmatic in Guatemala. Its origins are obscure, but it is generally accepted that he is a mischievous, evil saint, a powerful figure who can impregnate women, confront Christ, cure illnesses, and bring all sorts of misfortune to his enemies. He is said to be a combination of Judas Iscariot, the conquistador Pedro de Alvarado, and various Maya deities.

Though the cult of Maximón is widespread through the highlands of Guatemala, his physical appearance is remarkably consistent. At first sight he's a comical figure, a stunted statue with a wooden face that's unmistakably *ladino* in appearance, with stumpy legs and arms, a hat, a cigar in his mouth, and draped in scarves and a towel or two to soak up alcohol spillage. He is surrounded by a bevy of attendants who ensure his appetite for *aguardiente* liquor is satisfied and his cigars are regularly lit. Maximón's house is truly a den of iniquity: a smoky abode where the air is thick with candle and tobacco smoke and the floor littered with empty bottles and spittle.

The three best-known Maximón chapels are at Zunil, San Andrés Itzapa, and Santiago Atitlán, though many other highland villages share the cult – every village around Lago de Atitlán has its own figure. At Zunil (see page 143), near Quezaltenango, Maximón can often be seen wearing sunglasses and sporting a bandana, buccaneer-style. The San Andrés Itzapa Maximón entices hundreds of devotees daily, largely *ladinos*, who come to seek cures from illness and protection from their enemies. The walls are covered with plaques from all over Guatemala, and even Mexico and El Salvador, acknowledging his help. Uniquely, the San Andrés Maximón is especially popular with prostitutes.

In Santiago Atitlán, the Maximón cult involves a highly charged, symbolic confrontation with an image of Christ every Good Friday. To the sound of drums and a mournful brass band, Christ emerges from the colonial Catholic church, carried by the faithful, with hundreds crowding the plaza. The tension reaches fever pitch until Maximón appears, supported by his *telinel* (bearer), from a neighboring chapel and faces Christ across the plaza, a challenge that mirrors the conflict between the Maya *costumbristas* (traditionalists) and Catholic Action (mid-20th-century orthodox priests) for Santiago's hearts and minds.

It is essential to respect local etiquette when visiting Maximón – be careful not to offend local sensibilities. Maximón actually moves from house to house every year or so (except at San Andrés Itzapa), so you'll need a guide to take you to his current residence – plenty of children will offer to escort you there for a quetzal or two. Buy a small bottle of Venado or Quezalteca liquor to give to quench Maximón's thirst and a cigar or two for him to puff on. Before you enter Maximón's chapel greet his keepers and pay them a dollar or two to enter, and, crucially, ask their permission to take a photograph (which will involve a charge).

Maximón shrine in Santiago Atitlán.

Traditional clothing in Todos Santos Cuchumatán.

THE WESTERN HIGHLANDS

This is the heartland of the Guatemalan Maya, a place of living traditions amid the most beautiful landscape in the whole country.

The rugged mountain scenery and the absorbing Maya culture alive in the western highlands are the apex of most visitors' experience in Guatemala. The natural setting really is awesome, epitomized by the chain of volcanoes that strides through the heart of the land. There is Lago de Atitlán, one of the most beautiful lakes in the world, the Cuchumatanes mountain range to the north, and the hot springs and market villages around Quezaltenango.

This landscape would entice tourists anyway, but these highlands are also the heartland of Guatemala's Maya. The strength of indigenous culture is all-apparent in the peoples' costume, fiestas, religious practice, and language – a dozen different tongues (plus Spanish) are spoken in these mountains. If you can, get to a fiesta (see page 144) to see one of the many often somber, sometimes joyous, and always acutely symbolic Maya dances. Visit all the markets you can: the spectacle of Chichicastenango, the tranquility and hushed tones of Chajul, the frenetic hustle and commerce of San Francisco El Alto.

LAGO DE ATITLÁN

Of all Guatemala's natural attractions, perhaps the most beautiful is the volcanic caldera of **Lago de Atitlán** ❶ and its unforgettable highland setting, which have seduced travelers for centuries. Its various bays and inlets give the lake an irregular shape, but it measures about 19km (12 miles) long by 12km (7.5 miles) at its widest point. Atitlán is transcended by three towering volcanoes, its shores are dotted with Maya villages, and its 305-meter (1,000ft) deep waters conjure up a spectrum of shifting color changes.

Of all the 13 lakeside villages, Panajachel is the place that most people head for first, though in the last few

Main Attractions

Maps on pages 132, 141

Lago de Atitlán.

years a number of excellent hotels and lodges have mushroomed all around the shores of the lake. Each of the villages has its own character and appeal. Panajachel is the main resort, Santa Cruz is supremely peaceful and relaxing, San Pedro is a backpacker haven, Santiago Atitlán has a traditional feel, and San Marcos is a "new age" center. Santa Catarina and San Antonio Palopó are different again, both villages specializing in textile weaving, while tranquil San Juan has some excellent community tourism projects.

GRINGOTENANGO

Panajachel ❷, on the lake's northern shore, is where most people stay. Dubbed *Gringotenango* by the locals because of the heavy influx of tourists and the high density of Westerner-owned bars and cafes, "Pana" has become something of a boomtown since the turn of the millennium. It is the only lakeside village where tourism really dominates the economy. Yet, despite the vast lakeside kasbah of traditional textile shops and stalls and the dozens of hotels, restaurants, and cafés, Panajachel remains a pleasant place to relax and a good base to explore the rest of the lake. There are no sights to see in the town itself; Pana's appeal is all about its position overlooking the lake and volcanoes, and its inimitable laid-back atmosphere. Transportation

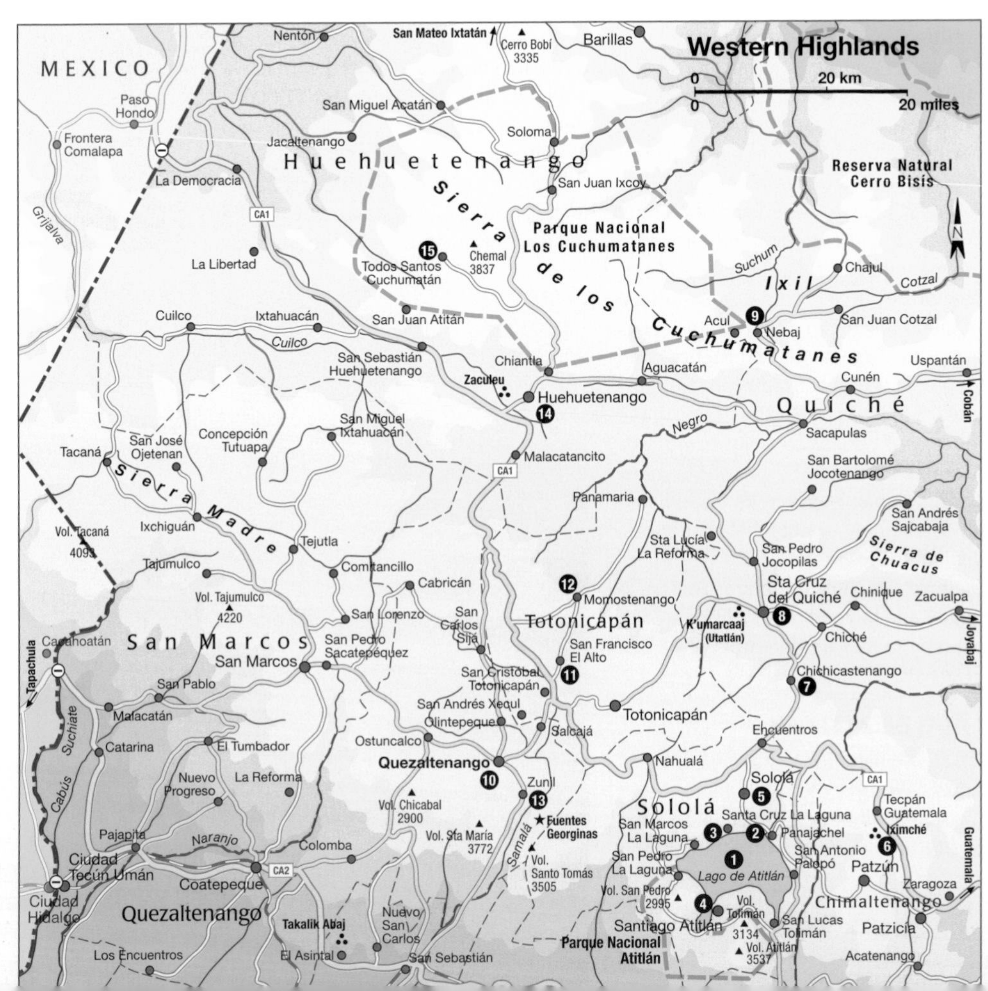

connections are also superb, with regular buses and shuttles running up to the Interamericana and a flotilla of boats linking Pana with the other lakeside villages.

Back in the 1960s, Panajachel was Guatemala's hippie mecca, and Atitlán a legendary place where ley lines were said to meet. This hippie consciousness has never quite left Panajachel, and today the town remains a magnet for a graying tribe of new agers clad in tie-dyes and *típicas* (Westernised traditional clothing) who run many of the cafés and export businesses in town. Westerners apart, Panajachel is a Kaqchikel Maya and *ladino* town.

The north shore of the lake is sparsely populated, almost road-free, and the perfect place to head for some real relaxation. The first place the boat heading west to San Pedro stops at is **Santa Cruz La Laguna ❸**, the main village high above the water, while its shoreside hotels, popular with independent travelers, make an excellent base for hiking, kayaking, and scuba-diving. There's quite a scene developing here in Santa Cruz, with yoga classes, holistic therapies, massage, a spa, and some good dining options. More lodge-style hotels have been constructed in Jaibalito and Tzununá, the next two tiny, very traditional settlements – ideal if you seek real isolation from the everyday world.

At **San Marcos La Laguna**, a larger village, the dense foliage has been left in an aromatic tangle of jocote, banana, mango, and avocado trees, and there's a meditation-yoga center and some excellent budget and mid-range hotels. There's not much to see or do in San Pablo, the next village, but pretty San Juan La Laguna close by wins the cleanest village on the lake award. Here you will find a weaving co-op run by the village women just up from the dock, an excellent village-based tourism initiative and a lovely, unexpected restaurant specializing in wine and cheese.

San Pedro La Laguna, a short distance beyond San Juan, attracts the second-greatest number of tourists

Santa Cruz La Laguna.

THE HISTORY OF LAKE ATITLÁN

The Maya probably first settled the Lake Atitlán area around 2000 BC when they formed small farming and fishing communities on its shores.

The region around Lago de Atitlán has probably been volcanic in character for at least 12 million years, when a colossal caldera, much larger than the present lake, extended several kilometers further to the north. More eruptions around 9 million years ago then formed another, slightly smaller, bowl-shaped caldera.

Lago de Atitlán's present outline is the result of a third volcanic explosion 85,000 years ago. This eruption blocked all access to the sea, so that the three rivers that tumble into the newly formed crater formed today's vast, high-altitude lake, some 1,562 meters (5,125ft) above sea level.

Lake Atitlán is a great place to observe traditional Guatemalan lifestyles.

Further volcanic energy then threw up the three huge cones – Atitlán, Tolimán, and San Pedro – which ring today's lake's waters. The final addition to the scene is the small cone called Cerro de Oro between the villages of San Lucas Tolimán and Santiago Atitlán.

New evidence collected by scuba-divers indicates there was once a Maya ceremonial center, dating back to around 50 BC, on the southern shore of Lago de Atitlán, though this was later flooded due to rising lake levels. When the first Europeans arrived in 1523 the lake was inhabited by Tz'utujil and Kaqchikel Maya. You can visit the modest remains of the old Tz'utujil capital, Chuitinamit, from the village of Santiago Atitlán – only a couple of altars survive, but they are still a place of worship for local people.

During the colonial period, Santiago Atitlán was the most important village on the lake, as its fine church from that era testifies, because of its position on the edge of the highlands and access to the Pacific.

In the last 100 years, the environment, economy, and character of the lake have radically changed. Firstly a new road from Sololá was completed in the 1930s. By the late 1960s the road had turned the previously sleepy lakeside village of Panajachel into a legendary hippie tourist retreat. Then in the 1970s, the lake environs became a battleground, as guerrillas and the Guatemalan army fought a protracted war on the volcanic slopes.

The lake's environment has been ravaged in recent years by population pressure (over 120,000 people now live around its shores), over-exploitation of land, and the effects of tourism. Fields are being planted higher and higher up the hillsides, and the waters are increasingly tainted with pesticide and sewage – leading to cyanobacteria outbreaks, in 2009 and again in 2015. Hundreds of vacation homes have been built. The Atitlán grebe, a flightless bird once endemic to the lake, is now extinct, its chicks all eaten by the black bass, a predatory fish that was introduced for sport fishing. And in the first decade of the 21st century, the level of the lake rose sharply, though the reasons are unclear, leading to the flooding of lakeside property.

after Panajachel, almost all young backpackers. Suitably, the hotels and restaurants here are some of the cheapest in the country, and if you plan to climb **Volcán San Pedro** this is the ideal base for an early-morning start.

A road runs around the east side of the lake, connecting Pana with another two interesting villages. **Santa Catarina Palopó**, the first place, 4km (2.5 miles) from Pana, is famous for its weavings. You will see the turquoise and purple *huipiles* at markets all over the highlands. There's not much to see in the village itself, though as ever the volcano views are magnificent. **San Antonio Palopó**, another 5km (3 miles) from Santa Catarina, shares a fine weaving tradition; here many men also wear *traje* (traditional dress) – interestingly the men's and women's shirts are nearly identical.

SHRINE OF MAXIMÓN

Continuing around the lake, on the south side is San Lucas Tolimán, the least interesting of the villages, but the best place from which to climb either of the nearby Atitlán or Tolimán volcanoes. Ask at your hotel or the town hall about hiring a guide, which is recommended as the paths are very difficult to follow. Much more interesting is **Santiago Atitlán** ❹, a Tz' utujil Maya village on one of the lake's inlets around the western flank of Volcán Tolimán, 20 minutes from Pana by fast *lancha* boats. A shrine is kept here to Maximón (see page 129), part evil saint, part pagan idol, said to be a combination of San Simón, Judas Iscariot, and Pedro de Alvarado the conquistador. Any young Atiteco will guide you to his abode for a quetzal; it is customary to make a donation for his upkeep. The two other points of interest are a small weaving museum to the left of the dock, and the Catholic church. Inside this imposing colonial structure there's a giant altar and a memorial to Father Stanley Rother, an American priest who served in the village between 1968 and 1981, and

Tip

If you are in Santiago Atitlán over Easter, you can watch the symbolic confrontation in the plaza between Jesus Christ and Maximón that always takes place on Good Friday.

Shrine of Maximón, Santiago Atitlán.

who was murdered here in 1981 by a paramilitary death squad.

SOLOLÁ AND IXIMCHÉ

Close to Lago de Atitlán are a number of other fascinating places, the nearest of which is **Sololá** ❺, just to the north of the lake. Unusually, Sololá has parallel Maya and *ladino* governments and is one of the largest indigenous towns in Guatemala. Despite its proximity to Atitlán, Sololá is bypassed by most travelers, leaving the huge Friday market almost wholly a local affair. The town itself is pretty unremarkable, but on market day (Tue and Fri) the whole place erupts in a frenzy of activity as traders and villagers besiege the plaza and surrounding streets. You cannot help but gawk at the iridescent local costume, worn by both sexes, though the men's outrageous "space cowboy" shirts are especially eye-catching.

Some 28km (17 miles) east of Sololá are the ruins of **Iximché** ❻ (daily 8.30am–4.30pm), former capital of the Kaqchikel Maya, who were allies of the Spanish. The ruins (in common with the remains of all the highland Maya cities) are not large in scale, consisting of a few pyramids, plazas, ball courts, and there is also a small museum showcasing artifacts found on the site. But the setting is beautiful, surrounded by stunning highland countryside, and the ruins are still used as a place of Maya worship. (Shamans here performed a cleansing ceremony after George W. Bush dropped by in 2007, declaring the need to remove "negative energy"!).

Just 3km (2 miles) away, the town of Tecpán was the first ever Guatemalan capital (1524–6). Unfortunately there's nothing here today to hint at this illustrious past.

QUICHÉ: THE MAYA HEARTLAND

North of Sololá is the mountainous department of Quiché, stretching from Chichicastenango northward as far as the Mexican border. As the name suggests, this is the heartland of the 2 million or so K'i che' Maya, the most numerous Maya group in

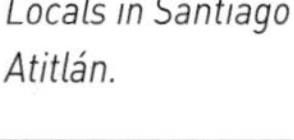

Locals in Santiago Atitlán.

Guatemala. Quiché has had a long history of bloodshed, from the days of the Conquest when, in 1524, Alvarado's men massacred Maya warriors after a final battle at K'umarcaaj, near Santa Cruz del Quiché, to the horrors of the "scorched earth" policy of the 1980s, when thousands of Maya civilians were massacred in a series of paramilitary operations. The department is crossed by several mountain ranges and travel to the Ixil region in the north is a long slog, taking up to three hours from Santa Cruz del Quiché on steep roads.

CHICHICASTENANGO

Turning off the Carretera Interamericana at the Los Encuentros junction, you enter Quiché department along a winding road, plunging down into river valleys, through pine forests, then zigzagging upward to dizzying passes. After some 20km (12.5 miles), you will reach **Chichicastenango** ❼, a quiet highland town with an intriguing past that has become one of the chief tourist destinations of the highlands. Twice a week, the normally calm "Chichi" hosts the most famous market in the entire Maya region, coming to life in a maelstrom of furious commerce.

From the dead of night every Thursday and Sunday, traders arrive to set up their stalls by candlelight, and by daylight the roads into town are crammed with trailers, trucks, and *camionetas* (buses). The market is a good place to buy *típica* textiles and handicrafts – short of venturing to their place of origin – if your haggling skills are well honed.

Sitting pretty in the main plaza, the whitewashed **Iglesia de Santo Tomás** is an overwhelming sight, the air around the crescent-shaped stone steps thick with the sweet, smoky aroma of smoldering pine-based incense called copal. The church, dating back to 1540, is one of the most fascinating in all Guatemala, a place where Maya religious traditions have long been tolerated and fused with Catholicism. Enter by the side door (the front door is reserved for priests and *cofrades* – religious

Friday market in Sololá.

Quote

"There is the original book and ancient writing, but he who reads and ponders it hides his face."

Foreword from the Popul Vuh

officials). The atmosphere inside is magical on Sundays, the aisles and the altar packed with Maya families and groups softly praying. Candles, *aguardiente* liquor wrapped in corn husks, and flowers are offered at different platforms spread around the church, each dedicated to the souls of the deceased. Photography is not allowed inside the church.

As you leave (again through the side door), the neighboring building holds the former monastery where, in about 1702, a Spanish priest, Francisco Ximénez, first discovered the *Popol Vuh*, the K'i che' sacred book, containing their story of creation involving the hero twins – it is considered one of the great literary masterpieces of the pre-Columbian Americas. On the south side of the main plaza is the **Museo Rossbach**, with an interesting collection of pre-Columbian ceramics and jade (Tue–Sun 8am–4pm).

The smaller church opposite Santo Tomás is El Calvario, another hallowed place where incense is burned and prayers are offered. A statue of Christ, kept in a glass case, heads a procession through the town during Holy Week.

There's another sacred site on a hill just outside Chichi: **Pascual Abaj**, (Sacrifice Stone), where sacrifices, flowers, cigarettes, and incense are regularly offered to the *Idolo*, a blackened pre-Columbian sculpture, in thanks for the earth's continuing fertility. It's a 20-minute walk from the plaza: go up 9 Calle and across a stream, then follow the signs through the yard of a workshop making wooden masks and continue up into the pine forest.

SANTA CRUZ DEL QUICHÉ

Heading north some 15km (9 miles) from Chichicastenango, the next stop is **Santa Cruz del Quiché** ❽, the departmental capital. As the town of Quiché is not especially interesting, it's best to head straight for **K'umarcaaj** (also called Utatlán), the former capital of the K'i che' Maya, 4km (2.5 miles) southwest of the plaza. Like all the highland Maya capitals, K'umarcaaj is set superbly in a defensive position,

A misty morning in Santiago Atitlán.

surrounded by pine trees and ravines, and the ruins are low-rise and lack initial impact. Yet this is the fortified capital where Pedro de Alvarado and the conquistadors burned alive two K'i che' kings in 1524 and sealed their control of the highlands.

Today K'umarcaaj remains an active site for Maya religious ceremonies and prayers, especially beneath the grassy plaza, where a long tunnel leads to an underground chamber. Maya priests frequently come here to pray, burn incense and candles, and offer liquor. As you approach the tunnel, if you hear prayers it is best to keep some distance; be careful if you decide to explore inside – some of the side tunnels end abruptly and plunge into oblivion. Take a flashlight or ask to borrow one from the site caretaker.

East of Santa Cruz del Quiché a good road passes through a string of small villages in the foothills of the Sierra de Chuacús for some 54km (34 miles) to the market town of **Joyabaj**. There is an excellent Sunday market here and one of the best fiestas in the country in the second week of August. Dances performed include the Palo Volador, a kind of Maya bungee jump, where men jump off a maypole and spin to the ground with a rope attached to their feet.

Chichicastenango's cemetery is as colorful as its market.

THE IXIL REGION

One of the most compelling regions of the highlands, the Ixil region is an extremely traditional and beautiful area that also saw some of the bloodiest conflicts of the civil war during much of the 1970s and 1980s (see page 81). Now the war is over, the Ixil region (Ixil is the language spoken in these parts, region refers to the three

Thursday market, Chichicastenango.

Lakeside view from San Marcos La Laguna.

main towns of Nebaj, Chajul, and Cotzal) is again welcoming a steady flow of visitors, especially hikers.

Getting to the Ixil involves an incredibly steep two-hour journey from Santa Cruz del Quiché, via the interesting town of **Sacapulas**, an ancient salt-producing center on the banks of the Río Negro, where there is a fine colonial church and a couple of reasonable restaurants. From Sacapulas, a lofty dirt road snakes eastward toward Uspantán, and then on to Cobán in Alta Verapaz.

There is little of interest in Uspantán, but the Maya Nobel Peace Prize laureate Rigoberta Menchú grew up in the mountains north of the town, and many chapters in her two-volume autobiography (see page 85) are set here.

NEBAJ

Nebaj ❾ is the largest of the Ixil towns, set dramatically in a broad green valley encircled by steep-sided ridges. The first thing you will notice is the startling costume worn by the Ixil women, arguably the finest in the entire Maya region: incredibly tightly woven white, green, and red *huipiles* and waist sashes, scarlet *cortes* (skirts) and Medusa-like headdresses of fabric and colorful woolen pom-poms. By contrast, most men are dressed in bland secondhand *ropa americana* (US clothing sold in the market), although on festival days colonial-style scarlet jackets are worn. Check out the Sunday market for its colorful bustle, but you'll find better prices for textiles at the co-operatives in the main plaza or from the women who regularly visit the town's *hospedajes* to sell their wares. There's an imposing colonial church in the plaza, but otherwise there is little of architectural interest to see in Nebaj itself. The hill-walking is tremendous, however. One hike takes you to the "model village" of **Acul**, a strategic hamlet two hours' walk from Nebaj, where villagers were resettled under pressure from the military during the civil war. Continuing through the village, just the other side you will come to the Finca San Antonio, a beautiful Italian-Guatemalan farm where some

Diverse wares arrive in Chichicastenango for the Thursday and Sunday markets.

of the best cheese in the country is made – and it is for sale.

CHAJUL AND COTZAL

The other two Ixil towns are about 40 minutes or so away by minibus from Nebaj. If you decide to go, try to travel on a market day when there is more to see. Chajul's market days are Tuesdays and Fridays, Cotzal's are Wednesdays and Saturdays. **Chajul** is the more interesting – and traditional – of the two villages, a scruffy but beautiful place dominated by the massive white basilica in the main plaza. The Chajul women also wear an elaborate costume of scarlet skirts, *huipiles* woven with images of animals and birds, pom-pom accessories, and earrings threaded with old coins.

Cotzal (officially San Juan Cotzal), the third town, is the least traditional of the trio, with a higher number of *ladinos* and more Spanish spoken. It is also set in a lovely valley, beneath the Cuchumatanes mountains, and again is a sleepy place best visited on market days. The weavings here are some of the finest in Guatemala. Tours of nearby villages and waterfalls can be organized by the village's tourism committee located behind the plaza.

QUEZALTENANGO

Southwest of Quiché, beyond the small department of Totonicapán, is the department of Quezaltenango, with its chief city of the same name, located high (over 2,300 meters/7,500ft) in a mountain range. Also Guatemala's second city, **Quezaltenango** ⓾ (population around 150,000) for centuries rivaled the capital as the country's most important business, banking, and cultural city, even declaring itself the capital of an independent state in 1820. By the 20th century, Quezaltenango (also known as Xela – pronounced "Shella" – from its Maya name Xelajú) was an impressive city, its wealth boosted by its pivotal position as a center for the coffee trade and a direct railtrack to the Pacific port of Champerico. But the stately architecture and theaters were all but destroyed by a colossal earthquake in 1902, and ever since

Fact

The Spanish attacked Nebaj and burned it to the ground in 1530; captive "rebels" were branded and sold into slavery.

The men outdress the women in Todos Santos Cuchumatán.

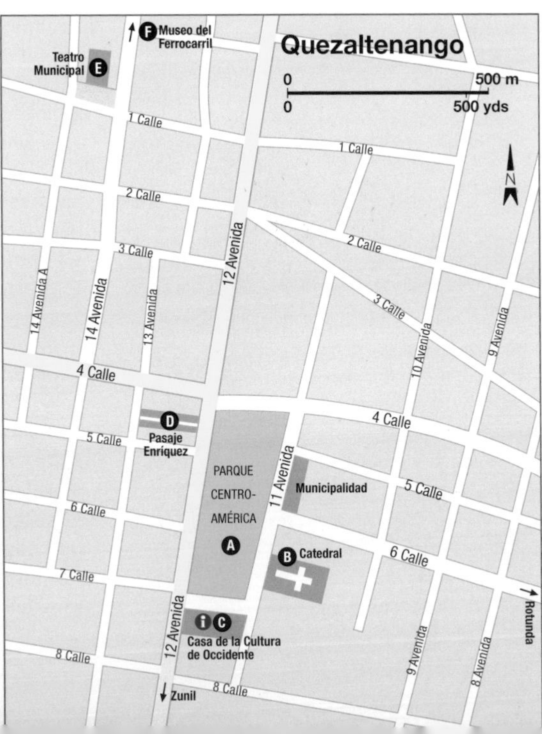

Tip

San Andrés Xecul, about 8km (5 miles) to the northeast of Quezaltenango, has a stunningly colorful church that is claimed to be the oldest in Central America (although the color scheme is 20th-century). The background color is yellow, decorated with brightly dressed angels and vines, while the dome resembles a stripy beach ball.

Quezaltenango has been relegated to second-division provincial status as a capital of the highlands, devoid of metropolitan swagger, but retaining a friendlier, less frenetic character.

Evenings and early mornings can be chilly in this high-altitude city, especially around Christmas. Looming above the buildings is the majestic Volcán Santa María, the most perfectly proportioned cone in Guatemala.

The heart of the city, the sprawling **Parque Centroamérica** Ⓐ, holds an impressive assortment of buildings, including some fine-looking banks, the Municipalidad (city hall), the cathedral, and, in the center of the square, a strange visual cocktail of neo-Grecian columns and stone benches. The **Catedral** Ⓑ is a modern concrete building, with only the facade remaining of the original. The Bishop of the Highlands, an important post, is stationed here. Inside the cathedral is an image of El Padre Eterno (The Eternal Father) housed in a silver case. The **Casa de la Cultura de Occidente** Ⓒ (Mon–Fri 8am–noon, 2–6pm), on the south of the square, harbors the Tourist Office (daily 7am–5pm), exhibits about the city's history and the **Museo de Historia Natural (Mon–Fri** 8am–noon and 2–6pm, Sat 9am–1pm), where there's an assortment of stuffed creatures, as well as some impressive pre-Columbian artifacts. Also of note is the small **Museum of Marimba** , dedicated to Guatemala's national instrument. Take a look at the fine shopping arcade, the **Pasaje Enríquez** Ⓓ in the northwest corner of the square as well – for years it was very run down, but is now looking much healthier and is home to several bars and restaurants including the ever-popular Salon Tecún. Away from the Parque Centroamérica, there is little to see in the center of town, though the **Teatro Municipal** Ⓔ, at the end of Avenida 14, on the corner of 1 Calle, is another stolid neo-colonial edifice. The theater faces a plaza, which contains various busts of local artists, including Guatemala's first Poet Laureate, Osmundo Arriola (1886–1958).

About 2km (1.2 miles) northwest of the centre, close to the Minerva bus

A highly skilled hand-weaver at work in Nebaj.

terminal, the city's old train station has been converted into the **Museo del Ferrocarril** Ⓕ (daily 8am–noon, 2–6pm), dedicated to the railway which connected Xela to the Pacific coast, though exhibits are not very well presented. Next door, in the same building, Museo Ixkik' (daily 9am–1pm, 3–6pm) deals with Maya costume from the highlands.

THE COUNTRYSIDE AROUND QUEZALTENANGO

Unlike the city itself, there is much of interest in the countryside around Xela. Going north of Xela for 17km (10.5 miles) up a steep hill, you come to the village of **San Francisco El Alto** ⓫, which hosts the biggest market in the entire Maya region. The Friday morning market is a wonderful spectacle and a real assault on the senses, as thousands of traders descend on the small village to buy and trade everything from honking hogs to fine fabrics. Textiles are bought here to be sold around the country, and some good bargains can be found here and in the town's many textile shops. Most of the market is given over to fruit and vegetables; however, for a bird's-eye view of the action, pay the main church's caretaker one quetzal to climb up to the roof.

A further 19km (12 miles) from San Francisco is another famous market town, **Momostenango** ⓬, this time specializing in *chamarras* (warm, woolen blankets) and carpets. Some good-quality textiles can be bought here, especially at its twice-weekly markets on Wednesday and Sunday. Momostenango is also a center for Maya religious study, with many shamans working here, attracting students from all over Guatemala.

Ten kilometers (6 miles) southeast of Xela is **Zunil** ⓭, another traditional K'i che' Maya village, where there is a shrine to Maximón (the idol's location is rotated yearly), a Monday market, and a good weaving co-operative close to the plaza. The village economy is based on the cultivation of vegetables, which thrive in the rich volcanic soil. From Zunil a steep road leads to **Fuentes Georginas**, a beautiful natural hot spring spa. Perched on the lush slopes of the Volcán Santo Tomás, it is smothered by dense ferns, moss, and other plants. There are seven rustic cabins and a restaurant (with wine available) here. Trails lead to the sister-volcanoes of Santo Tomás and Zunil.

THE CUCHUMATANES

In the far west of the country, the highland scenery becomes even more dramatic, dominated by the blunted peaks of the Cuchumatanes mountains. Above Huehuetenango there's a huge high-altitude plateau known as the *altiplano*, a dauntingly inhospitable environment where trees are stunted by the cold and little else will grow. In the valleys, the warmer climate permits a limited amount of corn, vegetables, and some fruit to be grown, but only enough to sustain a very small population, and many villagers are forced

Fact

Momostenango means "Citadel of the Altars," after the many altars found around the town and surrounding hills, and reflecting the longstanding religious devotion of many of the townspeople.

Huipile, waist sash, scarlet skirt, and headdress of fabric and pom-poms typically worn by women in the Ixil region.

Tip

There are two language schools in Todos Santos Cuchumatán. Nuevo Amanacer and Academia Hispano Maya (https://hispanomaya.weebly.com) both teach the local Mam language as well as Spanish. Summer residential courses are offered, for US$130 per week.

to leave and look for work elsewhere in the country or, increasingly, in the United States.

The Cuchumatanes have always been an isolated region – the Spanish had little interest in the area, and the inhospitable terrain has helped shield the overwhelmingly Maya inhabitants from changes that have affected villages closer to the Interamericana. In many villages, the Maya Haab and Tzolkin calendars are still observed by prayer keepers. Travel in the mountains is tough, hotels and restaurants are simple, but the spellbinding scenery is ample compensation.

GATEWAY TO THE MOUNTAINS

The first port of call for visitors to the Cuchumatanes is **Huehuetenango** ⓮, a pleasant town that's both a transport hub and a departmental capital. The main sight, however, is **Zaculeu**, Maya ruins 5km (3 miles) from the center of "Huehue." Zaculeu was the capital of the Mam nation, one of the main tribes that confronted the Spanish. The former capital, like the other highland Maya centers, was well fortified, and the Mam held out for six weeks before they surrendered.

Unfortunately, Zaculeu was insensitively rebuilt in 1947, the temples covered in an unsightly stucco finish, lacking any decorative detail. Despite this, it is still worth a visit – the ruins are surrounded by ravines on three sides, providing tremendous views, and there's also a small museum on site with exhibits of burial pieces (daily 8am–4pm).

North of Huehue a single road clings to the massive southern flank of the Cuchumatanes, passing a lookout point after 12km (7.5 miles), where, if it is clear, you can pick out the chain of volcanoes that rises over the epic Guatemalan highland landscape. About an hour and a half from Huehue the terrain tempers a little and the flat, chilly *altiplano* lands beckon. Continuing down this road you pass through the villages of San Juan Ixcoy and Soloma (where there are *hospedajes*), and then to San

The Ixil region costumes are some of the most beautiful in Guatemala.

TODOS SANTOS' FIESTA

At the end of every October, Todosanteros (men from Todos Santos Cuchumatán) return to the village from all over Guatemala – and even from the United States – to celebrate the festival of All Saints (Todos Santos), which is probably the most famous in the country.

The festivities start the week before the horse race, which takes place on the morning of November 1 (All Saints' Day). Music and dancing is held on October 31, in the costume of the next day's race. Riders, most of whom have been drinking hard liquor all night, must circumnavigate a course around the town, stopping to take another swig of *aguardiente* after each lap and struggling to hang on. The "race" in reality becomes a comical stampede, with the drunken jockeys urging their long-suffering steeds like demons possessed. The winner is the one who survives, still on his mount; all the riders gain considerable kudos, however, just for taking part.

On the next day, appropriately "the day of the dead," everyone moves to the cemetery for a day of eating, more drinking, and commemorating the lives of their dearly departed. Marimba bands play in the town center for days, and in the cemetery itself on November 2. Many traditional dances are performed, including the dance of the conquistadors. Absolute bedlam!

Mateo Ixtatán, the most interesting place on this isolated road. The circular design on the women's *huipiles* worn here is one of the most striking in Guatemala: a multicolored star-like emblem woven upon a white background (see Textiles feature on page 146). The small Maya ruins of Wajxaklajunh enjoy a superb position on the lower slopes of San Mateo and have some temples and a couple of stelae. Visit the village on its market days (Thursday or Sunday), when you can buy textiles much more cheaply than in Huehue.

TODOS SANTOS CUCHUMATÁN

The one village in the Cuchumatanes that draws a trickle of tourists is **Todos Santos Cuchumatán** ⓯, some 50km (31 miles) northwest of Huehue, a magical place that has a few basic hotels and a language school, but which is most famous for its three-day fiesta *(see box)*. Apart from this, the twin attractions are the sublime setting in a canyon-like valley beneath the 3,837-meter (12,589ft) peak of Chemal and the purity of Mam Maya culture here – it is extremely rare to see any Todosanteros not wearing traditional costume. The women wear beautiful purple and navy *huipiles* that are among the most tightly woven in the country, but it is the men who are the real peacocks – they wear an almost outrageous outfit of candy-striped trousers and thick cotton shirts with huge, flapping pink or purple collars. Both men and women wear similar straw hats.

The countryside around Todos Santos is perfect for some challenging hikes, including one route which takes you out of town, south past the minor ruins of Tojcunanchén, up on to the spine of the Cuchumatanes and on to the equally traditional Mam village of San Juan Atitán, six hours' walk away. The men in San Juan wear leather sandals almost identical to those worn by the ancient Maya. From San Juan Atitlán, pick-ups return regularly to the relative civilization of Huehuetenango.

The brightly decorated church of San Andrés Xecul.

RAINBOW COLORS OF GUATEMALAN COSTUME

Visit the markets and villages of the Guatemalan highlands and you will be dazzled by the glowing colors of the costumes worn by the Maya.

The most beautiful textiles in Guatemala are the traditional clothes Maya women make for themselves and their families.

The most intricate weavings are made on simple hip-strap looms identical to those used by the ancient Maya, which consist of nothing more than a series of sticks. The vertical foundation threads (the warp) are suspended between the two end-rods, one of which is tied to a post and the other to the strap which passes round the weaver's hips to control the tension. The remaining sticks are used to separate the layers of warp yarns, to interlace the horizontal (weft) threads with the warp to form the ground weave, and to beat the woven threads together.

MATERIALS

Cotton is still the most commonly used fiber, although it is now in the process of being replaced by brightly colored, shrink-resistant acrylic yarns, which started taking over from wool in the 1960s. Very little cotton thread is hand-spun today. Metallic threads and artificial silks are very popular as they give the weavings a luxurious look.

Chichicastenango's Thursday and Sunday markets are a great place to buy textiles and handicrafts, and to see them in traditional use.

Through the continued use of the hip-strap loom, Maya women preserve the tradition of hand-weaving their own multicolored costumes, seen here in Todos Santos Cuchumatán.

The age-old practice of hand-spinning cotton has, for the most part, given way today to a vast array of commercially produced threads and yarns.

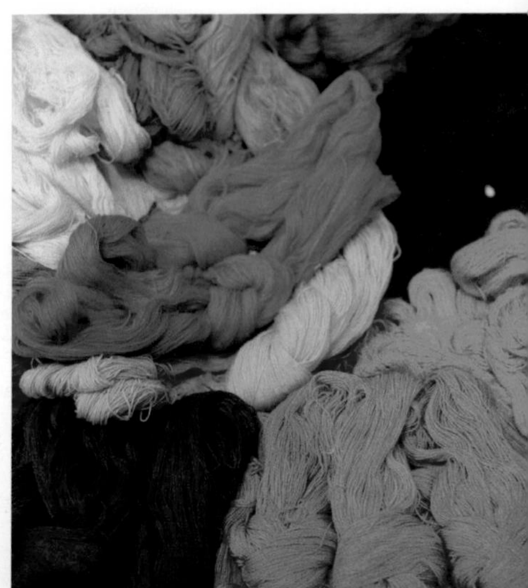

Maya weavers and embroiderers draw from a wide range of designs, using sacred and secular images, both ancient and modern.

Designs and Motifs

Highland costumes are decorated with a wide range of bird, animal, and plant motifs as well as geometric forms; some are recalled from memory, without the use of patterns. Some motifs, such as the horse, peacock, and chicken, are obviously post-Conquest, as these animals arrived in the Americas with the Spaniards. Other animals such as deer, coyotes, snakes, and double-headed birds figure in Maya mythology. It is said that the zigzag patterns symbolize Chac, the god of lightning and rain. Monkeys are associated with disaster, while the quetzal was the spiritual protector of the rulers. Some of the most impressive and varied designs are found in the beautiful *tzuts* (multi-purpose cloths) of Santa María de Jesús, near Antigua.

Today's artisans widen their range of designs by drawing from picture books and life around them. However, older designs are often preserved in ceremonial textiles. Tree, doll, and lyre motifs decorate many skirts. These patterns are traditionally produced by a dye-resistant method known locally as *jaspé*.

Short of heading to their place of origin, buying típicas (Westernized traditional clothing) and textiles at Chichicastenango's market is good if your haggling skills are well honed.

Many women still hand-wash their clothes at communal pilas (washing basins), such as this one at Iglesia Santa Clara in Antigua. It's a good excuse for a chat and gossip.

The clothes worn by women in Nebaj, in the Ixil region, combine tightly woven huipiles and waist sashes with scarlet skirts and Medusa-like headdresses of fabric and woolen pom-poms.

The Biotopo Monterrico-Hawaii protected wetlands.

THE PACIFIC COAST

Guatemala's longest coastline does not have the beaches to compete with the Yucatán, but it does have some surf, nature reserves, and a few unusual archeological sites.

Glance at a map of Guatemala, and the 300km (190-mile) long Pacific coastline might appear to be the perfect place to chill out, swim, and relax. But if you are dreaming of palm-fringed beach resorts and tropical cocktails, try the Caribbean. Guatemala's Pacific coast is the engine room of its agricultural economy, a sultry, humid strip of land that's almost entirely dominated by vast *fincas* devoted to sugar cane, cattle ranching, cotton, and bananas.

Attractions are few and far between. The beaches are all black sand, the climate is fiercely hot and humid, the few hotels and restaurants tend to be disappointing, and the sea is plagued by a dangerous undertow that makes swimming treacherous. Yet between the sugar plantations, you will find important (both Maya and Olmec) archeological remains at Takalik Abaj and in numerous sites around the town of Santa Lucía Cotzumalguapa, including the colossal stone heads in La Democracia. The scale of these sites cannot compete with the temples and pyramids of the Petén and Yucatán, but some of the sculpture is fascinating. Parts of the original rich coastal ecosystem of mangroves and forest have survived, especially around Monterrico, one of the nicer places on this coast.

Running parallel to the coast is Guatemala's fastest highway, the Carretera del Pacífico, and it is simple to get around this route by bus. To explore the region fully, however, you will need your own transportation, as many of the sights, and all the beaches, are a considerable distance off the highway.

FROM EL SALVADOR TO MONTERRICO

The border town of Ciudad Pedro de Alvarado is a quiet crossing. Tourist attractions are limited in this remote corner of the country, but close to the tiny settlement of Las Lisas is the beautifully situated Isleta de Gaia hotel. Pressing on down the Carretera del Pacífico, there's

Main Attractions

- Biotopo Monterrico-Hawaii
- Parque Auto Safari Chapín
- La Democracia
- El Paredón
- Santa Lucía Cotzumalguapa
- Takalik Abaj
- Tilapa

Map on page 150

Volleyball on Monterrico beach.

Kids

Just north of Retalhuleu is Parque Acuático Xocomil (Thu–Sun 9am–5pm; http://irtra.org.gt), a huge water park with 14 water slides – including the longest one in Central America – wave pools, a beach, and a lazy river: an aquatic paradise for children.

a spectacular section of the road with the volcanoes Moyuta and Cruz Quemada defining the highlands to the north.

The Carretera del Pacífico bypasses the cowboy town of **Chiquimulilla ❶**, 48km (30 miles) from the Salvadorean frontier, but if you need a break the town is quite interesting as it has a number of specialist stores selling superb leather goods. Taxisco is the next town, a nondescript place, but from here a branch road leads to **Monterrico ❷**, probably the most attractive place on the entire coast to spend a day or two. To access Monterrico from here you will have to cross the Chiquimulilla canal, which separates the beach from the hinterland. Regular ferries (which can take cars) make the connection from the village of La Avellana (or you can drive direct to Monterrico via a bridge that crosses the canal at Iztapa to the west).

MONTERRICO NATURE RESERVE

Much of the wetlands around Monterrico are protected as part of a national nature reserve, the **Biotopo Monterrico-Hawaii**, which forms an important habitat for herons, egrets, and migratory birds, iguana, alligators, opossums, raccoons, and anteaters. It is the three species of sea turtle that nest on these shores that make Monterrico really special, however. The green turtle (up to 1 meter/3ft in length) and olive ridley (reaching over 1 meter/3ft) nest here between July and November, and the leatherback (reaching over 2.5 meters/8ft) between mid-October and February. All the turtles crawl ashore at night to lay their clutch of 80–100 eggs, a laborious effort that sends the turtles into a trancelike, exhausted state.

Despite the protected status of the reserve, egg collectors comb the beaches at night, seeking out nesting turtles and taking the eggs, which are considered an aphrodisiac in Central America and so fetch a good price. Conservationists have set up two hatcheries on this section of the beach, however, and have had some success in persuading the egg collectors to donate a proportion of their cache. The collected eggs are protected until they hatch, when the baby turtles are released

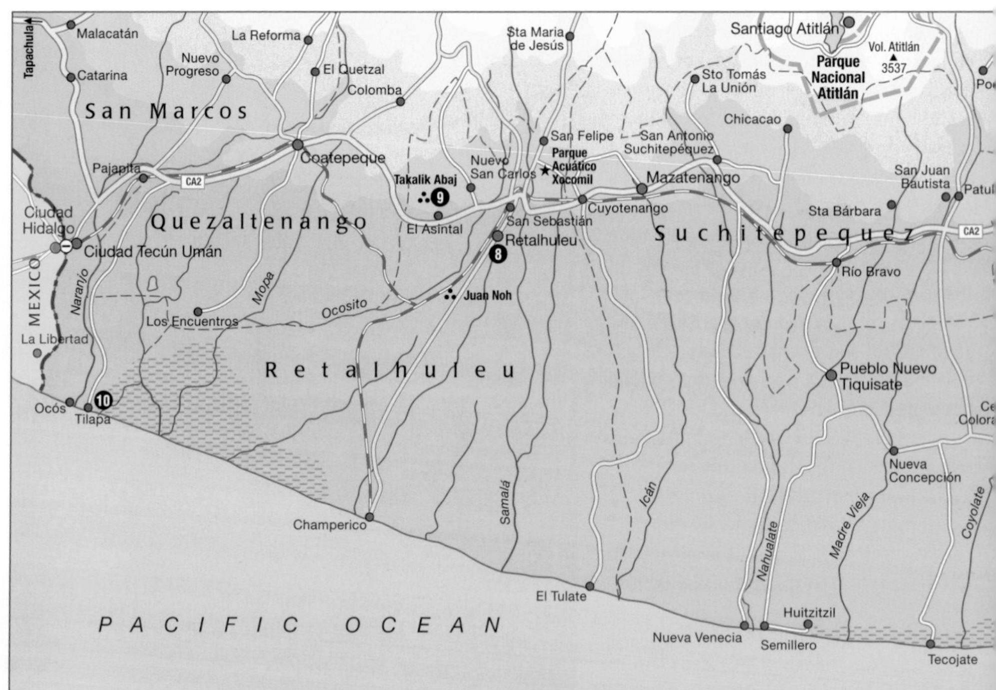

into the ocean. Around 10,000 baby turtles are released annually, though it is estimated only a few dozen of these will reach maturity and return to nest at Monterrico. Take care if you want a dip, as the ocean is savage and prone to a strong undertow.

CHAPÍN SAFARI PARK TO LA DEMOCRACIA

Back on the Carretera del Pacífico, heading west toward Mexico, the **Parque Auto Safari Chapín** ❸ is a popular attraction at Km 87.5, with a diverse range of wildlife, both endemic (jaguar and tapir) and foreign (rhinos and giraffes). There's a swimming pool here (www.autosafarichapin.com; Tue–Sun 9.30am–5pm). Escuintla is the next town on the highway, an ugly, sprawling place that's an important center for agri-commerce, with plenty of cheap hotels and restaurants, but with no esthetic or cultural merit.

From Escuintla a fast road runs south 38km (23.5 miles) to the formerly bustling **Puerto San José** ❹, the most popular "resort" on the entire coast, though this is entirely due to its proximity to the capital – the place itself is somewhat run-down. Around Puerto San José there are several other places that are more inviting. Just to the east, past the container port, Puerto Quetzal, is a marina where sailing and fishing trips can be organized, while farther east (12km/7.5 miles from Puerto San José), Iztapa has plenty of character, a more easy-going atmosphere, and several hotels geared to sport-fishers – the offshore seas here harbour sailfish and marlin.

Heading west again along the Pacific highway, a quick detour south takes you to the sleepy town of **La Democracia** ❺, where there is a unique collection of basalt stone heads known locally as *dioses gordos* (fat gods) in the main plaza. The heads, with carved faces grinning from ear to ear, were gathered from the nearby ruins of Monte Alto, and show strong Olmec influence. If you continue down this side road to the Pacific from La Democracia there's a near-deserted beach settlement called Sipacate some 42km (26 miles) away. Just 6km (4 miles) east of Sipacate, tiny **El Paredón** ❻ has arguably the best surfing conditions in Guatemala, a fine hotel in Paredón

Tip

If you feel in need of a cooling dip, spend a few hours in the sleepy resort of Champerico, south of Retalhuleu, but watch out for the dangerous undertow.

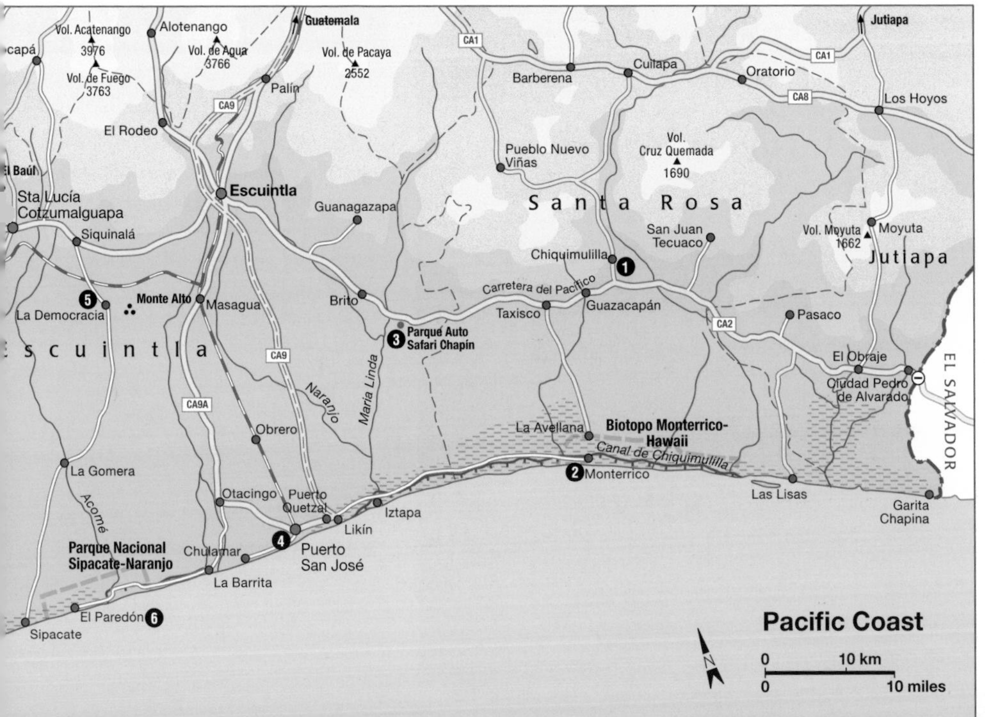

Offering prayers at a Maya altar in Takalik Abaj.

Surf House (www.paredonsurf.com), and a basic surf camp. Both these places offer instruction, board rental and boat trips to the surrounding mangroves.

AROUND SANTA LUCIA COTZUMALGUAPA

The hot town of **Santa Lucía Cotzumalguapa** ❼, some 17km (10.5 miles) northwest of La Democracia, holds no interest, but around it are some interesting Pipil archeological remains. Here the sights are spread out in the sugar-cane fields that surround the town; to explore them all you will need your own transport, or to hire a taxi in the main plaza. The Pipil were not great temple builders, but astonishingly adept sculptors, carving from basalt (volcanic) stone. The nearest sculptures, the Bilbao stones (known as *las piedras*), are just to the north of the town.

RETALHULEU AND TAKALIK ABAJ

Back on the highway, heading west toward Mexico for another 94km (58.5 miles), the road passes through a collection of dull lowland towns before the turnoff for **Retalhuleu** ❽, usually shortened to "Reu" (pronounced "RAY-oo"). Reu is a civilized place as far as the Pacific coast goes, with an attractive, shady plaza, a relaxed air, and a good Museo de Arqueología y Etnología (Tue–Sat 8am–noon and 2–5pm, Sun 9am–noon), which is full of historical photographs and anthropomorphic figurines.

West of Reu, near the small village of El Asintal, is **Takalik Abaj** ❾ (daily 7am–5pm), probably the most important ruins on the entire coast – though the Maya and Olmec-style temples have not survived well and lack visual impact. The stelae and altars are much more interesting, and a tomb is thought to be the burial place of the site's last Mayan king. There is also a small but worthwhile museum.

Continuing west along the highway there's a turnoff about 20km (12.5 miles) before the Mexican border for the coast. The village of **Tilapa** ❿ right on the Pacific is a slightly scruffy place with some basic hotels, but it does have some great fish restaurants right on a magnificent expanse of sands. This beach's profile is far less steep than most on this coastline, making it a safer place to swim.

Skull sculpture at El Baúl Museum.

EL BAÚL HILLTOP SITE

Just to the north of Santa Lucía Cotzumalguapa is **El Baúl**, a ceremonial center atop a small hill that's still used by Maya shamans. There are two sculptures at El Baúl: one stela of a human figure crowned with a dramatic headdress and inscribed with the date "8 deer" (equivalent to AD 36); the second a giant stone head, its face blackened by centuries of candle wax and copal (pine resin incense). At the third site, nearby at the Finca El Baúl, there's a collection of carvings and stone heads inside a small museum (Mon–Fri 8am–4pm, Sat 8am–noon; free). Finally, take a look at the small museum attached to the Finca Las Illusiones, 2km (1.2 miles) from the town center, just off the Carretera del Pacífico, where there are stelae, Olmec-style carvings, and pottery.

Horse riding on Monterrico beach.

Finely carved stela at Copán.

THE EAST

This varied region has some superb lakes, the wonderful carved stelae of Quiriguá and Copán, a quetzal reserve, and a fascinating Caribbean coastal culture.

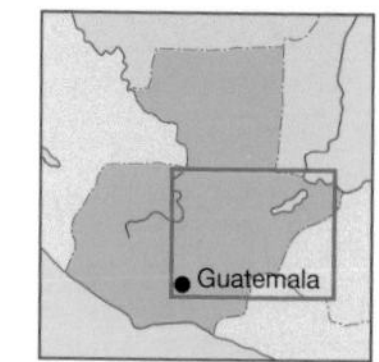

Eastern Guatemala only attracts a slim slice of the country's burgeoning tourist industry – it is a region that most visitors hurry through on their way to the ruins of Petén or Copán, just over the Honduran border. Yet there is plenty of interest here, most obviously the extreme juxtaposition of landscapes: desert, wetlands, both arid and humid mountain ranges, lowland jungle, tropical coastline, and even (this being Guatemala) a volcano or two. Creditably, a network of protected reserves has been established to safeguard these remarkable ecosystems, and the unique habitat of species like the manatee and the quetzal, the national bird – but this reserve status is all too often poorly enforced.

This chapter covers a vast swathe of land, which is divided into three distinct regions: the twin departments of Alta and Baja Verapaz, to the northeast of Guatemala City; the huge department of Izabal, which encompasses the Caribbean coast and Lago de Izabal; and finally the dry mountainous departments of Chiquimula, Zacapa, El Progreso, and Jalapa, known locally as "El Oriente."

Its population is as diverse as its landscape: most people are *ladinos*, but there are a number of Maya speakers (mainly Q' eqchi') and also a few Garífuna people on the coast. This is a sparsely populated area, overwhelmingly agricultural and devoid of a single city. Cattle ranching, bananas, and tobacco dominate the lowland economy; coffee and cardamom are the most important highland crops.

Historically, the Motagua River that flows through the heart of the region to the Caribbean Sea was a crucial trade route. Close to the banks of the Motagua were the largest jade deposits in the entire Maya area, contested and controlled by the Maya settlements of Quiriguá and Copán (see page 161). Today the ruins of both sites are essential visits for their astonishing sculptural remains.

Main Attractions

- Biotopo del Quetzal
- Cobán
- Semuc Champey
- Parque Nacional Laguna Lachuá
- Quiriguá
- Lago de Izabal
- Río Dulce
- Lívingston
- Copán

Maps on pages 156, 163

Canoeing expedition, Río Dulce.

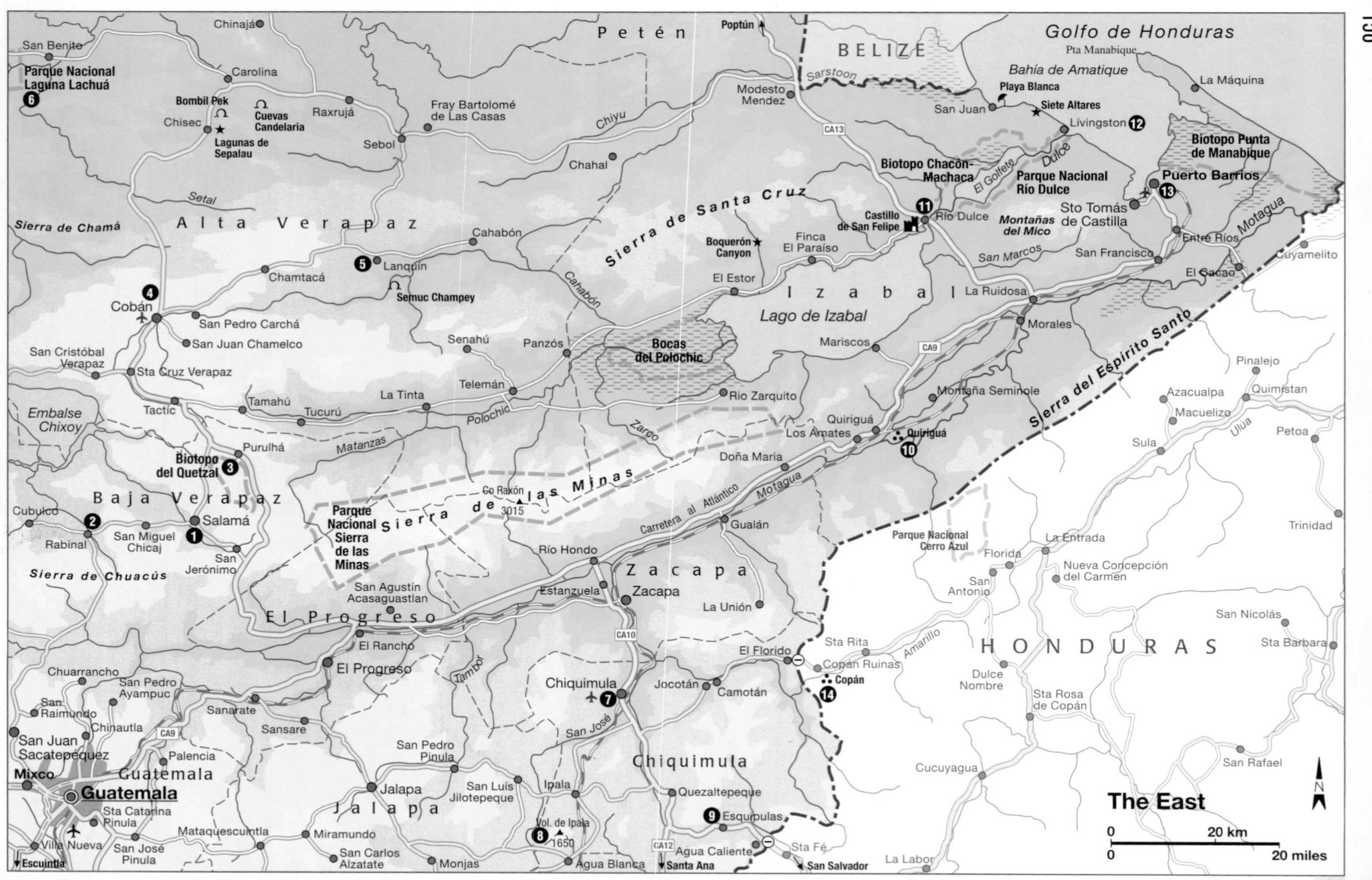
The East
0 20 km
0 20 miles
Golfo de Honduras
Pta Manabique
Bahía de Amatique
BELIZE
Petén
HONDURAS
Alta Verapaz
Baja Verapaz
Izabal
Lago de Izabal
Zacapa
Chiquimula
Jalapa
El Progreso
Guatemala
Sierra de Santa Cruz
Sierra de las Minas
Sierra del Espíritu Santo
Montañas del Mico
Sierra de Chamá
Sierra de Chuacús
Biotopo Punta de Manabique
Puerto Barrios
Lívingston
Siete Altares
Playa Blanca
San Juan
La Máquina
Parque Nacional Río Dulce
Biotopo Chacón-Machaca
El Golfete
Dulce
Río Dulce
Castillo de San Felipe
Sto Tomás de Castilla
Entre Ríos
El Cacao
Motagua
Guyamelito
San Francisco
San Marcos
Morales
La Ruidosa
Montaña Seminole
Quiriguá
Los Amates
Mariscos
Finca El Paraíso
Boquerón Canyon
El Estor
Bocas del Polochic
Río Zarquito
Zarco
Doña María
Gualán
Carretera al Atlántico
La Unión
Parque Nacional Cerro Azul
Copán Ruinas
Copán
Sta Rita
Amarillo
El Florido
Camotán
Jocotán
Esquipulas
Sta Fé
San Salvador
Agua Caliente
Santa Ana
Quezaltepeque
Chiquimula
San José
Agua Blanca
Vol. de Ipala 1650
Ipala
San Luís Jilotepeque
Monjas
San Pedro Pinula
Jalapa
San Carlos Alzatate
Miramundo
Mataquescuintla
San José Pinula
Villa Nueva
Escuintla
Sta Catarina Pinula
Palencia
Guatemala
Mixco
San Juan Sacatepéquez
San Raimundo
Chinautla
Chuarrancho
San Pedro Ayampuc
Sanarate
Sansare
Tambor
El Progreso
El Rancho
San Agustín Acasaguastlan
Parque Nacional Sierra de las Minas
Co Raxón 3015
Río Hondo
Estanzuela
Zacapa
Cahabón
Panzós
Senahú
Telemán
Polochic
La Tinta
Tucurú
Tamahú
Matanzas
Purulhá
Biotopo del Quetzal
Salamá
San Jerónimo
San Miguel Chicaj
Rabinal
Cubulco
Embalse Chixoy
San Cristóbal Verapaz
Sta Cruz Verapaz
Tactic
Cobán
San Pedro Carchá
San Juan Chamelco
Chamtacá
Lanquín
Semuc Champey
Fray Bartolomé de Las Casas
Sebol
Raxrujá
Cuevas Candelaria
Lagunas de Sepalau
Bombil Pek
Chisec
Carolina
Chinajá
Setal
San Benito
Parque Nacional Laguna Lachuá
Chahal
Chiyu
Modesto Mendez
Poptún
Sarstoon
Pinalejo
Quimistan
Azacualpa
Macuelizo
Sula
Ulúa
Petoa
Trinidad
La Entrada
Florida
San Antonio
Nueva Concepción del Carmen
San Nicolás
Sta Barbara
Dulce Nombre
Sta Rosa de Copán
Cucuyagua
San Rafael
La Labor
CA9
CA10
CA12
CA13

Leaving the capital down the busy Carretera al Atlántico, the scenery is an uninspiring deforested landscape of scrub bush that gradually gives way to succulents and cereus cacti. There's no reason to stop until the El Rancho junction, from where a good sealed road climbs into the Verapaz highlands and toward the town of Cobán.

THE VERAPACES

The twin departments of Baja and Alta Verapaz (*vera paz* meaning "true peace") were the last part of Guatemala to fall under Spanish control (apart from Flores), such was the ferocity of opposition from the indigenous Achi tribes, and dominance was only established in 1538 after a successful "softly-softly" approach pioneered by a group of Dominican priests led by Fray Bartolomé de Las Casas.

The Verapaces contain some of the most beautiful scenery in the country, in places almost Swiss alpine in appearance; a large spread of cloud forest, home to the elusive quetzal; some of the world's best coffee-growing country; and the fascinating market towns of Cobán, Salamá, Rabinal, and Cubulco.

HISTORIC SALAMÁ AND RABINAL

Salamá ❶, the first of the towns in Baja Verapaz and also the capital of the department, lies some 60km (37 miles) northeast of Guatemala City. The scenery around the town (altitude 940 meters/3,084ft) is a delightful mix of productive pastoral land (everything from oranges to olives are grown) and extensive pine forests. It is a historic place set in a wide river valley with an excellent Sunday market. The 17th-century colonial church in the plaza is an absolute gem, with no fewer than 14 gilded altars, and there's a rather dilapidated old colonial bridge on the edge of town, now only used by pedestrians.

Situated a further 19km (12 miles) west is **Rabinal ❷**, the town where the leader of the Achi tribe accepted Bartolomé de Las Casas and his Christian priests. It also has a fine colonial church, and another superb Sunday market that's a good place to buy *artesanías* (handicrafts), especially ceramics. About 1km (0.6 miles) north of Rabinal are the unreconstructed Achi ruins of Cahrup – there's not too much to see, but it makes a pleasant place for a picnic.

The final town out this way is Cubulco, famous for its July 25 fiesta, where the Palo Volador, a spectacular Mayan ritual high up in the air, is performed.

QUETZAL RESERVE

Baja Verapaz's other attraction is located just to the south of Purulhá, off the Cobán highway, where an area of dense cloud forest has been declared a quetzal reserve, the **Biotopo del Quetzal ❸** (daily 7am–4pm). The quetzal, once the spiritual talisman of the Maya lords, now Guatemala's national bird, is a beautiful but notoriously elusive creature that is now very rare throughout Central America (see page 99).

Tip

At the Finca Santa Margarita (see page 152), once owned by prominent German coffee grower Erwin Dieseldorff, the guided tour takes you step by step through the coffee-making process from propagation to roasting. You also have a chance to sample the different types of Arabica coffee blends, and to buy beans direct.

The beautiful quetzal.

Tip

You can climb the 131 steps of the Calvario church tower in Cobán for a fine view of the town and surrounding countryside.

The reserve (also called the Biotopo Mario Dary, after its founder, a conservationist who was murdered in 1981 whilst fighting to protect the area from loggers) is a permanently humid patch of forest thick with ferns, epiphytes, moss, and lichen. Dawn is the best time to spot a quetzal, which feasts on the fruit of the aguacatillo (wild avocado) tree, but there are at least another 87 species of birds to look out for. A map available on site details the two trails that meander through the ever-dripping foliage. The season for spotting the quetzal is just before and after the nesting season, between March and June.

COBÁN

The commercial center of the Verapaces is **Cobán** ❹, which, though founded by Las Casas in 1538, remained a slumbering backwater until the late 19th century, when large numbers of German immigrants arrived. The Germans were granted authority to plant coffee bushes, which thrived in the mild, moist Verapaz climate, and business prospered until World War II, when many of the coffee barons were expelled at the US's insistence because of their open support for Adolf Hitler.

Tranquil Cobán has a few attractions and makes an excellent base to explore the beautiful Verapaz scenery. Though the town maintains a sleepy demeanor, there are some good-value cafés and hotels, so visitors should enjoy their stay here. Take a stroll up to the Templo el Calvario, a fine old church dating from 1599, which is popular with Q' eqchi' and Poqomchi' Maya worshipers. Don't miss the exquisite carvings and artifacts inside the small **Museo El Príncipe Maya** (Mon–Sat 9am–6pm), or the chance to take a guided tour of the **Finca Santa Margarita** (Mon–Fri 8.30am–11pm, 2–4pm, Sat 8.30–11am), a coffee plantation 300 meters/yds southeast of the plaza.

Just out of town, 5km (3.10 miles) to the west, is the Orquigonia (daily 7am–4pm; http://orquigonia.blogspot.com), a specialist nursery where thousands of plants, including more than 600 species of orchid, are grown.

The stunning turquoise pools of Semuc Champey are a perfect natural water park.

SEMUC CHAMPEY

A cascade of cool turquoise and emerald-green pools surrounded by lush, tropical forest, Semuc Champey is one of eastern Guatemala's most spectacular sights and its top tourist attraction. The Río Cahabón eventually flows into Lago de Izabal, but at Semuc Champey most of its current plunges underground, leaving a great limestone bridge at the surface. A little river water spills over this natural shelf, creating a series of idyllic pools perfect for swimming, and a magical place to relax and enjoy the magnificent natural setting (keep your valuables with you). Climb the steep path (which can be slippery in parts) on the southern side of the valley to a *mirador* (lookout) for an eagle's perspective of the pools. Tour companies in Cobán run regular trips here (see Travel Tips, page 374).

CAVES AND LAGOONS

Far more dramatic, though, are the stunning natural wonders near the village of **Lanquín** ❺, situated 58km (36 miles) to the northeast. The gargantuan Lanquín caves are a speleologist's delight, stretching for several kilometers underground, while on the banks of the Río Cahabón south of Lanquín is **Semuc Champey**, one of the most beautiful places in Guatemala.

North of Lanquín, a poor dirt road winds through some spectacular Verapaz countryside, the first stretch almost alpine in appearance, then punctured by dramatic limestone hills as the route heads towards the Cruce del Pato junction. Near the isolated village of Raxrujá, the Candelaria caves are some of Guatemala's most impressive and include a 200-meter (650ft) chamber known as Tzul Tacca. There is a small charge.

Heading north of Cobán toward Petén, 60km (35 miles) along a smooth highway brings you to the small town of **Chisec**, which has two natural attractions close by. Just 2km (1.2 miles) north of town, **Bombil Pek** (painted cave) is a huge limestone sinkhole, which has a tiny cave adorned with faint images of monkeys that date from ancient Maya times. Some 8km (5 miles) east of Chisec are the **Lagunas de Sepalau**, two stunning turquoise lakes surrounded by dense rainforest.

Another 43km (27 miles) northwest from Chisec is the **Parque Nacional Laguna Lachuá** ❻, a spectacular circular lake. Ringed by rainforest, Lachuá is idyllic, if extremely remote, and a variety of wildlife, including otters and many birds, can be seen here. There's a good wooden guest lodge and camping facilities.

EL ORIENTE

Lying south of the Carretera al Atlántico is another highland region, known as El Oriente. This is the hottest part of Guatemala, a relentlessly uncompromising land where the thermometer regularly nudges 38°C (100°F). El Oriente is *ladino* country par excellence, the arid, dusty terrain the natural home to *campesinos*, cattle ranchers, and tobacco farmers. Probing the horizon are a scattering of ancient, extinct

Tip

There's another large cave system close to Semuc Champey called K'anba that can be explored; hotels in Lanquín offer tours. A river flows through the cave system, so be prepared to get thoroughly wet, and it is pitch dark – tours are often conducted by candlelight to add to the atmosphere.

Exploring the spectacular caves at Lanquín.

Tip

Boat cruises around El Golfete (usually departing from Lívingston) often stop at the hot springs that empty into the lagoon, so you can take a dip in the warm, sulfurous water. It is an idyllic spot, shaded by overhanging trees and surrounded by lush jungle vegetation.

volcanoes – though much smaller in scale and more weathered in appearance than the chain across the western highlands. You will have to cross through these eastern highlands if you plan to visit the ruins of Copán.

The main route into El Oriente branches off from the Carretera al Atlántico at the Río Hondo junction. Heading south, the first major town, **Chiquimula 7**, is archetypal of the region – hot, dusty, and featureless. Because of its location, it is well served by buses, and has a reasonable choice of places to stay and eat. The only building of architectural interest is an old colonial church, the Iglesia Vieja, on the edge of town, badly damaged by the earthquake in 1765 and now reduced to ruins.

Continuing south of Chiquimula, down near-empty roads, is **Volcán de Ipala 8**, a 1,650-meter (5,410ft) eroded volcano with an exquisite crater lake at its rounded summit. It is a fairly easy two-hour hike to the top from the closest village of Agua Blanca. If you have your own transportation, the most direct route is up a trail that begins at Km 26.5 on the Ipala–Agua Blanca road, near to a drinks stall in the tiny settlement of Sauce. Once here, you can walk all around the forest-fringed summit of the lake in a couple of hours.

Vicar blessing pilgrims in front of the Basilica of Esquipulas.

ESQUIPULAS

Some 33km (20 miles) south of Chiquimula, close to the border with El Salvador, **Esquipulas 9** is famous as the site of the biggest pilgrimage in Central America. The object of veneration is an image of El Cristo Negro, the Black Christ, which is housed in a colossal white basilica. Inside the church the atmosphere is heady with incense and smoky from burning candles, while a continuous procession of pilgrims lines up to receive a blessing, many on their knees and reciting prayers. The image itself, created from balsam wood, was carved by the fabled sculptor Quirio Cataño in the late 16th century, while the origins of the pilgrimage are thought to predate the Conquest. The main pilgrimage date is January 15, and there is a smaller event on March 9, but Esquipulas is busy throughout the whole year with pilgrims and devotees paying homage and seeking cures to ailments.

The town itself is rampantly commercial, geared to extract as much as possible from its short-term visitors – hotel prices double on Saturdays and there's an unholy heap of tacky souvenirs in market stalls outside the basilica.

IZABAL

Fringed by the Caribbean Sea, with Belize just to the north and the Honduran coastline to the south, the low-lying department of Izabal feels totally unlike the rest of the country. The population is a polyglot assortment of *ladinos*, Garífuna, Caribs, and Q' eqchi' Maya. The scenery is also different: the landscape is lush, and the heat and humidity are punishing at any time of year, creating a decidedly languid, tropical ambience.

Izabal is bounded by mountains: the Sierra del Merendón defining the Honduran border, the Sierra de las Minas to the southwest, and the Sierra de Santa Cruz to the north. In the very center of the department is **Lago de Izabal**, the biggest lake in the country, which drains into the Caribbean through the beautiful Río Dulce gorge. The economy has been geared around bananas for over a century, exported via the port towns of Puerto Barrios and Santo Tomás de Castilla to North America and Europe, though tourism centered upon the town of Río Dulce is also becoming more important, particularly for cruises on Lago de Izabal and El Golfete.

QUIRIGUÁ RUINS

The Carretera al Atlántico follows the Motagua River through much of the department, following the ancient trade route from the highlands to the Caribbean. The early Classic ruins of **Quiriguá** (daily 8am–4.30pm) ❿, set in a beautiful clearing just off the highway, are well worth investigating for their remarkable stone carvings of fine-grained sandstone stelae and giant flat boulders. Quiriguá had always been a minor site, possibly first settled in the early Classic period by an elite group from the northern Maya lowlands. It was subsequently dominated by nearby Copán, but in AD 737, the leader Cauac Sky (or Two-legged Sky) captured and sacrificed Copán's ruler 18 Rabbit, turning centuries of Maya power politics upside down.

To celebrate this success, Cauac Sky started rebuilding Quiriguá, commissioning the carving of the largest stelae anywhere in the Maya world, which were grouped around an enormous monumental plaza, enclosed on three sides by an acropolis.

The site's largest stela is Stela E, 8 meters (25ft) tall, which depicts Cauac Sky crowned with an elaborate headdress. There are 10 other stelae in the plaza, a small acropolis to the south, and a ball court. Don't miss the six fantastic carved boulders just below the acropolis, which are decorated with images of frogs, turtles, jaguars, and snakes, and a serene, Buddha-like figure on Zoomorph P.

Local girls in traditional costume, Río Dulce.

Beautiful carvings at Quiriguá.

Esquipulas is a popular site for Catholic pilgrimage.

LAKE IZABAL

North of Quiriguá is **Lago de Izabal**, a huge freshwater expanse which is steadily being opened up to tourism. The western environs of the lake are protected as part of the Bocas del Polochic reserve, where there are alligators, iguanas, and a riot of colorful birdlife. Most people stay at the eastern edge of the lake, however, near the massive concrete bridge, at the town of **Río Dulce** ⓫. The town, scattered on both sides of the bridge, is no beauty, functioning mainly as a transport hub, but unexpectedly close by there are some delightful hotels that are well placed for exploring the lake.

Back in the 16th and 17th centuries, British pirates caused mayhem around Izabal, raiding Spanish merchant caravans, and the Castillo de San Felipe (daily 7am–5pm), just 3km (2 miles) from Río Dulce town, was built to combat these marauding buccaneers. There's a lot more to see around the lake, including an incredible hot spring waterfall near Finca El Paraíso, which drops about 12 meters (40ft) into a deep pool, and the Boquerón canyon near the town of El Estor, originally called "the store," another reminder of English influence.

MANATEE RESERVE

Heading toward the Caribbean from Río Dulce town, the lakeside scenery opens up again into a lagoon called El Golfete, where there's a manatee habitat reserve, **Biotopo Chacón Machaca** (daily 7am–4pm), though you will be extremely fortunate to see one of the huge, timid mammals. The birdlife is usually much more in evidence, so keep your eyes peeled for pelicans, egrets, kingfishers, ospreys, and herons. The banks then close in as you enter the spectacular Río Dulce gorge, its soaring 100-meter (328ft) high walls covered in impenetrable rainforest, passing a bubbling underwater hot spring.

LÍVINGSTON

At the point where the Río Dulce meets the Bahía de Amatique is the Garífuna town of **Lívingston** ⓬, sometimes known locally as La Buga (The Mouth). Lívingston is one of the most

Fishing on the Río Dulce.

interesting villages in Guatemala, its atmosphere seemingly much more in tune with Jamaica or the Honduran Bay Islands than the Central American mainland. Connections with the rest of Guatemala are somewhat tentative, and not just culturally, as Lívingston can only be reached by boat from Puerto Barrios, Belize, or Honduras. With the melodic rhythms of reggae and Garífuna punta filling the village streets, it is easy to assume Lívingston is some lost laid-back Caribbean paradise. Not so – unemployment is very high, forcing many to emigrate, and allegedly more Lívingston-born men live in New York than in the village itself.

Good excursions from Lívingston include the impressive series of waterfalls called Siete Altares (best in the rainy season), the best beach in Guatemala, Playa Blanca, and even snorkeling trips to the edge of the Belizean reef system.

PUERTO BARRIOS

Puerto Barrios ⓭, located in the southeastern corner of Bahía de Amatique, is today little more than a transit point for tourists picking up boats for Punta Gorda in Belize or en route for Lívingston. For many years though, the town was the country's most important port. Now it has been eclipsed by the modern facilities available at Santo Tomás de Castilla, just 11km (7 miles) to the west around the bay.

Puerto Barrios was established by president Rufino Barrios in the late 19th century, but developed by the United Fruit Company in the 1900s as the company's exclusive port for the export of its bananas. The UFC modeled the town on urban North American lines, and it retains this legacy today, with broad streets and sprawling city blocks.

Most of the old wooden Caribbean buildings are crumbling and dilapidated now, unfortunately, replaced by faceless concrete constructions. The odd reminder of more prosperous times remains, however, and the town's one real sight is the atmospheric Hotel del Norte, right on the waterfront, an immaculately preserved – and charming – living monument, built entirely from wood.

Using a traditional canoe to navigate the Río Dulce.

Fruit and vegetable production has played a significant role in the nation's history.

⊙ THE UNITED FRUIT COMPANY

For more than half a century, all Guatemala's political and economic decisions were effectively supervised by the United Fruit Company, Central America's biggest employer, and dubbed *El Pulpo* ("The Octopus") because of its huge influence in the region. The UFC first began banana business in Guatemala in 1901, and quickly struck a deal to complete the Guatemala City–Puerto Barrios railroad line in exchange for almost complete tax exemption and land concessions. By 1930 the company was worth US$215 million, and its yellow tentacles controlled the country's railroads, the main port Puerto Barrios, and consequently had control over all the country's other exports.

This hegemony was largely unchecked until 1952, when President Arbenz drafted new reform laws, which redistributed land to peasants at a fraction of its market value. US interests were deemed to be under threat, and a plot was hatched by the CIA (whose director Allen Dulles was also on the UFC board) to support an invading force of Guatemalan exiles from Honduras, which overthrew Arbenz in 1954.

The new CIA-backed strongman, Carlos Castillo Armas, returned all the confiscated land to the UFC, which merged with United Brands in the 1960s and finally quit Guatemala in 1972, selling its remaining land to Del Monte.

COPÁN RUINS

One of the most impressive ancient sites in Mesoamerica is Copán, featuring some of the Mayan world's greatest treasures.

Copán ⓮, a restored Mayan city, is located on the banks of the Río Copán, only 12km (8 miles) into Honduras from the Guatemalan border town of El Florido.

The explorers John L. Stephens and Frederick Catherwood visited the site in 1839, at which time the magnificent stonework was smothered in jungle vegetation. Today, however, after more than 20 years' dramatic excavation work and study, the site has been spectacularly restored. An increasing number of visitors to Guatemala make a special detour to these superb ruins, whose carved stelae are widely considered the finest yet found in the Maya world.

Gigantic head of the god Pauahtun, near Temple 11.

HISTORY

At its peak in the 8th century AD, Copán was a powerful city-state which dominated the Motagua valley through its control of the important trade in jade, obsidian, cacao, and quetzal feathers. By this time the city was home to an estimated population of some 20,000 inhabitants.

There is evidence of human settlement in the Copán valley as early as 1300 BC, but it was not until AD 426 that a nobleman from Teotihuacán in central Mexico, Yax K'uk Mo', took control of the area and established a new royal dynasty which would rule Copán for almost the next 400 years.

The dynasty of Yax K'uk Mo' held political sway throughout the southeastern Maya region, including Quiriguá, another city-state in the southeast of present-day Guatemala (see page 161). Eventually, however, the warriors of Quiriguá rose up under their new king Cauac Sky and rebelled against Copán in a bid for independence, crushing the once invincible city. Following the capture and ritual sacrifice in AD 737 of its 13th ruler, 18 Rabbit, Copán's supremacy began to wane. The quality of its ceremonial architecture and carved stonework also began to deteriorate from this time on. The glorious dynasty founded by Yax K'uk Mo' struggled on under three more rulers before the city finally collapsed.

Copán's slow decline coincided with that of the rest of the lowland Maya world at the end of the Classic period, c. AD 800. The city of Copán was abandoned in the early 9th century, although a small population remained in the valley for some time afterward.

Archeological work at Copán has been in continuous progress since 1975, and there were several earlier expeditions that mapped and excavated the site. To date, a large portion of the city center has been excavated and restored, with many monuments re-erected in their original positions. Over 1,000 structures have been found in this urban core alone, covering an area of 1.3 sq km (0.5 sq miles), which represents only the nucleus of the majestic city of Copán.

The visual impact of the city lies above all in the artistic achievements of its craftsmen, and the site boasts some of the most ornate carving to be found in Mesoamerica. Copán's masons developed an extremely fine and detailed form of high relief sculpture using the local stone: a greenish andesite that was very soft and thus the ideal material for the intricately formed figures of humans, animals, and birds.

The sculptures also contain a myriad of symbolic texts and images demonstrating what Aldous Huxley described as the Maya's "extraordinary preoccupation with time." Scribes were revered by the Maya, and the knowledge and use of hieroglyphics were vital to Copán's rulers for the affirmation of elite legitimacy and to ensure the continuation of the dominant ideology in future generations.

THE SITE TODAY

Copán is a well-kept site, which you could visit on a long day trip from Guatemala City, but it is better to take your time and spend at least one night in the delightful nearby town of Copán Ruinas. As you enter the site from the **Visitors' Center**, a main pathway takes you into the **Great Plaza**, a vast open space which, at one time, would have been paved. The Great Plaza houses some of the site's most beautiful sculpted stelae, many of which depict King 18 Rabbit, including stelae A, B, C, D, F, H, and 4. Stela A is particularly impressive, with deep carving and 52 glyphs decorating its sides. It is a reproduction of the original, which is kept, together with most of the other original stelae, in the on-site **Museum of Maya Sculpture**. Stela C has faces carved on both sides, and an altar in the shape of a turtle at its base.

To the south of the Great Plaza lies the **Acropolis**, a colossal man-made mound upon which several successive pyramids, temples, terraces, and plazas were built over the centuries. Altar Q, at the base of Pyramid 16, is one of Copán's most famous sculptures, its sides decorated with 16 seated figures, carved in exquisite relief. Together with the Great Plaza, the Acropolis constitutes what would have been the main hub of activity in the ancient city.

Just to the north of the Acropolis is perhaps the most exceptional structure in Copán, which is known as the **Hieroglyphic Stairway**. Built by the city's 15th ruler, Smoke Shell, in AD 756, the stairway was dedicated to the honor of his dynastic predecessors. Smoke Shell also hoped the achievement would serve to regain the support of his people and reaffirm the status of his dynasty after the earlier, humiliating defeat of 18 Rabbit.

With 62 carved steps leading up a pyramid, and adorned with six richly decorated figures representing the city's rulers, the Hieroglyphic Stairway contains the longest inscription known in ancient Mesoamerica, the meaning of which is still challenging epigraphers. The partial collapse of the structure at some point before its excavation left a "jigsaw in stone" of some 20,000 individual hieroglyphic inscriptions. At the base of the stairway is Stela M, depicting a royal figure in a feathered cloak, while at the front a plumed serpent swallows a human head.

The ruins of Copán are open daily (daily 8am–4pm; www.ihah.hn). The **Museum of Maya Sculpture**, next to the Visitors' Center, is well worth a visit (charge) – best before you see the ruins themselves – containing many of the original stelae, and a full-size reproduction of the startlingly colorful **Rosalilia Temple**, discovered intact beneath Temple 16 in 1989.

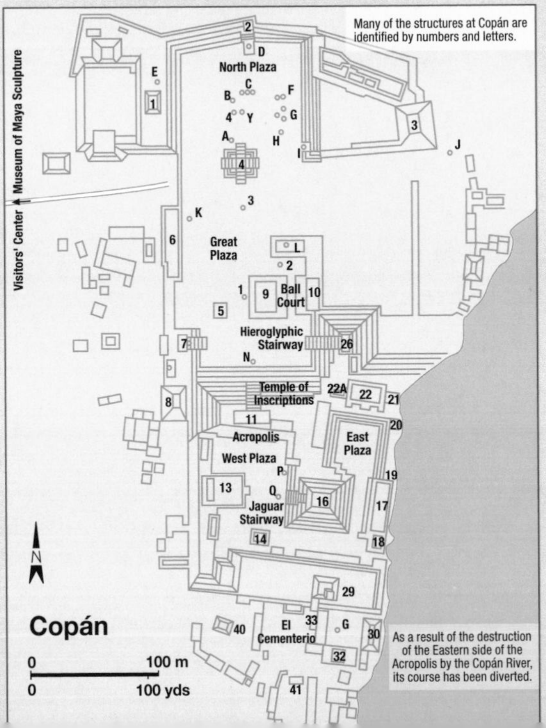

Copán

Many of the structures at Copán are identified by numbers and letters.

As a result of the destruction of the Eastern side of the Acropolis by the Copán River, its course has been diverted.

View from Temple IV at Tikal, whose ruins are swathed in jungle.

PETÉN

Hidden in this vast northern jungle department are some of the most spectacular Maya cities, including the indisputable, dazzling jewel in their crown: Tikal.

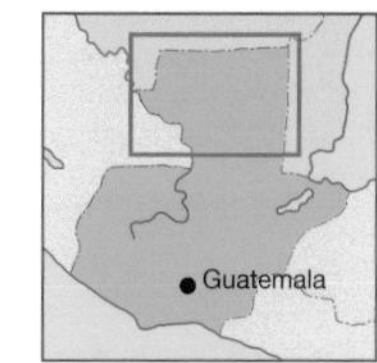

Between 750 BC and around AD 900, arguably the greatest of all pre-Columbian cultures, the Maya civilization, evolved, excelled, and ultimately collapsed in the lowland subtropical forests of what is now northern Guatemala. It was in the jungles and savannas of the department of Petén, which covers a third of the country, that the Maya city-states succeeded in creating some of the greatest human advances in the continent: a precise calendrical system, pioneering astronomy, a complex writing system, breathtaking artistry, and towering architectural triumphs.

There's compelling evidence that a combination of environmental and social factors (including overpopulation, warfare, and revolt) prompted the disaster of the Maya collapse, but the exact reasons are still subject to animated academic debate. Whatever the truth, the jungle reclaimed the temples, plazas, and palaces, so that by the time the 19th-century explorers arrived, buildings were choked with over 1,000 years of forest growth.

PENETRATING THE PETÉN

The Spanish all but ignored the area until, in 1697, they finally defeated the tiny isolated Itzá Maya tribe that lived on the shores of Lago de Petén Itzá. Most of the entire department of Petén was all but inaccessible until the 1960s, when the hellish trails that sneaked through the trees between the capital and Flores were upgraded to dirt roads. At this time, most of Petén was still covered in pristine forest, with only a few thousand human inhabitants. Government schemes opened up the forests to land-hungry settlers, loggers, and oil prospectors, and the population spiraled (now estimated to be over 600,000). As much as 50 percent of the forest may have already been cut, with destructive "slash and burn" farming and logging, at first clearing the

The tropical flower heliconia.

Main Attractions

Flores
Tikal
Uaxactún
El Mirador
Lago de Petexbatún
Yaxhá

Maps on pages 168, 172

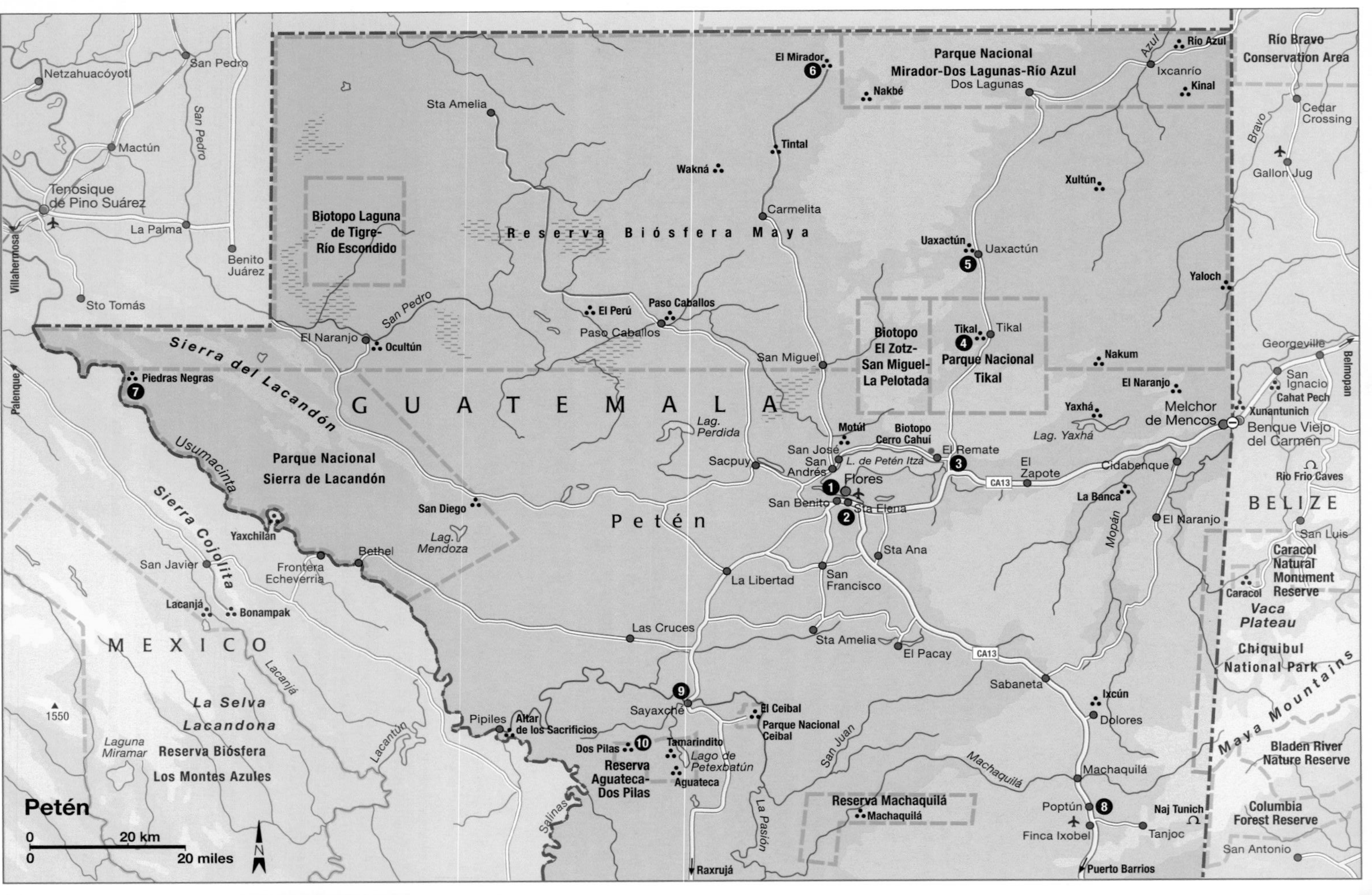
Petén
0 20 km
0 20 miles
N
Netzahuacóyotl
San Pedro
Mactún
San Pedro
Tenosique de Pino Suárez
La Palma
Benito Juárez
Villahermosa
Sto Tomás
Palenque
Sta Amelia
El Mirador
Parque Nacional Mirador-Dos Lagunas-Río Azul
Nakbé
Dos Lagunas
Azul
Río Azul
Ixcanrío
Kinal
Río Bravo Conservation Area
Cedar Crossing
Bravo
Gallon Jug
Tintal
Wakná
Xultún
Carmelita
Biotopo Laguna de Tigre-Río Escondido
Reserva Biósfera Maya
Uaxactún
Yaloch
El Perú
Paso Caballos
San Pedro
El Naranjo
Ocultún
Biotopo El Zotz-San Miguel-La Pelotada
Tikal
Parque Nacional Tikal
Nakum
Georgeville
Belmopan
San Ignacio
Cahal Pech
Xunantunich
Sierra del Lacandón
Piedras Negras
San Miguel
El Naranjo
G U A T E M A L A
Yaxhá
Melchor de Mencos
Benque Viejo del Carmen
Lag. Perdida
Motúl
Biotopo Cerro Cahuí
Lag. Yaxhá
San José
El Remate
Usumacinta
Parque Nacional Sierra de Lacandón
Sacpuy
San Andrés
L. de Petén Itzá
El Zapote
Cidabenque
Río Frío Caves
Flores
CA13
La Banca
Sierra Cojolita
San Diego
San Benito
Sta Elena
BELIZE
Petén
El Naranjo
Mopán
San Luis
Yaxchilán
Lag. Mendoza
Bethel
Sta Ana
Caracol Natural Monument Reserve
Caracol
San Javier
Frontera Echeverría
La Libertad
San Francisco
Vaca Plateau
Lacanjá
Bonampak
Las Cruces
Sta Amelia
El Pacay
CA13
Chiquibul National Park
MEXICO
Lacanjá
Sabaneta
Maya Mountains
Ixcún
1550
La Selva Lacandona
Sayaxché
El Ceibal
Pipiles
Altar de los Sacrificios
Parque Nacional Ceibal
Dolores
Laguna Miramar
Reserva Biósfera Los Montes Azules
Lacantún
Dos Pilas
Tamarindito
Lago de Petexbatún
San Juan
Machaquilá
Machaquilá
Bladen River Nature Reserve
Reserva Aguateca-Dos Pilas
Aguateca
Salinas
La Pasión
Reserva Machaquilá
Machaquilá
Poptún
Naj Tunich
Columbia Forest Reserve
Finca Ixobel
Tanjoc
San Antonio
Raxrujá
Puerto Barrios

trees, then moving on and leaving the degraded land to cattle ranchers.

The Petén is still Guatemala's wild frontier province, and transportation, communications, hotels, and restaurants are generally pretty basic away from the main town of Flores. To get to Maya sites like El Mirador takes time (unless you take a heli-tour!), planning, and local expertise – there are a number of excellent local organizations that operate expeditions to the remote ruins. The Petén climate is perennially hot and humid. The rainy season can extend until December, and can disrupt overland travel to isolated areas. Tikal and Flores are always accessible nevertheless.

FLORES

Set on a natural island in Lago de Petén Itzá, connected via a small causeway to shore, **Flores** ❶ (population 13,000) is a peaceful, civilized place now largely dependent on tourism. It is a small, tranquil, and historic town that's by far the most pleasant urban center in the department. Today's town stands on the remains of the old Itzá Maya capital, Tayasal, which was first visited by Hernán Cortés in 1525, left alone, and only conquered in 1697. The Spanish had no appetite for jungle life, and Flores retained closer contact with Belize and Mexico until the road links to the rest of Guatemala improved in the late 20th century.

The best way to explore Flores is to stroll around the lane that circumscribes the shoreline – it will take you about 15 minutes to walk around the cobbled streets and lanes of the town. Some of its architecture is delightful: the older houses are brightly painted wooden and adobe constructions, many of the hotels have been painted in harmonious pastel shades, and there's a fine plaza in the center of town that boasts a twin-domed cathedral.

Just across the causeway, the ugly urban sprawl of **Santa Elena** ❷ and San Benito (combined population around 90,000) could not present more of a contrast. These are rough and ready frontier towns, typical of a region where laws can be ignored and the authorities bribed if necessary.

PETÉN'S WILDLIFE

Despite illegal logging and environmental damage, vast areas of the Petén forest remain intact, and this is still one of the best places in Central America to see some spectacular wildlife. A number of national parks and reserves have been established (and combined as the Maya Biosphere Reserve) to protect the subtropical habitat of over 4,000 plant species and animals that include jaguars, crocodiles, tapirs, ocelots, collared peccaries, armadillos, boa constrictors, blue morpho butterflies, and 450 resident and migratory birds. Even if you only make it to Tikal, you should hear the deafening roar of the howler monkey, glimpse toucans and parrots squabbling in the forest canopy, and perhaps spot an ocellated turkey or a gray fox in the undergrowth (see page 179).

Scarlet macaws can be seen around Petén.

Tip

Boat trips are available from Flores to the surrounding sights, including traditional villages such as San José and San Andrés, the ARCAS wildlife rescue center next to the zoo, ruins, and Aktun Kan caves.

Development is ramshackle, and the streets are thick with dust and dirt. There's no reason to be here except to visit a bank (there are a couple in Flores anyway) or catch a bus out of town.

AROUND FLORES

On the banks of Lago de Petén Itzá, around Flores, there's a number of things to see, most of which are best visited by boat – you will find boatmen by the Hotel Santana and on the Santa Elena side of the causeway. The **Petencito zoo** (daily 8am–5pm) and a lookout point on a small island are the most popular destinations, but if you want to see a traditional Petén village, head for San Andrés on the north shore. The neighboring village of San José, 2km (1.2 miles) away, is another friendly place, where efforts are being made to preserve the Itzá Maya language. Some 4km (2.5 miles) beyond San José are the minor ruins of Motúl, where there are some small pyramids and a stela to see.

Some 2km (1.2 miles) south of Santa Elena, the caves of Aktun Kan have some bizarre formations that vaguely resemble animals, plus plenty of stalactites, stalagmites, and the odd bat.

The small but spread-out village of **El Remate** ❸ is another good base for exploring Tikal, with a burgeoning number of hotels. It is 30km (18.5 miles) from Santa Elena/Flores and particularly convenient if you are approaching the ruins from Belize.

About 3km (2 miles) from the center of the village is a small nature reserve, the **Biotopo Cerro Cahuí** (7am–4pm). The reserve is home to a remarkable diversity of plant life (mahogany, *ceiba*, and *sapodilla* trees, orchids and epiphytes), animals (spider and howler monkeys, armadillos, and ocelots) and particularly an exceptional quantity of birds, with hundreds of species recorded here.

TIKAL

Entombed in dense jungle, where the inanimate air is periodically shattered by the roars of howler monkeys, the phenomenal, towering ruins of **Tikal** ❹ (6am–6pm; www.tikalnationalpark.org) are

It's a steep climb to the top of Temple II at Tikal.

one of the wonders of the Americas. Five magnificent temple-pyramids soar above the forest canopy, finely carved stelae and altars in the plaza eulogize the city's glorious history, giant stucco masks adorn monuments, and stone-flagged causeways lead toward other ruined cities lying even deeper in the jungle.

Tikal's scale is awesome. In the Classic period its population grew to almost 100,000. Trade routes connected the city with Teotihuacán (near modern-day Mexico City), the Caribbean and Pacific coasts. Temple IV was built to a height of around 65 meters (213ft), complete with its enormous roof comb. Exquisite jade masks, ceramics, jewelry, and sculptures were created. There were ball courts, sweat baths, colorfully painted royal palaces, and another 4,000 buildings to house the artisans, astrologers, farmers, and warriors of the greatest city of the Classic Maya civilization.

Most travelers concur that Tikal is the most visually sensational of all the Maya sites. To get the most out of your visit, try to stay overnight at one of the three hotels close to the ruins, to witness the electric atmosphere at dawn and dusk when the calls of toucans, frogs, monkeys, and other mammals echo around the surrounding jungle. The temperature and humidity are punishing at any time of year, so make sure you take plenty of water, and also insect repellent.

HISTORY

Tikal is one of the oldest Maya sites: only some of the Mirador Basin sites and Cuello (in Belize) predate it. It's located in the central lowland Maya zone, the cradle of Maya civilization, in a dense subtropical forest environment. The earliest evidence of human habitation at Tikal is around 700 BC, in the Preclassic period. By 500 BC the first simple structures were constructed, but Tikal would have been little more than a small village at this time and Nakbé, some 55km (34 miles) to the north, was the dominant power in the region.

By the time Tikal's first substantial ceremonial structures were built (the North Acropolis and the Great Pyramid) about 200 BC, powerful new cities had emerged, above all the enormous El Mirador, 64km (40 miles) to the north and connected by a *sacbé* raised causeway.

By the start of the Classic period in AD 250, El Mirador and Nakbé had faded and Tikal had grown to be one of the most important Maya cities, along with Uaxactún. The great Tikal leader Great Jaguar Paw and his general Smoking Frog defeated Uaxactún in AD 376, bringing on an era when Tikal and rival "superpower" Calakmul contested dominance of the Maya region for another two centuries. Huge advances were made in the study of astronomy, calendrics, and arithmetics under Stormy Sky (AD 426–57). But disaster struck in 562 when upstart Caracol (in Belize) defeated Double

A coatimundi (known as a pizote in Guatemala) near Tikal.

The pretty town of Flores, on Lake Petén Itzá.

Fact

After the death of a Maya ruler, the stelae describing his life were often broken up and placed in his tomb, as they were considered personal records rather than public monuments.

Bird of Tikal and forged a crucial alliance with Calakmul that was to humble Tikal for 120 years – no stelae at all were carved in this time.

Tikal's renaissance was sparked by Ah Cacau or Lord Chocolate (682–734) and continued by his son Caan Chac, who ordered the construction of most of the temples that bestride the ruins today, which are taller and grander than earlier buildings. Caan Chac also reassumed control of the core Maya area, eclipsing bitter rival Calakmul. Tikal continued to control the region, enjoying unsurpassed stability and prosperity into the 9th century; it faded quickly by AD 900, however, along with all the other lowland sites.

THE SITE

Before (or after) you enter the site, have a look in the **Visitors' Center** Ⓐ, where the **Museo Lítico** has an excellent collection of stelae and carvings; opposite is the **Museo Morley**, where the exhibits include ceramics, jade, the burial ornaments of Lord Chocolate, and Stela 29, the oldest found at Tikal (both museums are open daily 8am–6pm).

The **Great Plaza** Ⓑ is the first place to head for, the nerve center of the city for 1,500 years. The grassy plaza is framed by the perfectly proportioned Temples I and II to the east and west, the North Acropolis, and the Central Acropolis to the south. In Classic Maya days, these monumental limestone buildings would have been painted vivid colors, predominantly red, with clouds of incense smoke smoldering from the upper platforms. Civic and religious ceremonies, frequently including human sacrifice, would have been directed by priests and kings from the top of the temples.

Temple I Ⓒ (also known as the Temple of the Giant Jaguar because of a jaguar carved in its door lintel), was built to honor Lord Chocolate, who was buried in a tomb beneath the 44-meter (144ft) high structure with a stately collection of goods (now exhibited in the Morley Museum). Three small rooms on top of the temple were probably the preserve of priests and kings, adorned

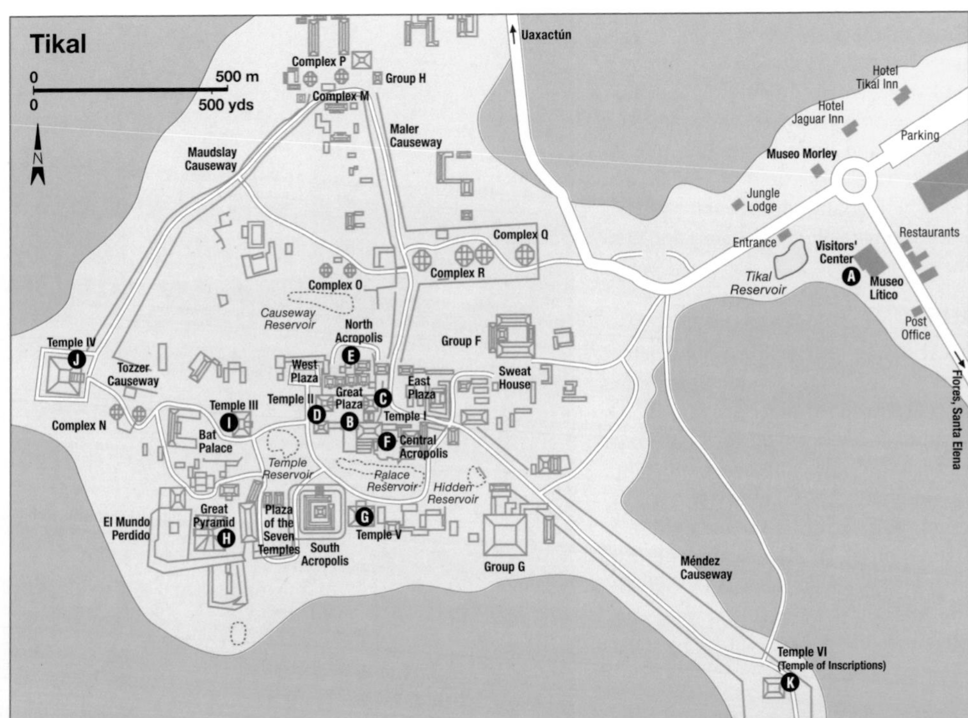

with beautifully carved zapote wood beams and lintels. Facing Temple I across the plaza is **Temple II** **D** (also known as the Temple of the Masks), slightly smaller at 38 meters (125ft) tall, and a little less visually impressive, too, because part of its massive roof comb is missing. Both temples were constructed around AD 740.

Between the two mighty edifices, on the north side of the plaza is a twin row of stelae and altars, about 60 in all. Many date from Classic Maya times, but were moved here from other parts of the site by post-Classic people in a revivalist effort – Stela 5 has some particularly fine glyphs. Behind the stelae is the untidy bulk of the **North Acropolis** **E**, a jumble of disparate masonry composed of some 16 temples and an estimated 100 buildings buried underneath, parts of which are some of the oldest constructions at Tikal, dating back to 250 BC. Most of the temple structures are late Classic, and missing elaborate roof combs, but all are built over much earlier foundations. Among the remains are two colossal Preclassic stucco masks.

On the south side of the plaza is the **Central Acropolis** **F**, a maze of buildings thought to function as the rulers' palace, grouped around six small courtyards. In front of the Central Acropolis is a small ball court, and behind it to the south are the palace reservoir and the restored 58-meter (190ft) **Temple V** **G**. A very steep staircase ascends this temple (which may be closed following heavy rain), and from its summit there's an astonishing view of the entire site.

THE LOST WORLD

Reached by a trail from Temple V, El Mundo Perdido (The Lost World) is a beautiful, atmospheric complex of buildings, dominated by the mighty **Great Pyramid** **H**, a 32-meter (105ft) high Preclassic monument that's Tikal's oldest known structure. It is also an ideal base from which to watch sunrise or sunset. **Temple III** **I**, north from here, peaks at 55 meters (180ft) and remains cloaked in jungle, while

Efforts are being made to preserve the Itzá Maya language in the villages around Lago de Petén Itzá.

View from Temple V at Tikal.

Tip

Your entry ticket into the ruins at Tikal is officially only valid for one day, but if you enter the site after 3pm, your ticket will automatically be stamped for the following day, allowing you another full day to explore at no extra cost.

Temple IV ❶ has been half-cleared of vegetation. Temple IV is the tallest of all Tikal's monuments, at around 64 meters (210ft), or 70 meters (230ft) if you include its platform, making it the second-highest pre-Columbian structure ever built – only the Danta temple at El Mirador eclipses it. Getting to the top involves a tricky climb up a ladder, but the view from the summit really is astounding – mile after mile of rainforest, broken only by the roof combs of the other temples.

There are thousands of other structures to explore – some considerable like Temple VI, also known as the **Temple of Inscriptions** Ⓚ, down the Méndez causeway leading from Temple I, with its 12-meter (39ft) high roof comb and intricate glyphs – most much more modest, the homes of the workers and farmers. Take a good map and great care if you go for a walk in the forest; people get lost every year.

THE NORTHERN RUINS

In the thick jungle of the Maya Biosphere Reserve in the extreme north of Guatemala, there are dozens more Maya ruins, most almost completely unexcavated. The easiest to get to is **Uaxactún** ❺, 24km (15 miles) away, and connected to Tikal by a dirt road, served by one daily bus from Flores/Santa Elena. If you can, visit Uaxactún before Tikal because the ruins are much smaller. Uaxactún rivaled Tikal for many years in the early Classic era, but was finally defeated in a battle on January 16, AD 378. Today there is an interesting observatory comprising three temples built side by side (Group E), numerous fine stelae, simple accommodation, and, of course, the jungle to explore and admire.

Just a couple of kilometers from the Mexican border, the Preclassic metropolis of **El Mirador** ❻ matches Tikal in scale and may yet be found to exceed it. Unless you take a pricey helicopter tour, it is only accessible by foot. Other remote ruins, including **Nakbé** and Río Azul, right on the tripartite border where Belize, Mexico, and Guatemala meet, can also be found here (for full details see page 177).

Temple II – the temples sit in clearings in thick jungle.

Finally, way over on the other side of the Maya Biosphere Reserve on the Río Usumacinta is the extremely isolated **Piedras Negras** ❼. The site, which towers over the Guatemalan bank of the river, can only be accessed by boat, with trips organized in Guatemala City (see page 117). Some of the finest stelae in the Maya world were carved at Piedras Negras, and there is a megalithic stairway and substantial ruins to admire, including a sweat bath and an impressive acropolis, with extensive rooms and courtyards.

SOUTH AND EAST OF FLORES

Two roads creep through the jungle south of Flores, the busier of which heads past **Poptún** ❽, a dusty, featureless town 113km (70 miles) away, where a fine ranch makes an idyllic place to stay. At the American-owned Finca Ixobel, a short distance out of town, there are many opportunities to explore the region's cave and river systems and enjoy great company, while the home-cooked food is delicious.

Taking the other route south, 62km (38 miles) from Flores is the town of **Sayaxché** ❾, a frontier settlement by the Río de la Pasión. This is an ideal base to visit the ruins of **El Ceibal**, set in a patch of rainforest 17km (10.5 miles) away, which was a large city dating from Preclassic times. Much remains unreconstructed, but there's a fine plaza and stelae, an astronomy platform, and many noisy howler monkeys. South of Sayaxché is the lovely, forest-fringed **Lago de Petexbatún**, with three interesting ruins close by. **Aguateca** is the most accessible, positioned high above the lake; the partly restored ruins are scattered around a natural chasm. **Dos Pilas** ❿ is a bigger site with some fine altars, a ball court, and four short hieroglyphic stairways.

Finally, 73km (45 miles) east of Flores are the substantial ruins of **Yaxhá**, which are steadily being restored. Structure 216, which tops 30 meters (98ft), is Yaxhá's most impressive construction. There's also a fine Preclassic temple cluster, with three large pyramids arranged in a triadic formation, and two giant stucco masks.

Fact

One of the buildings at Uaxactún, the unimaginatively named E-VII in Group E, functioned as an observatory in Preclassic Maya times (one of the first ever built) and was built to align with the sunrise on the summer and winter solstices.

Detail on stelae in Museo Tikal.

THE MIRADOR BASIN RUINS

Buried in the densest jungles of the region in the extreme north of Guatemala are the remains of dozens of ancient cities that were the birthplace of the Maya civilization.

The terrain is very difficult to access – there are no roads into the Mirador Basin, and the marshland and forest become so saturated that archeological excavations can only be attempted for half the year. Nevertheless a trickle of visitors makes it to the region, either using mule tracks that operate on ancient *sacbé* causeways built by the Maya, or on helicopter trips (which are becoming increasingly popular and affordable).

For travelers, the main draw is the colossal site of El Mirador, the first Maya superpower, famed for its towering triadic temple complexes which peak at over 70 meters (230 feet). At its peak around the time of Christ, Mirador's Kaan dynasty ruled over hundreds of thousands more subjects in the Basin region – then one of the most densely inhabited places on earth – and millions more in the Maya world paid tribute to this great power.

El Mirador is only one of a cluster of fascinating sites. As yet most of these ruined cities have only been investigated by archeologists, and there's been little reconstruction, so most temples and palaces, marketplaces and residences remain choked by giant roots and rainforest. Nevertheless, exploring the cities can be deeply rewarding, allowing travelers to view these ruined remains just as the early explorers like Maudslay encountered Tikal. Nakbé was the prototype, the first city to emerge in the basin (around 1000 BC), and its triadic temples remain an imposing sight. Wakná (which was only discovered in 1998) boasts more striking early Maya architecture, while the huge site of Tintal matches Tikal for scale.

A snail kite, found around tropical marshlands.

RAINFOREST AND WILDLIFE

Enveloping these myriad ruined cities, the Mirador Basin rainforest is an incredibly rich and biodiverse habitat. The forests contain all the big cats of Central America, including healthy numbers of jaguar (around 400) and puma, howler and spider monkeys, while the birdlife is exceptional. This ecosystem is under constant threat from a formidable collection of landless *campesinos*, timber-hungry loggers, cattle ranchers, tomb looters, and *narcos* (drug smugglers). Environmentalists and archeologists are fighting to get the entire Mirador region, 2,169 sq km (837 sq miles) of forest, declared the Mirador Basin National Park. Guatemala's ex-President Colom backed the scheme in 2008, yet the national park has yet to be established.

Protection is essential, according to Mirador's principal archeologist, Dr Richard Hansen, "otherwise we'd lose the whole city." He wants to promote ecotourism, with visitors entering the basin via a narrow-gauge railroad, as the way to preserve the ruins and the rainforest. Powerful logging and farming interests oppose the idea of a strictly enforced national park, however.

EL MIRADOR

Archeologists are only starting to understand the history and importance of El Mirador, perhaps the most evocative of all Maya sites. We are not even certain of its name – *El Mirador* means "the lookout" in Spanish due to its position on a hilltop – but it could have been Ox Te Tun (Birthplace of the Gods). We do know that the city was a Preclassic superpower of unprecedented scale, and that it was first settled around 1000 BC. The city's zenith was between 350 BC and AD 100, when it was home to over 100,000 Maya and was the greatest trading centre in Mesoamerica, with stone causeways, some up to 20 meters (65 feet) wide, linking it to dozens of other cities in its empire.

The core of the ancient city is between two massive temple complexes, the Tigre and Danta groups. This would have be the home of the elite, the ruling Kaan kings.

On the western side, the Tigre Complex's triadic design reaches 55 meters (180ft) in height, the temple adorned with huge jaguar masks made from stucco. South of Tigre, Structure 34 is a smaller temple embellished with giant jaguar claws. Dating back to around 200 BC, Structure 34 has been restored and sits under a protective polycarbonate roof.

A wonderful sculptured panel depicting the Maya creation myth was found close by in 2009 with imagery from the Maya creation story, the Popol Vuh.

East of the ceremonial core is the vast La Danta complex, the largest structure ever built in the Maya world. This triadic temple sits on a stone base platform measuring 600 meters by 300 meters (2,000ft by 1,000ft), its summit 79 meters (259ft) above the forest floor. Climb the staircase for a view of unbroken tropical forest with only the tops of temples of distant sites of Nakbé and Calakmul peeking above the canopy.

NAKBÉ

Around 12km (7.5 miles) southeast of El Mirador, Nakbé was the first city to emerge in the Maya world – by 400 BC it was a city of many thousands. Structure I here is 45 meters (148ft) high, and you can see the earliest-known ball court, built around 450 BC, as well as many curious *chultunes* (storage chambers cut into the limestone bedrock).

TINTAL AND OTHER RUINS

Tintal, another vast site south of El Mirador, is often used as a campsite by hikers en route to Mirador. Though severely looted, there are two main temple complexes, both with impressive stucco masks, and you can climb the Catzin pyramid for awesome jungle views. There are more than 20 other sites in the Mirador Basin, virtually all Preclassic, including Wakná, which was only rediscovered in 1998 and can be visited by hikers.

GETTING TO THE MIRADOR BASIN

There's no road access to the Mirador Basin, so getting here involves either a tough jungle hike through the rainforest (minimum five days) or a helicopter trip. Both should be organized well in advance.

On foot, the hike is best attempted from mid-January to July (February to April is the driest period). You will need to contact an agency in Flores or Carmelita to organize a guide, pack horses or mules, food, water, and camping gear. Rates start from around US$250 per head for a five-day trek (slightly less if you take a tour from Carmelita). Bring insect repellent, plasters for blisters, a resilient mindset, and a sense of humor. For details, contact tour operators in Flores.

Helicopter tours to El Mirador are a possibility for those short on time, though these only offer about six hours at the site; day trips start at US$450.

El Mirador ruins.

TIKAL – JEWEL IN THE MAYA CROWN

Possibly the most visually impressive of all the Maya cities, Tikal stands majestically in the Petén jungle, occupied now only by monkeys, toucans, and other exotica.

As the first sunlight filtered through the early morning mist, the high priest, Iahca Na, emerged from the inner sanctum of Temple I. Yik'in Chan K'awiil, waiting to be crowned the 27th ruler of the great city, was clad in jaguar pelt and jade jewels, awaiting approval from the shaman who had consulted the gods for their blessing. A discreet nod from the priest confirmed Yik'in Chan's accession and the expectant multitude gathered in the plaza below erupted in celebration, heralding a new era for Tikal.

Temple I: being closer to heaven, the small room at the top of the temples was used for sacred rituals and ceremonies.

COSMOPOLITAN CITY

As you walk through the ruins today, it is easy to forget that it was previously a thriving metropolis with a population of around 100,000. The Maya city was home to a multi-layered society: as well as the nobility there was a large middle class, comprising merchants, craftsmen, and bureaucrats, and a workers' class, which included farmers, builders, and servants.

Tikal represents over 1,200 years of continuous construction. Wherever you stand, beneath your feet lie many layers of previous eras; more than 100 structures lie beneath the North Acropolis as we see it today.

A Mayan Classic-period censer of a deity holding a human head in Museo Tikal.

Carved stelae depicted major events in Tikal's history and tales from Maya mythology.

As seen from the top of Temple IV, the tallest of all the Tikal structures, the massive temple roof combs rise out of the dense tree canopy.

The ceiba is a symbol of national pride in modern Guatemala. In ancient times, the sacred tree was seen as a link to heaven.

Birdlife, such as this colorful montezuma oropendola, is abundant around the temples of Tikal.

Tikal's Natural Wonders

In addition to its awesome archeological heritage, the Tikal National Park offers visitors one of the richest rainforest environments in Central America. The protected territory saves trees, hundreds of years old, from logging, and rare animals from both the black market and the dining table.

Tikal has an incredible variety of animal life, and as you wander around the site, you can tell that they have made it their home. Racoon-like coatimundis scurry around the undergrowth, and troupes of spider monkeys playfully pelt you with berries from the treetops. The park is also home to over 300 species of birds, such as the keel-billed toucan, the ocellated turkey, parrots, and eagles. Most thrilling of all are five of the world's rarest wildcats that live in the area; you might be lucky enough to catch sight of a jaguar, puma, ocelot, jaguarundi, or margay. As you enter the site, pause by the Tikal reservoir, which is a good place to spot a turtle or even a small alligator.

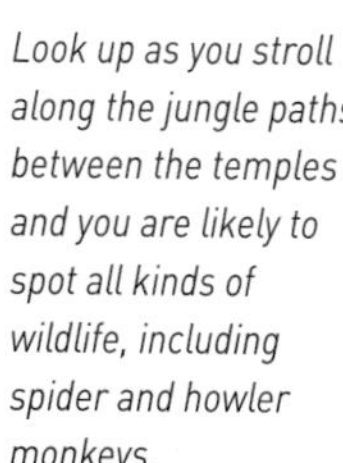

Look up as you stroll along the jungle paths between the temples and you are likely to spot all kinds of wildlife, including spider and howler monkeys.

Exploring the collection of small rooms and courtyards at the Cahal Pech ruins near San Ignacio.

Coconut seller on Caye Caulker.

On the road in San Miguel, a village on the foothills of the Maya Mountains.

El Pescador Resort, south of San Pedro on Ambergris Caye.

BELIZE

This tiny Central American country, although only about the size of Massachusetts or Wales, is an eco-tourism paradise.

The Cayo district, home to San Ignacio, is largely agricultural and bananas are a main crop.

With so few people and so much space, Belize's main attraction for the visitor is its incredible, largely untouched natural environment. The steamy rainforest and spectacular coral reef, along with a chain of tiny paradise islands, are within touching distance of the US, with Miami only a two-hour flight away. Above all, Belize's greatest natural attraction is its superb coral reef, which shadows its entire coastline, the longest in the western hemisphere. The reef's dazzling underwater landscape hosts an astonishing array of sea life and acts as a barrier, calming the inshore waters and creating excellent conditions for watersports. There are more than 200 small offshore islands and three coral atolls.

THE CLIMATE

Belize has a subtropical climate, with distinct wet and dry seasons. It is most often hot and humid, particularly during the rainy season from May to December. The dry season is a cooler and more bearable time. There's a hurricane risk from September to November – Belize has suffered a direct hit from a hurricane on average once every 40 years, but the country does have an excellent warning system in place.

The jetty at Caye Caulker.

THE GOVERNMENT AND THE ECONOMY

Belize usually gets lumped in with the other English-speaking Caribbean nations because of its British colonial heritage and contemporary status as part of the British Commonwealth. The present government, the UDP (United Democratic Party), is led by the country's first black PM Dean Barrow, who has won three consecutive general elections in 2008, 2012, and 2015.

Although the economy is still heavily reliant on the export of cash crops – sugar, citrus, and bananas being the most important – tourism has now overtaken agriculture as the largest foreign-currency earner. Tourism drives over 34 percent of all jobs in the country, and is directly responsible for over 14 percent of Belize's GDP. Other industries, such as oil extraction, are also emerging, but the stability of Belize's economy is largely reliant on the health of the world's economy as a whole.

THE LAND AND THE PEOPLE

One of the main reasons that the Belizean environment and wildlife have been able to survive and thrive is the country's tiny population – just 400,000. Its fellow Central American republic of El Salvador is smaller but has a population of more than 6 million. Belize has an area of 22,965 sq km (8,867 sq miles), only about one-fifth the size of neighboring Guatemala. Belizeans are a polyglot, culturally diverse people. The main groups are Creoles and Latinos, with smaller numbers of Maya, Garífuna, East Asians, and whites. Many thousands of refugees, mainly from El Salvador and Guatemala, settled in Belize in the early 1980s, fleeing civil war and altering the racial balance of the country – now more people speak Spanish than English as a first language. The northern towns of Belize are mainly Spanish-speaking, with a population of *mestizos* (of mixed Spanish and Maya descent) and Yucatec Maya who fled from Mexico after the Caste Wars in the mid-19th century. Most farm sugar cane. In the far south of the country are a few thousand indigenous K' ekchi (Q' eqchi') and Mopán Maya, who live mainly in isolated hill villages and practice subsistence farming.

Tobacco Caye.

Creoles today form just under a quarter of Belize's population, but they still dominate the country's largest town, Belize City. Belizean Creoles are descended from black African slaves and British buccaneers. The first European settlers or "Baymen" (because they were mostly based around the Bay of Honduras) arrived in the 17th century and set up mahogany-logging camps along the main rivers. Villages grew up around the camps, but the end of the logging industry in the 1960s left many of these communities in poverty. Some have struggled on as subsistence farming communities, others have moved to Belize City.

Mennonites often visit the cayes to sell produce.

Most of Belize's southern coastal towns and villages – Dangriga, Hopkins, Seine Beight, Punta Gorda, and Barranco – are home to the Garífuna people (see page 247), deported by the British from St Vincent to Roatán (off Honduras) in the 18th century. Displaying remarkable resilience, they retained their mixed Carib and African culture and identity, and quickly established communities along the coast of Central America.

Belize is also home to a sizeable Mennonite community of around 12,000, who migrated from Mexico in the 1950s, drawn by promises of plentiful land and an official drive to develop agricultural production. The industrious Mennonites (see page 197) have helped Belize become self-sufficient in chicken, dairy products, and corn, the country's main foods.

Xunantunich Maya ruins near San Ignacio.

Mennonite girls playing outside school, Spanish Lookout.

Troops keep an eye on the locals at the Port of Belize in what was British Honduras, 1837.

MODERN HISTORY OF BELIZE

It took Belize many years to win its independence. Even then, it was a good few years before the country achieved true political freedom.

After the decline of the Maya settlements in Belize, it was British settlers – known as "Baymen" – and their slaves from the Caribbean who began to occupy the territory in the 17th century. These new inhabitants were interested above all in the timber to be found in Belize's forests, especially logwood, then much in demand in Europe as the basis for fabric dyes, and mahogany for furniture making. These loggers founded the first settlement on St George's Caye, a small island off the southern coast. Some time later, a larger colony was set up at the mouth of the Belize River, where the main city now stands.

In 1765, Admiral Sir William Burnaby, the commander of the British Navy in Jamaica, wrote a first constitution for the territory. This became known as "Burnaby's Code" and was the basis of the government in Belize for many years.

Captain Morgan, one of the most infamous pirates of the Caribbean.

Two further waves of immigration at the end of the 18th century changed the make-up of the population considerably: 2,000 people from the Mosquito Shore, a British settlement in Honduras and Nicaragua, were brought in; then, from 1800 onward, the Garífuna, or people of mixed Amerindian and African blood, began to arrive after being deported from the island of St Vincent; since then they have formed a strong and distinct group in the south of the country.

COLONIAL CONFLICTS

Relations with the Spanish rulers of neighboring Guatemala were frequently tense throughout the 17th and 18th centuries, as British pirate ships used Belize's sheltered waters as harbors from which to attack Spanish ships. As a result of the American War of Independence, Spain declared war on Britain and in 1779 a sizeable Spanish force attacked St George's Caye, burning it and Belize Town to the ground. The settlement was rebuilt, but in 1798 the Spanish attacked again. Despite the fact that the Spanish force had far superior firepower, a decisive sea battle was fought at St George's Caye, and the Spanish were soundly defeated.

Following this victory, the local inhabitants considered themselves part of the British empire, although officially the colony still did not exist. In 1802, Spain was obliged to acknowledge

> *When Guatemala became independent in 1821, it claimed Belizean home rule was a "flagrant violation of the sovereign rights of Guatemala," and threatened to go to war over the territory.*

British sovereignty over the area in the Treaty of Amiens. When Guatemala and Mexico won their independence from Spain in 1821, both laid claim to the territory of Belize.

The volunteer guard boosted Belize's defenses when Guatemalan invasion was feared in the 1980s.

FEAR OF INVASION

By the middle of the 19th century, the Guatemalan authorities were more concerned with a possible invasion by the United States. They were therefore willing in 1859 to accept a Convention with Great Britain which recognized the boundaries of Belize. Another article in the Convention called for Britain to help build a road from Guatemala City to the Atlantic seaboard in Belize, a promise which was never fulfilled. Three years later, in 1862, Britain finally recognized Belize as the Colony of British Honduras, and in 1871 it became a Crown Colony. A treaty signed with Mexico in 1893 saw the end of its claim to the territory, but successive Guatemalan governments upheld their right to sovereignty over the land. This claim lasted even after Belize was granted independence from the United Kingdom in 1981. It was not until the return of civilian government to Guatemala in 1986 that the position changed. In 1991 the Guatemalan government recognized the right of the Belizean people to "self-determination" while, in response, Belize limited its claim to territorial waters in the south to 3 miles (5km), so ensuring Guatemalan access to the Caribbean. In 1992 the Guatemalan Congress officially ratified the decision to recognize Belize. This led to a final pull-out of the British garrison in 1993.

THE FIGHT FOR INDEPENDENCE

The struggle within Belize to gain independence from Britain began in earnest after World War II. The People's United Party (PUP), under leader George Price, was founded in 1950. After universal adult suffrage was introduced in 1954, the People's United Party won huge majorities in the assemblies elected in 1954 and 1957, and in 1961 George Price became the colony's First Minister.

Price also became the first Belizean prime minister after self-government was granted in 1964, and he and the People's United Party began to press for complete independence.

THE HURRICANE HITS

On October 31, 1961, Belize was devastated by Hurricane Hattie. This particularly affected Belize City, the town on the coast which had been the capital since the 18th century. The hurricane killed hundreds of people and destroyed property to the value of millions of dollars. The authorities decided it was time to build a new capital, away from the coast and therefore less threatened by the hurricanes. The name Belmopan was chosen for the new city, in honor of the Mopa, the Maya tribe who had resisted the Spanish conquistadors, and "Bel" for Belize.

By 1970, a new National Assembly building, government buildings and offices, and a national police headquarters had been constructed. The English firm which carried out the work declared that their intention was to create a similar experience to seeing one of the country's Maya temples for the first time, so the gray concrete National Assembly building is flanked by the government offices in a long green court reminiscent of Classic Maya sites,

Hurricane Dean's wind and waves ravaged the coast of Corozal in 2007.

THE CHICLEROS OR THE CHEWING-GUM MEN

There have been many extraordinary figures in the rediscovery of the Maya civilization. Perhaps the oddest were the *chicleros*, the men who went into the jungles of Belize, the Petén region of Guatemala, and the Yucatán Peninsula to gather *chicle* gum. As the habit of chewing gum became widespread in the US early in the 20th century, demand grew for the gum from the sapodilla tree and the *chicle macho* that was used in its manufacture. This *chicle*, obtained by slashing the trunks of the trees, was collected in the rainy season, when the sap is flowing, by a band of men many of whom were Maya or Waika indigenous people who had come to Belize from the Mosquito Coast. They also had intimate knowledge of the trails through the dense jungle where the Maya sites had been hidden for centuries. It was thanks to the *chicle*-hunters that the Austrian explorer Teobert Maler was able to find and photograph such important sites as Tikal, Yaxchilan, Piedras Negras, and Naranjo.

At the end of their expeditions, the *chicleros* would bring back 10kg (22lb) blocks of boiled gum for export to the US. The gum industry was badly hit in the 1950s, when an artificial substitute superseded the natural *chicle*. But, with the recent renewed demand for *chicle* gum, Maya and others are again being employed in this strange trade, and stumbling on yet more ancient sites not seen for hundreds of years.

and its entrance is at the top of a flight of low, wide steps.

Belmopan soon became a symbol of the new, independent Belize, although admittedly it has struggled over the years to evolve from an administrative center to a thriving city where ordinary Belizeans want to live.

INDEPENDENCE AND BEYOND

The long-sought independence from Britain was eventually won in 1981, and George Price of the PUP was elected as the first prime minister of the newly independent country, now officially known as Belize. Since then the PUP and rival United Democratic Party (UDP), a more Conservative political grouping, have battled it out with the electorate. Dean Barrow was elected the nation's first black prime minister in 2008, and repeated his success in the following two elections, in 2012 and 2015, pledging to stamp out corruption, improve infrastructure, tackle crime, and address poverty.

In its short lifespan since independence Belize has developed into a relatively prosperous and stable country, particularly given its neighborhood in turbulent Central America. Commendably, over 40 percent of its territory has been protected as national parkland, land and marine reserves, and wildlife sanctuaries, a world-class achievement. This concentration on environmental protection has reaped benefits, and the nation's tourism industry is now a huge income generator, as the nation is seen as a clean, green land rich in rainforest and Caribbean marine parks: some 1.2 million tourists visited Belize in 2016, boosting hard currency revenues and bringing prosperity to many.

The campaign for full national independence received wide public support.

Yet away from the resorts in the rural hinterland, many Belizeans have little stake in the tourist dollar, and near-subsistence living affects many (more than 40 percent live below the poverty line, unemployment is around 13 percent – higher than the country's average of 8 percent – and the cost of living is punishing).

Crime and corruption are other key issues. The country has become a major transit point for narco gangs moving cocaine from South to North America (it was black-listed as such by the US in 2011), and gang culture affects urban areas. Belize was ranked 109th in the Corruption Perceptions Index in 2008, the last year for which statistics were available for Belize, perceived as more corrupt than India, Mali or Gabon. Foreigners are extremely unlikely to be troubled by these drug and gang issues, however.

THE MENNONITES

Belize's Mennonite community is a resilient, religious sect that traces its roots to the 16th-century Netherlands.

They stand out in any Belizean crowd: blond, blue-eyed men in denim overalls and cowboy hats; modestly dressed women whose home-made outfits – ankle-length, long-sleeved frocks and wide-brimmed hats tied down with black scarves – defy the tropical heat. Polite and reserved, they talk quietly among themselves, not in Spanish, English, or Creole, but in guttural German.

These are part of Belize's Mennonite community, who take their name from a Dutch priest, Menno Simons. Mennonites live in isolated farming communities, calling themselves *die Stillen im Lande*, the Unobtrusive Ones. They reject state interference in their affairs and are committed pacifists.

Belize is the latest stop in a three-century odyssey – their beliefs have often led to persecution, driving them from the Netherlands to Prussia in the 1600s, to southern Russia, and, when the Russian government suggested military conscription in the 1870s, to Canada.

After World War I, the Canadian government demanded that only English be taught in Mennonite schools and, spurred on by anti-German feeling, reconsidered conscription. Again, many of the Mennonites moved on, this time to Mexico – only for the Mexican government then to try to include them in a new social security program.

Around 100,000 Mennonites remain in Mexico, including a community in Campeche, but others have moved into Belize, where their farming skills have proved successful. In colonial times few Belizeans farmed the land – even eggs were imported from abroad.

In 1958, the first of 3,500 Mennonites arrived, to begin hacking roads through the forest, clearing a vast wilderness of land to create their farmsteads in the jungle. But, after centuries of traumatic upheaval, though the Mennonite religion's core had survived intact, deep cultural divisions had opened up. Conservative groups spoke German and used only farming implements available in the early 1900s, while progressive Mennonites had learned English in Canada, and were happy to use tractors and fertilizer.

Settlements spread throughout Belize reflecting this cultural diversity: the progressive "Kleine Gemeinde" (Small Community) settled around Spanish Walk near San Ignacio; the conservative "Altkolonier" (Old Colonists) opted for the wilderness at Blue Creek on the corner of Mexico and Guatemala. Another contingent settled near Orange Walk Town at Shipyard and Richmond Hill.

A Mennonite man from the progressive community of Spanish Lookout.

The Mennonites are today the most successful farmers in Belize. They supply much of the country's food, including chicken, dairy products, and eggs, and make most of the country's furniture. The modern Mennonite town at Spanish Lookout would not look out of place in the US.

There are two settlements of conservative Mennonites at Barton Creek in Cayo District. Despite their isolation, they are happy to meet interested visitors. There is one caveat: strict Mennonites object to having their photographs taken, believing no memory should be left of a person after they die.

The colorful keel-billed toucan.

FLORA AND FAUNA OF BELIZE

Belying its tiny size, Belize has an impressive range of abundant ecosystems, supporting great bird diversity and animals from jaguars to tree frogs.

For centuries, Belize's small population, limited agricultural land, and lack of industry caused it to be left behind in the race for development. This has worked to its advantage in many ways: Belize boasts the most accessible tropical wilderness in the western hemisphere, and wildlife that lures travelers from around the world. Though not as biologically rich as the Amazon or Costa Rica, Belize is, for its size, unique in the number of different habitats and species within its borders.

The reasons for this diversity can be traced to its climate and geological history. Set in northern Central America, Belize is part of a landmass bridging two great continents. North and South America were separated until roughly 2 million years ago, when giant continental plates began to rotate, grinding against each other and thrusting upward to form mountains. As water became caught in the poles' colossal ice sheets, the seas receded, exposing new land. Central America became a bridge between the two continents, opening an avenue of migration. The resultant mixture of endemic and immigrant creatures spawned one of the most varied faunas on earth.

Belize boasts around 280 species of orchid.

FOREST TYPES

As a result of its complex geological history, Belize's landscape mixes mountains, savannas, and coastal lagoons in an area smaller than New Hampshire in the United States, while the tropical climate provides wet and dry seasons, hurricanes, and heat. The resulting environmental mix creates an astonishing variety of animal and vegetable habitats: Belize has more than 4,000 species of flowering plants, and more than 750 species of trees. In contrast, the whole of the US and Canada put together supports only 730 tree species, giving Belize on average a 1,000 times greater diversity of trees per square mile.

Scientists have catalogued over 70 kinds of forest in Belize, grouping them into three basic types: 16–17 percent are open forests of pine and savanna; less than 5 percent are mangroves and other coastal habitats; while by far the largest type, 68 percent, is broadleaf forests. Vegetation, which is largely determined by soil, in turn determines to a large extent which animals will thrive, and where they will do so.

INTO THE RAINFOREST

The broadleaf forests (or, in Belize, all rainforests) support by far the greatest diversity of wildlife. They are the result of optimal conditions for life on land in this area – abundant sunlight, warmth, and moisture. The essential core of a rainforest is its dense canopy, formed by the interlaced crowns of trees. One to three layers of trees and, in the undergrowth, shrubs, twined together by twisting vines, create virtually a separate climate within, saving moisture and cooling temperatures.

Leaves, fallen branches, and fungi litter the forest floor, where they are quickly broken down into minerals by soil decomposers. The secret of the rainforest is that most of the nutrients are stored not in the soil, but in its living biomass – the roots, trunks, leaves, flowers, and fruits, as well as the animals. The nutrients are cycled and recycled throughout the system's plant and animal components.

Despite this, visitors to the tropics may be disappointed with the apparent lack of wildlife. Although the animals are definitely there, most creatures of the rainforests sense human intruders long before they themselves are noticed, and they take advantage of the innumerable hiding places in the towering walls of green. But if you are patient, birds in particular will eventually reveal themselves in all their splendor.

A red-eyed tree frog.

BAIRD'S TAPIR

Belize's national animal, Baird's tapir, known locally as the "mountain cow," is the largest in the forest. Although weighing up to 650lbs (300kg) and measuring 6.5ft (2 meters) in length, tapirs can dissolve silently into the forest at the first sign of danger. A distinctive feature of these tapirs is their long prehensile lip, used to forage for leaves.

Tapirs prefer rainforest pools and swamps, although they may be seen in other habitats. Despite its adaptiveness, the tapir is endangered throughout its range (Mexico to Ecuador) by hunting and deforestation. Belize is one of the last remaining strongholds of this magnificent creature.

For birders and all wildlife watchers, the best time to visit such a forest is at sunrise, when the air is cool and filled with the sounds of birds feeding and declaring their territories. The broadleaf forest yields tremendous bird biodiversity – more than any other habitat on earth.

On the ground, it's easiest to spot leafcutter ("wee wee") ants, each carrying a leaf along the wide, clean highways they have cleared on the forest floor. The ants place the pieces of leaves in underground chambers, where they are chewed and processed to grow fungus. The fungus in turn feeds the ants. This relationship is so finely evolved that the fungus can no longer reproduce without the ants.

If you are lucky, you might spot snakes on the forest floor. The luck lies in the fact that 45

Spiders are some of the most conspicuous creatures encountered at night, the glinting reflections from their multiple eyes visible up to 50ft (15 meters) away.

of Belize's 54 species are harmless, and even the most poisonous ones would rather slither away than fight. The surest way to steer clear of snakes lurking in the undergrowth is to stay on fallen logs. Most nocturnal animals have big eyes that enable them to see in moonlight; point a flashlight at a rustling in the leaves and you might see a bright pair of eyes.

The paca, known as the gibnut in Belize, is a nocturnal rodent the size of a large rabbit. It can sometimes be heard chewing on cohune nuts and thrashing around the litter of the forest floor at night. Gibnut has traditionally been a popular dish in local restaurants, but the eating of wild species is now discouraged – and it is also hunted by the five species of Belizean wild cats.

The shy tapir is Belize's national animal.

the trails; unless you are sure of identification, it is best not to interfere with them.

RAINFOREST NIGHTS

After sunset, rainforests come alive with a new, nocturnal shift of creeping, crawling, flying, and jumping creatures, making the night a perfect time to scrutinize the vegetation on well-marked trails. Tree frogs, gaudily colored lizards, and a varied multitude of insects and spiders awake and roam the dark jungle in search of sustenance.

The night is also a good time to view mammals. Bats dart above trails, gathering insects while startling hikers. Opossums, armadillos, kinkajous, and anteaters are all nocturnal creatures that forage the forest's stream banks and

FAMOUS FELINES

As Central America's largest spotted cat, the jaguar is probably the most celebrated creature of the rainforest – Belize created the world's first jaguar sanctuary at Cockscomb Basin (see page 245) specifically to protect it. Roaming beneath the rainforest canopy and along the banks of mountain streams, four other wildcats share the territory: jaguarundi, margay, ocelot, and puma. All are endangered throughout their ranges, but Belize supports healthy populations. That five species of cat, so similar in their ecological needs, can coexist and thrive within the same rainforest is a tribute to the health of the Belizean habitat.

One of the smaller wild cats (and the most abundant), the jaguarundi moves like a fleeting shadow. Its long, lanky body, slender tail, and short legs make it unmistakable. No bigger than a domestic cat, this animal feeds mainly during daylight hours on small rodents, birds, and insects.

The shy, nocturnal margay has very large eyes, the extremely bright shine of which attests to its highly developed night vision. Superlative balance and great leaping ability make the margay ideally adapted for life in the forest canopy. Margays prefer primary or old-growth forests, but are rarely seen in the wild.

A jaguarundi on the lookout for prey.

The ocelot's name comes from the Aztecan word *tlalocelotl*, meaning "field tiger," although it prefers second-growth or recently cut forests. Known locally as the tiger cat, the beautiful spotted ocelot – which was hunted nearly to extinction for its fur – is about the size of a medium dog. It keeps to the forest floor, feeding occasionally on prey such as anteaters and brocket deer.

Of the larger cats, the jaguar inhabits lowland forests near streams and swamps, whereas the puma (known as the cougar or mountain lion in the United States) prefers the highlands and drier ridge areas of the forest. As a result, the two rarely encounter each other.

BLACK HOWLER MONKEYS

Another celebrated inhabitant of the Belizean rainforest is the black howler monkey, whose aggressive and alarming roar is frequently mistaken for that of a jaguar. "Baboons," as they are known in Belize, live in troops of between four and eight, and carve out a territory of favorite food trees. They defend their territories from intruding rival troops with their guttural roars, which advise other black howlers of their presence. Howlers often begin and end their days with a roar – a noise that can carry for several miles.

The black howler monkey's range is limited to southern Mexico, northern Guatemala, and Belize, and throughout this area, the populations are rapidly declining due to deforestation. Belize supports one of the last strongholds of baboons in the region: at the Community Baboon Sanctuary (www.belizehowlermonkeys.org), where landowners have

RISKS AND RULES

Though a naturalist's heaven, Belize can become purgatory for those ill-informed about the dangers of tropical wildernesses, so stay safe by following a few simple, basic rules:

Don't go alone. All forests begin to look alike once you are off the trail, and if you chase a bird or a red-eyed tree frog into the forest, it can be very easy to lose your orientation. It is best to hire a licensed guide.

Stay on the trails. You are not only less likely to get lost, but also much less likely to stumble over nasties such as the deadly fer-de-lance and coral snakes that live among the litter of the forest floor. (Don't panic: most snakes are non-venomous, and all will avoid you if they can.)

Watch where you place your hands and feet. Some palm trees have needle-like thorns sticking out horizontally from their trunks, which will cause a nasty wound. Avoid unexpected meetings with snakes by looking to see what is on the other side before stepping over fallen logs. And check for ants before sitting down.

Carry sunscreen. You need only leave the protection of the broadleaf canopy for a short time to get burned. Do not underestimate the power of the tropical sun.

The multitude of insects in Belizean forests is generally more of a nuisance than a serious hazard so don't forget to apply repellent on all exposed areas.

The Manatee Road, running between Belize City and Dangriga, meanders through some of the most beautiful savannas in Belize.

agreed to manage their properties in ways that will not be detrimental to the baboons. There are an estimated 2,000 monkeys here and an excellent visitor center (see page 233). It is hoped that some of them will be transferred from the sanctuary back to their former homes, including the Cockscomb Basin Wildlife Sanctuary.

IN THE SAVANNA FORESTS

Savannas are grasslands with trees, ranging from a few clumps to dense stands, embedded in them. With the exception of the high Mountain Pine Ridge in the Cayo district, most savannas are along the level lowlands of the north and on a strip east of the Maya mountains, behind the coast. Islands of limestone, surrounded by oceans of wind-blown grasses and knurled trees, attest to the harshness of the habitat.

Savanna flora in Belize evolved to subsist in extremes of climate and soil. Plants must deal alternately with water-logging during the rainy season and severe drought during the dry season. Savanna soils are poorly drained, acidic, and nutrient-poor, allowing only hardy plants such as pines, oaks, craboo, and palmettos to flourish. (The craboo is a small tree that produces a yellow, cherry-sized fruit that Belizeans use in jams, ice cream, and wine.)

Caribbean pine is a prominent feature of the coastal savanna. Driving along stretches of the Northern Highway, the new coastal road, and much of the Southern Highway, formations of this pine align themselves like silent sentries awaiting review.

Many larger pines are protected by their thick bark, while the seeds of many shrubs and other trees actually need to be scorched in order to germinate. For this reason savanna plants are often referred to as pyrophytes. Though the practice is discouraged, hunters will often light fires to flush out deer and other game, or to clear land for other use. Savanna land is increasing in area in Belize, and the Savanna Forest Reserve off the Southern Highway near Big Creek is the ideal place to view this habitat.

Despite the inhospitable appearance of savannas, many mammal species forage there. The gray fox, one of the most common mammals in Belize, is about the size of a house cat, with a large bushy tail. The white-tailed deer is found in savanna areas as it emerges during the early morning to search for tender new shoots.

UNMISSABLE BIRDS

The savanna's wide-open spaces are ideal for birding, and harbor over 100 species. The striking vermilion flycatcher, a sparrow-sized bright-

Frigate birds engage in an eye-catching courtship display.

red bird, is often seen making repeated sorties to nab flying insects. The fork-tailed flycatcher, whose aerial acrobatics make it an unmistakable inhabitant of the savanna, sports 10in (25cm) long tail feathers, which make up half to two-thirds of this small bird's total length.

The most spectacular bird of the wet savanna is the jabirú, the largest stork in the Americas. Standing nearly 5ft (1.5 meters) tall, the jabirú is white with a black head and a red band around the neck. It constructs a distinctive 8ft (2.4-meter) diameter nest atop a pine, which is visible from a considerable distance away. In pre-protection days, this exposed nest made the endangered stork easy prey for hunters. Now fully protected, the jabirú is the symbol of the Central Bank of Belize.

BELIZE – A MODEL FOR ECOTOURISM?

Belize offers some of the most pristine habitats in Central America. The question is how to exploit such a bountiful legacy without ruining it in the process.

Belize's barrier reef, atolls, rivers, mountains, and tropical forest, along with its imposing Maya ruins and vibrant contemporary culture, make it ideal for the development of eco-tourism. This small Central American state of only 400,000 people has a low population density that has allowed a combination of state and private reserves to protect more than 40 percent of Belize's territory.

TOURISM WITHOUT TEARS

In the mid-1980s, the government recognized that small-scale, low-impact tourism was the way to provide stable economic growth while still safeguarding the environment. Rather than follow the mass-tourism path of Cancún 250 miles (400km) to the north, Belize decided to follow one that would allow as many Belizeans as possible to participate in the tourism industry as stakeholders.

The development of a small number of upscale lodges in the spectacular interior of Belize has provided a model of sustainable tourism that has both set standards and inspired many Belizeans to develop a network of accommodation and services to support the burgeoning industry.

Tourism is now Belize's number one foreign revenue earner, and around 35 percent of all jobs in the country are within or related to the industry. Still, stakeholders must always balance the economic benefits of mass tourism with its potential damage to the environment and sites of cultural value.

Many local fishermen benefit from tourism by using their boats to conduct snorkeling trips to the nearby reefs. Don't remove any of the shells and coral though.

Kick back in many people's idea of paradise, thanks to Belizeans being committed to conserving their country's stunning natural areas.

The steep climb up the impressive El Castillo at Lamanai.

nesco has awarded World Heritage status to the Belize arrier Reef, and miles of these delicate ecosystems have en designated as marine reserves.

a kayaking, Tobacco Caye.

Belize's numerous reserves and parks make it an eco-tourism paradise.

Belize Audubon Society

The Belize Audubon Society (BAS; www.belizeaudubon.org), formed in 1969, is Belize's foremost environmental organization. It aims to maintain a balance between the needs of the nation's people and the environment through sustainable management of natural resources and public education programmes. The society has over 1,400 members and a staff of more than 40 dedicated professionals. The society manages over 192,000 acres (77,000 hectares) of protected land in nine separate areas, including Crooked Tree Wildlife Sanctuary, Guanacaste National Park, St Herman's Blue Hole National Park, Cockscomb Basin Wildlife Sanctuary, Blue Hole Natural Monument, and Tapir Mountain Nature Reserve. The society engages with communities bordering on the protected zones, offering training in tourism-oriented services, such as scuba-diving and tour guiding, and providing vital environmental education.

With the help of a guide, trail systems can be explored throughout Belize on horseback, mountain bike, or on foot.

The incredible beauty and biodiversity of the reef.

BELIZE'S BARRIER REEF

Immerse yourself in a spectacular underwater world of colorful corals, tropical fish, huge rays, barracudas, sharks, and turtles.

The seaward rim of Belize's barrier reef, referred to as the fore-reef, is a popular destination for scuba-divers and snorkelers. It is not hard to understand why: imagine floating along an underwater mountain ridge; to the east stretches an abyss of indigo, below lies a 60-degree slope covered by a quilt of colorful coral plates and swaying fronds. A formation of eagle rays cruises past, their meter-long wings lazily flapping, grace in slow motion; groupers lurk in the shadow of coral heads, their skins darkening to blend into the surroundings; tiny damsel fish defend their territories against intruders (including divers); and parrotfish, the grazers of the sea, browse among the algae attached to dead corals while fluorescent blue chromis float above coral gardens.

Goff's Caye, part of the enormous reef system.

UNDERSTANDING THE BARRIER REEF

If coral reefs are visual poems that fill a diver's sense of sight with form, color, and patterns, then Belize is a master poet, and the Belize barrier reef a colossal epic.

The variety of reef types and marine life within their borders is unequaled in the northern hemisphere. Belizean waters are perfect for coral growth. Corals are finicky and they require warm, salty, clear water, steady sunlight, and a shallow, firm foundation on which to grow.

The barrier reef and its offshore atolls lie perched atop underwater geological formations that appeared toward the end of the Cretaceous period about 65 million years ago. Coral has formed a crust on the shallow portions of three of these fault escarpments, separated by deep cuts.

Windward of the best-developed scarp – off southern Belize – the sea floor lies more than 3,300ft (1,000 meters) beneath the surface. Relatively recent reef growth commenced 5,000–8,000 years ago as sea water was gradually released from Ice Age glaciers.

Relics can still be seen, as scientists discovered when they drilled deep into the reefs. Closer to the surface, along the northern shore of Ambergris Caye, lies further evidence of these ancient reefs. Sharp, skeletal remains of staghorn, elkhorn, and brain corals lie exposed

At 185 miles (300km) in length, and dotted with around 1,200 cayes, Belize's barrier reef forms part of the second-largest system in the world after Australia's Great Barrier Reef.

onshore, cemented together in a matrix of coral, sand, and shells. These eroded fossils conjure up images of prehistoric landscapes; but you will not have to go far to see them come to life.

HARD AND SOFT CORAL

South of these formations, hard coral begins to form a true barrier reef as it snakes toward the Bay of Honduras. Its structural framework is composed of limestone, on which billions of individual coral polyps form colonies connected by living tissue. Each polyp consists of

The reef is home to green, hawksbill, and loggerhead turtles.

a set of tentacles, a mouth, and a gut perched atop a limestone skeleton. The polyps have cells on the outside of their bodies that secrete calcium carbonate. As the colony grows, the polyps build their skeletons from underneath, pushing themselves up or out into a myriad of sizes and shapes. Growth rates vary with different species and conditions, but coral reefs in warm, tropical waters tend to grow upward by only about half an inch (10mm) every year.

A coral reef, then, is actually a thin layer of life on top of ever-accumulating pieces of limestone. When an inattentive swimmer or errant boat hits or brushes against a piece of coral, the damage may not be immediately apparent; but, much like a small wound on a human which can become infected if not properly treated, a coral wound may allow disease or infection to develop. Since the entire colony is connected by living tissue, a small, seemingly inconsequential injury may eventually wipe out a whole coral colony, one that took hundreds of years to develop.

Soft corals, close relatives, also secrete calcium carbonate, but they contain tiny pieces of limestone, protected by a leathery coat, inside their bodies. Soft corals can be distinguished by the branches that wave gracefully in the water currents. They come in a range of hues – including yellows, reds, and purples – and form colorful underwater forests.

DIVING ON THE REEF

The Belize barrier reef (which comprises the central section of the Great Maya Reef that stretches between the Yucatán and Honduras) is split into segments separated by relatively deep channels. Oxygen and plankton (free-floating microscopic plants and animals) carried by tides flush the Belize coastal zone twice daily through these channels, thereby feeding billions of hungry coral polyps and other reef creatures. As a result, the reef attracts large numbers of fish and is consequently excellent for diving and snorkeling.

Hundreds of species of fish are visible to snorkelers and divers over the coral reefs. Most ignore humans, unless the area has been heavily spear-fished. But there are exceptions. Barracudas have an unnerving habit of approaching and even following swimmers. This is pure curiosity – they normally move away when approached. Moray eels have a nasty reputation; alarmingly, they open and close their mouths as if about to bite, when they are merely pumping water through their gills. Be careful nevertheless: morays can inflict a nasty bite if annoyed. Sharks will sense you long before you see them, and usually move away. However, all sharks should be treated with caution. Even the nurse shark can become aggressive if molested.

Fire coral lives in shallow water. Characterized by a smooth surface and a uniform mustard color, it grows in two distinct forms: plate-like and encrusting. If touched, both cause intense stinging and welting. Some sponges also cause irritation, as do bristle worms and hydroids.

CORAL ATOLLS

Lying as close as 10 miles (16km) off the barrier reef are three of the very finest coral atolls in the Caribbean: Turneffe Islands (see page 253), Glover's Reef (see page 256), and Lighthouse Reef (see page 254), whose combined reef systems comprise almost 140 miles (225km) of coral growth. Surrounding the atolls lie thousands of patch reefs; Turneffe, the largest of the atolls, includes some 175 small mangrove-covered islands. These three atolls provide some of the finest wall diving in the world.

Snorkeling amongst tropical fish.

THE MANGROVE COASTLINE

Coral reefs do not exist in isolation. Mangroves line much of the Belizean coastline, the *cayes* and lower reaches of the rivers. Seagrass beds, their blades swaying in the current like the long grass of spring meadows, blanket the sea floor between reef and shore. These mangrove and seagrass beds may not look as spectacular as coral reefs but, as giant marine nurseries, they form the foundation of the continuing long-term health of the country's coastal zone. The quiet water protected by the reef – a self-repairing breakwater – supports mangrove roots and grass blades, which provide plentiful food and shelter for countless juvenile marine organisms. Most of the seafood caught off Belize depends on mangroves or seagrass. Swallow Caye (see page 253) has some superb mangroves that are home to manatee, but you will find fine examples all along the coast.

As well as stabilizing the coastline against erosion and presenting a natural buffer against destructive hurricane winds, mangroves link rich nutrients on land with the billions of hungry mouths at sea. Every year Belizean rivers transport tons of sediment and debris to the sea from deep within the interior. The nutrients in these loads, deposited along the coast, may be in forms unavailable to

RESEARCH ON THE REEF

The basic structure of the barrier reef is consistent all along its 185-mile (300km) length. At Carrie Bow Caye, a marine lab perched atop the edge of the barrier reef, scientists from the Smithsonian Institution have divided the reef up into basic zones or habitats. These are distinguished by conditions such as current, slope, and type of bottom. Support communities of plant and animal life have adapted to these variable conditions. Four major and 12 minor zones have been established along an east–west line north of Carrie Bow Caye. These zones include grass beds, reef flats, and spur and groove formations, each with its own specialized life forms.

marine life. Mangroves, which thrive on these frequent deposits, produce new foliage while protecting delicate polyps from sediment and pollution.

When a mangrove leaf drops into the waters below, the process of decomposition begins. Millions of voracious micro-organisms attack the leaf, slowly releasing the nutrients within for coming generations. Small invertebrates such as worms, shrimps, and crabs feed on these nutrients and microbes; these are in turn eaten by larger creatures, until the nutrients within are passed on through the food chain.

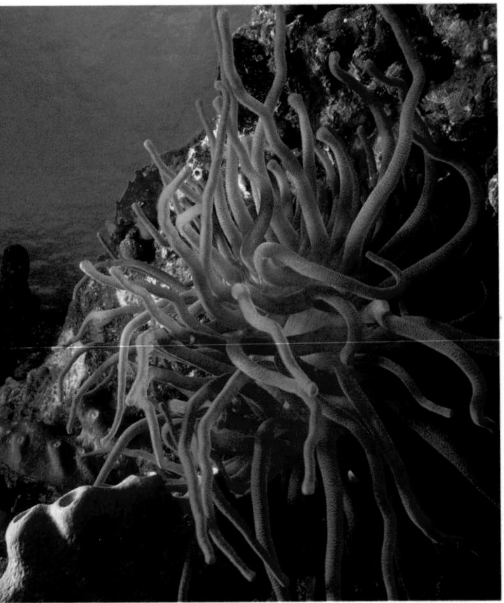

A pink sea anemone.

Many of these smaller fish become prey to the flocks of wading birds that comb the surf line for food. Roseate spoonbills, ibises, herons, and cormorants nest on the small mangrove islands in Chetumal Bay, leeward of Ambergris, while magnificent frigate birds, boobies, and terns have established nesting colonies on *cayes* to the south. Man-O-War Caye, 10 miles (16km) east of Dangriga, has one of the largest colonies of frigate birds in the Caribbean. Ospreys build nests, or rather loose piles of sticks, in the highest trees on the *cayes*.

JEWELS OF EVOLUTION

The entire coastal zone of Belize is awash with life. Jewels of evolution are continually being found. For example, Smithsonian scientists have stumbled upon a tiny bay that may be unique in the Caribbean. A quirk of nature allows mangroves to grow on the edge of a series of deep sinkholes. Healthy colonies of lettuce coral carpet the steep slopes of the depressions. As the slopes rise into shallow water, the multicolored scene explodes into activity: crinoid arms perform silent ballets between tall loggerhead sponges; star and brain corals flourish among seagrasses and mangrove roots. Researchers have identified an incredible 43 different tunicates in this one location, more than was previously discovered throughout the entire Caribbean. The fish are so abundant that they form layers, with the smaller ones near the surface, the larger specimens a level down, and the fat-bodied herrings blanketing the carpet of lettuce coral.

The location of this bay will stay a closely guarded secret until scientists, the government, and conservation groups can agree on proper management of the area. The risks cannot be overestimated. These organisms evolved over millions of years in a stable or gradually changing environment. Any sudden stress – from pollution, overfishing, or injuries inflicted by a careless diver – can be devastating. A visitor might not even be conscious of kicking a piece of coral; for the coral it is a matter of life and death, and for Belizeans it is slow destruction of a priceless resource. The bay is a gauge of the local marine system's health. Areas such as this expose Belize as a raw wilderness, below the waves no less than in the rainforest.

EFFECTS OF CLIMATE CHANGE

Up to 40 percent of Belize's coral reefs have suffered damage over the past 15 years. The country's reefs are well managed and protected, and the damage has not been caused by local pollution or overfishing. Instead, scientists believe the coral is being killed as a result of something local people have almost no control over – climate change.

Unless something is done to curb climate change the outlook for Belize's reefs is bleak. Caribbean waters are already close to the upper end of the temperature range in which coral can grow, and an increase of even a couple of degrees could spell disaster for this magnificent ecosystem.

A red longjaw squirrelfish stands out from the horse-eye jacks at Lighthouse Reef.

MUSIC AND DANCE

Belize has some raw music talent, with a large range of styles, from the *punta* rock of the Garífuna to the home-grown sounds of "brukdown".

Dancing to punta rock.

Reflecting the diversity of the nation, the music scene is vibrant and eclectic, with Creoles heading to bass-driven sound systems that feature dancehall reggae imports from Jamaica, Latinos dancing to the latest salsa, merengue and reggaetón hits from Puerto Rico and Colombia, Maya partying to marimba at their festivals, and the whole nation soaking up hip-hop, soul, R 'n' B from all over the world. But if there's one sound that seems to define Belize, and puts the nation on the musical map, it's *punta*.

Based on the traditional Garífuna drum beats of the country's south, *punta* evolved during the 1980s to become the Belizean sound and is now enjoying enormous popularity. Some of *punta*'s most famous names – the late Andy Palacio, Bredda David, Chico Ramos – have been joined more recently by Griga Boyz and Super G, who often use sound systems rather than live musicians. *Punta* has been exported to North America and Europe with considerable success. Locally, it has won the hearts of virtually every ethnic group in the country and is the one native sound that manages to kick the imports off the radio and dance floors. The *punta*, an erotic mating ritual full of passion and spirit, has returned steamy romance to the dance floor and become the national dance.

THE SOUND OF "BRUKDOWN"

The local music scene was a lot more vibrant during the logging days of the 19th century. Then the country's community let its hair down by "bramming" – groups of revelers would travel from house to house, push the furniture against the walls and use any available household object as a musical instrument on which to play "brukdown" music. In addition to drums, banjos, guitars, accordions, and cow bells, purveyors of brukdown would utilize broom handles, wash basins, metal graters, and even an ass's jawbone. The Creole lyrics, spontaneously thought up on the spot, tended to be about famous people or local happenings. The undisputed king of brukdown was Wilfred Peters, an accordionist who performed live with his Boom and Chime band for over 20 years. When he passed away in 2010, the president and prime minister attended his funeral.

In place of an ass's jawbone, Belize's festive partygoers are these days more likely to bring out the modern equivalent, the karaoke machine. Nearly every bar in town in Belize has karaoke, and a night out isn't complete without at least one singalong session. These are fronted by a growing number of semi-professional karaoke singers, backed by aspiring vocalists plucked from the crowd.

The karaoke singers' inspiration most probably comes from local radio stations. Love FM and BCB play a wide range of music, while specialist stations such as Estereo Amor (the station for Latin lovers) cater specifically for certain ethnic groups. Hip-hop is also very influential with Creole youngsters.

ANNUAL FESTIVALS

Party time in Belize peaks during the annual September festivities, when the two most significant events in the country's history are celebrated: the Battle of St George's Caye Day on September 10 commemorates the 1798 sea battle which finally saw off Spanish claims to Belize, while Independence Day on September 21 marks the day that British rule came to an end in 1981.

Music plays a vital role in the celebrations, and every year an assortment of favorite old Tenth Songs – mainly patriotic march tunes and sentimental ballads – hits the airwaves.

Also featuring in the festivities are performances by Francis Reneau, probably Belize's most talented classical musician and composer, who wrote his first major work, *Mass in Blues*, when he was just 17. In 1994, Reneau was commissioned to write an album drawing together all the country's musical threads: the resulting *Celebration* features Maya harp and marimba, Creole laments and humor, Garífuna singing and drumming, and Latin boleros and salsa, all performed by five generations of Belize's top musicians. Reneau is frequently asked to compose music for Belizean Independence Day celebrations; in 2011 his *Hymn to Belize* was performed to a rapturous reception in Belmopan.

Throughout the country people hold parties on the eve of the September public holidays. Trucks bearing huge speakers are followed by dancing crowds. While the flag-raising at the courthouse on Independence Eve and the official ceremonies the next morning are very solemn events, a party atmosphere prevails later in the day as people swarm the parks or main streets for the "jump up," or street fair, with lots of food and music.

Keeping the party going, Garífuna Settlement Day, on November 19, commemorates the 1832 arrival of the largest group of Garífuna to Belize's southern shores, and is a non-stop fiesta. The best place to enjoy this is in Dangriga, where the celebratory music and dancing starts on the evening before Settlement Day. At dawn the following morning there is a re-enactment of the arrival of the early settlers in their *dories*. As they enter town the travelers are greeted by women singing, drums beating, and the waving of the distinctive yellow, black, and white Garífuna flags.

Both Garífuna Settlement Day and Christmas are greeted in Garífuna towns with Joncunu (John Canoe) dancers. Outfitted in pink wire masks, white tunics with flowing ribbons, elaborate crowns with tall feathers, and hundreds of tiny shells attached to their knees, the dancers go from door to door dancing the *wanaragua*, with arms outstretched and legs together. Some say the dance is meant to imitate the behavior of white slave-holders, which might explain why it has traditionally been popular at Christmas, when master–slave relations would, for a short time, be more relaxed.

Punta rock musicians in Dangriga.

The *mestizo* and Maya communities have their own religious and other events, particularly at Easter time – costume parades begin the weekend before Lent. In Orange Walk, Las Mascaradas wear scary disguises and drag chains through the streets, while others perform skits or *comparsas* door to door. Most *mestizo* and Maya villages have an annual fiesta in honor of their patron saint, the largest of which is held in July in Benque Viejo del Carmen, near the Guatemalan border.

Sunrise in Dangriga.

BABY
Baby Arriah

The spectacular Blue Hole off the coast of Belize.

The Maya ruins at Lamanai, deep in the jungle.

Climbing El Castillo at Lamanai.

BELIZE PLACES

A detailed guide to the entire country, with principal sites clearly cross-referenced by number to the maps.

Sunset at Ambergris Caye.

Belizeans like to tell you that that once you have drunk fresh Belize creek water and tasted rice and beans, their staple diet, you are certain to come back. Even if you don't succumb to these particular culinary temptations, once you have dived the rainbow-colored water world around Belize's spectacular coral reef, traced the ancient footsteps of Maya priests to the top of great pyramids, and swum in crystal-clear pools in the rainforest, it is still more than likely you will want to return for a second helping.

Belize City is the hub, the whole nation under one roof, distilled down into this bustling, ramshackle port town by the Caribbean Sea.

North of the City, riverside Creole communities left slumbering since the end of the logging industry in the 1960s are waking up to help unlock Belize's environmental treasure chest. Situated in vast wetlands and pristine rainforest, you can see more wildlife here in one day than in most other parts of the world in a year.

Jungle view from the top of Lamanai's El Castillo.

In the forested northwest, Maya cities hidden for centuries by the jungle are coming back to life, their mysteries painstakingly being unraveled by teams of archeologists from around the world.

Heading west into the hills around San Ignacio, a welcome drop in temperature is accompanied by a booming network of comfortable jungle lodges, and it is possible to adventure here in style. Capped by the Mountain Pine Ridge, home of the great Maya city of Caracol, the region has become Belize's main inland eco-tourism center.

In Placencia, one of the fastest-developing of all Belize's holiday destinations, the locals retain a defiantly laid-back lifestyle. More adventurous souls can head for the interior of the deep south and Belize's only true tropical rainforest, where Maya villages coexist with nature in a way that has not changed in thousands of years.

Finally, and the highlight for most visitors to Belize, are the *cayes* (pronounced keys), a necklace of islands strung the length of the coral reef. Unforgettable islands, the *cayes* range from upbeat tourist spots to stranded desert isles offering the best diving, snorkeling, and fishing.

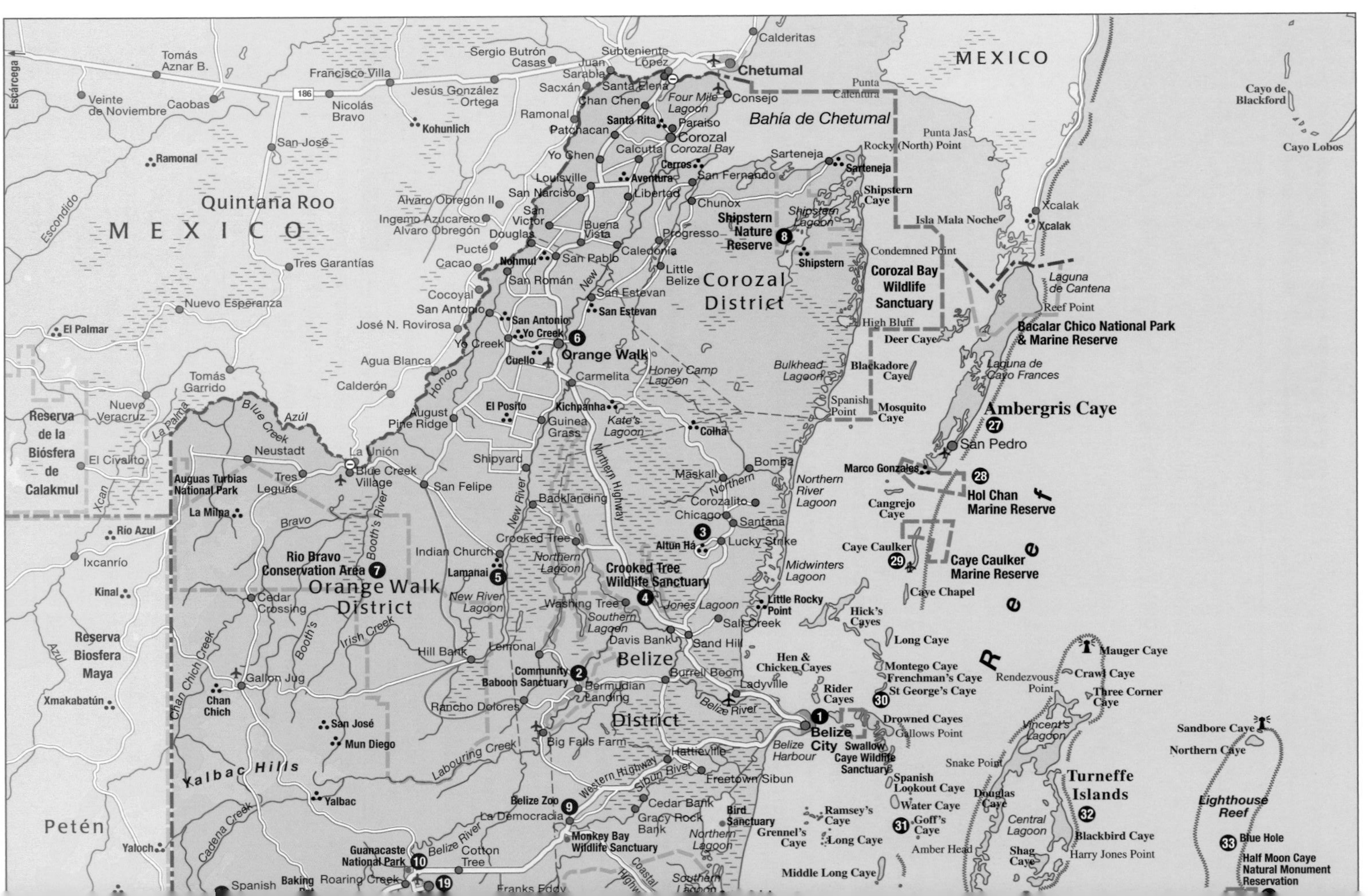
MEXICO
Cayo de Blackford
Cayo Lobos
Chetumal
Calderitas
Bahía de Chetumal
Punta Calentura
Punta Jas
Rocky (North) Point
Isla Mala Noche
Xcalak
Laguna de Cantena
Reef Point
Bacalar Chico National Park & Marine Reserve
Laguna de Cayo Frances
Ambergris Caye
San Pedro
Hol Chan Marine Reserve
Caye Caulker Marine Reserve
Caye Chapel
Caye Caulker
Cangrejo Caye
Marco Gonzales
Corozal Bay Wildlife Sanctuary
Condemned Point
High Bluff
Deer Caye
Blackadore Caye
Mosquito Caye
Spanish Point
Shipstern Caye
Sarteneja
Shipstern Lagoon
Shipstern
Shipstern Nature Reserve
Corozal District
Consejo
Corozal
Four Mile Lagoon
Corozal Bay
Paraiso
Santa Rita
San Fernando
Chunox
Cerros
Progresso
Little Belize
Bulkhead Lagoon
Honey Camp Lagoon
Colha
Bomba
Northern River Lagoon
Maskall
Northern
Corozalito
Santana
Chicago
Altun Há
Lucky Strike
Midwinters Lagoon
Little Rocky Point
Salt Creek
Crooked Tree Wildlife Sanctuary
Jones Lagoon
Sand Hill
Burrell Boom
Ladyville
Hen & Chicken Cayes
Hick's Cayes
Belize River
Belize City
Belize Harbour
Rider Cayes
Swallow Caye Wildlife Sanctuary
Long Caye
Montego Caye
Frenchman's Caye
St George's Caye
Drowned Cayes
Gallows Point
Mauger Caye
Crawl Caye
Three Corner Caye
Rendezvous Point
Vincent's Lagoon
Reef
Turneffe Islands
Blackbird Caye
Harry Jones Point
Central Lagoon
Shag Caye
Douglas Caye
Snake Point
Spanish Lookout Caye
Water Caye
Goff's Caye
Amber Head
Ramsey's Caye
Long Caye
Grennel's Caye
Middle Long Caye
Sandbore Caye
Northern Caye
Lighthouse Reef
Blue Hole
Half Moon Caye Natural Monument Reservation
Freetown Sibun
Bird Sanctuary
Northern Lagoon
Southern Lagoon
Hattieville
Cedar Bank
Gracy Rock Bank
Monkey Bay Wildlife Sanctuary
Western Highway
Sibun River
Coastal Highway
Big Falls Farm
Belize District
Davis Bank
Bermudian Landing
Community Baboon Sanctuary
Washing Tree
Southern Lagoon
Belize Zoo
La Democracia
Belize River
Cotton Tree
Guanacaste National Park
Roaring Creek
Baking Pot
Spanish Lookout
Labouring Creek
Rancho Dolores
Lemonal
Hill Bank
Northern Highway
Kate's Lagoon
Kichpanha
Guinea Grass
Backlanding
Crooked Tree
Northern Lagoon
New River
Lamanai
Indian Church
New River Lagoon
Orange Walk District
Shipyard
El Posito
Carmelita
Orange Walk
San Estevan
Yo Creek
San Antonio
Cuello
San Román
Nohmul
Caledonia
San Pablo
Buena Vista
Libertad
Calcutta
Aventura
San Narciso
Louisville
Yo Chen
Patchacan
Chan Chen
Santa Elena
San Victor
Douglas
San Felipe
August Pine Ridge
Blue Creek Village
La Unión
Booth's River
Rio Bravo Conservation Area
Irish Creek
Booth's
Bravo
Tres Leguas
Neustadt
Blue Creek
Azúl
Cedar Crossing
Gallon Jug
Chan Chich
Chan Chich Creek
Yalbac Hills
Yalbac
San José
Mun Diego
Cadena Creek
Auguas Turbias National Park
La Milpa
Hondo
Quintana Roo
MEXICO
Subteniente López
Juan Sarabia
Sacxán
Ramonal
Sergio Butrón Casas
Jesús González Ortega
Kohunlich
Francisco Villa
Nicolás Bravo
186
San José
Alvaro Obregón II
Ingemo Azucarero Alvaro Obregón
Pucté
Cacao
Cocoyal
San Antonio
José N. Rovirosa
Agua Blanca
Calderón
Tres Garantías
Nuevo Esperanza
Tomás Garrido
Tomás Aznar B.
Caobas
Ramonal
Veinte de Noviembre
El Palmar
Escondido
Escárcega
Nuevo Veracruz
El Civalito
Reserva de la Biósfera de Calakmul
La Palma
Xcan
Rio Azul
Ixcanrío
Kinal
Reserva Biosfera Maya
Azul
Xmakabatún
Petén
Yaloch
Franks Eddy

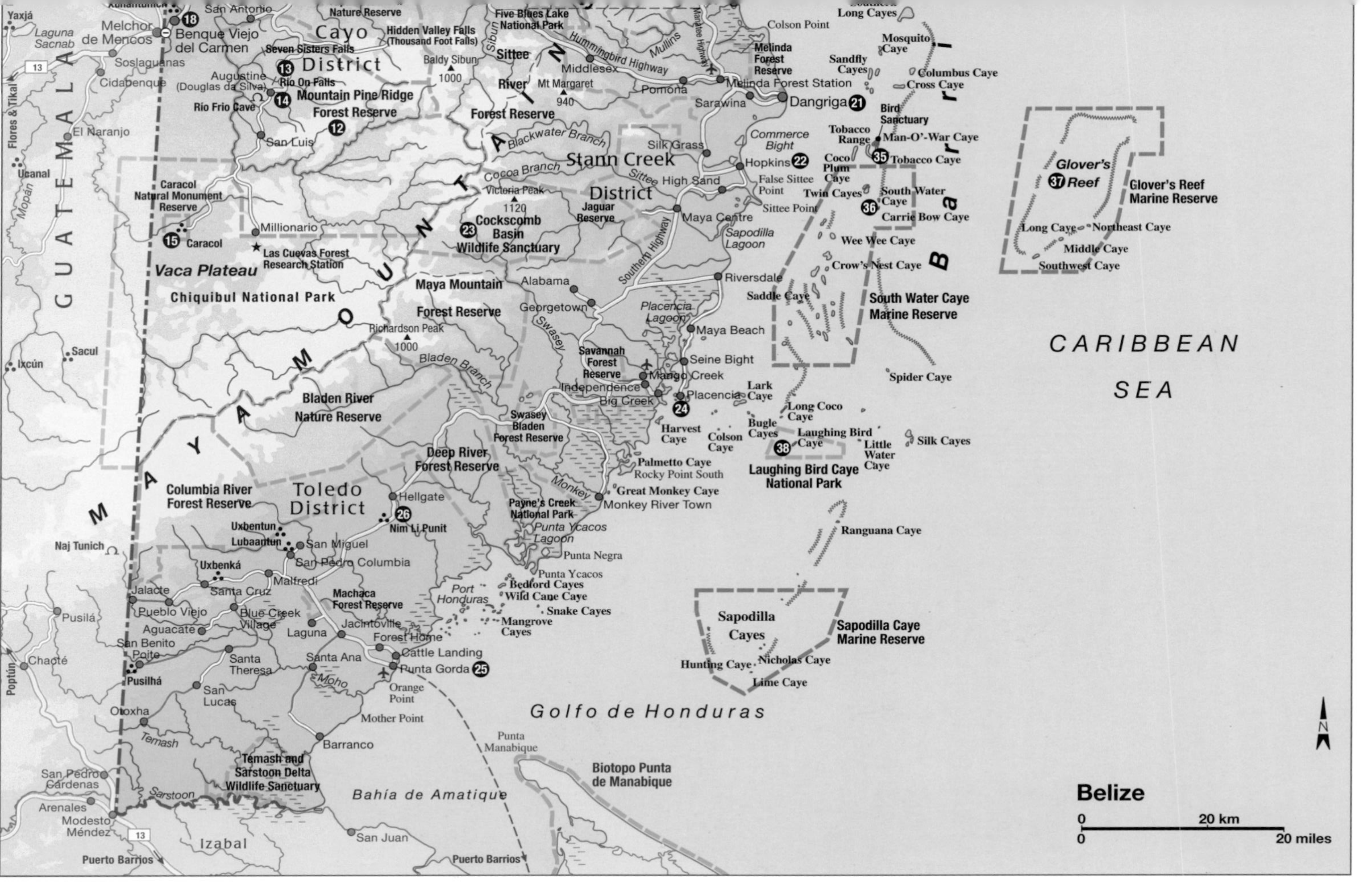
Belize
0 20 km
0 20 miles
CARIBBEAN SEA
Golfo de Honduras
Bahía de Amatique
GUATEMALA
MAYA MOUNTAINS
Cayo District
Stann Creek District
Toledo District
Izabal
Glover's Reef
Glover's Reef Marine Reserve
Northeast Caye
Middle Caye
Long Caye
Southwest Caye
South Water Caye Marine Reserve
Sapodilla Caye Marine Reserve
Sapodilla Cayes
Hunting Caye
Nicholas Caye
Lime Caye
Laughing Bird Caye National Park
Laughing Bird Caye
Ranguana Caye
Silk Cayes
Little Water Caye
Spider Caye
Crow's Nest Caye
Wee Wee Caye
Carrie Bow Caye
Tobacco Caye
Man-O'-War Caye
Bird Sanctuary
Columbus Caye
Cross Caye
Mosquito Caye
Sandfly Cayes
Long Cayes
Tobacco Range
Coco Plum Caye
Twin Cayes
South Water Caye
Saddle Caye
Long Coco Caye
Lark Caye
Bugle Cayes
Colson Caye
Harvest Caye
Palmetto Caye
Rocky Point South
Great Monkey Caye
Dangriga
Melinda Forest Station
Melinda Forest Reserve
Colson Point
Commerce Bight
Hopkins
False Sittee Point
Sittee Point
Sapodilla Lagoon
Riversdale
Maya Beach
Seine Bight
Placencia
Placencia Lagoon
Mango Creek
Independence
Big Creek
Monkey River Town
Savannah Forest Reserve
Southern Highway
Hummingbird Highway
Manatee Highway
Sarawina
Pomona
Middlesex
Silk Grass
Sittee High Sand
Maya Centre
Jaguar Reserve
Cockscomb Basin Wildlife Sanctuary
Victoria Peak 1120
Mt Margaret 940
Five Blues Lake National Park
Sittee River Forest Reserve
Alabama
Georgetown
Swasey Bladen Forest Reserve
Maya Mountain Forest Reserve
Bladen River Nature Reserve
Deep River Forest Reserve
Payne's Creek National Park
Punta Ycacos Lagoon
Punta Negra
Punta Ycacos
Bedford Cayes
Wild Cane Caye
Snake Cayes
Mangrove Cayes
Port Honduras
Cattle Landing
Punta Gorda
Orange Point
Mother Point
Hellgate
Nim Li Punit
San Pedro Columbia
San Miguel
Machaca Forest Reserve
Jacintoville
Forest Home
Santa Ana
Laguna
Barranco
Temash and Sarstoon Delta Wildlife Sanctuary
Columbia River Forest Reserve
Lubaantun
Uxbentun
Malfredi
Blue Creek Village
Santa Cruz
Uxbenká
Santa Theresa
San Lucas
Pueblo Viejo
Jalacte
Aguacate
San Benito Poite
Pusilhá
Otoxha
Sarstoon
Temash
Biotopo Punta de Manabique
Punta Manabique
Puerto Barrios
San Juan
Modesto Méndez
Arenales
San Pedro Cárdenas
Chacté
Pusilá
Naj Tunich
Poptún
Ixcún
Sacul
Ucanal
Flores & Tikal
Mopán
Yaxjá
Laguna Sacnab
El Naranjo
Melchor de Mencos
Cidabenque
Soslaguanas
Benque Viejo del Carmen
San Antonio
Augustine (Douglas da Silva)
Río Frio Cave
Río On Pools
Seven Sisters Falls
Mountain Pine Ridge Forest Reserve
San Luis
Hidden Valley Falls (Thousand Foot Falls)
Baldy Sibun 1000
Caracol
Caracol Natural Monument Reserve
Vaca Plateau
Chiquibul National Park
Millionario
Las Cuevas Forest Research Station
Richardson Peak 1000
Bladen Branch
Blackwater Branch
Cocoa Branch
Swasey
Monkey
Moho

The old post office.

BELIZE CITY

The hidden charms of Belize's largest and inimitably ramshackle city are all in its non-stop street life: chaotic but laid-back, and unmistakably Caribbean.

Unlike the debauched pirate town of Port Royal in Jamaica, which fell into the sea following an earthquake, **Belize City** ❶, which was equally uninhibited in its buccaneer heyday, was literally raised from the sea on top of empty rum bottles. Built on a swamp, divided in two by the Haulover Creek, and surrounded on three sides by the Caribbean Sea, Belize City often seems to be more water than land and is fighting an ongoing battle against drowning – fortunes are spent every year keeping it out of the mud. Yet its 57,000-strong population, drawn from just about every ethnic group under the sun, manages to keep the city afloat, combining to create a metropolis all of its own.

HISTORY

The city was founded in the early 1700s by British "Baymen" – former pirates who had settled in the Bay of Honduras in the 17th century (see page 193). The Baymen made their first Belizean settlement on St George's Caye, a few miles off the coast of Belize, succeeded by a settlement at the mouth of the Belize River, which developed into Belize City, the country's commercial capital. The city grew with the development of the timber trade – first logwood, which grew nearer the coast, and then mahogany, found farther inland.

Belize City was the country's capital until another in a regular series of devastating hurricanes in 1961 killed hundreds of people and flattened many of its buildings. The seat of government was subsequently moved inland to a purpose-built site at Belmopan.

Visitors usually only stay in the city begrudgingly, put off by its bad reputation and neglected appearance. Yet Belize City is worth a visit, if only for a day or two. It remains the commercial and cultural center of the country, and has some excellent museums covering

Main Attractions

- Swing Bridge
- Image Factory
- Museum of Belize
- Memorial Park
- House of Culture
- Yarborough Cemetery
- Old Belize

Maps on pages 222, 227

A British-style red post box.

Tip

Belize City has a high crime rate and parts of the city are affected by gang culture. There is little risk during daylight hours, but it is wise to keep valuables out of sight. Take taxis after dark.

the country's rich marine ecology and archeology. Throughout a turbulent history of hurricanes, floods, fires, disease, and violence, the capital has retained a distinctive Caribbean charm.

THE CITY CENTER

At the heart of the city is the **Swing Bridge** Ⓐ, the busiest crossing point across Haulover Creek, so named because cows and other large objects had to be hauled over the creek by the original settlers. The Swing Bridge is the world's oldest operational manual swing bridge, assembled in 1923 from parts shipped from Liverpool, England. Once cranked open every morning and evening so tall boats could sail up the river, it is now only opened by special request. Adjacent to the bridge, on the east side of the creek, is the Marine Terminal, from which speedboats depart regularly, taking passengers to the *cayes*. A short walk east of the Marine Terminal is the riverside **Image Factory** Ⓑ (tel: 223 4093; www.imagefactorybelize.com; Mon–Fri 9am–5pm; free), at 91 North Front Street, an art gallery run by Yasser Musa, a popular Belizean artist and poet. The gallery is worth checking out as it often runs shows by some of Belize's most talented modern artists, who sometimes drop in and are glad to discuss their work. There's a great gift shop selling art, books, and Belizean music CDs here too.

The **Museum of Belize** Ⓒ (Tue–Fri 9am–5pm, Sat 9am–4pm; www.nichbelize.org/mob/the-museum-of-belize.html), to the north on Gaol Lane at its corner with Gabourel Lane (in the Central Bank Compound), is housed in a former prison building. The brick structure dates to the early 19th century and was Belize's only correctional facility until as recently as 1993. One of the original prison cells has been preserved as part of the restoration, and there are displays with photographs of the gallows used for hanging people convicted of capital offenses.

The museum contains two permanent exhibitions: a collection of artifacts found at ancient Maya sites throughout the country and a historical tour of Belize City, featuring old photographs of the town showing the ravages of the 1931 and 1961 hurricanes, as well as various antiques. There is also an extensive collection of preserved insects and butterflies, old coins and bottles, and antiques, and a display of Belizean stamps.

Schoolchildren looking at the stamp collection in the Museum of Belize.

COLONIAL QUARTER

South of here down Marine Parade Boulevard is **Memorial Park** Ⓓ, in a pretty seafront location, amidst a cluster of grand edifices. The park, with its stage and bandstand, has been at the center of many historic occasions. Music concerts and other events are held here, especially during the September holiday period. The surrounding wooden colonial buildings, including the former Mexican Embassy building, contribute to make this the city's most graceful quarter.

Unfortunately the city lost one of its oldest and most elegant buildings, the Chateau Caribbean Hotel, to fire in 2016.

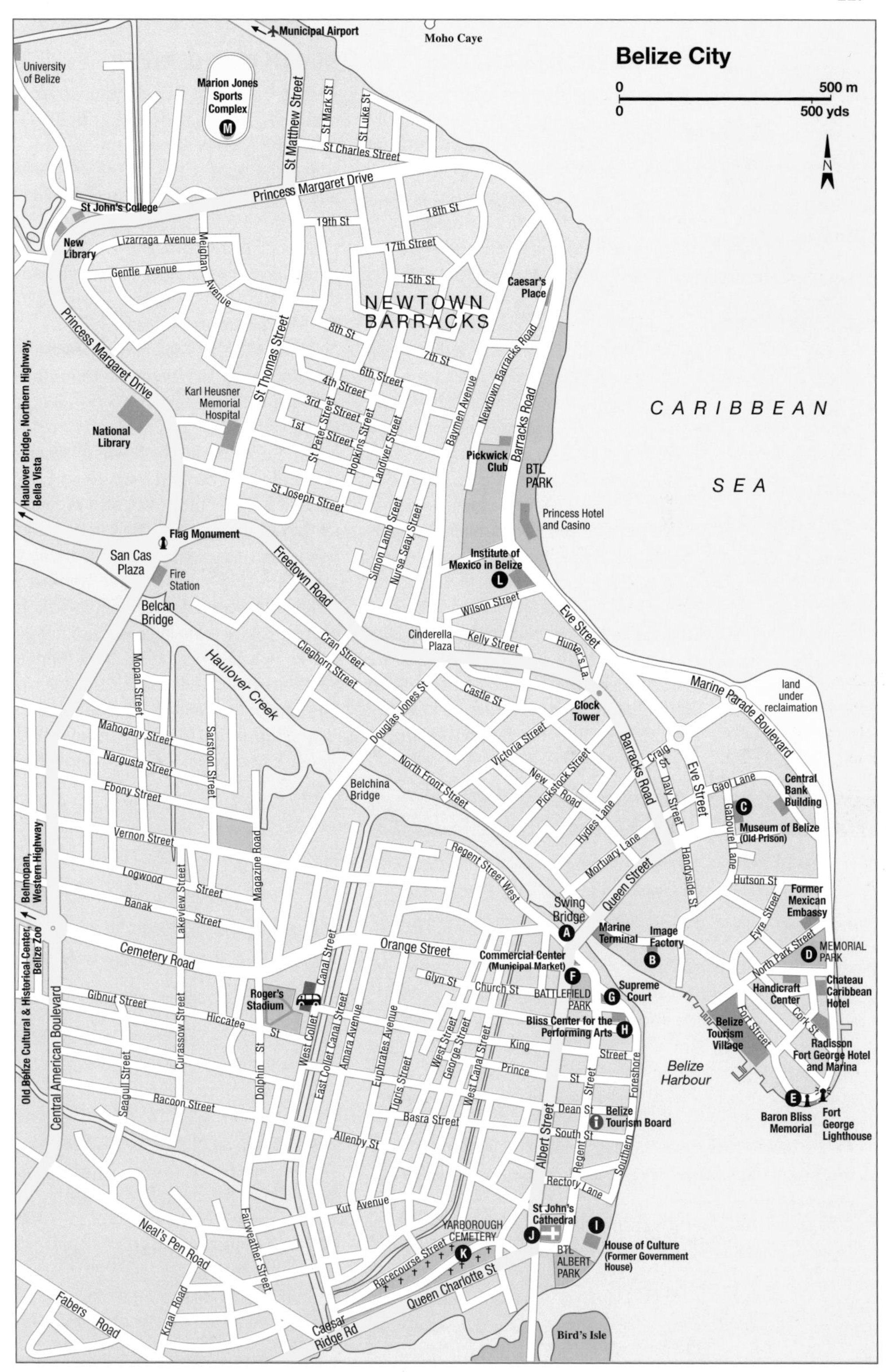

Belize City
0
500 m
0
500 yds
N
CARIBBEAN SEA
NEWTOWN BARRACKS
Municipal Airport
Moho Caye
University of Belize
Marion Jones Sports Complex
St John's College
New Library
National Library
Karl Heusner Memorial Hospital
Flag Monument
San Cas Plaza
Fire Station
Belcan Bridge
Caesar's Place
Pickwick Club
BTL PARK
Princess Hotel and Casino
Institute of Mexico in Belize
Cinderella Plaza
Clock Tower
land under reclamation
Belchina Bridge
Central Bank Building
Museum of Belize (Old Prison)
Former Mexican Embassy
MEMORIAL PARK
Swing Bridge
Marine Terminal
Image Factory
Commercial Center (Municipal Market)
Supreme Court
BATTLEFIELD PARK
Bliss Center for the Performing Arts
Handicraft Center
Chateau Caribbean Hotel
Belize Tourism Village
Radisson Fort George Hotel and Marina
Belize Harbour
Baron Bliss Memorial
Fort George Lighthouse
Belize Tourism Board
Roger's Stadium
St John's Cathedral
YARBOROUGH CEMETERY
House of Culture (Former Government House)
BTL ALBERT PARK
Bird's Isle
Haulover Bridge, Northern Highway, Bella Vista
Belmopan, Western Highway
Old Belize Cultural & Historical Center, Belize Zoo
Haulover Creek

Jade mosaic masks dating from AD 150–300 found in Corozal district and now displayed in the Museum of Belize.

THE HARBOR ENTRANCE

A few blocks south of Memorial Park brings you to where the Fort George Lighthouse dominates the sea wall at the entrance to the harbor. Beneath the lighthouse, the **Baron Bliss Memorial** Ⓔ commemorates a wealthy British yachtsman and fisherman who fell in love with Belize from the sea and became its generous benefactor.

Down the street from the Baron Bliss Memorial and commanding a large strip of land along the harbor entrance is the Tourism Village, a terminal for arriving cruise-ship passengers lined with small gift and duty-free shops and restaurants. However, access is restricted to people with valid ship passes.

Dozens of tour companies and taxis operate just outside the village and provide package tours or trips to Belize Zoo, Altun Há, Community Baboon Sanctuary, and other destinations in the Belize or Cayo districts. Be sure to negotiate fares and prices of trips before setting off. All tour guides are required to have certification from the Tourism Board, so ask to see their credentials.

SOUTH OF THE RIVER

Across the Swing Bridge, pedestrians, cyclists, and cars fight noisily for space along the narrow streets and walkways which characterize the Southside. This part of town is regularly gridlocked – when the offices and shops open and shut at 8am and 5pm, and at either end of the lunch hour. Lunch is the big meal of the day, so don't expect anything to be open between noon and 1pm.

Downstairs at the modern **Municipal Market** Ⓕ (officially the Commercial Center), at the foot of the Swing Bridge, the stubborn survivors of the site's old market, which was dismantled and taken away, remain to give the place its character. Here, at the popular Big Daddy's Diner, there's rice and beans and cow foot soup. Downstairs are shops and fruit stalls, as well as a range of bush medicines, including the ever-popular cleansing bitters. Another market worth a visit is **Michael Finnegan Market** located next to the Novelo's Bus Station on West Collect Canal.

A couple of blocks south down Regent Street is Belize's **Supreme**

Fishing off the sea wall by the Fort George Lighthouse that marks the spot of the Baron Bliss memorial.

THE BOUNTIFUL BARON BLISS

Visiting Belize in 1926 in order to recuperate from a serious bout of food poisoning caught in Trinidad, Henry Edward Ernest Victor Bliss, a wealthy businessman and sailor from Buckinghamshire, England, with a Portuguese title, discovered a passion for the country that kept him here for the rest of his life.

He spent several months in Belize's coastal waters, living aboard his yacht, the *Sea King*, fishing and hoping for his health to improve, while enjoying the calm, unspoiled surroundings and Belizean hospitality.

However, his health eventually failed him, and on March 9, 1927, he died peacefully aboard his yacht. So impressed had the baron been by the beauty of the Belizean coast and *cayes*, and the kindness shown to him by the people during these difficult months, that he left in his will a trust fund of US$2 million established for the benefit of the people of Belize. This became the Bliss Trust.

Without once being well enough to step ashore, the baron endowed the people of Belize with a legacy from which health clinics, libraries, and museums continue to benefit, and the Bliss School of Nursing was created. In recognition of this generosity, March 9, the anniversary of his death, is a national holiday celebrated every year with a regatta in the harbor.

Court G. With its elaborate wrought ironwork capped off by the town clock, the building is a reconstruction of the wooden original destroyed by fire in 1926. Next to the Supreme Court, the Treasury Building marks the commercial center of town, where most of the banks, as well as Belize's only department store, Brodie's, are located.

Behind the Supreme Court and Treasury, the walk along the Southern Foreshore beside the river gives the best view of the harbor, and has a boat service to the *cayes* from Court House Wharf. The very modern **Bliss Center for the Performing Arts** H (known as the Bliss Institute) at 2 Southern Foreshore is Belize's main cultural venue and home to the National Arts Council. You can see a good range of theater productions here.

HOUSE OF CULTURE

At the end of Regent Street, in an idyllic seashore setting, is the **House of Culture** I (formerly Government House), the city's grandest building, with its wide, sweeping staircases and paneled oak interior (Mon–Fri 8.30am–5pm). After independence in 1981, the governor general, the Crown's representative in Belize, moved to Belmopan. In 1996 Government House was converted into a museum and renamed the House of Culture. The museum's displays include collections of silver and glassware and colonial furniture, and the house's beautiful gardens are a haven for birds. Opposite Government House, on Albert Street, **St John's Cathedral** J is the oldest Anglican cathedral in Central America (daily 6am–6pm; free). It was built by slaves in the 1800s from English bricks brought to Belize as ballast. St John's competes with the Holy Redeemer Catholic Church on North Front Street as the dominant place of worship.

YARBOROUGH

To the west of St John's Cathedral is Yarborough, once a wealthy neighborhood, but now the gateway into the poorer parts of town, where it is wise not to wander off alone. Running along the Southside Canal, just west of the cathedral,

The Supreme Court is one of the city's finest old buildings.

Crossing the world's oldest operational swing bridge.

Tip

The newer areas of Belize City are more spread out, and you would be advised to take a car to visit them. Taking a taxi ride can be quite an adventure here with the cabs racing through the streets, narrowly missing pedestrians, and rocketing across bridges. (On the plus side, cab drivers – as everywhere – like talking and can be a good source of recommendations for the latest restaurants and sightseeing.)

Yarborough Cemetery Ⓚ is famous for tales of old Belize now secreted away in the illegible inscriptions of headstones dating from centuries past. Named for the magistrate James Yarborough, who owned the land, it was used as a cemetery between 1781 and 1882, first as a burial ground for the colony's prominent personages and later opened up to the masses. Close by the cemetery is a statue of Belize's first self-made millionaire, Emmanuel Isaiah Morter, a follower of Marcus Garvey and owner of much of Barracks Road, who left a great deal of his fortune to the United Negro Improvement Association. The monument also marks the entrance to what was Eboe Town in the 19th century.

FURTHER ATTRACTIONS

Newtown Barracks, a short taxi ride north from the city center, is the place to enjoy some sea breeze after the heat and hustle of downtown, with a good selection of parks, restaurants, and nightclubs. To get acquainted with things Mexican before journeying north, it is worth looking in at the **Institute of Mexico in Belize** Ⓛ, which often has art and photographic exhibitions featuring Mexican culture and traditional Mexican music concerts. It is open daily 8am–5pm and entrance is usually free, except for certain events such as concerts, when a ticket may need to be purchased in advance.

A drive past the Newtown Barracks, which eventually become Princess Margaret Drive, takes you past the **Marion Jones Sports Complex** Ⓜ, named after the American track athlete Marion Jones who is of Belizean origin, and built by the Marylebone Cricket Club of Great Britain. This is where all the big cricket matches were once played. Today, cricket is rarely played here and soccer has taken over as the crowd-pulling Sunday afternoon event. The stadium is also sometimes used for concerts or cultural events.

The King's Park area around Princess Margaret Drive is where the more prosperous Belizeans live and where many of the city's schools are located, including St John's College, established by Jesuits in 1887. The exclusive Belize Pickwick Club is a members-only sporting facility with tennis courts and one of the city's few swimming pools.

St John's Cathedral.

OLD BELIZE

Lying 5 miles (8km) southwest of the city is the **Old Belize Cultural and Historical Center** at Cucumber Beach Marina (tel: 222 4129; www.oldbelize.com), which has an exhibit detailing the history of the country. Visitors enter through a mahogany tree, the national tree of Belize and vitally important to the early development of the settlement. In turn you visit a rainforest, a Maya village, a logging camp complete with steam engine, used for hauling logs, a *chiclero* camp, and a sugar mill. The highlight is an authentic-looking reconstruction of an early 20th-century street in Belize City. There is also a short zipline tour, where you are clipped into a harness and whizz 65ft (20 meters) above the beach and the sea.

BELIZE ZOO

There is one place in Belize where you can be sure of seeing scarlet macaws, jaguars, or a Baird's tapir in a natural setting.

Belize Zoo (www.belizezoo.org; daily 8.30am–5pm) is an oasis of ponds, forests, and flowers among the sprawling savannas 29 miles (47km) west of Belize City. More than 60 indigenous Belizean animals live here in large, natural enclosures.

Around midday, many of the animals slumber, and are difficult to see through the dense green foliage. If you can, try to visit the zoo first thing or late in the afternoon.

You will often feel that you are in the forest, peering through a tangle of vines and shrubs to catch a glimpse of a puma, jaguarundi, or ocelot. Patience and persistence are necessary to view the creatures here, but your patience will be rewarded: a glimpse of a jaguar staking out his dominion, time in the company of curious and lively kinkajous, or eye-to-eye contact with the towering jabirú stork. Other star attractions include a pair of harpy eagles, the largest eagles in the world, which are nearly extinct in Central America. They are an awesome sight, and of great conservation importance: Panama, the male, is father to several fledglings reintroduced to Belize.

There's also a reptile area where you can see Belizeans snakes including the very venomous fer-de-lance and the boa constrictor. The Belize Zoo education programs concentrate on informing visitors about snakes and their beneficial role in the ecosystem, helping to control rats and other rodents.

The animals and grounds are meticulously cared for, and fun signs spell out the natural habits of each animal and its endangered status, reminding visitors that "Belize is my home too!". Raised gravel paths lead from exhibit to exhibit through natural savanna and pine ridge vegetation, as well as transplanted rainforest. Belize Zoo is as much a botanical garden as it is a zoo, and it is a focal point for environmental awareness in Belize. It operates on strict environmentally friendly principles, with composting and lots of recycling.

Sharon Matola, the North American founder and driving force behind the zoo, arrived in Belize after a colorful career that included time as a lion-tamer in Romania and on a circus tour in Mexico. She started the zoo to provide a home for animals that were used in a wildlife documentary she worked on. Today the focus of the zoo is on research and conservation – with projects that range from educating schoolchildren about harpy eagles to organizing a national day for the tapir.

Belize Zoo now covers 30 acres (12 hectares), and is part of a larger complex that includes a Tropical Education and Research Center; you can stay here, too, in the Belize Zoo Jungle Lodge (tel: 822 8000), which includes an unmissable night tour of the zoo. As many animals are nocturnal, including wild cats and most mammals, you have a good chance of observing them at their most active.

The jaguar, Central America's largest and most elusive wild cat.

A black howler monkey.

NORTHERN DISTRICTS

Wide open spaces – vast forests, wetlands, fields of sugar cane – and the magical mix of environmental and archeological treasures make northern Belize a rewarding destination.

The north of Belize is the most agriculturally developed region of the country but also the least appealing for visitors. Probably the main reason the people here have been slow to promote the attractions of their part of the country is because they are too busy growing sugar cane, Belize's main crop. Beyond sugar, though, there's plenty to see and do, and the north is home to the country's most successful, privately run conservation projects.

North of Belize City, the Northern Highway winds between the Belize River and the deep blue sea to Ladyville, a village dominated by the International Airport, and Price Barracks, home of the Belize Defence Force.

COMMUNITY BABOON SANCTUARY

Five miles (8km) past Ladyville, a left turn signposted to Burrell Boom and Bermudian Landing is the start of a paved road which winds west through quiet Creole villages created and then abandoned by the logging industry.

Bermudian Landing hosts the **Community Baboon Sanctuary ❷**, a conservation project established in 1985 by an American zoologist backed by the Worldwide Fund for Nature. Persuading local farmers to sign to a plan protecting the broadleaf forest habitat of local black howler monkeys (known in Belize as "baboons"), the project has spread to eight neighboring riverside villages and reversed an alarming fall in monkey numbers.

Tours of the sanctuary can be arranged from the visitors' center (www.belizehowlermonkeys.org; daily 8am–5pm; charge for entry and tour). Led by local guides, the tours explore the forest, with the highlight being the chance to hear a howler's howl, a frighteningly loud noise which sounds more like what you might expect a jaguar's roar to be.

Main Attractions

Community Baboon Sanctuary
Altun Há
Crooked Tree Wildlife Sanctuary
Lamanai
Río Bravo Conservation Area
Shipstern Nature Reserve

Guest accommodation at the Crooked Tree Wildlife Sanctuary.

Jabirú storks, cormorants, white ibis, and several types of egret wade in the lagoon at the Crooked Tree Wildlife Sanctuary.

ALTUN HÁ

Back on the Northern Highway, past the village of Sand Hill, a turning on the right is signposted to Maskall and Orange Walk. This is the Old Northern Highway, and 12 miles (19km) along this one-track, pot-holed lane is a turn-off that leads to the impressively restored Maya ruins of **Altun Há** ❸ (daily 8am–5pm; www.nichbelize.org/ia-maya-sites/altun-ha.html).

Altun Há, Mayan for "stone water," was first excavated in 1957, but extensive work did not start until the discovery of a jade pendant in 1963, which excited a great deal more interest. Archeological excavations unearthed a jade replica of the head of the Maya sun god Kinich Ahau, found in the Temple of the Masonry Altars (also known as Temple of the Sun God). At 6in (15cm) high and weighing 9.75lbs (4.4kg), it is the largest carved jade object ever found in the Maya world.

Altun Há is made up of two plazas surrounded by temples. Plaza A is the first you come to, and beneath Temple A-1 is a magnificent temple, the Temple of the Green Tomb. More than 300 pieces were unearthed here, including jade, jewelry, flints, and jaguar skins.

Plaza B has the site's largest temple, B-4, the Temple of the Masonry Altars (which is depicted on the Belikin beer label). A single stairway leads to an altar at the top. The discoveries at Altun Há have pointed to its importance as a coastal trading base and ceremonial center, though the final fate of the settlement, which was suddenly and mysteriously abandoned, has never been discovered.

CROOKED TREE WILDLIFE SANCTUARY

At Mile 33 (Km 52) on the Northern Highway is a left turn signposted to the village of Crooked Tree and the **Crooked Tree Wildlife Sanctuary** ❹ (daily 8am–4.30pm; www.belizeaudubon.org). Crooked Tree, built on a freshwater island, is the largest of Belize's Creole villages and the oldest inland community. The growing popularity of its developing Wildlife Sanctuary has given it a new lease of life. However, since most of the 900 people who live here rely on either their

Temple of the Masonry Altars at Altun Há.

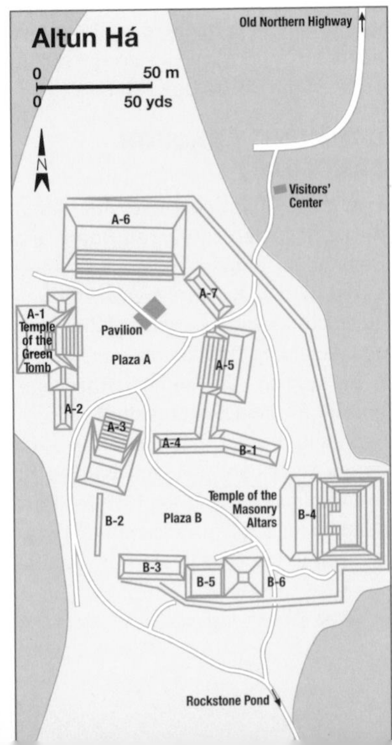

feet or their horse to get around, it is in no danger of getting busy.

The 36,480-acre (14,760-hectare) sanctuary opened in late 1984 and is run by local volunteers with support from the Belize Audubon Society. The sanctuary's lagoons, rivers, and wetlands provide perfect habitats for more than 300 species of birds and waterfowl, including ospreys, snail kites, and kingfishers, as well as other wildlife, including crocodiles and turtles. The rarest of all is the jabirú stork, a tall, prehistoric-looking monster of a bird, which makes an unnerving rattle with its long beak if it becomes agitated.

To help you get the most from the sanctuary there is a visitors' center at the end of the 3-mile (5km) causeway linking the Northern Highway to Crooked Tree village, which has displays and maps, and can advise on lodgings and tours.

Crooked Tree also hosts the annual Crooked Tree Cashew Festival. Held in May, this has grown into one of the area's biggest annual events, showcasing Belize's culture, products, and above all the ability of locals to have a good time. Ostensibly to celebrate the cashew harvest, the festival is really just a good opportunity to eat, drink, and make merry on home-made Creole food and wine.

LAMANAI

Approaching Orange Walk on the Northern Highway, some 22 miles (35km) from Crooked Tree is the Tower Hill Toll Bridge. On the New River, by the bridge, boats wait to take you along the scenic river journey to Lamanai.

On the west shore of the New River Lagoon, **Lamanai** ❺ (daily 8am–5pm), which translates as "submerged crocodile" (though "place of the mosquito swarm" would be an equally appropriate name), was one of the longest continually inhabited settlements anywhere in the Maya world, dating back to at least 1500 BC. As well as the Maya ruins, excavations have uncovered the remains of two 16th-century Spanish missions destroyed by the Maya, who apparently rejected this attempt to convert them to Christianity.

Most of the stelae, relating the lives of the city's Maya rulers, were found

Tip

The one-hour boat trip to Lamanai is worth making even without the lure of the Maya ruins. Plants, birds, and the occasional crocodile give the expert tour guides plenty to talk about, as the boat slowly drifts through the Mennonite colony at Shipyard, past old deserted logging camps, before opening out onto the New River Lagoon.

A three-month-old black howler monkey at the Community Baboon Sanctuary.

A child by New River, near Lamanai.

scattered, burned, and broken amongst the ruins. One of the most elaborate, Stela 9 (showing Lord Smoking Shell), was discovered intact, however, and is now on display under a thatched canopy, near the site's main temple. An impressive visitors' center and museum contains pottery and other artifacts dug from the site, as well as details of plant and animal life around Lamanai, which doubles as a wildlife and botanical reserve with rare untouched tracts of jungle and savanna.

ORANGE WALK

Back on the Northern Highway, **Orange Walk ❻**, 57 miles (92km) north of Belize City, is Belize's second commercial center, and the working-class heart of the sugar industry. Nearby is the Tower Hill Sugar Refinery, which handles all Belize's sugar cane, and at harvest time the rumble of trucks can be heard from dawn to dusk, pulling the precious cane to the factory.

From Orange Walk and beyond the culture perceptibly changes from Creole to Hispanic – this part of the country was settled by *mestizos* fleeing the Yucatán Caste Wars in the 1860s, and for a long time, until the Northern Highways were built, the people here had closer ties with Mexico than with the rest of Belize.

RÍO BRAVO CONSERVATION AREA

Farther southwest is the Mennonite settlement at Blue Creek, famed for having built its own hydroelectric plant out of parts salvaged from an airplane wreck. South of Blue Creek is one of Belize's most successful environmental conservation projects. The **Program for Belize** was launched in 1988 by the Massachusetts Audubon Society and has established the 260,000-acre (105,000-hectare) **Río Bravo Conservation Area ❼**. The lands were acquired through donations inspired by its distinctive "sponsor an acre of rainforest" fund-raising appeal.

With more than 240 species of trees, 390 species of birds, and over 70 known species of mammal, Río Bravo represents one of Belize's highest concentrations of biodiversity. To generate further income, the program has

A rare sighting of a jaguar.

entered the eco-tourism industry and offers on-site accommodations and meals at two field stations: La Milpa and Hill Bank, located at opposite ends of the reserve.

COROZAL

Some 90 miles (145km) north of Belize City, Corozal is a seaside town (no beach) with a quiet and welcoming character. The name derives from the Spanish for the cohune palm tree, a Maya symbol of fertility, and reflects Corozal's fertile soils and benign climate. On a wall inside the Corozal Town Hall, the town's history is told through the colorful mural by Manuel Villamor Reyes, which traces events from the original settlement in 1849 by refugees fleeing a massacre in the town of Bacalar in Mexico's Yucatán Peninsula.

SHIPSTERN NATURE RESERVE

About 15 miles (24km) southeast from Corozal is the 27,000-acre (11,000-hectare) **Shipstern Nature Reserve** ❽ (daily 8am–4pm). The trees on the Shipstern Peninsula were flattened by Hurricane Janet in 1955 but, thanks to the assistance of the International Tropical Conservation Foundation, the nature reserve and forest here have made a remarkable recovery.

This is one of the most remote and untouched areas in Belize and native mammals found here include tapirs, peccaries, coatimundi, wild cats, and birdlife including egrets, teals, keel-billed toucans, and collared aracari. The camouflaged treehouses and new 65ft (20-meter) observation tower enable you to observe wildlife without disturbing the animals, but you will need to be accompanied by a guide.

The reserve can be reached by boat or plane from San Pedro, Ambergris Caye, or Corozal (via the village of Sarteneja). Alternatively, there is a rough road from Orange Walk, via Little Belize and then on to Chunox and Sarteneja. The reserve headquarters are 3 miles (5km) before Sarteneja, and tours can be arranged from here. Accommodation is available at the lodge located next to the visitors' center and reserve's headquarters.

Tip

To find out more about the Shipstern Nature Reserve before visiting, check the comprehensive website (www.visitshipstern.com). There is plenty of information on the plants and animals you can see here, and details of the ongoing conservation efforts and research program.

Excavating Maya artifacts from within a pyramid.

CUELLO MAYA RUIN

The route west of Orange Walk passes by the small Cuello Maya ruin, which is on land owned by the Cuello brothers' distillery, whose permission is needed to visit the site (tel: 322 2183; http://cuellosdistilleryltd.bz). While there is not much for the casual observer to see (excavations are filled in after research has been completed), the site has become of pivotal importance in understanding the history of the Maya.

Cuello has been systematically explored and researched from 1973 to the present day, led by Norman Hammond of Cambridge University, who found the site had been continuously occupied from at least 1000 BC until AD 1500. The findings were startling for historians, because the earliest known Maya civilization before then had only dated from 600 BC. Compounding this discovery, previously unknown trade artifacts (probably obtained in exchange for local bird feathers and animal skins) found at Cuello have led Hammond to suggest the Maya may have had other unknown influences independent of the Olmec peoples from whose culture the Maya way of life is usually believed to descend.

There is no visitors' center, nor any other source of information at the site, but background information can be obtained from Banquitas House of Culture in Orange Walk and the Institute of Archeology in Belmopan. The site is open every day except Sunday.

Canoeing trip on Barton Creek.

THE SOUTH

The south of Belize is blossoming after years of isolation. From archeological revelations to new life forms discovered in vast caves and plants found deep in the forest, it is a region full of surprises.

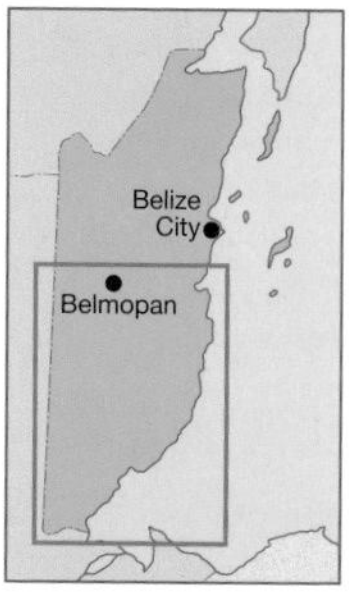

Lightly populated and replete with interest for travellers, this region contains three diverse districts: Cayo, which dominates the center-west of the country, and Stann Creek and Toledo, which cover the coastal strip south from Belize City to Belize's southern border with Guatemala.

The journey south begins on the 76-mile (122km) Western Highway, which slices Belize in half, soon leaving Belize district behind for Cayo, where the monotony of the flat coastal plain is quickly transformed into a luscious landscape of hills and rivers. Cayo is the heart of Belize, embracing all the country's landscapes and cultures and a perfect antidote to the heat and bustle of Belize City; the air is cooler, the people calmer, the pace gentler. And a short journey south from western Cayo into the Mountain Pine Ridge opens a world of environmental treasures here in the foothills of the majestic Maya mountains.

Venturing farther south, the paved Hummingbird Highway cuts a spectacular route back east through the mountains to reach the southern coast. Alternatively, the unpaved Coastal Road takes a more direct route south, starting near Belize Zoo, driving close to the shore and through some stunning savanna scenery. Either way the destination is Stann Creek district, where citrus and banana plantations squeeze onto the slopes and fringes of the Maya mountains, and Garífuna fishing communities "ketch and kill" a living from the sea. South of Stann Creek, Toledo district is Belize's last frontier, where the "real world" gets left behind for something even more real.

BELIZE ZOO

At Mile 30 (Km 48), the road passes one of Belize's major tourist attractions, **Belize Zoo** ❾ (see page 231). The zoo was founded as a home for animals abandoned after the making of

A margay in Belize Zoo.

Main Attractions

- Belize Zoo
- Guanacaste National Park
- Spanish Lookout
- Caracol
- Xunantunich
- St Herman's Blue Hole National Park
- Hopkins
- Cockscomb Basin Wildlife Sanctuary
- Placencia

Maps on pages 222, 242, 244

> **Tip**
>
> Roaring Creek flows into the Belize River at Guanacaste National Park's western boundary – an excellent spot for relaxation, swimming, and picnics. Buses stop right outside the park, making it easily accessible.

a natural wildlife film, *Path of the Raingods*. With its sister Tropical Education Center, it plays an important role in environmental education in Belize (daily 8.30am–5pm; www.belizezoo.org).

The **Caves Branch Archeological Reserve** (daily 8am–5pm), near Frank's Eddy Village (turn off at Jaguar Paw on the Western Highway), is part of a spectacular 4-mile (6km) underground cave system. Visitors can rent rubber inner tubes and travel downriver exploring what the ancient Maya considered to be the entrance to the underworld. Although the river is shallow through the caves, participants should be able swimmers, since tubing occurs in total darkness and the river moves swiftly in places. Expect long lines.

Another 20 miles (30km) along the Western Highway is the intersection with the Hummingbird Highway. Sitting on this junction is the entrance to the small **Guanacaste National Park** ⑩ (daily 8am–4.30pm; www.belizeaudubon.org), which is managed by the Belize Audubon Society and named after an ancient guanacaste tree that once stood near the entrance. The 52-acre (21-hectare) park is packed with birdlife, orchids, bromeliads, ferns, lizards, and small mammals such as gibnut, agouti, and kinkajou. A network of nature trails is mapped out on a leaflet available from the visitors' center.

SPANISH LOOKOUT

A right turn shortly after the village of Blackman Eddy leads to the Mennonite settlement at **Spanish Lookout** ⑪. The dirt track first crosses the Belize River and then Iguana Creek, and plows on through Mennonite farmland before reaching the outskirts of Spanish Lookout. Here, the most modern of Belize's Mennonites have created a surreal-looking American Midwest-style farming community (see page 197). People in Spanish Lookout are very friendly, although quite reserved. The town is self-contained, running its own churches and schools, and is also incredibly productive, supplying Belize with much of its corn, chicken, and dairy. Spanish Lookout is also the location of one of Belize's two oilfields, in production since 2006. The road

Snappy advice, Belize Zoo.

emerges onto the Western Highway between Central Farm and Esperanza Village, and the highlight is the ride back across the Belize River on the ancient wooden ferry. Three cars at a time can squeeze on before the ferry is hand-winched back across the river.

MOUNTAIN PINE RIDGE

At Georgeville, 10 miles (16km) west of Belmopan on the Western Highway, a road runs south toward the hilly region known as Mountain Pine Ridge. A side road on the way to the reserve leads to the spectacular **Barton Creek Cave**, near the traditional Mennonite farming community of Upper Barton Creek. The limestone cave, in which Maya artifacts have been found, is only accessible by river; canoe trips are organized in San Ignacio.

The **Mountain Pine Ridge Forest Reserve** ⓬ is named for the expanses of temperate pine forest which dominate what was once an ecological "island" raised above the rest of Belize. The vast reserve includes tracts of pristine pine and hardwood forest liberally sprinkled with bromeliads and orchids, rivers, waterfalls, and extensive, little-explored limestone cave systems. The ongoing excavations at the enormous Caracol Maya site deep in the Mountain Pine Ridge have led to road improvements, making the area more accessible.

An entrance checkpoint at the top of the climb into the mountains marks the beginning of the reserve. A couple of kilometers farther is the Baldy Beacon junction, and the main road continues south parallel to the Guatemalan border. Some 18 miles (29km) from the Western Highway, the **Río On Falls** ⓭ are a tributary of the Macal River, where clear waters cascade over smooth-as-glass boulders and granite slabs, creating water slides and chutes, and jacuzzi-sized pools of bubbling water. East at the junction toward Baldy Beacon, on the northern side of the ridge, are the equally awesome **Hidden Valley Falls** (or "Thousand Foot Falls"). The waterfalls are 1,600ft (490 meters) high, the tallest in Central America. A viewing platform has been built nearby at the end of a short track, leading north off the main road.

A short drive beyond the Río On Falls is the Douglas da Silva Forest Station based in **Augustine** ⓮. Until recently Augustine was the only settlement in the Mountain Pine Ridge, but today the wooden houses that stand amongst the trees are mostly deserted. You (or your guide) can pick up a free permit from the Forestry Department building here to visit Caracol and the Chiquibul National Park.

Shortly after Augustine and 5 miles (8km) after the Río On Falls, signs point to the **Río Frio Cave**, once used by the Maya as a ceremonial center, and the largest of several caves in the immediate vicinity. The cave can easily be reached along a 1-mile (1.6km) track off the main road, or alternatively by taking the 45-minute Río Frio Nature Trail. A 280yd/meter-long tunnel carved through solid limestone, the cave is light enough to be accessible without flashlights and suitable

Fact

In Plaza B, at Caracol, you will find the massive Caana complex, or "sky palace," counted among the greatest Maya structures of Mesoamerica. It was only completely cleared of vegetation in 2005, and contains palaces, courtyards, and pyramids. The view from the top is amazing.

The hand-cranked ferry crossing to Xunantunich.

for inexperienced spelunkers wanting to experience the awesome shapes and colors sculpted into the rock by centuries of erosion and mineral deposits.

CARACOL

Beyond Río Frio, the road drives ever deeper into the forest, with few signposts. It eventually forks, with the right turn leading to **Caracol** ⓯ (daily 8am–5pm), about a 90-minute drive from Augustine village. Uncovered in 1937, the ancient Maya city of Caracol (snail in Spanish), was one of the most powerful in the Maya world. Caracol's 138ft (42-meter) high *Caana* or "sky palace" is the tallest Mayan structure in the country. The site is immense – 55 sq miles (142 sq km) – with an estimated 35,000 buildings in total, though only a small fraction have so far been excavated. At the center are five plazas, 32 large structures, and an astronomical observatory with main plazas linked by causeways to the outlying ruins. There was no reliable water supply – only the ingenuity of the Maya engineers' reservoir and irrigation systems kept Caracol alive during the long dry seasons each spring. There are few facilities at the site, so bring refreshments. Due to a series of hold-ups along the Caracol road in the past, a convoy is now in operation from Augustine, with vehicles leaving daily at 9.30am and returning from the site at 2pm. The Belize Defense Force usually accompanies the convoy. You can also drive there on your own or as part of a tour; plenty of tour agencies in San Ignacio offer trips to Caracol.

SAN IGNACIO AND SANTA ELENA

Returning to the Western Highway at Georgeville, the road continues 6 miles (10km) to Santa Elena and San Ignacio. These twin towns are separated by the Macal River, which flows under the Hawksworth Bridge, a single-lane suspension bridge (a miniature model of the Brooklyn Bridge) used by vehicles heading east; traffic into town crosses the river on a low wooden bridge. **San Ignacio** ⓰ is a lively town with a single main street, Burn's Avenue, with all its shops and eating places. San Ignacio

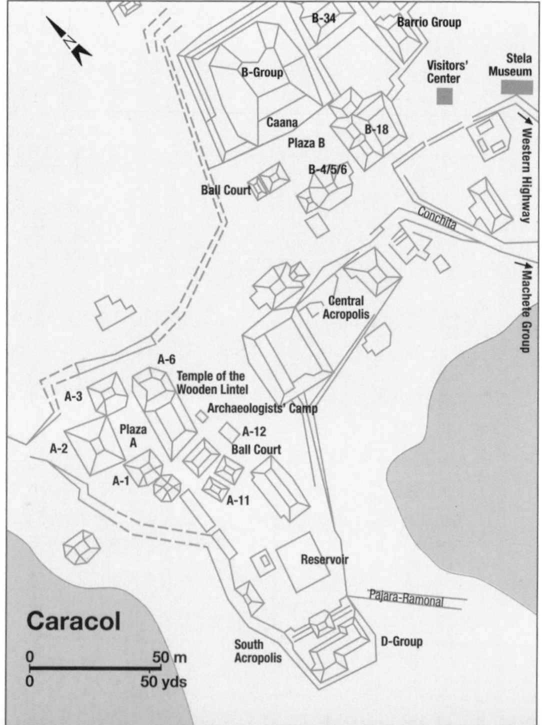

Caracol.

was the last frontier town on one of the obscure corners of the British empire, and several of its buildings retain a faded colonial charm.

On the hills overlooking San Ignacio are the haunting ruins of **Cahal Pech** (daily 8am–5pm). This small hilltop Maya site has several temples (including imposing Structure A1) and the remains of palaces grouped around several courtyard-like plazas. There's a visitors' center which explains the relevance of Cahal Pech in the wider Maya world (it is thought to be the oldest settlement in the Cayo region, dating back to around 1250 BC).

XUNANTUNICH AND BENQUE VIEJO

Heading west toward the Guatemalan border, 7 miles (11km) outside San Ignacio is the village of San José Succotz. Here is the crossing point over the river to reach the road that continues for about 2 miles (3km) on to Xunantunich (meaning Stone Maiden). The Xunantunich road is steep but paved; most vehicles will be able to make it up to the car park a few hundred yards' climb from the site. The highlight of **Xunantunich** ⑰ (daily 8am–5pm), once an important ceremonial center, is the view from the top of the 130ft (40-meter) El Castillo temple, from where a jungle landscape spreads out for miles around over the Mopán River valley and into Guatemala. El Castillo dominates the three adjacent plazas at the heart of Xunantunich, which were flanked by many temples and a ball court. Little is known about the site despite extensive excavations in 1959–60, which have yielded objects of stone, obsidian, shells, and jade, and a jeweler's workshop with flint hammers and stone chisels. Wrapped around the eastern wall of El Castillo is a reproduction of a spectacular carved frieze depicting astronomical symbols, human faces, and jaguars' heads. Also on display are three well-preserved stelae. Archeologists believe earthquake damage may have weakened Xunantunich's influence around AD 850, but it was not abandoned until about AD 1000. Facilities include a site museum, a small visitors' center, and a shop.

On 2 miles (3km) from San José Succotz, **Benque Viejo del Carmen** ⑱

The idyllic pool of St Herman's Blue Hole National Park.

Tip

A few miles inland from Dangriga, near Melinda Forest Station, is the Marie Sharp's Factory, makers of the hot pepper sauces and tropical jams and jellies famous throughout Belize since the 1980s (www.mariesharps.bz).

is the last town before the border. Benque is a quiet place except during fiesta days, in mid-July, and Easter, when its streets throng with crowds. The Durán family, Spanish expatriates, have established Cubola (Belize's main book publishers) and Stonetree Records (Belize's main music producers), tucked away in this corner of the country. There is also a small art gallery and monthly lectures and classes.

BELMOPAN

The tiny, modern capital of Belize is reached from the junction on the Western Highway opposite Guanacaste National Park. **Belmopan** 19 was born when the government and part of the diplomatic community relocated from Belize City following Hurricane Hattie. Belmopan has few facilities for tourists and the town is dominated by government offices, arranged in the style of a Maya plaza.

HUMMINGBIRD HIGHWAY TO DANGRIGA

Heading south on the Hummingbird Highway, 12 miles (19km) past Belmopan is **St Herman's Blue Hole National Park** 20 (daily 8am–4.30pm). Within the park are the entrances to both St Herman's Cave and Mountain Cow Cave, as well as Petroglyph Cave, which contains ancient rock drawings. While St Herman's Cave is open to the public, both Mountain Cow and Petroglyph require Department of Archeology approval to visit. The centerpiece of the park is the Blue Hole, a brilliantly clear pool created as mountain streams rise to fill a sinkhole before flowing back into the earth and eventually into the Sibun River. It makes an excellent location for birdwatching and swimming, though beware the fast-moving waters. Accommodations are available at the nearby Ian Anderson's Caves Branch Jungle Lodge (www.cavesbranch.com).

The journey along the Hummingbird Highway from here is spectacular, as the road carves its way over and through the Maya mountains. Just over 50 miles (80km) out of Belmopan the road ends at the Garífuna town of **Dangriga** 21, in a beautiful location and with a fascinating Garífuna heartbeat.

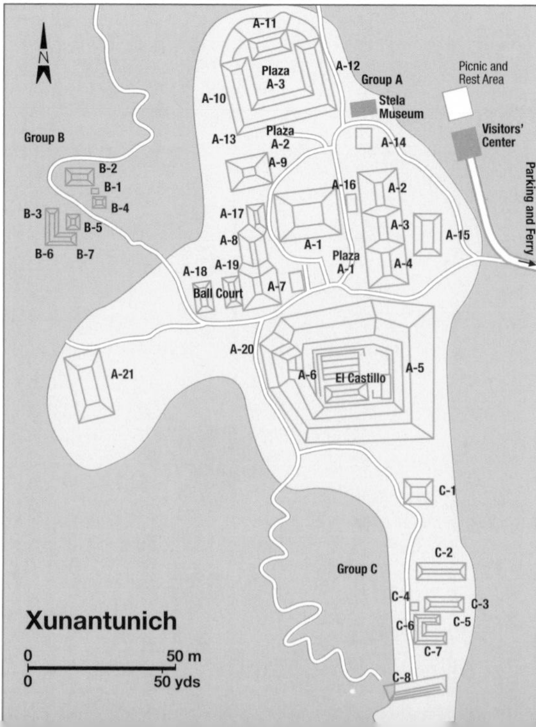

Carvings on the El Castillo temple at Xunantunich.

The best time to be in Dangriga is on and around Garífuna Settlement Day (November 19), when the first coming ashore of the Garífuna people is re-enacted amidst great festivity.

SOUTHERN HIGHWAY

The Southern Highway begins 6 miles (9.5km) before Dangriga. Ten miles (16km) along this road a left turn leads to the low-key village of **Hopkins** ㉒, the best place to enjoy traditional Garífuna hospitality. Be sure to drop by the Lebeha cultural center (http://lebeha.com) where there are Garífuna drumming sessions, gigs (nightly from around 7pm), and percussion lessons. Lots of tours can be set up here, including dirt bike and mountain bike excursions, snorkeling, fishing, and hiking. Four miles (6km) farther south along the Southern Highway, the village of Maya Centre marks the entrance to the **Cockscomb Basin Wildlife Sanctuary** ㉓ (see page 56), the world's only designated jaguar reserve (daily 8am–4.30pm; www.belizeaudubon.org). A rough 5-mile (8km) road leads off the highway to the visitors' center. Established in 1984 as a small forest reserve, the sanctuary soon evolved into a reserve of over 128,000 acres (52,000 hectares); there are thought to be around 50 jaguar in this and adjacent protected areas. This world-renowned sanctuary is also a haven for many other rare and endangered species such as puma, ocelot, margay, and scarlet macaw. Simple, inexpensive accommodations are available at the park administration center and well-maintained trails are constantly being expanded. Many of the park rangers are from the nearby Maya Centre, where there is a medicinal plant trail and crafts shop.

At Mile 23 (Km 37) on the Southern Highway is the left turn to **Placencia** ㉔, which is second only to Ambergris Caye as a tourist hotspot. The route branches east, hits the coast, and then runs south along a narrow peninsula to Placencia at the very tip. Sparkling sandy beaches, vibrant social life, and a budding art scene attract holidaymakers. Placencia is a mix of traditional wooden stilt-houses that

Heliconia flowers are found in the tropical forests of the south.

TOLEDO ECOTOURISM PROGRAMS

One especially rewarding way of visiting Toledo district is through several village projects offering accommodations and guided visits to local attractions. The projects provide villagers with a livelihood, and an alternative to the timber industry that is causing deforestation in the region at an alarming rate.

The **Toledo Peoples Eco-Park Plan** (formerly known as the Toledo Guesthouse and Eco-Trail Program but now much enlarged), is run by a grassroots organization of Mopan, K' ekchi' Maya and Garífuna leaders (Toledo Ecotourism Association, Punta Gorda; tel: 702 2096). Guesthouses sleeping several people in bunk beds or hammocks have been constructed in five local villages, where families (chosen on a rotating basis) host visitors. The accommodations are simple, built of local rainforest hardwoods and covered with a traditional thatch roof. Nature trails, planned and constructed by the villagers, lead to local sites of interest, such as waterfalls, caves, and ruins, and visitors can engage in various adventurous activities, including mountain treks, canoe trips, and caving.

The villagers have a wealth of knowledge in herbal medicine, flora and fauna, and Maya folklore, which they are proud to share with visitors, enabling you to gain a unique experience of this traditional way of Mayan life.

are juxtaposed with an ever-expanding number of swanky new villas and hotels. Aside from the tourist boom, this is still a working fishing village, and the annual Lobsterfest in July celebrates both a bountiful harvest and fishing as a way of life.

About 40 miles (60km) along the Southern Highway, the road branches sharply right to continue for another 40 miles through the only rainforest in Belize, and into **Punta Gorda** ㉕, a quiet place called "PG" locally with beautiful views out to sea. Most visitors come through here to catch the ferry boats to Puerto Barrios and Lívingston in Guatemala.

Hidden in the hills around Punta Gorda are numerous Maya villages. It is possible to stay in these villages (see page 245), and there are Maya sites in the area, including **Lubaantun** ("Fallen Stones"), the most important site in southern Belize – built from crystalline limestone blocks with no visible mortar – and **Uxbentun** ("Ancient Stones"), a largely unexcavated site to the northwest.

Nim Li Punit ㉖ ("The Big Hat"), with the tallest and best-preserved carved stelae in Belize, is an impressive site high on a ridge just half a mile (1km) off the Southern Highway near the villages of Golden Stream and Indian Creek in the Toledo district. The stelae and other objects from the site are preserved in a modern Visitors' Center.

Southwest of Nim Li Punit and a few miles from the Guatemalan border, in the K' ekchí Maya village of San Benito Poité, **Pusilhá** lies at the confluence of two fast-flowing rivers. The palace buildings of the Gateway Hill Acropolis, built on a rocky outcrop, tower 262ft (80 meters) above the river. Perhaps even more notable are the remains of a rare Maya bridge; the ancient Maya even paved the riverbed beneath it.

Discoveries in recent years have brought the Toledo district to the vanguard of archeological knowledge: the only canoe paddle found in the Maya world was pulled from the mud in Payne's Creek National Park, while inland at **Uxbenká** what is believed to be a ceremonial canoe was found in a hilltop cave.

Relaxing on the beach at Placencia.

THE GARÍFUNA

The Garífuna (or Garinagu) are descendants of Carib, Arawak, and Africans, who trace their history back to the island of St Vincent.

The story of the Garífuna begins on the island of St Vincent, where, years before the Europeans arrived, Carib Indians had sailed north from South America to explore the Caribbean territories of the indigenous Arawak tribes. The Caribs raided Arawak territories, killing the men and taking the women for wives, and over time a language evolved with a female Arawak version and a male Carib version, understood by both sexes.

English and French sailors first ventured into the Caribbean in 1625. A treaty between the British and the Caribs guaranteeing the latter perpetual possession of the islands of St Vincent and Dominica was broken by the British a few years later. As the British began to settle the islands, the independent Caribs grew closer to the French military, who saw them as a useful ally in their colonial wars with the British. French words found their way into the Carib language, and the Caribs gradually converted to Roman Catholicism.

Meanwhile, in 1635, two Spanish ships carrying captured African slaves were shipwrecked just off the St Vincent coast. Some of the captives managed to swim ashore and found shelter in Carib settlements. The relationship between the indigenous Caribs and marooned Africans followed a stormy course over the next century and a half, ranging from reluctant acceptance to intermittent warfare and finally resulting in a wholesale fusion of the two cultures.

By 1773, this hybrid people, the Garinagu (whose culture is "Garífuna") was the dominant population of St Vincent. Yet more and more British settlers landed on St Vincent, until it was clear the colonial forces would never tolerate a free black community at the very heart of their own slave plantations.

Following repeated raids on the British settlers, in 1795 the Black Caribs attempted one final all-out attack, led by Chief Joseph Chatoyer. His fatal wounding by a British soldier in a sword duel eventually led to the Garinagu surrender in June 1796.

Less than a year later, fearful of a resurgence of the Black Carib power, Britain deported 2,000 Garinagu to the island of Roatán off the northern coast of Honduras. While many died of disease on the journey, and the rest were abandoned with supplies for only three months, this marooned population not only survived but flourished, establishing fishing and farming communities along the coastline of the Honduras mainland.

An abortive takeover by royalists against the republican government of Honduras in 1823 found the Garinagu siding with the losing faction and facing continued persecution. They began to move up the coast to British Honduras (now Belize) and, in 1832, led by Alejo Benji, a large group of Garinagu landed at Stann Creek.

Today, they are a thriving community along the southern coast, and Garífuna Settlement Day on November 19 each year commemorates this landing. Nearly all Garinagu are trilingual, speaking English and Spanish along with their own language. Traditional activities such as the *dugu*, a sacred ceremony involving ancestral spirit worship, are reminders of a distinctive heritage, while modern Garífuna culture has created "*punta* rock", a lively dance music based on Garífuna drum rhythms.

Garífuna boy from Dangriga, flying his kite.

Sunrise on Ambergris Caye.

THE CAYES

The Belizean *cayes* are an exceptional destination for divers and snorkelers but also ideal for just kicking back on the beach with a book and a rum punch.

Belize has the world's biggest and best aquarium, encompassing hundreds of square miles of the Caribbean Sea around the 185-mile (300km) coral reef which skirts her coastline. Here you can swim in clear waters packed with a kaleidoscope of flirting tropical fish, dive vast underwater walls spun through with tunnels and caves, sail alongside playful schools of inquisitive dolphins, kayak in coral lagoons flocked with pelicans, egrets, and herons, or try to reel in the blue marlin of your dreams.

Exploring this wonderful aquarium is becoming easier as more and more of Belize's *cayes*, the sand and palm islands which dot the perfect blues and greens of the sea around the reef, provide springboards to the underwater world. From simple campsites with basic facilities to luxurious resorts offering full-service diving and fishing packages, the *cayes* are perfect places to base your adventures.

Previously bases for Maya traders, Spanish conquistadors, and British pirates, the *cayes* were until recently either sleepy fishing villages, or uninhabited patches of mangrove, sand, and coconut palms. Then word caught on that this was one of the world's most exciting diving and sports fishing locations. The late French filmmaker and marine biologist Jacques Cousteau popularized the diving at Lighthouse Reef's Blue Hole in a 1972 documentary, and more and more people began to arrive packing wetsuits and fins.

Two *cayes*, Ambergris Caye and Caye Caulker, have gone on to develop into Belize's main "commercial" tourist resorts, but by most yardsticks they remain quiet and genuine, and are totally absorbing. They retain the essential ingredients of Belize – warm and hospitable people, things tending not to happen quite "on time" or "as planned," and an experience guaranteed to be the real deal.

Main Attractions

- Ambergris Caye
- Hol Chan Marine Reserve
- Caye Caulker
- Turneffe Islands
- Blue Hole
- Half Moon Caye Natural Monument
- Tobacco Caye
- South Water Caye
- Glover's Reef

Map on page 222

High-rise beach huts.

Canine companion on a fishing trip at Tobacco Caye.

AMBERGRIS

The northernmost and largest of Belize's *cayes*, **Ambergris** ㉗ is a strip of land and lagoons 25 miles long by 4 miles wide (40km by 2.5km) which would be in Mexico but for a thin sliver of a channel which sets it adrift. The island is in two parts separated by the River Cut, a 60ft (18-meter) wide channel about 1 mile (1.6km) north of San Pedro. Most of the 3,000-strong population live in San Pedro, a few streets of colorful wooden clapperboard houses on the southeast corner of the island. The locals are nearly all *mestizos,* so Spanish is the local language, though English is widely spoken.

San Pedro only has three main streets, Barrier Reef Drive, Pescador Drive, and Angel Coral Street – more commonly known to locals by their pre-tourism names, Front, Middle, and Back streets – so finding your way around is easy. Arriving by scheduled plane (20 minutes) or water taxi (1.5 hours) from Belize City puts you right in the center of town, and most resorts are within easy walking distance.

The soft sandy streets of San Pedro town encourage most people to go barefoot, while, for exploring farther afield, electric golf carts and bicycles are available. Sea kayaks can be rented for exploring the coastline, and the island's 13 lagoons are ideal paddling spots. Most other watersports can easily be organized through tour operators and resorts, including surfing, water-skiing, fishing, snorkeling, and scuba-diving. There are also banks, a post office, pharmacy, library, and stores on the island.

On the lagoon (west) side of the island, even the most inexperienced birdwatcher is likely to see flamingos, pelicans, herons, egrets, and frigate birds. However, be sure to take plenty of mosquito repellent and sunscreen.

BEACH LIFE

Beach lovers will appreciate Belizean laws that insist all beaches are open to the public. The best are to the south of San Pedro town, so simply stroll down along the shore until you find somewhere you like. For added comfort, most beachfront resorts have their own supply

The perfect spot for relaxation on Ambergris Caye.

of hammocks and sun loungers for resident guests, and will usually be more than happy to lend or rent these out to you. For fueling up, there is no shortage of restaurants – San Pedro is a festival of culinary delights compared to the rest of Belize. A good way to start a day in the sun and on the sea is with a traditional *cayes* breakfast of fry jacks (fried dough), eggs, and bacon, washed down with a freshly squeezed fruit juice – try soursop or watermelon, which are both delicious.

HOL CHAN

San Pedro's main attraction, though, is its ability to launch you off into the world of the reef. While the best diving is farther out at the atolls, there's excellent diving close to Ambergris. Most takes place in and around the 5 sq miles (13 sq km) of the **Hol Chan** (Maya for "little channel") **Marine Reserve** ㉘ (www.holchanbelize.org), established in 1987 and the first of its kind in Central America. Daily trips to Hol Chan are run by most of the tour operators in San Pedro, normally in small skiffs – twin-engined speedboats – or sailboats. Tours leave only when the boat is full, so expect some waiting around if the captain has to hustle up extra passengers. For more independent-minded snorkelers and explorers, hiring a sea kayak is worth considering because it provides an alternative mode of transport for do-it-yourself trips around the island and the reef. Whichever way you go, check out the Hol Chan visitors' center on San Pedro's Caribeña Street for brochures and other information on Belize's marine life (daily 9am–5pm).

There are other good reefs around Ambergris – Mexican Rocks on the windward side of the reef is recommended, as is Coral Garden – and a full-day snorkeling or diving trip can also take in lunch at the neighboring island of Caye Caulker.

CAYE CAULKER

Only 45 minutes by boat from Belize City, **Caye Caulker** ㉙ is a smaller, slightly less developed version of Ambergris, 5 miles (8km) long by 650yds/meters wide at its broadest point. It is split in two along a channel created by Hurricane Hattie in 1961.

Fact

The Maya and their ancestors were the first settlers of the *cayes*, using many of the islands as trans-shipment centers for their extensive regional trade network. The northern *cayes* were strategically important, guarding the entrance to Chetumal and Corozal bays, and there are a number of Mayan sites on Ambergris Caye.

HOL CHAN RESERVE

The Hol Chan Marine Reserve (from the Maya word meaning "little channel") is based on a 30ft (9-meter) deep cut in the reef, the sides of which are lined with caves and sinkholes. One of these is the incredible Boca Ciega, an underwater cave and fresh spring crammed full of tropical fish, including parrot fish, horse-eye jacks, blue-striped grunts, gray angels, and yellowtail snappers. Because there's so much here, Hol Chan is equally rewarding for inexperienced snorkelers and veteran divers alike. It is also possible to ride over the reef in a glass-bottom boat to see spectacular sights without getting wet. Trips to Hol Chan also usually take in another part of the reserve, Shark Ray Alley – where locals have bribed rays and 10ft (3-meter) nurse sharks with fish feeds to gather in a convenient spot.

Aerial view of the cut through the reef.

Meteorological prediction, Caye Caulker-style.

The majority of the 1,300 or so population live in the southern part of the island, in the roughly mile-long stretch from the southern tip to the River Cut. Here it is altogether less busy than Ambergris, prices are a little lower, and accommodations more homely. Many resorts are between the airstrip on the island's southern tip and the main settlement just to the north, on sandy beaches and streets looking straight out through tall coconut palms onto the Caribbean Sea.

Caulker is often referred to by the locals by its original Spanish name Hicaco, which British pirates and settlers anglicized to Caulker. It has a simple street arrangement – Front Street, Centre Street, and Back Street, now renamed Hicaco, Langosta and Mangle (mangrove) respectively. Basic amenities include a bank, phone office, grocery, souvenir stalls, and laundry places.

The beaches are narrow, and in most places the water is too shallow for swimming. The best places to swim are from the various piers and at the "Split" at the north end of the south island – although currents are strong here and there's a busy boat lane, so while it's not deep, you do need to be careful.

The sea-based activities available on Caye Caulker including scuba-diving, snorkeling, kayaking, fishing, windsurfing, and kitesurfing. Boat tours to Swallow Caye to observe manatees and sailing trips to the southern *cayes* are also available. The best known of the diving operations are Frenchie's Diving Services (tel: 226 0234; www.frenchiesdivingbelize.com) and Belize Diving Services (tel: 226 0143; http://belizedivingservices.net), but there are lots of other dive schools and adventure sports operators (see page 368).

CAYES AROUND BELIZE CITY

Farther south, only 9 miles (14km) out from Belize City, **St George's Caye** 30

Cleaning fish after the day's catch – watched by expectant pelicans.

was once home base to pirate Edward "Blackbeard" Teach. It is also famous for being Belize's first capital, as it was the scene of a sea battle in 1798 which finally put paid to Spanish claims on Belize. There are some fine colonial buildings here but it is not publicly accessible unless you are staying at one of its two upscale resorts.

A popular day-trip destination from Belize City is **Goff's Caye** ㉛, a patch of sand and coconut palms perched on the edge of the reef. Snorkeling and fishing in the area are excellent, and there are several equally attractive *cayes* nearby, including Gallows, Sergeant's, and English *cayes*.

Buccaneers used to spy on Spanish galleons from tiny Spanish Lookout Caye, 10 miles (16km) southeast of Belize City. Now free from pirates, the island is a highly recommended destination for divers with a keen interest in environmental conservation.

On the Drowned Cayes, just a 10-minute boat ride from Belize City, **Swallow Caye Wildlife Sanctuary** (tel: 226 0567; http://swallowcaye.org) provides a refuge for the endangered West Indian manatee, also known as a "sea cow." Belize has the largest population of these gentle herbivores. The reserve is co-managed by the Friends of Swallow Caye, based on Caye Caulker, and visitors can arrange trips from there – but you are not allowed to swim with the manatees.

THE TURNEFFE ISLANDS

The largest of Belize's three atolls, the **Turneffe Islands** ㉜ are also the easiest to get to – only about 90 minutes by boat from Belize City. The largest and most visited resort is Blackbird Caye (www.blackbirdresort.com), which has become a renowned international marine science facility as well as offering the usual facilities you would expect at a *cayes* resort.

The main attraction at Turneffe is sports fishing, while for divers the southern tip of the atoll has one of the best wall dives around – "The Elbow." Considered an advanced dive because of strong currents, the drop-off is sensational, as are the rippling herds of eagle rays which gather together here.

Fact

In the early 20th century, small groups of settlers made their living on Turneffe from trading sponges and coconuts, but now, after a succession of hurricanes and plant diseases, the atoll's economy is dominated instead by fishing and dive resorts.

The beachfront at Blackbird Caye in the Turneffe Islands.

Fact

One of the two lighthouses at Lighthouse Reef is on Sandbore Caye, at the northern end of the reef. The waters in this area are especially treacherous for shipping, as the many wrecks on the seabed testify. On one such doomed voyage, the Spanish trade ship Juan Bautista went down off Sandbore Caye in 1822, and is said to have taken with it a cargo of still unrecovered gold and silver bullion.

The reef on the western side of Turneffe is wide and gently sloping, ideal for snorkeling and shallow dives. Also on this side is the wreck of the Sayonara, a cargo boat which sank in 1985 and is a good place to practice wreck diving.

THE BLUE HOLE AND HALF MOON CAYE

Lying some 60 miles (100km) east of Belize City, **Lighthouse Reef** can be reached in about 1.5–2.5 hours by fast boat from Belize City or San Pedro; Tropic Air also offers scenic flights of the area. At the center of Lighthouse Reef is one of Belize's best-known "landmarks," the **Blue Hole** 33, now protected as a Natural Monument. From the air the Blue Hole can be clearly seen as a dark blue circle fringed by the lighter blue of shallow waters. This 400ft (120-meter) deep circular sinkhole was created by the collapse of an underwater cavern some 12,000 years ago and since Jacques Cousteau's visit in 1972 has become one of the world's most famous dive sites. While there is not much marine life in this vivid blue shaft of water, the geological formations and encircling coral are spectacular. You can visit Lighthouse Reef from San Pedro or Caye Caulker for a day or overnight stay, with a range of all-inclusive fishing and diving packages on offer.

Belize's first national reserve, **Half Moon Caye Natural Monument** 34 was created back in 1982 to protect the threatened red-footed booby bird. Now a thriving nature colony, loggerhead turtles and mangrove warblers, amongst others, keep the booby birds company. Diving and snorkeling here are particularly enjoyable because of better-than-average visibility. The Half Moon Caye drop-off is a classic wall dive plunging from a coral ridge 30ft (9 meters) below the surface, the drop broken by an ever-changing seascape of mysterious caves and tunnels. For more information on Half Moon Caye and the Blue Hole, check out the Belize Audubon Society's website, www.belizeaudubon.org.

TOBACCO CAYE

A few miles offshore farther south at Dangriga are a number of *cayes* where

Paddling past Tobacco Caye.

tourism is only just beginning to take off. If you want to know what Caye Caulker was like a few years back, try visiting **Tobacco Caye** 35, a tiny speck in a turquoise sea (it is only 200yds/meters long) but the largest of the *cayes* in Tobacco Range. Despite the late entry into the tourism market, the *cayes* of Tobacco Range have been well used over the years by both fishermen and traders. Puritans set up shop here over 300 years ago to trade tobacco and other goods with visiting mariners.

The half-dozen hotels on Tobacco Caye are typically rustic, usually run by local fishing families to supplement their fisherman's wage. As prices tend to be lower than elsewhere, the camping facilities make Tobacco a favorite of budget travelers. The absence here of the sort of luxury you might expect at upscale resorts is well compensated for by reasonably priced boat trips and some excellent tour guides who have an intimate knowledge of the sea and the reef.

SOUTH WATER CAYE

Nearby **South Water Caye** 36, 12 acres (5 hectares) of desert island sitting right on the reef, is another first-rate diving and fishing location. It also boasts some fine sandy beaches and is the center of local and international marine research. Across the South Water Cut on Carrie Bow Caye, Washington DC's Smithsonian Institution operates a major marine research station; hotels (all are upmarket, there are no budget places) can arrange visits.

Carrie Bow used to be twice its current 1-acre (0.4-hectare) size, but storms and mangrove clearing have taken their toll. The reef around Carrie Bow gives some of the best snorkeling in the entire Caribbean. It has also been used by the Smithsonian's scientists to track how Belize's fragile reef is reacting to the chemicals washed into the sea from the citrus and banana industries, overfishing, and tourism.

The Smithsonian lease the *caye* from its owners, Tony Rath – photographer and creator of several Belize websites – and Therese Bowman-Rath, who also own part of South Water Caye and run Dangriga's best-known resort, Pelican Beach, from where trips to South Water can be organized.

Morgan's Inn on Caye Caulker consists of three self-catered beachfront cabins with large covered porches.

Blue Hole at Lighthouse Reef.

Some distance farther out to sea, **Glover's Reef** ❸❼ is named after the British pirate John Glover, who "traded" from its southeast *cayes*. As well as sports fishing, Glover's has exceptionally good snorkeling and diving. Emerald Forest Reef is a shallow spot suitable for novices, while Southwest Caye and Long Caye both have excellent wall dives. As Glover's is less than a mile from the deep water of the continental shelf, pelagic sea life is frequently encountered, including sharks and rays. For longer stays on the atolls, Glover's Atoll Resort on Northeast Caye has the most reasonably priced accommodations.

THE SOUTHERN CAYES

The *cayes* in the far south are quieter still, with only a few offering accommodations. The atoll-like "faro" (elongated ridge of reef) of **Laughing Bird Caye** ❸❽ is a favorite destination for local and visiting day-trippers from Placencia, and this tiny island can get very busy. Partly in response to this and to try to prevent the resident laughing gulls from being frightened away again, it has been declared a national park. The gulls abandoned their rookery here once before, back in the 1980s, and have only begun to return since 1990. They share the *caye* with flocks of green herons, brown pelicans, and melodious blackbirds, but increasing numbers of visitors make it more than likely that they will fly the roost again.

Instead of bothering the gulls, try the other equally beautiful *cayes* in this area – favorites include Colson, Silk, Bugle, and Lark *cayes*. It is possible to stay overnight on Ranguana Caye, which has upscale accommodations and sea kayaks for rent, or at nearby Wippari and Little Water *cayes*.

Beyond this, the Sapodilla Cayes off Punta Gorda remain little-explored except by local fishermen, scientists, and Guatemalan holidaymakers, for whom the few resorts that operate here predominantly cater. Nicholas and Lime *cayes* both have accommodations. Wild Cane Caye, just off the coast of Punta Gorda, was once a major Maya ceremonial site and is in the process of being excavated, while Frenchman Caye is famed for its manatee population.

Some cayes are so tiny they only have one or two buildings.

Exploring the reef depths.

Turquoise waters at Xel-Há cenote.

Enjoying the shallow waters at Playa Norte, Isla Mujeres.

Uxmal, one of the most impressive ruins in the Maya world.

The Iglesia de Jesús (also known as La Tercera Orden) in Mérida, built with stones from Maya temples.

THE YUCATÁN

The Yucatán Peninsula contains a wealth of cultural and ecological treasures – and, of course, miles of beautiful beaches.

Strolling in Campeche.

Believed to be an island by the first Spanish conquistadors in the 16th century, the Yucatán Peninsula has always been a different, detached region of Mexico. It has a unique landscape: the three states of the peninsula – Campeche, Yucatán, and Quintana Roo – sit on a giant, flat limestone plain, sometimes only a meter or two above sea level. There are no surface rivers anywhere north of Champotón, on the west coast, and the Belize border on the east. Rainwater sinks straight through the rock, and the Yucatán is honeycombed with caves and sinkholes *(cenotes)*, including the longest underwater cave systems in the world. Above ground, dense subtropical dry forest covers the south of the peninsula, while in the north the environment is even drier and the forest more sparse and scrub-like.

The elusiveness of water has always marked life in the Yucatán. In much of the region it can only be obtained for most of the year from *cenotes*, either through tunnels that lead down into majestic water-filled caverns, or from deep, open pools formed when the limestone surface collapses, exposing water beneath. *Cenotes* and the Yucatán's caverns are magical places, and have always had great significance for the Maya, particularly associated with the rain god Chac. At his first sight of a *cenote*, early explorer John L. Stephens raved about "a spectacle of extraordinary beauty...a bathing place for Diana and her nymphs."

Swimming in Cenote Samula, Valladolid.

THE MODERN ECONOMY

The characteristic Yucatecan rural landscape is of whitewashed thatch-roofed houses, rough-hewn Franciscan churches, and rambling *haciendas*, once the homes of henequen (agave fiber) planters who supplied most of the world's sisal rope until the advent of synthetics. Henequen is still grown on a small scale, but the era when the industry's millions paid for mansions along Mérida's Paseo de Montejo are long gone. Today, many *haciendas* have been restored as luxury hotels.

The Yucatán's income mainly comes from two incompatible sources: oil and tourism, with the former fortunately restricted to the offshore rigs south of Campeche. The latter spreads across the peninsula from its great base in the 130km (80-mile) strip of Caribbean coast from Cancún to Tulum, now known as the *Riviera Maya*. Cancún is the mighty modern-day temple of the sun, a resort selected by bureaucrats and literally hacked out of the jungle, and which now attracts more than 6 million visitors every year. But as interest grows in ancient Maya civilization, hitherto ignored jungle ruins also attract attention, while better-known sites such as Uxmal, Chichén Itzá, and Tulum can barely cope with the hordes of visitors.

Meanwhile, agribusiness is replacing traditional agriculture, with wider markets being developed for chili peppers, tomatoes, and cantaloupes. To the east of Progreso, the port of Mérida, the region's main fishing harbor at Yukalpetén, has huge seafood-processing facilities.

The Magician's Pyramid, Uxmal.

ENVIRONMENTAL TREASURES

Perhaps the continent's greatest living treasure is the Great Maya Reef, which stretches from north of Cancún down through the reefs off Belize to the Bay Islands of Honduras. The reef is host to thousands of species of coral creatures (plus many sunken galleons) and visiting pelagics: dolphins, whales, tarpon, tuna, turtles, and whale sharks. It is easy to plunge into this sub-aqua paradise with the help of the dive schools of Isla Mujeres, Cozumel, Playa del Carmen, and Tulum.

Inland, fortunately, the forests that have always characterized the peninsula are still relatively pristine in huge areas. Deep in the interior there are also enough ancient sites to keep archeologists busy for several lifetimes. The largest Maya city of the Classic era, Calakmul in the jungles of southern Campeche, has only been extensively excavated since the 1990s.

It is in the nature of modern tourism always to seek out new places to build, and to build the same things everywhere – resort complexes, golf courses. However, local conservation groups are increasingly well organized. Much conservation work centers on the biosphere concept, the idea that a protected area, rather than just being closed off, should be managed in a way that can harmonize the interests of conservation, local communities, and tourism – keeping the last of these to a non-destructive scale. The giant condo-complexes do not always get their own way.

A dive shop in Cozumel.

CLIMATE

The Yucatán's climate is tropical, with daily highs between 28°C and 35°C (82–95°F) most of the year, though November to February is a little cooler. Sea breezes moderate temperatures near the coast, though here the humidity can be punishing. The rainy season is between May and September, and hurricanes are a risk from late August to November.

The Yucatán's east coast has one of the world's richest underwater environments.

Maya ruins meet the sea in the Yucatán.

Chichén Itzá.

THE MAYA IN THE YUCATÁN

Some of the Maya's greatest cities were built in the Yucatán, despite the obstacles of isolation and lack of water.

Maya settlements in Mexico's Yucatán Peninsula expanded a little later than those farther south in Guatemala and Chiapas: the dry limestone terrain made the region less attractive for village communities. However, the Maya had established themselves here from early times, settling near *cenotes* – the pools or caves where rainfall collected. Some of the first evidence of human habitation has been found at the caves of Loltún, in the central Yucatán, thought to have been inhabited since around 8000 BC.

OLMEC ORIGINS

Knowledge of the Maya has exploded since the 1960s, and new discoveries are adding to our understanding all the time. From early days the Maya farming villages around the Yucatán and Chiapas had trading and cultural contacts with other peoples of Mesoamerica (the historic region covering Mexico and Central America). One of the earliest influences came from the Olmecs, who lived around the Gulf of Mexico from about 1600 to 400 BC.

The "mother culture" of Mesoamerica, the Olmecs were the first people to move from living in simple villages to a more complex society centered on ceremonial complexes. From around 600 BC the Maya too began to create larger communities with dramatic ritual architecture. The main Preclassic Maya cities, such as Nakbé and El Mirador, were just to the south of the Yucatán, but by about 250 BC a cluster of significant settlements had emerged close to modern-day Campeche, including Edzná, Dzibilchaltún, and Oxkintok.

CENTERS OF CIVILIZATION

The elements of Classic Maya civilization were in place by around AD 200. It was based on

The Nunnery Quadrangle at Uxmal.

separate city-communities, each ruled by a dynasty of *ahauob* or "holy lords," glorified as the community's sacred channel to the gods. The Classic Maya had the most complex calendar of ancient Mesoamerica, the "Long Count," and its only complete system of glyph writing. Their intricate beliefs included the idea that, in the same way that gods fed men with rain and corn, the gods too needed to be fed – most powerfully with human blood, hence the importance of human sacrifice. Maya cities were also often at war.

In the 8th century AD, the Classic heartland from the Usumacinta valley in Chiapas through the Petén to modern Belize was probably the most densely populated region anywhere in the world. Calakmul was one of the greatest cities, with perhaps 80,000 people. Its eternal rival was Tikal, and the two fought titanic battles through the 6th and 7th centuries.

The several main areas of Maya development and settlement reveal a fascinating diversity. The northern Yucatán long appeared to have been a backwater for most of the Classic era, but there were significant major Classic cities in the north, notably Dzibilchaltún and – largest by far – Cobá, believed to have been an ally of Calakmul.

The grand palacio at Sayil.

PUUC SPLENDOR

However, the most celebrated Maya cities in the northern Yucatán did not begin to make their mark until after AD 600. It is thought overpopulation and environmental pressures in the Petén drove people north, bringing an influx of migrants and Classic Maya culture to the Puuc region.

Puuc is Yucatec Maya for hill, and refers to a range of low hills that stand out in the flatness of the Yucatán. They have very good soils, but the usual problems of finding water in the Yucatán are made far worse by the height; there are no accessible *cenotes*, so to retain water for the dry season the Maya had to build huge ceramic *chultunes* or cisterns in the ground. In this unpropitious setting the Maya of the Puuc created a string of impressive communities – not just Uxmal but Kabah, Sayil, Labná, and more – which flourished for a brief 300-year period between about 650 and 950.

Maya architects at Uxmal used finely cut stone to build delicate arches, and covered the exteriors of their buildings with intricate carvings, riotous ornamentation, and rhythmic designs. Naturalistic sculptures and the typical "hooknose" motif – often placed on corners, and thought to represent the rain god Chac – demonstrate the prowess of local carvers.

Uxmal and the other Puuc communities retained many elements of Classic Maya culture, notably rule by a single dynasty. Uxmal's finest buildings – such as the Governors' Palace and the Nunnery – were all completed in the reign of a single ruler, commonly referred to as Lord Chak, who reigned around 890–910.

CHICHÉN AND ITS POWER

By this time a very different city had arisen to the east, Chichén Itzá. Its origins have long been debated. From the moment the first archeologists saw it, it was recognized that its largest buildings – above all the pyramid of Kukulcán

– are unlike most Maya structures and much more like those of central Mexico. The name Chichén Itzá means "Well of the Itzaes." The sacred pool or cenote around which it was built was a place of pilgrimage – and sacrifice – for several hundred years. In the 16th century, Bishop Landa related how the local Maya of his time still spoke of this pool: "It was the custom to throw live persons into the pool at times of drought; these persons were thought not to die, although they were never seen again. They also threw in many valuable objects."

Bishop Landa spoke favorably of Quetzalcoatl: "He was regarded in Mexico as one of their gods... [and] a god in Yucatán on account of his being a just statesman."

The elaborate Maya carving of the long-nosed rain god Chac, at Chichén Itzá.

Legends told to the Spaniards described the city as having been founded by a "foreign," non-Maya people called the Itzaes, who worshiped the god Kukulcán or Quetzalcoatl. This encouraged the theory that the "Mexican" buildings of Chichén were the work of the Toltecs, originally from Tula, north of Mexico City, who were said to have invaded the Yucatán around AD 1100.

However, the "Toltec migration" theory does not match well with known dates. Moreover, there are plenty of entirely Maya buildings at Chichén – the Nunnery complex – and recent research has shown that they and the "Mexican" temples were mostly built around the same time, between about 750 and 900. Instead of a product of separate invasions, Chichén Itzá seems always to have been a hybrid community, created by local Maya and migrants from central Mexico in the disrupted world of the Terminal Classic.

Chichén differed in all kinds of ways from Classic Maya cities. They are full of monuments to named, individual rulers; there is not one at Chichén, but instead there are images of huge numbers of people, as in the Temple of the Warriors. Chichén Itzá did not have a ruling dynasty, but a kind of collective leadership, shared between the heads of several lineages.

Chichén's style of operation gave it extra strength and flexibility, and it dominated trade in important commodities such as salt, honey, and cotton. Around 860, Chichén crushed its greatest enemy, Cobá. After the decline of Uxmal, Chichén Itzá had no challengers to its domination of the northern Yucatán.

THE COLLAPSE MOVES NORTH

Even Chichén Itzá, though, could not avoid the catastrophe that swept over Classic Maya culture after 800. The "Maya Collapse" is a great enigma of history, but it seems fairly clear the Classic Maya fell victim to a spiral of environmental decline and political disasters.

Soaring population growth led to land being over-exploited, and productivity fell over a period of time. Maya rulers responded with more warfare, which only made things worse. Chronic crises led to a fall in confidence in the sacred *ahau*-kings. Between around 800 and 870 all the dynasties of the southern cities collapsed, and whole cities such as Palenque were abandoned over the next 200 years.

The ruins of Tulum overlooking the beach.

The Collapse came later to the north and was never as complete, but still had its casualties. Most prominent were the Puuc cities; as in the south, rapid growth seems to have accelerated land exhaustion, and from around 920 Uxmal and the Puuc communities fell into a rapid decline. Chichén Itzá survived longer, but around 1200, according to Maya chronicles, its last ruler, Chac Xib Chac, was expelled by a lord from a new city, Mayapán.

Tulum's modern name, from the Yucatec Maya for fence or enclosure, refers to the walls around the site. Its old name was probably Zama, "Place of the Dawn," a lyrical evocation of its fabulous view of the ocean sunrise.

POSTCLASSIC REVIVAL

From the 13th century Maya culture revived on a far smaller scale in the northern Yucatán, in the Postclassic era. At its center for 200 years was Mayapán, the last "capital" of the Yucatán Maya. The Postclassic Maya seem to have been in awe of earlier achievements, for architecturally much of Mayapán is almost a smaller "copy" of Chichén Itzá. Its political organization was also similar, as authority was shared and sometimes rotated between different lords. This system was always unstable, and around 1440 Mayapán fell apart, and the Yucatán split into 19 often warring local chiefdoms.

This did not prevent economic development, particularly around the coast, which benefited from expanding trade between the Aztec empire and Central and South America. The most impressive of the Postclassic coastal centers is Tulum, now on the *Riviera Maya* (see page 338).

THE SPANISH ARRIVE

The first Spaniards to penetrate the Yucatán were two shipwrecked sailors, survivors of Valdivia's expedition, which sank off Jamaica in 1511. One, Gonzalo Guerrero, spent the rest of his life among the Maya; the other, Jerónimo de Aguilar, became Hernán Cortés's interpreter and went with him on the conquest of central Mexico. The first proper Spanish expedition to the Yucatán arrived in 1517, led by Francisco Hernández de Córdoba.

Juan de Grijalvabecame the first European to see the temples of Tulum in 1518. The next year it was the turn of Hernán Cortés, who landed on Cozumel, where he celebrated the first Mass. In 1527, conquest of the Yucatán Maya began in earnest, led by Francisco de Montejo.

The House of Pigeons at Uxmul: the roofcombs suggest dovecotes.

Leaving a dance display, Izamal.

A corrida (bullfight) in Cuzamá.

MODERN HISTORY OF THE YUCATÁN

Mexican independence brought freedom from the Spanish to the Yucatán, but it also led to a bloody civil war and continued hardship for the Maya.

Under Spanish colonial rule, the Yucatán – which then included all the peninsula's three modern Mexican states – had its own governors and administration or *audiencia*, with little interference from the viceroys of "New Spain" in Mexico City. There was no land link with central Mexico, and contacts were carried on by ship. Hence, when the Spanish empire in Mexico collapsed in 1821, many in the white elites of the Yucatán were as suspicious of "Mexicans" as they had been of Spaniards, and only grudgingly agreed to join the new state. Farther south, by contrast, Chiapas, which under Spain had been governed from Guatemala, broke away and petitioned to become part of Mexico, which ever since has given it a special aura for Mexican patriots.

An ancient Maya riddle reflects perfectly their deep-rooted stoicism. "What do you call a man on the road?" it asks. "Time," comes the reply.

Mexico's first "empire" under General Iturbide was soon replaced by a federal republic, in 1823. In the Yucatán the elites squabbled endlessly among themselves and with the central government, and in 1838 a revolt led to the Yucatán declaring itself an independent republic. The dictator General Santa Anna sent an army to re-establish Mexican rule in 1842, but they were beaten off at Campeche. The Yucatán did not agree to return to the national fold until 1849, after the greatest crisis in the region's post-Conquest history.

Iglesia Dulce Nombre de Jesús, Campeche.

WAR OF THE CASTES

This crisis arose out of the greatest-ever revolt by the Yucatán Maya – which was, too, the widest-reaching, most concerted rebellion of any indigenous people anywhere in the Americas since the Conquest, and almost succeeded. The situation for the Maya of the Yucatán had changed for the worse over the previous 100 years, and particularly after independence. The disappearance of Spanish rule carried away a series of Crown and Church institutions that since the Conquest had protected the Maya, at least a little, from the greed of their white and *mestizo* neighbors. The Maya could now be taxed, while white planters found it far easier to grab Maya communal village lands for their own estates.

Ownership of the best land became concentrated in fewer and fewer hands. At the same time, the *ladino* Yucateco elite, confident in their power, broke one of the cardinal rules of the Spanish governors, by giving the Maya weapons and recruiting them as foot soldiers in their petty wars.

The result was an explosion of long-pent-up rage against the *dzulob*, or whites. In early 1847 Maya recruited as soldiers in the east of the Yucatán disobeyed their officers and rioted in Valladolid, considered a bastion of racism. In reprisal a Maya leader, Manuel Antonio Ay, was executed, but this only sparked off a general rebellion, which began with a massacre of non-Maya in the small town of Tepich.

Porfirio Díaz, the president of Mexico from 1876–80 and 1884–1911.

Soon, a fierce war was raging through the countryside, as white and *mestizo* Yucatecans retreated to towns for safety. But the Maya had able leaders, notably Jacinto Pat and Cecilio Chi, and took town after town. In March 1848 they seized Valladolid itself, after a bloody siege, before advancing on Mérida. Such was the state of panic in the city that letters were sent to Britain, Spain, and the USA, offering sovereignty over the Yucatán to whoever would "save the civilized population from their fate." By May, everyone who could was trying to get on a boat to Veracruz, but then Mérida had a remarkable deliverance. Winged ants appeared, which to Maya farmers meant that rains would come early, and so this was the time to go back to their villages to plant, if they did not want their families to starve. Pat and other leaders pleaded with their men to finish the job, but most of the Maya army faded away.

White and *mestizo* Yucatecans could not believe their luck, and confidence soared. No foreign power had been interested in taking on the Yucatán, but they could hope for assistance from Mexico, if they would only toe the line. The Yucatán's elite, chastened, agreed to return to the republic; a later Mexican government, still suspicious of Mérida's pretensions, made Campeche a separate state in 1863. In the meantime, federal and Yucatecan troops pursued the rebel Maya, carrying out reprisals equally as bloody as rebel attacks. According to some estimates, the Yucatán lost half its population during the Caste War.

THE *CRUZOB*

The war never had a tidy end. In 1850 groups of rebel Maya retreating into the empty forests south of Valladolid were rallied by one of their leaders, José María Barrera. He announced he had seen a vision of a cross in a tree, and that this (apparently with the help of a ventriloquist) had begun talking to him. The holy cross had assured him, Barrera said, that if they followed its guidance they would ultimately be victorious. This "talking cross" gave the rebels new spirit and cohesion. The *Cruzob* or "people of the cross," as they were known, continued the fight for another 50 years.

The *Cruzob* established their own "capital" at Chan Santa Cruz, now Felipe Carrillo Puerto. In the 1860s authorities in Mérida decided that, while they still could not conquer the *Cruz* Maya, they were no longer much of a threat either, and so they were left to themselves for years on end. The Maya forged an ambiguous relationship with British Honduras (now Belize), from where they illegally obtained weapons.

It was an 1895 agreement between Mexico and Britain to end this trade that finally led to the *Cruzob*'s defeat. The sudden demand for *chicle*, the natural ingredient of chewing gum, had made the forests of the eastern Yucatán valuable, and increased interest in them from the government of Mexican dictator Porfirio Díaz. To the annoyance of Mérida politicians, the area was made a separate territory under federal control, called Quintana Roo (it did not become a state until 1974). In 1901, federal troops marched into Chan Santa Cruz without resistance.

Even this was not the end of the story, for the troops were withdrawn during the Revolution, and most of the *Cruz* Maya did not agree, peacefully, to accept Mexican rule until 1930. To this day, north of Felipe Carrillo Puerto, a few villages refuse to consider themselves part of the country.

THE YUCATÁN'S GILDED AGE

Despite this trouble on the frontier, the late 19th century was a boom time for the Yucatán, with a prosperity based on "green gold," henequen from the agave plant, used to make the rope known as sisal. Such was the demand from Europe's and the United States' farms, ships, and factories for sisal rope that the Yucatán became the wealthiest state in Mexico, and around 1900 Mérida could boast more millionaires per capita than any other city in the world. A broad new avenue was created, Paseo Montejo, flanked by mansions in ornate European styles. Railroads were built for exporting the rope, and politicians hailed the sisal boom as the triumph of progress.

At the same time, the Maya peasants employed on henequen plantations were cruelly abused in near-slave status, and often paid in tokens that could be exchanged only in stores owned by the landowners. The situation in rural Mexico under the Díaz regime was exposed by American journalist John Kenneth Turner in his 1910 book *Barbarous Mexico*. This led even the London *Daily Mail* to protest: "If Mexico is half as bad as she is painted by Mr Turner, she is covered with the leprosy of a slavery worse than that of San Thome or Peru, and should be regarded as unclean by all the free peoples of the world."

REVOLUTION AND RADICALISM

Turner predicted that the tide of opposition was rising quickly. In the Yucatán, as in other parts of Mexico, the Revolution broke out in 1910. Once again, the flashpoint was Valladolid. However, in the first years of the Revolution, the Yucatán's wealthy *hacendados* were still able to keep a tight rein on the situation, retaining local power and resisting any attempts at land redistribution.

Change finally came in 1915, when President Carranza sent a federal army under General

Old henequen hacienda at Yaxcopoil near Mérida.

PAINTING THE RUINS

Miss Adela Catherine Breton, the daughter of an English officer, was one of the most intrepid early recorders of the Maya sites in the Yucatán Peninsula.

Born in 1849, she was already well into her forties when she first visited the site of Chichén Itzá. She returned many times up to 1907, painting delicate and extremely accurate watercolors of the mural paintings and making plaster casts. Miss Breton also carried out an important full-color drawing of the elaborate stucco relief at Acanceh, to the southeast of Mérida. She was never to visit the Yucatán again after 1908, and died in 1923 at the age of 73 in Rio de Janeiro.

Salvador Alvarado. Yucatecan Conservatives attempted to rally around a new call for "Independence," but were easily routed. A stern moralist, Alvarado pacified the Yucatán, and closed churches when priests were accused of opposing the Revolution. He ended debt-slavery on *haciendas*, and imposed a single, state-run authority to market Yucatán sisal. With the proceeds, Alvarado set about creating 1,000 new schools.

Alvarado was succeeded a few years later by Felipe Carrillo Puerto, a native Yucateco who

ADO Bus Station, Cancún.

had fought for the Revolution alongside the peasant revolutionary Emiliano Zapata. In 1922 he was elected the Yucatán's first (and only) Socialist governor. A flamboyant figure, Carrillo Puerto built roads, distributed land to thousands of families, and founded rural schools and the Yucatán's university. In 1924, however, he was murdered in a failed coup, and further radical change was stalled.

It was not until the 1930s, under the reforming government of President Lázaro Cárdenas, that another major effort was made to bring more social justice to the region. In 1937 President Cárdenas redistributed almost half of the large henequen plantations among peasant farmers. This was enormously popular, and

> *The Socialist government of Felipe Carrillo Puerto gave Yucatán state one of the world's most liberal divorce laws. This led to a first tourist influx from the US in the 1920s, of couples in search of quickie divorces.*

gave many Yucatán villages the shape they still have today, but by this time the international market for sisal had slumped, and the move did little to increase the region's wealth. The Yucatán continued to be one of the poorest areas of Mexico.

TOURISM UNPACKS

Everything began to change in the 1970s, and development has been accelerating ever since. The Mexican government decided on tourism as a foreign currency earner, and chose the beaches of the eastern Yucatán, especially the near-deserted island of Cancún, as ideal sites for development. Since then, Cancún has become a world resort, and the once-remote beaches to the south have been dubbed the *Riviera Maya*.

Yet, not far from the tourist resorts, many Yucatán Maya live in much the same way as they have for centuries. There are almost half a million Maya in the region, most of whom speak Yucatec Maya. In more remote areas, many still own and farm the land communally. They cultivate maize, chili peppers, and beans as they have always done, and most families have beehives for the Yucatán's celebrated honey.

The Maya today still have a profound religious spirit. This has been channeled into Catholicism and Evangelical Protestant sects, but interwoven with Christian practices many Maya continue rites that their people have practiced for hundreds of years. Many of the feast days celebrated through the year would be recognizable to the ancient Maya, as they are closely related to the seasons and gods of rain and fertility.

THE STRUGGLE FOR LAND RIGHTS

Nevertheless the Maya still have to struggle to survive. Traditional farming gives only a meager income. The tourism boom has, naturally, provided new kinds of work; new tourist towns like Playa del Carmen are full of Yucatecan migrants, and many Maya spend a few months each year on the coast, working in construction or hotels, before returning home with their savings. But the average family economy is still very unstable, and this way of life creates its own set of problems, damaging community cohesion.

The more fluid political situation in Mexico since the ending of the one-party rule of the PRI in 2000 has made it a little easier for village people to be heard, but the Maya's right to own and farm land is still constantly threatened by development. Maya cultural traditions are often seen only as a picturesque part of the tourist industry. Although they are the most Mexican of Mexico's inhabitants, they are still often excluded socially and treated as outcasts in their own land.

To the south in Chiapas, conflicts have been and are far more intense, and led to the revolt by the Zapatista National Liberation Army (EZLN) in 1994, when, as so often in the past, the Maya emerged from remote jungle areas and took over towns to press their claims for more land and other social demands. This conflict – known worldwide thanks in good part to the role of the Zapatistas' eloquent, witty spokesman Subcomandante Marcos – has dragged on ever since. Currently, it is in a state of never-ending standoff, with the Zapatistas declaring their willingness to develop their autonomous communities (called caracoles, or snails) by themselves – rather like the *Cruz* Maya years before them – and no formal contacts between the opposing sides.

When Pope Francis visited Chiapas in 2016, he denounced the repression of Mexico's indigenous people, giving the Maya struggle yet another impulse. Recently, the Mayas and other indigenous people of Mexico, who form the National Indigenous Congress (CNI), have decided for the first time in the country's history to put forward their own, independent candidate for the 2018 Mexican presidential elections.

Emiliano Zapata (left), father of the Zapatista Movement.

MAYA RELIGIOUS FESTIVALS

In the Yucatán, the two main village festivals are related to rain and fire. The rain ceremony is known as *Cha-Chaac* and takes place at the start of the maize-growing season in February. The ceremony is led by a shaman or *H-men* who prepares the traditional drink of *balche*, a mildly intoxicating beverage made from a mixture of honey, water, and secret plant roots that the participants consume before ritual dancing and chants. It is believed to possess magical powers.

The *Tumbul Kak* or New Fire ceremony has also been performed since the beginning of Maya civilization. According to the Maya calendar, each historical cycle comes to an end after 52 years. This was a very dangerous moment, when the sun might be extinguished, ending life on earth. In order to prevent this, when the planet Venus appears in the heavens, the shaman lights a new fire, which is then taken out to each of the houses, underlining that fire and life are shared by all in the community.

As with many other Maya religious practices, the ritual has been adapted to Christian beliefs brought by Spanish missionaries. It now takes place on Easter Saturday, during the hours when, according to Christian tradition, Jesus had died on the Cross and not yet been resurrected. In this, as in many other ways, Maya culture has learned to borrow from sources outside itself, but has transformed them into something meaningful for its own people.

The beach at Tulum.

THE COAST OF THE YUCATÁN

Coral reefs, white sand beaches, fascinating fauna, and tranquil fishing villages: these are the highlights of the Yucatán coastline.

The Yucatán Peninsula is famous for many reasons, not least its indigenous Maya culture, unique landscape formations such as *petenes* (hardwood "islands" within mangrove swamps) and *cenotes* (sinkholes in limestone rock), prehistoric caves, and subterranean rivers. It is also a major stop for millions of migratory birds. But what catches the attention of most first-time visitors is its magnificent coastline, stretching for 1,830km (1,140 miles). Bordered on the west and north by the tranquil green waters of the Gulf of Mexico, and on the east by the turquoise blue of the Caribbean, much of this coast is lined by broad, uninterrupted expanses of fabulous white silicate sand, powder-soft and always cool underfoot even in temperatures above 35°C (95°F).

Large areas of superb natural habitats along the Yucatán coast have been marked out as protected reserves. The main conservation strategy used here is the biosphere concept, which promotes rational use rather than a "hands off" policy. By putting wetlands, forests, and coral reefs under protection, rules can be established for the use of natural resources between competing economic activities – for the most part, fishing and tourism.

The reserves of the Yucatán vary in official status. Starting in the west, full *Reserva de la Biósfera* status is held by several coastal reserves: Los Petenes and Ría Celestún in Campeche; Río Lagartos in Yucatán state and Sian Ka'an and Banco Chinchorro in Quintana Roo. Areas with *Parque Nacional* (national park) status are the Alacranes reef off Yucatán state, Isla Mujeres and its reefs, Isla Contoy, the Cozumel reefs, Puerto Morelos and its reefs, Tulum, and the lagoons and reefs of Xcalak. A few reserves have the lesser status of a protected

Isla Holbox, a sanctuary to thousands of birds.

area for flora and fauna (APFF): for example Yum Balum, which includes Isla Holbox and the lagoon around it.

CRATERS AND CORAL REEFS

Since the turn of the century, the village of Chicxulub, on the north coast near Progreso, has been under international scientific scrutiny. It has been determined that it was here that a meteor – more than 10km (6 miles) in diameter – impacted on the earth some 65 million years ago, creating a crater over 180km (110 miles) across. This cataclysmic event appears to have provoked the extinction of the dinosaurs; in their place birds and mammals prospered. The north–south divide created by the rim of this vast, ancient crater is what today causes the subterranean rivers of the peninsula to deposit their water in either the Gulf of Mexico or the Caribbean Sea. The brackish mixture of fresh and salt water is responsible for carving out the picturesque inlets or *caletas*, found behind coral sand beaches at points along the Caribbean coast.

The Yucatán's east coast also hosts a magnificent coral barrier reef, stretching 550km (340 miles) from northern Quintana Roo to Honduras. The offshore islands of Isla Contoy, Isla Mujeres, and Cozumel, and Banco Chinchorro in the south, are all part of this vast system. The north coast is not entirely void of reef formations either. One, Arrecife Alacranes, 60km (38 miles) north of Progreso, is actually an atoll composed of five separate islands, especially valuable for its flora and fauna.

The other offshore islands of the Campeche Bank in the Gulf of Mexico are enormous sandbars, used both by nesting seabirds and as bases for oil exploration. Along the coast, northerly winds have created long sandbars parallel to the shore, varying from a few meters to half a kilometer (540yds) in width. They act as limits to kilometer after kilometer of coastal lagoons and salt flats.

The natural wonders of the reef are a joy for divers.

ANCIENT INDUSTRIES AND VILLAGES

Maya fishermen have used these coastal lagoons for fishing and salt-making for at least 2,000 years. Not a whole lot has changed – fishing and saltworks are still primary economic activities. From the 16th to the 19th centuries, dyewood was extracted from the forests of Tabasco, Campeche, and Belize. In the first half of the 20th century, coconut plantations replaced native vegetation along large extensions of the coast from Veracruz to Belize, and *chicle* was exported from inland forests before the development of synthetic gum. Tourism is the latest growth industry, coinciding with the depletion of forest products and fish populations.

The natural, easy-going atmosphere of the fishing villages along the Gulf coast – such as Celestún, Río Lagartos, or El Cuyo – have made them favored destinations for independent travelers. As already mentioned, several are now surrounded by reserves and protected areas.

The lagoons behind the Yucatán sandbars are of major importance to science as well as to local fishermen. They serve as natural nurseries for an abundance of fish, crab, and mollusk species, and are used as shelters by fishermen for their boats, just as the ancient Maya used them when they plied the coastal waters in dugout canoes,

The water off the long sandbar that lines the north and west coasts of the Yucatán is so shallow that there are no natural harbors able to admit large-scale ships.

trading goods from the Gulf all the way to Central America. Many present-day settlements can trace their origins back to ancient times, when their locations were first chosen because they offered a good site for fishing or salt-making, or had natural openings through the reef.

Brown pelicans are ever-present around the Yucatán coast.

AROUND THE COAST

The giant, mangrove-lined Laguna de Términos, behind Isla del Carmen in Campeche, is the largest bay on Mexico's Gulf coast. Oil exploration has caused severe pollution problems in parts of the lagoon, but much of it is still a natural nursery for shrimp larva, the basis for the area's large shrimping industry. It also harbors fish species such as tarpon, sought by saltwater fly-fishermen.

Heading north along the coast, you come to Champotón, which sits at the mouth of the only surface-flowing river on the west coast of the peninsula. In the early 16th century, it boasted as many as 8,000 houses. It has shrunk, and grown, depending on the health of the local fisheries. The same is true of many coastal villages, although in recent years it has been tourism rather than fishing that has brought new life to these communities. North of Campeche city and running up to the Yucatán state border, the reserve of the Petenes – a name that refers to its characteristic little islands of higher ground with forest trees, within a vast expanse of mangrove – harbors a wealth of fauna, from jaguars to the rare jabirú stork.

FLAMINGOS AND TURTLES

On the coast directly west of Mérida is the placid village of Celestún, on a beachhead between the Gulf and a broad coastal lagoon system. It is an example of the effects of increasing visitor numbers. Fishing is still a major economic activity, but now tourism comes a close second, drawn by the beauty of the mangrove-lined lagoon and its colorful inhabitants. The big attraction is the non-breeding colony of some 3,000 American flamingos, which can be seen in the estuary almost any time of year, with boat trips from Celestún's *embarcadero*. Kayaking tours can also be arranged. The flamingos and the abundant migratory waterfowl in the wetlands, along with endangered reptile and mammal species in the *petenes* beyond, are the major reasons why the Ría Celestún has been made a biosphere reserve.

Northeast of Celestún is Mérida's port town of Progreso, which hosts the migration of *Meridanos* to its long beaches each summer, when they seek relief from the heat of the state capital 36km (22 miles) inland. Canadians, looking for warmth, settle into the same homes in winter. But the real charm of this coast is found in fishing villages farther east such as San Felipe, at the mouth of the Río Lagartos lagoon. It is not far from the old port of El Cerrito, once used by

Snorkeling at Xcaret.

the Maya city of Chichén Itzá. The major export in ancient times was the same as today's – salt, produced in the flats behind Las Coloradas.

The primary nesting site of Mexico's population of the American flamingo is within the long mangrove lagoons of the Río Lagartos Biosphere Reserve, extending eastward to the remote village of El Cuyo. Its coastal vegetation mixes Gulf coast and Caribbean species, so important to the endemic Yucatán wren and millions of migrating land birds that fill the estuaries behind the coastal sandbar during their spring and fall passages. El Cuyo, on the border with Quintana Roo, is still small and quaint, yet has opened its gates to tourism. Actually, it has received visitors for years, as green and tortoiseshell sea turtles come ashore each summer to bury their eggs in the soft, white sand.

Off the northeastern corner of the peninsula is tiny, idyllic Isla Holbox, within the Yum Balam protected area, which has become a destination for visitors aiming to escape the crowds. Holbox also still hosts nesting sea turtles, as well as large concentrations of migratory shore and land birds. It offers wonderful opportunities to snorkel, fish, and view marine and wading birds, on islands in adjacent Yalahau Lagoon. Holbox is also the nearest point to a remarkable natural phenomenon, the massing of whale sharks off nearby Cabo Catoche, which occurs between May and September. In late May, more than 400 have been observed in a small patch of the ocean, an aggregation on a scale that is thought to be unique in the world. The sharks gather to gorge themselves on the eggs of tunny fish, which spawn at this time of year. Snorkel trips to see these silent, harmless giants can be set up in either Isla Mujeres or Holbox; a distance of 2m (6.5ft) must be maintained between snorkeler and shark.

DOWN THE RIVIERA

Rounding Cabo Catoche at the northeastern tip of the peninsula, you enter the Caribbean, and Isla Contoy National Park – a bird sanctuary – becomes visible. It is visited by boat trips from Isla Mujeres and Cancún. Farther south, the two largest islands of Isla Mujeres and Cozumel both have, along their sheltered west coasts facing the mainland, lines of spectacular coral reefs – from inshore reefs a few meters below the surface to

FRONTIER DAYS

Before the creation of Cancún began in 1969, the only communities anywhere on the mainland of northern Quintana Roo that amounted to more than a few huts were just two villages, at Puerto Juárez, with the boat landing for Isla Mujeres, and Puerto Morelos, with boats from Cozumel.

Puerto Morelos was first founded in the 1890s as a *chicle*-tappers' camp, and for many years had to defend itself against attacks from rebel *Cruzob* Maya (see page 280). When archeologist Professor Sylvanus Morley first came to investigate Tulum in 1914, he did so by boat from the island of Cozumel, with an armed guard.

massive undersea caverns – long famed as containing some of the best diving sites in the world. The transformation of another island, Cancún – site of a Postclassic Maya trading town 500 years ago – to a modern mega-resort has been complete, as has that of the one-time fishing village of Playa del Carmen farther south again.

EFFECTS OF TOURISM

The 130km (80-mile) strip of coast now labeled the *Riviera Maya* has, of course, been changed in many ways by its conversion into one of the world's biggest tourist attractions – as it has, too, by powerful recent hurricanes. The very softness of the Yucatán's sand that makes its beaches so attractive also makes it shifting and unstable, and beaches can change shape noticeably after a major storm. Hurricane Wilma in 2005, one of the biggest on record, stripped away most of Cancún beach itself, and the region's most famous asset was only restored by a massive program of dredging up sand from the seabed and "robbing" sand from other parts of the Riviera. Many resort owners employ a variety of barriers and other methods in an attempt to stabilize "their" beaches.

The effects of massive tourist growth are less obvious but still enormous. Cruise-ship traffic, now a staple of Cozumel's economy, damages precious coral reefs. Onshore, resort-building along the coastline often interrupts the natural flow of life and nutrients between the mangrove lagoons and the sea, and inadequately filtered waste damages reefs and marine life.

PROTECTED AREAS

One of the best-protected areas is around Puerto Morelos, between Cancún and Playa del Carmen, where the local reefs now form a marine park. The little port's location has long been popular with fishermen due to the existence of natural *quebradas*, or reef openings, offshore. Puerto Morelos is still home to fishermen, though some are turning in their boats to become waiters or dive masters.

The central coast of Quintana Roo, south of the Riviera's end at Tulum, is a massive wetland of international importance, with a coral reef to the east and swathes of tropical forest inland, which together make up the Sian Ka'an Biosphere Reserve, a Unesco World Heritage Site. Two very wide, shallow bays, Ascension Bay and Espíritu Santo, cut into the coastline and host important sea and wading bird colonies. Lobster fisheries have traditionally been the main support for tiny communities such as Punta Allen, at the entrance to Ascension Bay, and the area is world-renowned for saltwater fly-fishing.

The south side of the Sian Ka'an reserve is still more sparsely populated, but change has arrived here too, with the building of a cruise ship pier at Mahahual, reached via a paved road from Highway 307. This area is now dubbed the

The cruise ship terminal at Cozumel.

Costa Maya, to differentiate it from the Riviera. The pier was destroyed by Hurricane Dean in 2007, but has been rebuilt on a bigger scale. The road through Mahahual leads down to the tiny sand-street village of Xcalak, on the Belize border. Offshore is Banco Chinchorro, one of the largest, richest parts of the whole Maya Reef. Tourism here remains mostly small-scale and low-key, much of it geared toward scuba-diving, though local operators also accommodate birdwatchers and kayak trips through the mangroves.

Tourism has brought great change – both favorable and negative – but it is hoped that the protected areas will limit economic activities, and tourists will be better informed.

YUCATÁN'S NATURAL WONDERLAND

The Yucatán Peninsula and its Caribbean coast harbor magnificent natural treasures – hundreds of species of birds, animals and colorful marine life, forming a diver's paradise.

Visitors to the Yucatán Peninsula often spend their time clambering over its awe-inspiring Maya ruins, sunning themselves on its gorgeous beaches, or exploring old colonial towns, but many birders, divers, and snorkelers flock here above all for its uniquely rich and diverse natural environment. The immense limestone slab that makes up the Yucatán is flanked for long kilometers by vast, virtually uninhabited fresh- and saltwater coastal lagoons, which as well as being home to a great many resident birds, provide winter quarters for millions of migrants from across North America. The Yucatán's *cenote* water holes, beautiful and mysterious, and the huge underwater rivers beneath them, filter minerals from the rock as they flow out to sea, providing rich nutrients for the Great Maya Reef, along the Caribbean coast. This is part of the second-longest coral reef system in the world, stretching along the east coast of Yucatán and south past Belize to Honduras. Although narrower than the Australian Great Barrier Reef, this system reaches depths of over 40 meters (130ft) around Cozumel, and at times the remarkable transparency of the water provides visibility up to 27 meters (90ft).

The Caribbean is one of the richest regions on earth in coral formations. Reefs, in turn, harbor an incredible variety and density of marine life. Over 50 species of coral, 400 of fish, and 30 gorgonians have been identified in the Yucatán reefs, along with hundreds of mollusks, crustaceans, sponges, and algae.

Tiny jellyfish are quite easy to avoid when swimming in the perfectly clear sea.

The Great Maya reef is home to thousands of plant and animal species, from brilliantly colored exotic fish to rare sea turtles.

From turquoise to deep blue, the colors of the Caribbean waters are hypnotic.

A heron in a mangrove lagoon.

Diving Destinations

There are many well-equipped locations from which to explore the Yucatán's underwater garden and coral mountains. Cozumel generally has the biggest variety of reefs, from shallow and ideal for beginners to giant wall dives, dropping sheer into the depths. Isla Mujeres, though sometimes crowded, also offers a good range of dives. On the mainland, friendly Puerto Morelos and busier Playa del Carmen are both excellent dive centers, while Akumal and Tulum, as well as having good open-water operators, are now major locations for cave diving in nearby *cenotes*. The small dive operations on the Costa Maya, near Mahahual and Xcalak, offer a complete escape from any crowds (for slightly higher prices), and the chance to explore the vast, pristine Banco Chinchorro reef.

In general, the farther south, the better condition the reef will be in. Recent hurricanes, notably Wilma in 2005, have done considerable damage to the coral, especially on Cozumel's inshore reefs. More long-term damage is being done by overdevelopment, particularly the constant building of resort hotels down the Riviera Maya. These often obstruct the natural flow of nutrients out to sea from the mangroves and underground rivers, causing rapid coral deterioration. Only restrictions on building will halt this process.

The loggerhead is one of the five species of sea turtle that come to the Yucatán to nest on the beaches from May to September.

Divers in the upper caverns of the Dos Ojos cenote, near Tulum.

Pink flamingos breed in many of the shallow mangrove lagoons around the Yucatán coast, especially at Celestún and Río Lagartos.

The hotel strip, Cancún.

TOURIST TRAP – OR PARADISE?

The turnover of the region to tourism may have brought much-needed wealth – but at what cost?

Bathed with water so turquoise it seems to define the Caribbean dream, blessed with mile after mile of ravishing sandy beaches and boasting a climate that's utterly tropical, it is easy to understand the meteoric rise of Cancún from desert island to über-resort.

Bright lights and advertising hoardings can make parts of the Riviera seem quite urban. Their fast growth has caught many creatures unawares: jaguars are still spotted wandering through the woods behind Playa del Carmen.

Present-day visitors will probably have trouble imagining how pristine the area was back in the 1960s, thanks to the tens of thousands of hotel rooms, restaurants, marinas, golf courses, malls, and entertainment centers that cover almost every inch of the island.

The night is young: bright lights of the North Riviera.

THE UNSTOPPABLE RIVIERA

The statistics of Cancún and the *Riviera Maya* – a tag only dreamed up in 1998, but which has become an inescapable part of the scenery – defy the imagination. The growth of Cancún in 30 years from a few first hotels to a city of 750,000 is widely recognized; it is less well known that neighboring Playa del Carmen (see page 335), which in 1995 could still be talked about as a sleepy off-Cancún retreat, has grown in population by over 500 percent in little over 10 years, and now contains around 230,000 people.

Much is made of the idea that Cancún's creation came about through a rational, planned process, after Mexican officials came to the conclusion that (as was maybe a little obvious) the northern Quintana Roo coast was one of the most beautiful places on earth, and ideally located for easy access from North America and Europe.

It is unlikely the planners foresaw just how successful their project would be. The explosive expansion of the Riviera has created a new world, one in which tourists have everything on tap and can speak English wherever they go.

Elsewhere, it has created new urban realities, in downtown Cancún – conceived as just a "dormitory" for hotel workers, but now very much a real city – or the sprawl of Playa del Carmen.

Tourism is now well and truly inseparable from the Yucatán, its economic motor. There are few people who have not benefited in some way from the income it provides, from middle-class car-rental agents to the Maya farmers who spend a few months each year working on construction sites – although the wealth from tourism is distributed extremely unequally, as wages remain low and many jobs are very insecure.

Unsustainable tourism leads to environmental degradation.

LIMITS TO GROWTH

The big potential problems of the Riviera – beyond the open sore of inequality – stem from its sheer, unceasing momentum. Many developers seem to work on the assumption that there are no limits to tourist growth, and that making do with what has been done already is not an option.

Many people sneer at Cancún on taste grounds, but as a source of environmental damage it is less significant than all the self-contained, all-inclusive resorts spreading down the coast. Many are built right on the beach, blocking the flow of nutrients between the mangroves and the reefs that is essential for the survival of coral and fish. And the Riviera's people – tourists and residents – produce vast amounts of garbage, and local authorities are running out of places to put it.

There are now nearly 20 golf courses dotted around the Riviera, although this is actually one of the worst places in the world to build one. All tropical golf courses are surrounded by a cocktail of chemicals to keep back the natural vegetation; in the Yucatán, this quickly sinks through the thin limestone subsoil into the water courses below ground and into the sea.

Some local voices are loudly saying that an awareness of long-term prospects is desperately needed, and are trying to develop alternatives.

> *Resorts commonly attach the "eco" tag to their names, but very few have really adequate drainage systems, taking advantage of lax government controls.*

For tourists, there are of course other ways of enjoying the region than going straight from the airport to an enclosed resort, such as diving or taking wildlife tours with small-scale operators. Many such operations are based around reserves and work closely with the local Maya communities, aiming to ensure a more equitable distribution of the tourist dollar.

BASIC NEEDS FOR SUSTAINABILITY

Non-utopian environmentalists suggest there are three essential measures needed on the *Riviera Maya*: a solution to the garbage problem; a complete ban on new building within half a kilometer of the coast; and strict enforcement of proper, filtered drainage standards.

Many developers may only think in terms of their first five-year results, but the future of this coast is tied to its ability to supply its visitors with a beautiful natural environment, and allow its inhabitants, ultimately, to share in the benefits.

Boulevard Kukulcán, Cancún.

Admiring the murals inside Mérida's Palacio del Gobierno.

Hotel-heavy Cancún.

Ik Kal cenote, near Chichén Itzá.

One of the giant mascarones at Kohunlich.

YUCATÁN PLACES

A detailed guide to the entire region, with principal sites clearly cross-referenced by number to the maps.

Structure I, Calakmul.

With seemingly endless sunshine, a glittering coastline, and all the luxurious allure that modern resorts can dream up to entice visitors, the Yucatán is now a global travel destination, attracting visitors from every part of the world. Away from the resorts, the inland Yucatán changes at a much slower pace, and many Maya continue to farm *milpas* (cornfields), planting the maize and beans that have been harvested here for perhaps five millennia. The land they farm is not especially productive, and for many Maya it is an annual struggle to work the harsh conditions – arid lowlands and scrub bush – under the relentless sun.

CULTURAL SIGHTS

The Yucatán's Maya ruins can be found all over the peninsula, many of them still only partially excavated, or even buried in the forest. Despite their primitive tools, the Maya were great stone builders, using simple obsidian chisels to shape the huge blocks, which were then carved and dated, commemorating gods, myths, lords, and events through the various periods of Maya history. "Maya arches," corbeled vaults in which walls got progressively thicker until meeting at the top or in which cantilevered stones overhung each other, were a characteristic architectural feature. This system, noted US art historian George Kubler, was "inherently unstable" despite being strengthened with wooden tie rods, cement corners, and boot-shaped stones. Unstable or not, an enormous amount of it has endured.

The walled city of Becán.

Southwest Yucatán state, between the two cities of Campeche and Mérida, holds perhaps the region's greatest concentration of superb sites, including Uxmal, with its stunning Pyramid of the Magician and Nunnery Quadrangle (see page 315), and the other Puuc sites of Kabáh, Sayil, and Labná, with many more minor ruins close by.

No visit to the Yucatán is complete without a good look at Chichén Itzá, perhaps the most famous ruin in the Maya world (see page 320), and, despite the crowds, its Castillo temple, sacred *cenote* sacrificial pool, and the group of a Thousand Columns are still inspirational, unforgettable sights.

The Yucatán
0 50 km
0 50 miles
N
GULF OF
Bahía de Campeche
Progreso
Mérida
Celestún
Campeche
Champotón
Ciudad del Carmen
Isla del Carmen
Laguna de Términos
Izamal
Uxmal
Kabáh
Mayapán
Edzná
Calakmul
Reserva de la Biosfera Ría Celestún
Reserva de la Biosfera Petenes
Reserva de la Biosfera de Calakmul
Reserva de la Biosfera de Zohlaguna
Meseta de Zohlaguna
Campeche
Chiapas
GUATEMALA
MEXICO
Yucatán
Palenque
Bonampak
Yaxchilán

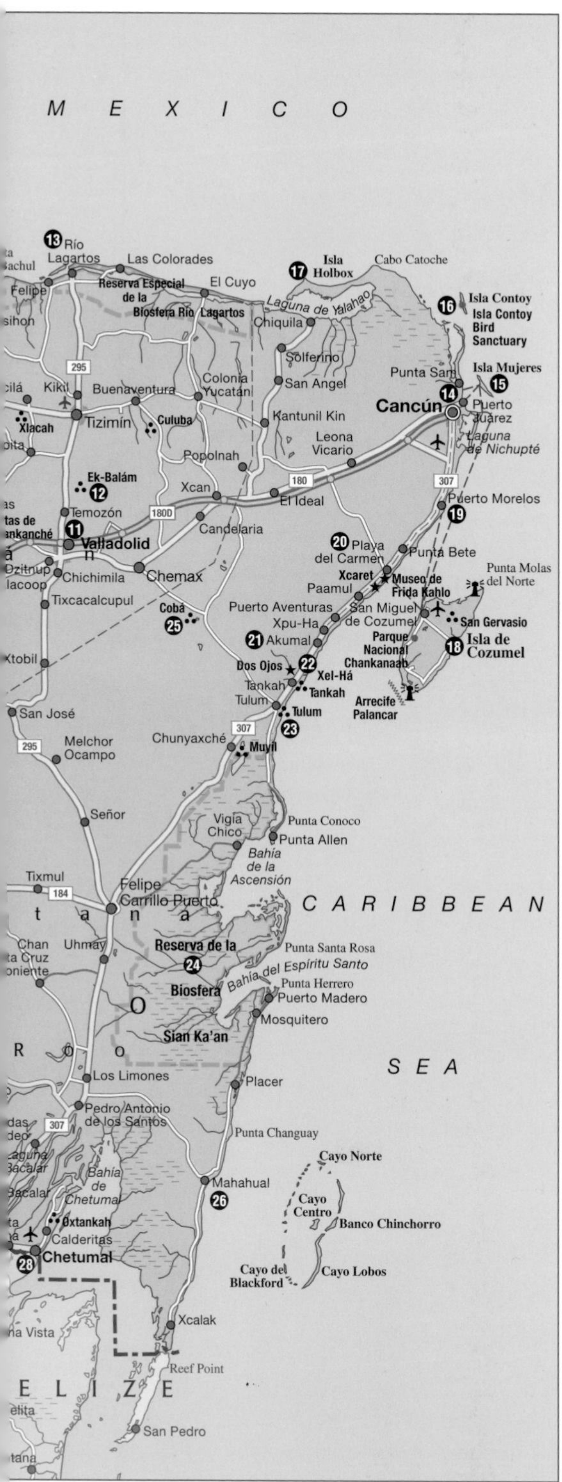

More wonders abound elsewhere in the peninsula, away from Chichén Itzá and the Puuc sites. Edzná, in the west and to the south of Campeche, has a remarkable five-story temple. Tulum, a minor site in every sense, has an incomparable location, framed with white-sand Caribbean beaches and turquoise waters. In the far south of the Yucatán, beyond the several sites of the Río Bec area, are the remains of Calakmul, one of the two superpowers of the Classic Maya era (along with Tikal), which at one time had a population of some 80,000 and a network of subsidiary cities connected by a network of stone causeways. Aside from the Maya ruins, there is a generous slice of Spanish colonial charm on offer here too, especially in the majestic core of historic Mérida and pastel-painted buildings of Campeche. Few of the henequen plantations that once brought great wealth to Yucatán landowners are still operating today; some have been abandoned, and left in atmospheric ruin (see page 310), while other colonial *haciendas* have been resurrected as utterly seductive luxury rural hotels.

THE COAST AND COUNTRYSIDE

The Yucatán's Caribbean coastline is stunning. The white beaches and azure waters between Cancún and Tulum attract the most visitors, and there are many delightful beaches and lagoons down this way, such as Akumal or Tankah. Offshore is the island of Cozumel, its coral walls the talk of dive magazines the world over, and the more intimate beaches of tiny Isla Mujeres. Much farther south, Laguna Bacalar is another jewel, a lovely lake just to the north of Chetumal.

National parks and reserves are extensive and varied. Most impressive is the Calakmul Biosphere Reserve with its pristine jungle and wildlife. The Sian Ka'an Biosphere Reserve is another vast protected territory, whose boundaries also include the offshore reef. The Río Lagartos and Celestún wetlands are superb for birders, especially for the flocks of flamingos. Finally, there are hundreds of atmospheric *cenotes* across the Yucatán: a swim in a *cenote* is a must-do experience for any visitor.

The Pyramid of Kukulcán at Chichén Itzá.

NORTHERN YUCATÁN

This is Mexico's Maya heartland, centered on two of its greatest cities, Chichén Itzá and Uxmal, both within a short hop from Mérida, the elegant colonial state capital of the Yucatán.

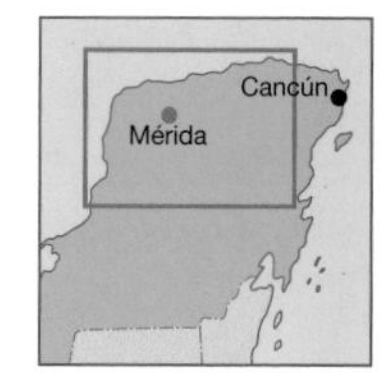

Main Attractions
- Mérida
- Celestún
- The Puuc Route
- Grutas de Loltún
- Uxmal
- Izamal
- Chichén Itzá
- Valladolid
- Ek-Balam
- Río Lagartos

Maps on pages 304, 308, 315, 320

The northern section of the Yucatán Peninsula is occupied largely by the wedge-shaped state of Yucatán. The landscape up here is flat, dry, and covered in scrub bush. The sacred *cenotes* of the Maya (deep natural wells in the limestone crust) provided the only access to fresh water. Second to the peninsula's Caribbean beach resorts, this is the region that draws the most visitors for its sheer quantity of superb archeological sites, crowned by the magnificent Chichén Itzá and Uxmal, and for the special charm of the Yucatecan way of life. The nature reserves at Celestún and Río Lagartos offer rich pickings for birders, in a tranquil setting that contrasts with the glitz of Cancún.

MÉRIDA

The ideal base for exploring the Yucatán is its elegant colonial capital, **Mérida** ❶. Formerly the home of millionaires who made their riches during the henequen heydays, today this thriving city is visited by nearly 4 million people who come to the state of Yucatán annually. In 2017, the city was nominated American Capital of Culture, with a variety cultural events held across town throughout the year.

In spite of this year-round human traffic, Mérida remains a pleasant city. Once enclosed by walls, Mérida's downtown area is compact, its narrow streets and closely packed buildings originally laid out in the era of the horse and buggy, and now filled by motor traffic. It operates on a grid plan with numbered streets: even numbers run north–south, odd numbers east–west.

AROUND THE PLAZA GRANDE

At the heart of the city center, the wonderfully shady **Plaza de la Independencia** (popularly known as **Plaza Grande**) Ⓐ is bound by calles 61 and 63, and 60 and 62. On its northern side, the Pasaje Picheta leads to an internal plaza with

Mérida's cathedral.

Fact

Mérida has long been known as the White City, possibly because of the many white buildings once here, or the white clothes worn by the inhabitants, or even from the white lime used to make the rooftops watertight.

cafe tables under a glass roof. Across on the south side of the laurel-shaded plaza is the **Museo Casa de Montejo** **B** (Tue–Sat 10am–7pm, until 2pm on Sun; free; http://casasdeculturabanamex.com). Built in 1549 for the first Spanish governor of the Yucatán, Francisco de Montejo, the now thoroughly renovated mansion features a collection of 19th- and 20th-century furniture, as well as temporary painting exhibitions and a museum shop/library. The house retains its extraordinary Renaissance portico, with carvings of armed warriors standing on screaming heads, who have always been thought to represent the defeated Maya. Montejo lived in his mansion only for eight years, after which, disillusioned with his surroundings, he left.

The Maya name for the city on the site, Tihó, means "the Place of the Five Temples," and its impressive appearance reminded the conquistadors of the Roman ruins of Mérida in Spain. Their admiration for the buildings, however, did not extend to preserving them. Many of their stones were used to erect the **Catedral de San Ildefonso** **C**, diagonally opposite the Montejo mansion on the northeast corner. Built from 1562 to 1598, this was only the second cathedral built anywhere in the Americas, after Santo Domingo in the Dominican Republic. The cathedral's interior was stripped during the Mexican Revolution in 1915, apart from a sculpture known as *Cristo de las Ampollas* (Christ of the Blisters), supposedly carved from a tree in the village of Ichmul that smouldered unharmed all night after being struck by lightning.

Next to the cathedral, housed in the former archbishop's palace, is the **Museo Fernando García Ponce-MACAY** **D**, Mérida's major modern art museum, containing an important collection of works from local and national artists, and lively temporary exhibits (tel: 999 928 3258, www.macay.org; Wed–Mon 10am–6pm; free) that also feature international artists.

On the plaza's northern side is the **Palacio del Gobierno** **E** (Governor's Palace), built in 1892, on whose murals Fernando Castro Pacheco worked for 25 years, including one which recalls

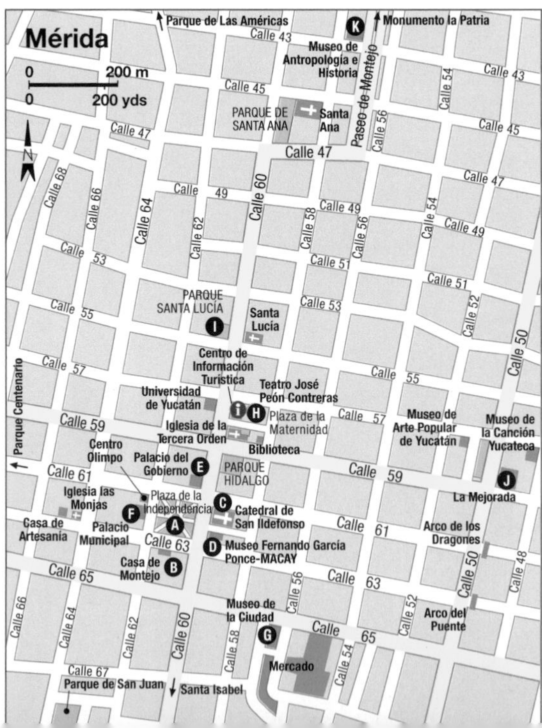

Food stalls outside the Catedral de San Ildefonso.

the infamous destruction of the Maya codices by Bishop Diego de Landa at Maní in 1562. Beside being the seat of the regional authorities it also houses a tourist information point (daily 8am–8pm). The restored **Teatro Armando Manzanero (tel: 924 0040)**, in an Art Deco building around the corner on Calle 62, is a cultural centre with a movie theater and two auditoriums. The west side of the square is dominated by the **Palacio Municipal** **F** or city hall, with an elegant 18th-century colonnaded facade. Next to it, the corner of Calle 61 is now occupied by the **Centro Cultural de Olimpo** (Mon–Sat 10am–8pm), an attractive modern cultural center, with a planetarium (shows Tue–Sun). Every Sunday, too, the plaza and Calle 60 to the north are closed to traffic for *Mérida en Domingo*, Mérida on Sunday, an all-day free fiesta with music and dancing, in which vendors set up all kinds of food and souvenir stalls.

CALLE 60 AND AROUND

Running across the east side of the Plaza Mayor in front of the cathedral, Calle 60 is Mérida's traditional main street, and you will find many sights on and just off this thoroughfare. East of Calle 60 is the traditional commercial heart of the city, the giant **Mercado** (Lucas de Galvéz Municipal Market; daily 5am–6pm) on Calle 65, where shops and stalls sell products ranging from traditional hammocks, panama hats, and embroidery to electronics and giant cooking pots. At the corner of calles 65 and 56, the former post office is now the **Museo de la Ciudad** **G**, which traces the history of the city, and hosts contemporary art shows (tel: 999 924 4264; Mon 9am–8pm, Tue–Fri 9am–6pm, Sat–Sun 9am–2pm; free).

Calle 60 north of the Plaza Mayor has a more tranquil atmosphere. One block north of the cathedral, the **Parque Hidalgo** is dominated by the Jesuit-built church of **La Tercera Orden**, completed in 1618 and containing a painting that depicts the meeting in 1542 of Montejo and Tutul Xiú, the first Maya ruler to convert to Christianity. The sparsely equipped **tourist office** is in the domed **Teatro José Peón**

Fact

Mérida's conquistador families were very keen to build the first cathedral on the mainland of the American continent. Nearby, around the church now known as Las Monjas, they also built a closed convent of nuns, so that their pious daughters could be kept close by.

Sculpture court at the MACAY.

Yucatecan folk dancing at a Mérida festival.

Contreras H (built in 1900), with an ornate marble staircase designed by the Italian architect Enrico Deserti, who was also responsible for the city's Anthropology Museum.

Opposite the theatre stands the **University of Yucatán**. A block farther north is charming, arcaded **Parque Santa Lucía** I, once the city's stagecoach terminus. Tour buses depart from this little park, which hosts free *Serenatas* of Yucatecan music and dance every Thursday (at 9pm), and other events in Mérida's free fiesta every Sunday. At the corner of the arcade leading off the park, a poets' corner contains busts of Mérida's famous musicians and writers.

FARTHER AFIELD IN MÉRIDA

A few blocks east at calles 50 and 59 is the typically austere Franciscan church of **La Mejorada** J, facing an attractive square of the same name. On the opposite side of the square a gracious old mansion has been restored as the **Museo de Arte Popular de Yucatán** (tel: 999 928 5263; Tue–Sat 9.30am–6.30pm, Sun 9am–2pm), with a brilliantly colorful display of folk art and a delightful shop. Just around the corner on Calle 57 is another charming museum, the **Museo de la Canción Yucateca** (tel: 999 923 7224; Tue–Fri 9am–5pm, Sat–Sun 9am–3pm; www.museodelacancionyucateca.com), dedicated to the Yucatán's popular music. The **Arco de los Dragones**, one of only three remaining Spanish arches – once there were 13 – which formed the entrances to the city, is two blocks south on Calle 61. (Another arch is on Calle 63, and the last is on Calle 64, just south of the **Parque de San Juan**.)

Several blocks northwest, starting at calles 56 and 47, is **Paseo de Montejo**, a wide, shady boulevard created in the early 1900s as Mérida's answer to Mexico City's Paseo de la Reforma and the Champs-Elysées of Paris.

A food stall in central Mérida.

President Porfirio Díaz attended the boulevard's grand opening in 1906, and many of its impressive mansions still stand. At the corner of the Paseo and Calle 43, the **Museo de Antropología e Historia** **K** (tel: 999 923 0557; Tue–Sun 8am–5pm; Sun free) is the region's most important collection of Maya artifacts, housed in a splendid former palace built in 1911 and superbly restored. Highlights include remarkable ceramics from Mayapán, informative displays on Maya ideas of beauty (including tattooing and some bizarre dental work), a dramatic carving of a standard bearer from Chichén Itzá and excellent displays about *cenotes*.

It is a lengthy walk from the Plaza Mayor to the Paseo, providing the ideal opportunity to ride a *calesa* (buggy) and study the mansions and the statues. One such statue is of Felipe Carrillo Puerto – tagged the Yucatán's Red Governor – who was assassinated in 1923 after he had introduced radical reforms intended to improve the lives of the Maya. Although married, he fell in love with US journalist Alma Reed, leaving his family to live openly with her, a tremendous scandal at the time. One of the most famous love songs in Mexico, *La Peregrina* (The Wanderer), was written at his request in her honor. The boulevard ends with the **Monumento a la Patria** (Monument to the Nation), created by Colombian sculptor Rómulo Roza in 1946, and portraying the history of Mexico from the days of the Maya to the Spanish Conquest.

MÉRIDA TO THE WEST COAST

The main attraction on the west coast is its flamingos. Take Highway 281 for 92km (57 miles) to the fishing port of **Celestún** **2**, on a narrow peninsula connected to the mainland by a causeway across a lagoon. The lagoon now forms the **Reserva de la Biosfera Ría Celestún**, home to abundant birdlife including flamingos (most numerous between November and May) and herons, as well as plenty of other wildlife. Flamingos, males and females virtually identical in appearance, form monogamous couples, and live as long as 30 years or even more. They obtain

Flamingos at the Ría Celestún Biosphere Reserve.

YUCATECAN ARCHITECTURE

The Yucatán is dotted with many ornate Baroque churches, imposing Franciscan monasteries, and aristocratic colonial *haciendas*.

The legacy of the past is never far away on the Yucatán Peninsula. Ancient pyramids coexist with Christian monasteries and ruined *haciendas*. The Spanish Conquest was followed by a campaign of religious conversion. Missionary friars were the most prolific builders of the 16th century. In the Yucatán, the Franciscans used Maya labor to build severely simple monasteries. Immense and majestic, with few carvings or moldings to distract the eye, they conformed to Franciscan principles of asceticism. Big timbers were scarce, but there was a plentiful supply of stone. Often, the friars reused the "pagan" temple-platforms and Maya stonework.

The Franciscan Convent of San Antonio de Padua, Izamal.

By 1560, six Franciscan monasteries had been completed at Mérida, Campeche, Maní, Izamal, Dzidzantun, and Valladolid. Of these, the most imposing and spacious is the monastery at Izamal (see page 319). Here, as at other centers of Christian worship, Maya converts gathered in great numbers inside the large walled atrium. A thatched and open-sided shelter, called a *ramada*, offered protection from strong sun and rain. In each corner of the atrium was a small, chapel-like sanctuary where Mass was said and the sacrament given. Often referred to as *capillas de índios*, these "chapels for indians" accommodated vast congregations.

The Spanish population of the Yucatán, greatly outnumbered by the Maya, created few large urban centers. The city of Mérida, founded in 1542, retains a rare and celebrated example of civil Plateresque (ornate Baroque) architecture. Facing the main plaza, the Casa de Montejo was completed in 1549. The entrance, surmounted by a coat of arms, is flanked on either side by a conquistador in full armor. In Mérida and in the neighborhood of Valladolid, some fine churches were built with elaborate *retablos* (altarpieces) to meet the spiritual needs of Spanish families. At Izamal, during the 17th century, arcades were added round the edge of the atrium for the benefit of worshipers.

Geographically and culturally, however, the peninsula remained isolated from changing architectural fashions. Only the rise of sisal exports in the 19th century brought conspicuous consumption to the region. With profits won from vast henequen plantations, landowners built opulent and eclectically designed villas in Mérida, giving it a European aura that it retains today. The decorative style incorporated rococo, neoclassical, and neo-Baroque traits. Meanwhile, in the countryside, Moorish-style double archways like that at Yaxcopoil marked the entrance to huge estates. Autonomous and self-sufficient *haciendas* operated along feudal lines. Included in the *hacienda* complex was the *casa grande* (main house), the processing plant, warehouses and work yards, a church, the *tienda de raya* (estate shop), and the humble dwellings of the laborers. After 1910, many *hacienda* buildings were sacked or destroyed by revolutionaries. These once imposing structures stood roofless and abandoned, but many of these crumbling houses have now been restored as hotels or tourist attractions.

food by filtering plankton through the sensitive hairs on their tongue. Boats (US$16 per head for a two-hour tour) leave frequently from the *embarcadero* beside the bridge leading into the town to explore the mangrove-fringed lagoon and its inlets, offering possible sightings of turtles, crocodiles, pelicans, egrets, and sometimes spider monkeys. North of Celestún a bumpy sand road, only passable with a 4x4, runs through empty dunes for 40km (25 miles) to the windblown village of **Sisal**.

SOUTHERN ROUTES

Two popular tour itineraries to the south of Mérida are "**The Puuc Route**" *(La Ruta Puuc)* and "The Route of the Convents" (La Ruta de los Conventos). To some degree they overlap, both going through the village of **Umán** and past **Yaxcopoil** ❸, a preserved *hacienda* (with a small museum) about 40km (25 miles) from Mérida, which demonstrates how wealthy henequen tycoons lived a century ago (tel: 999 900 1193; Mon–Sat 8am–6pm, Sun 9am–3pm; http://yaxcopoil.com/).

To follow the Puuc Route (the name refers to the low-lying hills of the region), from **Muna** you can either stay on Highway 261 to head straight to Uxmal, or – to do the route in a counterclockwise direction – turn southeast on Ruta 184 through one of the most characterful areas of Yucatán countryside, a region of citrus groves and banana trees, and *milpas* (cornfields) farmed by campesinos.

From Muna, Highway 184 runs for about 40km (25 miles) through the charming little town of **Ticul** to **Oxkutzcab** ("land rich in turkeys"), today known as "The Garden of Yucatán" for the many fruits that are sold in the busy market. A turn south here leads to the **Grutas de Loltún** ❹, giant caverns (daily, entrance by tour only at 9.30am, 11am, 12.30pm, 2pm, 3pm, and 4pm) that stretch underground for almost a mile. This is the oldest Maya site of all, for the earliest evidence of human habitation in the Yucatán was found here, from around 8000 BC, as well as relics from every era since then. Guided tours take about two hours: some of the caverns are

Tip

The town of Ticul, near Oxkutzcab, is famed for the quality of its embroidered *huipiles*; shoes, hats and ceramics (especially the distinctive red clay planters that are in evidence everywhere) are also made here. In most cases you can buy direct from the craftspeople.

A henequen field.

THE HENEQUEN BOOM

At the turn of the 20th century a dizzying economic boom swept the Yucatán, based on the cultivation of henequen. The spiky relative of the agave plant was grown on huge plantations in the countryside to the south of Mérida, and harvested for the sisal fiber to make rope.

This was the oil of another era, creating scores of millionaires. Henequen plantation owners lived like kings, their children educated at the best schools in Europe, their wives dressed in the latest Parisian finery – all attained, however, at the expense of their Maya laborers, who were practically slaves. Henequen was exported and the French bricks and tiles that came back as ballast were used to build mansions for the tycoons in Mérida.

Today, many of the plantation *haciendas* lie abandoned and crumbling, but some are open to visitors, such as the one at Yaxcopoil (www.yaxcopoil.com), which offers tours, a restaurant, and accommodations. A giant Moorish-style double arch on the highway leads to the main house, a series of large, airy rooms full of period furniture; next to the private chapel with its shiny marble floor, an ancient kitchen opens onto a garden of citrus trees and banana plants. Other *haciendas*, such as Temozón between Mérida and Uxmal, or San José Cholul toward Izamal, have now been turned into the Yucatán's most distinctive luxury hotels.

Fact

Maya expert Sylvanus Morley called the Governor's Palace at Uxmal "simply the most magnificent, the most spectacular single building in all pre-Columbian America."

over 45 meters (125ft) high, with bizarre rock formations, strange colors, and changes of temperature. Along the way you can see rocks smoke-blackened by ancient cooking fires, nests of bats, and fortifications built by rebel Maya who sheltered here during the 19th-century War of the Castes.

The Puuc Route road runs west from Loltún, leading to a quartet of ancient sites all bearing the characteristic features of the Puuc style, the most refined of all the Maya architectural styles: elegant arches, plain walls topped by elaborately carved friezes, roll-nosed masks of Chac, the god of rain, and apparently abstract designs that mimic physical features, such as the drum columns imitating the stick-walls of Maya huts. The first site, **Labná** (daily 8am–5pm), has a palace with dozens of rooms and virtually unweathered Chac masks, connected by a *sacbé* or stone causeway to a second area with an observatory and perhaps the finest of all Maya arches, adorned with a stone frieze of geometrical patterns. Nearby **Xlapak** (same hours) is a small site with just one restored building.

The great attraction of **Sayil** (daily 8am–5pm) is its three-level Great Palace, punctuated with short, Puuc-style columns, which towers over a large open space. Many more Chac masks and a stone sky serpent peer from above, and a path leads to other structures, such as the older pyramid known as the *Mirador* ("Watchtower"). The surrounding forest is rich in wildlife – look out for monkeys in the treetops and coati in the undergrowth.

A short distance northwest, **Kabáh** (daily 8am–5pm) is set majestically above two grassy plazas at different levels. The main building, a rectangular palace with 30 rooms, dominates the site, but equally striking is the adjacent *Codz Poop* ("rolled straw mat"), whose west facade is covered with Chac masks. Dozens of other grinning stone faces are jumbled at the foot of the steps. Kabáh's Arch, on the other side of Highway 261, marked the start of what was once a *sacbé* to Uxmal. These highly durable roads were prepared from a type of white earth, *sahcab*, which, when wetted and spread out, quickly solidified.

Serving up fish and seafood tacos.

UXMAL

About 20km (12 miles) north of Kabáh, you come to **Uxmal** ❺ (daily 8am–5pm), one of the most impressive ruins in the Maya world and a Unesco World Heritage Site. Uxmal was the most important Puuc center, reaching its peak between 800 and 1000, and its architecture is stunning. In 1840, the US explorer John Lloyd Stephens compared the **Palacio del Gobernador** Ⓐ (Governor's Palace) favorably with Grecian, Roman, and Egyptian art. "The designs are strange and incomprehensible, very elaborate, sometimes grotesque, but often simple, tasteful, beautiful," he wrote. The palace, 100 meters (330ft) wide, sits atop a hill with an impressive facade. The Puuc style of building was to face rubble-filled walls with cement and cover the whole with limestone mosaic panels, in this case 20,000 of them.

To the north of the palace is the 39-meter (128ft) high **Pyramid of the Magician**, legendarily built in one night by an *alux*, a spirit that was the son of a witch, but actually the product of several generations of builders (Uxmal means "three times built"). Visitors are no longer allowed to climb up its precipitously steep steps to enjoy the view, but you can still appreciate its dramatic structure from the bottom. The unusual rounded contours of this pyramid, according to one story, were created so that the wind god would not hurt himself on any sharp edges when he blew over the structure.

Immediately west is the 74-room quadrangle referred to as the **Cuadrángulo de las Monjas** Ⓑ (Nunnery Quadrangle), because its form reminded the Spanish priest Father Diego López de Cogolludo, who named Uxmal's main buildings, of a convent. Though made up of four separate buildings, it forms an elegant ensemble; the entire complex is built on an elevated man-made platform and typifies the Puuc architectural style, which is based on the Maya hut, the *na*, with its wooden walls and high-peaked thatch roof. The Quadrangle was built between about 895 and 910, and seems to have been a special space for government business and public rituals

Eat

El Príncipe Tutul Xiu restaurant in Maní (named after a Maya chief) specializes in a local delicacy, Poc-chuc, a tasty pork loin marinated in bitter orange juice.

Detail from the ruins at Sayil, one of the Maya sites displaying the Puuc architectural style.

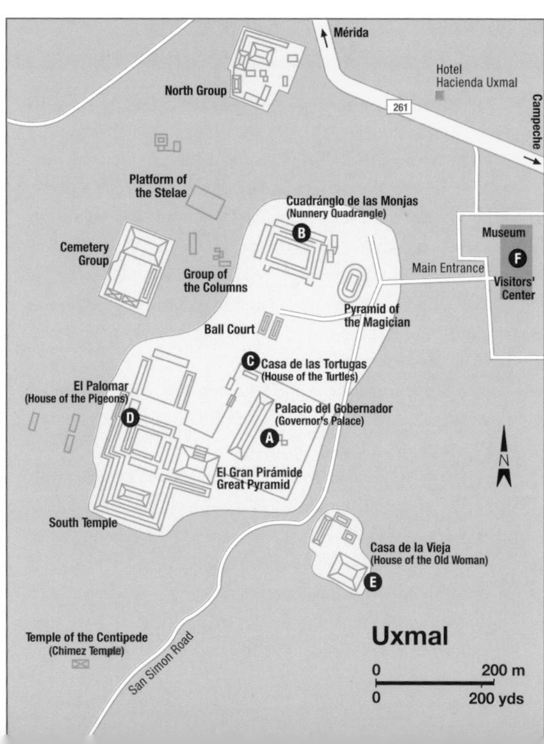

Quote

"Maya thought did not conceive of any empty spaces. Each corner and every moment was inhabited by men, gods, animals, and plants in an order strictly hierarchical."

Dzibilchaltún Museum

for the lords of the Uxmal. To the south of the Nunnery is a ball court, beyond which, sharing the Governor's Palace platform, is **Casa de las Tortugas** C (House of the Turtles), which gets its name from the turtle carvings on the cornice, an animal associated with rain in Maya legend. The rain god Chac was of course significant in this dry area, and his image in stucco masks is ubiquitous, at one point even taking the form of a doorway.

West of the pyramid is **El Palomar** D (House of the Pigeons), so named because the holes in its lofty roofcomb suggested a dovecote to Father Cogolludo. Away to one side, southeast of the Governor's Palace, is the pyramid called the **Casa de la Vieja** E (House of the Old Woman), which Maya legend avers was the house of the sorcerer-mother of the dwarf magician who built Uxmal.

The **Visitors' Center** F at the entrance includes a shop, museum, and restaurant. The 45-minute sound and light show is at 8pm (Nov–Mar 7pm); an English translation is provided through headphones. Regular buses (on average five times daily) leaving from TAME terminal on 69 street connect the site with Mérida.

TRAGIC MANÍ

The Puuc route and the Route of the Convents intersect at Oxkutzcab, with the latter itinerary heading north to **Maní** 6, where, in 1562, the bishop of the Yucatán, Father Diego de Landa, burned a pile of Maya sacred texts and idols. Maní was the first of all the Franciscan monasteries in the Yucatán, completed in 1549, and its massive gray stone cloister and well – built over a *cenote* – are enormously impressive.

Northwest, on Highway 18 back to Mérida, is **Mayapán** (daily 8am–5pm), considered the last Maya city, with its **Temple of Kukulcán** resembling a smaller copy of the Castillo-Pyramid at Chichén Itzá. From around 1250 Mayápan was the "capital" of Postclassic Yucatán, the center of a confederacy that included nearly all the peninsula's communities and their lords. However, this system fell apart when the Cocom dynasty, principal lords of Mayapán,

The remains of one of the four Maya codices still in existence.

ERASING MAYA HISTORY

Northeast of Oxkutzcab is the small town of **Maní**, whose sorrowful name in Maya means "the place where everything has stopped."

In 1562 it was at Maní that Father Diego de Landa gathered together hundreds of "idols" and all he could find – but could not read – of the Maya manuscripts and burned them as "works of the devil," destroying virtually the whole of Maya written culture in a single act. Landa had himself taken charge of instructing the sons of prominent local families in Christianity, and when he discovered that many were still performing old rituals in secret he was enraged. Today, there are only four Maya codices or bark books in existence.

As first head of the Franciscans and second bishop of the province, Diego de Landa (1524–79) hunted down and punished participants in native rites. Nevertheless, Landa admired the virtues of courage and willpower which the Maya shared with Christianity, and he was awed with their earlier accomplishments. "This country, although it is a good land, is not at present such as it appears to have been in the prosperous time, when so many and such remarkable buildings were built." He went on to write the *Relación de las Cosas de Yucatán* (Account of the Affairs of Yucatán), which, ironically, is an essential source for what we now know about the Maya.

were deposed by an uprising led by the Xiu of Maní, who claimed descent from the lords of Uxmal. According to the Maya chronicle the *Chilam Balam*, this happened in 1441.

These inter-Maya struggles were a major factor in enabling the invading Spaniards finally to take control of the Yucatán in the following century, after 20 years of trying: the first Maya lord to accept Spanish rule was Tutul Xiu of Maní, while the last to be subdued was Nachi Cocom, lord of Sotuta. A great deal has been discovered at Mayapán in recent years, including fine stucco carvings and remains of fresco paintings. The round **Observatory** is a smaller version of the one at Chichén Itzá.

Continuing north, a few other stops along the route are worth the pilgrim's time. At **Telchaquillo** a staircase in the town park leads to an attractive *cenote* and the Franciscan church whose facade was worked by Maya artisans. There's another *cenote* with fascinating caves at **Tecoh**, where a former convent, the Virgin of the Ascension, is based on what may have been a Maya pyramid. And at **Acanceh** the 16th-century Franciscan church adjoins the Plaza de las Tres Culturas, which has one of the oldest Maya pyramids in the Yucatán, begun before AD 300.

FROM MÉRIDA TO THE NORTH COAST

Heading north from Mérida on the Progreso road, just outside the city a road turns east that leads 3km (2 miles) to the ruins of **Dzibilchaltún** – meaning "where there is writing on flat rocks" – site of one of the oldest Maya settlements, continually occupied from as early as 500 BC until the Spanish Conquest. A lot of restoration work ongoing here, and thousands of structures, all joined by broad causeways, have been mapped. Around 20,000 people once lived here, with an economy based on fishing and salt panning.

On one side of Dzibilchaltún is the **Cenote Xlacah**, explored by divers in the 1950s, which is over 44 meters (144ft) deep and has yielded up thousands of Maya sacrificial offerings. It

Tip

Many Meridano families only use their holiday homes on the north coast during July and August, and on some holiday weekends. The rest of the time they can often be rented at very good rates, and many Canadian "snowbirds" spend their winters here.

Dzibilchaltún ruins.

Drink

One of the Yucatán's most deliciously refreshing specialties is *agua de Jamaica* – hibiscus water, an infusion made from flowers, best drunk with ice and mixed with a little lemon.

was also an ideal town watering-hole, and today the *cenote* is open to the public for swimming until 4pm; it can get very busy at weekends.

To the right of the site entrance is a 9.5-meter (30ft) pyramid with stairs on two sides; to the left a walkway leads to an excellent museum (closed for refurbishment at the time of research). Beyond the elaborately carved stones from a ball court and other Maya artifacts another gallery deals with post-Conquest history, including the 19th-century Caste War. On the east side of the site an impressive *sacbé* path leads to the **Templo de las Siete Muñecas** (Temple of the Seven Dolls), a low structure with a small temple with doors on both sides, through which the rising sun strikes directly in a line along the *sacbé* at dawn on the spring and autumn equinoxes, March 21 and September 21. The seven clay dolls for which it was named currently reside in a museum in Mexico City.

Contemporary visitors might marvel at such ruins spread over immense areas but, as an exhibit at the museum explains: "Maya communities are today thought to have been garden cities with large plantings in the interior to sustain a large concentration of inhabitants."

Strolling past the Thousand Columns, Chichén Itzá.

Continuing north, Yucatán state's port of **Progreso** ❼ lies 36km (22 miles) from Mérida. The highway into town becomes Calle 80, just east of the famous long wharf the **Muelle de Altura**, the actual harbor of Progreso, a 6km (4-mile) concrete pier built to compensate for the shallow sea. At weekends half of Mérida hits Progreso's beachfront, which is lined with great seafood restaurants.

East of Progreso, on the long road along the sandbar dividing the Gulf from the coastal lagoons, are a string of villages popular with Meridanos as locations for holiday beach houses. The classiest are near the little fishing village of **Chicxulub**, thought to be the location of a crater left by a meteorite 65 million years ago, which may have led to the extinction of the dinosaurs (see page 285). Along the way, on the landward side, there are wonderful opportunities for spotting water birds.

Not far before the larger village of Telchac a road turns inland for 3.7km (2 miles) past salt flats to a small Maya site at **Xcambo**, or X'tampu as some signs say (the Maya X is pronounced "sh"). As well as a typical Maya plaza, it has an early Catholic chapel built next to one of its pyramids. A further 60km (27 miles) take you to **Motúl**, a neat and tidy little town. Horse-drawn *calesas* roam the streets, and the tower of the convent (adjoining the distinctive church) offers fine views. In the market, women wearing *huipiles* sell bags of *nanzes*, a grape-sized yellow fruit that tastes like a soft apple and is used for jams and desserts. In season you will find fruit drinks of *pitahaya*, a red peach-sized fruit that ripens midsummer on the spiky cereus cactus. Pitahaya juice mixed with fresh lime and mineral water makes a very special mocktail.

INLAND TO IZAMAL

Turn off the Mérida–Valladolid Highway 180 after 26km (16 miles), near the village of Tixcobob, to follow signs to **Aké** ❽, one of the most unusual Maya ruins. Already a significant site before AD 300, Aké was occupied until the 15th century: its main buildings have a unique style, especially one huge platform ascended by 27 steps and topped with 30 massive stone pillars that once supported a palm roof. Equally strange is that a later village and henequen *hacienda* were built among and sometimes on top of the ruins. The *hacienda* was still working, and churning out reels of straw-colored rope and twine, in 2002, when it was destroyed by Hurricane Isidore.

A short distance farther east is **Izamal** ❾, known as the *ciudad dorada* or golden city because of the ochre-yellow color of its old houses. This is perhaps the most charming of all the Yucatán's colonial towns. Unhurried, historic, and visually attractive, it makes a delightful base for a couple of days and has some charming hotels and B&Bs. At its heart is the largest of all the Spanish monasteries in the region, painted yellow like the town, **San Antonio de Padua**, begun on the orders of Father Diego de Landa in 1549. The Franciscans made Izamal their headquarters because it was already a sacred place for the Maya, with 16 pyramids, and built the new monastery on the largest of them, a giant platform known as the *Paphol'chac* or "Home of Chac." Its size can be gauged from that of the *atrio* or porticoed square in front of the monastery, the largest church square in Mexico. At the foot of the steps leading up to the *atrio* from the plaza below a plaque commemorates the visit of "Papa Juan Pablo II" (Pope John Paul) in 1993. The Franciscans did not manage to destroy all Izamal's pyramids, and a few blocks north one can still walk up the huge **Kinich Kak Mo** pyramid for a view over the town.

Back on the main square, opposite the monastery, an old town house has been attractively restored as the **Centro Cultural y Artesanal** (tel: 988 954 1012; Mon–Sat 9am–6pm, Sun

Fact

The ancient Maya fasted and abstained from sex during the crucial equinox periods, still celebrated today at Chichén Itzá.

Chichén Itzá's Pyramid of Kukulcán (El Castillo).

Tip

Allow yourself at least one whole day to look around all of Chichén Itzá; it is an enormous site and gets very hot and crowded by midday, but your entry ticket allows you to go in and out as often as you want.

until 5pm), with a beautiful display of folk art and a shop with high-quality craftwork. Maps available at the tourist office on the plaza will direct you to many other craft workshops around the town, including hammock-makers and mask shops.

CHICHÉN ITZÁ

Just off Highway 180 about 116km (72 miles) east of Mérida is **Chichén Itzá** ⑩ (from the Yucatec Maya *chi* = mouths; *chen* = wells; *Itza* = the people believed to have settled here), the best known of all Maya sites. It is a Unesco World Heritage Site and was also voted one of the "New Seven Wonders of the World" in 2007.

Curiously, Chichén Itzá is a very atypical Maya site. Its largest buildings – the Pyramid of Kukulcán, the Temple of the Warriors – are very "un-Maya" in style, and much more similar to buildings in central Mexico. It used to be thought that Chichén Itzá had initially been a purely Maya city, which around the year 1000 was taken over by warlike invaders from central Mexico called the Toltecs, who were later replaced by another non-Maya people, the Itzaes. However, as more and more of the blanks in Maya history have been partially filled in, this theory has been largely discredited, as the successive invasions do not seem to match with any established dates. Instead, Chichén Itzá seems from its beginnings to have been a mixed community, combining Maya traditions with those of migrants from central Mexico (see page 273). It grew up late in the Classic Maya era, around 700, but from around 800 dominated the north-central Yucatán for several centuries. The city declined more slowly than other Maya centers, and only finally disintegrated as a political entity around 1200. Nevertheless, the memory of the power of Chichén was such that it has occupied a central role in Yucatecan folklore.

The site was first brought to the attention of the outside world by John Lloyd Stephens in 1840. His account, and the detailed drawings of Frederick Catherwood, prompted further explorations. In 1904 the American consul in Mérida, Edward Thompson, bought the site and began rather amateur excavations.

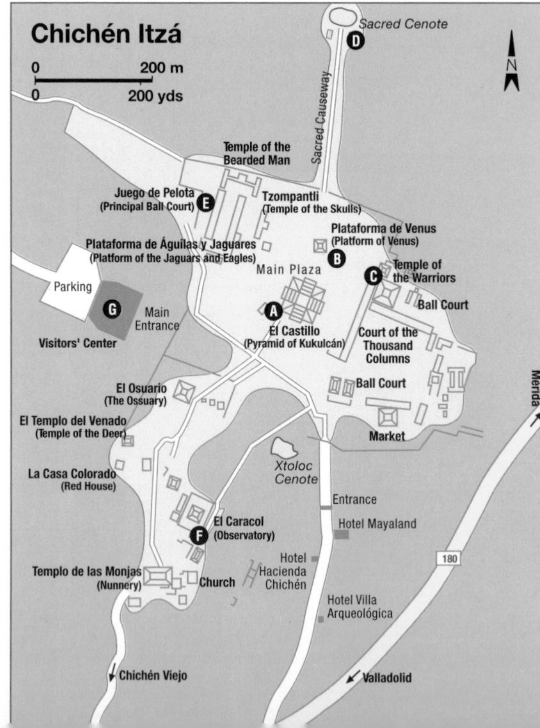

El Caracol (observatory), Chichén Itzá.

He described Chichén Itzá as having "scattered carved and square stones in countless thousands and fallen columns by the hundreds... Facades, though gray and haggard with age and seamed by time, sustain the claim that Chichén Itzá is one of the world's greatest monuments of antiquity."

Thompson was particularly interested in the Sacred *Cenote*, drawn by stories of virgin sacrifice, and imported dredging equipment (now on view in the site museum) which brought up a vast collection of offerings: incense statues, jade, amber, gold, and engraved metal discs, but, to his disappointment, only a few human skeletons, some of whom may have just fallen in.

EXPLORING THE SITE

As one enters Chichén the view is dominated by the 24-meter (80ft) high **Pyramid of Kukulcán (El Castillo) A**. It represents the Maya calendar, with four 91-step staircases plus a single step at the top, adding up to 365. Eighteen terraces divide the nine levels that represent the 18 months, each 20 days long. The nine terraces symbolize the nine underground worlds. Each side has 52 panels, representing the 52-year cosmic cycle, the point at which the Mayas' two calendars coincided and they considered that a cycle ended, only to begin anew.

The giant carved serpents beside the great stairway are picked out by sunlight at sunset during the spring equinox, interpreted as a time to sow the crops, just as the snake's apparent ascension of the pyramid at the fall equinox signified harvest time. Thousands of visitors come to see this phenomenon – known as the "Descent (or Ascent) of Kukulcán," from the Maya name for the plumed serpent god Quetzalcoatl – on March 21 and September 21 every year. The illusion, which lasts more than three hours, is imitated more briefly every night during the *Luz y Sonido* (Light and Sound) show (Nov–Mar 7pm, Apr–Oct 8pm).

Due to pressure of numbers, sadly, visitors to Chichén are no longer allowed to try what used to be a highlight of any visit – the climb up to the top of the great Pyramid. From the

Fact

The conquistador Francisco de Montejo tried to create a stronghold amid the ruins of Chichén Itzá in 1531, but was driven away by the Maya.

Detail of the Temple of the Warriors.

DÉSIRÉ CHARNAY

One of the most influential early explorers of Maya sites was the Frenchman Désiré Charnay. It was he who first photographed Palenque, Uxmal, and Chichén Itzá, and these superb photographs and lithographs led the way for the first scientific archeological expeditions.

Charnay first became interested in the Maya ruins when he heard of Stephens and Catherwood's trips to the region while he was teaching in New Orleans. A few years later, in 1857, he succeeded in persuading the French education ministry to pay for a lengthy trip to take photographs and papier-mâché casts of the Maya civilization. By 1860, using the immensely cumbersome collodion wet plate method, he managed to complete a volume of 47 plates published as *Cités et ruines américaines*, which became famous in France and throughout Europe.

It was only 20 years later, in 1880, that Charnay returned to the Maya region. By now, the photographic process had been simplified, and he was able to take many photographs, not only of monuments but of the local people and scenes of the exuberant jungles of southern Mexico. These were published as engravings in magazines and books back in France, and were a great contribution to spreading knowledge of the region. A flamboyant figure, Charnay also made sure that his own face and distinctive moustache appeared in many pictures.

Tip

A sign outside the cathedral at Valladolid asks visitors to "Avoid child exploitation. Do not buy anything from them. Do not give them money. Encourage them to go to school. They deserve a better future."

upper temple a stairway – also now normally closed off – leads down to an inner sanctuary, part of an early pyramid around which the later one was built, with an altar in the shape of a bright-red jaguar with jade spots, eyes and teeth. There is also a Chac-Mool figure, reclining and holding a shallow bowl on its chest, which held the heart of many a human victim. The Chac-Mool, messenger of the gods and provider of rain, was a ubiquitous image at Chichén Itzá and many later Postclassic Maya sites, because water was in such short supply.

The enormous growth in our knowledge of the ancient Maya, including the decipherment of glyph inscriptions, has revealed much more about their warlike customs, and the role of sacrifice. Maya cities waged war with their neighbors both to demand tribute and to seize prisoners for sacrifice. It was believed that it was essential to "feed" the spirit world with human blood, to ensure the balance of nature and the favor of the gods. In Classic Maya cities kings and their families themselves took part in sacrifice, drawing blood from their genitals or tongues which was soaked up in bark paper that was burned to carry the offerings to the gods. In Chichén Itzá, it seems that sacrifices were not carried out a few at a time, as was usual in older Maya cities, but in large numbers, a practice common in central Mexico and one that horrified the Spaniards when they saw it among the Aztecs.

The High Priest's Grave, El Osuario.

Centers of sacrifice at Chichén were the three small platforms in the great plaza to the north of the main pyramid, the **Plataforma de Venus** B (with stairways at each side guarded by feathered serpents), the **Plataforma de Águilas y Jaguares** (with relief carvings of eagles and jaguars holding human hearts), and the **Tzompantli**, from which human heads were hung. Around it are carved grinning stone skulls in horizontal rows, on all four sides.

The east side of the plaza is filled by the **Temple of the Warriors** C, another of the most imposing buildings at Chichén. This is another that you are no longer allowed to climb up, to see the most famous of all the Chac-Mool sculptures at Chichén Itzá. The temple takes its name from the rows of columns in front of it, carved with over 200 separate images of warriors, priests, and other figures of Chichén, each one different, almost like a "picture gallery" of the city. The Warriors' columns form a corner with the plainer pillars of the huge quadrangle called the **Court of the Thousand Columns**, which probably served as a market and center for public business in Chichén Itzá. Like the Warriors' columns, the pillars were probably once topped by wood and palm roofs.

A *sacbé*-style path to the left of the Warriors temple leads through woods to the **Sacred *Cenote*** D, 60 meters (197ft) in diameter and 35 meters (115ft) deep. Whether or not the legends of sacrifices here are true, it is a wonderfully mysterious, deep pool in the rock.

THE BALL GAME

The enormous **Juego de Pelota** Ⓔ (96 meters/314ft long, 30 meters/98ft wide) or ball court of Chichén Itzá, completed in the year 864, is the largest ancient ball court in Mesoamerica, and on a vastly different scale from the courts usually found in Maya cities. On either side it has stone rings high on the walls, and it seems likely players had to get the solid latex ball through them to score, which added extra pressure even to the usual difficulty of the Mesomerican ball game. In all forms of the game, players were not allowed to use their hands, but in the older Maya game they had only to get the ball past the opponent and out the far end of the court.

"They struck (the ball) with any part of their body, as it happened, or they could most conveniently," recorded one 16th-century observer quoted by Totten in his *Maya Architecture*, "and sometimes he touched it with any other part but his hip, which was looked upon among them as the greatest Dexterity; and to this effect that the ball might rebound the better, they fastened a piece of stiff leather on their Hips." The carved panels around the base of the court show images associated with the game, including one depicting a player (the winning captain?) holding a ritual knife and a decapitated head, for the game was also inseparable from beliefs on death and rebirth.

There are several other structures around the site, particularly to the south of the great plaza. **El Osuario**, a 10-meter (33ft) tall pyramid that seems almost a "model" for the later Castillo, contains an opulent tomb, the origin of its alternative name "The High Priest's Grave"; **La Casa Colorada**, the Red House, was named for the red paint on its doorway mural. **El Caracol** Ⓕ, the fascinating observatory of Chichén Itzá, is a domed, circular tower shaped like a snail (hence its name), with roof slits through which astronomical observations could be made with remarkable precision. Farther south again, the complex the Spaniards called **Las Monjas** (the Nunnery) is purely Maya in style, with fantastically elaborate carved friezes, made-up stone Chac

The pool at Cenote Samula, Valladolid.

Las Monjas (the Nunnery), Chichén Itzá.

Fact

Roadside offerings can occasionally be seen around the Yucatán, left by farmers for the aluxes – Maya "gnomes" – who are presumed to help look after their crops (and who may steal their tools if they are not appeased).

masks and mythological *bacabs* symbolized by snails, turtles, armadillos, and crabs – the creation spirits reputed to hold up the sky.

At the entrance to the ruins (daily 8am–5pm) is a large **Visitors' Center** **G**, with shops, restaurants, and a museum. Chichén Itzá is inundated with tourist buses every day of the year, but regular buses from Mérida and Valladolid also pass the site or stop in the nearby village of **Piste**, on the highway 1.5km (2 miles) before the site, about US$2 by taxi. In addition to the main entrance, there is another entrance farther east beside the larger hotels. Other accommodations are available in Piste.

THE CAVES OF BALANKANCHÉ

Five kilometres (3 miles) east of Chichén Itzá are the **Grutas de Balankanché**, another of the spectacular cave systems that have been visited and used by the Maya for millennia. A guide accompanies visitors through the caves, up and down 320 irregular steps over a distance of some 900 meters (3,000ft). It is a hot and sweaty route past stalactites, stalagmites, and dank pools, the ceiling sometimes closing in, forcing you to crouch, and at other times soaring up to cathedral-like heights (daily, guided tours in Spanish at 9am, noon, 2pm, and 4pm, and English at 11am, 1pm, and 3pm).

Discovered accidentally in 1959, the caves were reopened with a special ceremony, *Tzicult'an ti yunti yunts'loob* ("a respectful message to the gods"), and traditional Chac rain ceremonies still take place in times of drought. A wooden altar is constructed with an arch of leaves and baked bread, and other food offerings are placed on beds of sacred *ceiba* leaves, arranged in specific patterns. The shaman faces east while offering prayers and food to the gods. This is then distributed and eaten, along with a drink of *balche*, made from water, honey, cinnamon, and anise, a slightly intoxicating beverage. Small boys squat at each table leg making croaking sounds to imitate frogs.

A number of small villages, each with multiple sets of *topes* (speed bumps), punctuate the otherwise monotonous landscape between the caves and Valladolid.

The Paseo de Montejo, Mérida's version of Paris's Champs-Elysées.

VALLADOLID

Valladolid **11** (population over 80,000), some 40km (25 miles) east of Chichén Itzá, was once a Maya center called Zaci, but was taken over by the Spaniards in 1545. Its attractively calm feel today belies its dramatic history, as Valladolid was the scene of a historic massacre of most of its white citizens during the War of the Castes, the great Maya uprising that began nearby in 1847 (see page 279).

This bitterness is scarcely evident in modern Valladolid, but the city's colonial atmosphere is maintained by its well-preserved churches and mansions. The convent-church of **San Bernardino Sisal** is one of the oldest churches in the Yucatán (1552), and sits at the end of a row of colonial houses leading from the center, Calle 41-A or the *Calzada de los Frailes* (Street of the Friars). The **Museo San Roque**, just east of the plaza on Calle 41, has an engaging display of local relics (daily 9am–9pm; free). Valladolid still has its town *cenote*, **Cenote Zaci** (daily 8am–6pm) at the junction of calles 36 and 39, which is fine for a refreshing dip, though its waters are a little murky. Nearby, however, there is one of the great must-sees of the Yucatán, **Cenote Dzitnup**, 7km (4.5 miles) west and well signposted off the highway. Beyond a few souvenir stands, a narrow passageway leads down into a fabulous, arching cavern, a natural cathedral above a perfect, turquoise-blue pool lit by a narrow shaft of light from the cave roof.

EK-BALAM AND RÍO LAGARTOS

Highway 295 runs straight north from Valladolid to the coast. After about 18km (11 miles) it passes a turning on the right for **Ek-Balam** ⓬. This was one of the Yucatán's most neglected Maya sites, until excavations in 1998–2000 revealed extraordinary treasures, including some stupendous sculpture and stucco carving. Its pyramid-platforms are unusually tall and steep: the largest, Structure 1, has halfway up it **El Trono** ("The Throne"), a huge temple entrance in the form of a monster-mouth – its teeth circle the floor – surrounded by some of the finest Maya carving in, again, a unique style. There is also a curious spiral-shaped temple, a large ball court, wonderful stucco frieze and a beautifully carved stela to take in at the site (daily 8am–5pm).

Beyond Ek-Balam the road rolls on through Yucatán state's second-largest city, **Tizimin**, center of cattle-ranching in the state. From there, after another 53km (33 miles) it reaches **Río Lagartos** ⓭, 103km (64 miles) from Valladolid. The coastal region here is now a biosphere reserve, famous for the thousands of flamingos that nest there. Named "Crocodile River" by the Spaniards for the alligators that once infested the area (but are now rare), Río Lagartos is a rather scruffy fishing village with narrow streets and multihued houses on an estuary rife with egrets, herons, white ibis, spoonbills, and flamingos. As well as guides to the lagoons it has enjoyable restaurants, and there are decent, inexpensive hotels both there and in the prettier village of San Felipe, another 12km (7 miles) west.

Flamingos arrive in April in the lagoon to make nests, lay eggs in June, and depart in September for Celestún and other estuaries. Turtles also use the beaches annually for laying their eggs. Boat trips leave Río Lagartos early in the mornings to visit the flamingos (if traveling independently, get there the night before to arrange a trip). There is also good tarpon fishing off the coast.

A blue heron at Río Lagartos Biosphere Reserve.

Bacalar Lake.

THE CARIBBEAN COAST

Dominated by the mega-resort of Cancún, the Yucatán's Caribbean coastline also contains tranquil island retreats, and spectacular diving and snorkeling off the coral reef.

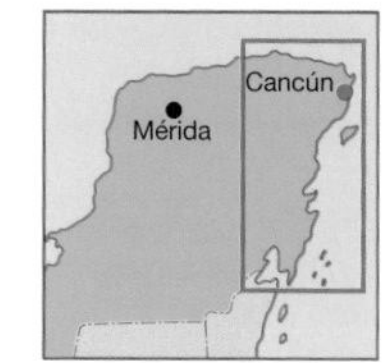

Mexico's Caribbean coast is best known for **Cancún** ⓮, the country's purpose-built global resort with its enormous hotels lining dazzling beaches, and the 130km (80-mile) strip of coast to the south now known as the *Riviera Maya*, with more fabulous beaches and resorts of different sizes running all the way down to the spectacular Maya ruins of Tulum. Tourists flood to Cancún and the Riviera year-round, drawn by their turquoise waters and white sands, the range of outdoor leisure activities, and glitzy nightlife. The sun-soaked coastline offers numerous attractions: tranquil islands such as Isla Mujeres, fascinating archeological sites such as Tulum, Cobá, and Kohunlich, and pristine wildlife reserves such as Sian Ka'an in the south.

CANCÚN'S HISTORICAL ROOTS

In the 1840s, US writer and explorer John Lloyd Stephens noted: "In the afternoon we steered for the mainland, passing the island of Kancune, a barren strip of land with sand hills and stone buildings visible upon it."

The buildings were some Maya sites which, against all odds, have survived: the major one **El Rey** Ⓐ, now stands beside the Hilton Hotel golf course. Like Tulum to the south, most of El Rey dates from the Postclassic era of Maya civilization just before the Spanish Conquest, when it was one of several communities around the coast that prospered thanks to the trade route between central Mexico and Central America. Its Spanish name refers to a large stucco head found there, which looked like a king to its first discoverers. Though small, El Rey is an interesting site, with a neat plaza where one can easily imagine Maya merchants coming and going. In the lagoon nearby it is still possible to observe exotic wading birds and sometimes even crocodiles.

Opened in 2012 in a stunning modern building, Museo Maya de Cancún (Av.

Main Attractions

Cancún
Isla Mujeres
Cozumel
Puerto Morelos
Playa del Carmen
Xcaret
Akumal
Tulum
Sian Ka'an Reserve
Cobá
Costa Maya
Xcalak

Maps on pages 304, 328

The coast is popular with scuba-divers.

Tip

Cancún's big nightclubs usually have a high, all-in-one entry charge of between US$30–70, with all drinks included – although waiters expect hefty tips too. To cut costs, take advantage of happy hours and girls-go-free nights.

Kulkulkán km 16.5; Tue–Sun 9am–6pm) is also must for all Maya aficionados. Its wonderful exhibits come from across the Maya world including Palenque, Chichén Itzá, and Comalcalco. The admission ticket also gives access to the adjacent archeological site of San Miguelito.

Modern Cancún was born in 1969, after the government agency Fonatur was set up to identify potential new tourist sites, draw master plans, and solicit investment. At first there was only jungle here, and a narrow sand strip enclosing the brackish Laguna de Nichupté. A tiny village at the northwestern end of the number 7-shaped island was transformed into a modern town to house all the workers needed to service the big hotels – the first of which opened in 1971 – and bridges connected the island to the mainland at both ends. Building has continued ever since, with ever-bigger hotels replacing the first ones of the 1970s. The population is now around 800,000, and around 6.2 million visitors arrive every year, from the US, Europe, and increasingly from the rest of the world too.

CANCÚN'S HOTEL STRIP

For those in search of a lazily luxurious vacation, sunbathing on a soft white beach and swimming in glorious turquoise waters (or your own pool), Cancún is tailor-made. Honeymooners are not the only people who check into a world-class hotel and rarely leave it. All the hotels are huge and, although next to each other, getting between them can be such a trek it hardly seems worthwhile to go visiting. Most hotels are self-contained, with restaurants, pools, beachfront, discos, lobby bars with soaring atriums, and shopping arcades, and more and more operate on an all-inclusive plan. The hotel strip has just one long street, Boulevard Kukulcán, with no street numbers but kilometer indicators (counting from the north end) to help locate addresses.

These monumental resort hotels have been built in every conceivable architectural style, from the verdant lobby of the **Gran Meliá Cancún** at Km 16.5, whose leafy plant tendrils drift over the balconies to create a lush

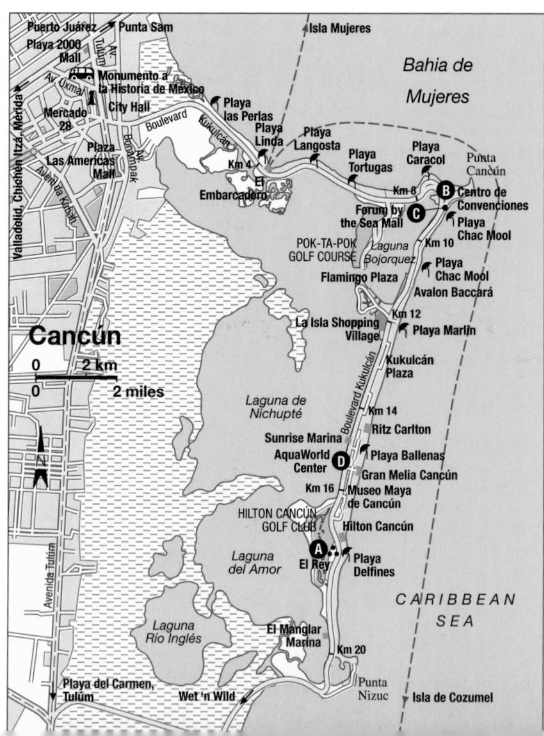

Heron at Isla Holbox.

tropical atmosphere, to the modernist landmark **Dreams Cancún Resort** at Km 9.5 with a design clearly inspired by the sloping walls of Maya pyramids.

Just before the halfway point where the boulevard turns sharp right is the **Centro de Convenciones** Ⓑ (Km 9; http://cancunicc.com), the scene of concerts and other cultural and business events. Across the boulevard from the Convention Center is another very important part of Cancún, its main nightlife hub (at Km 9.5), around the **Forum by the Sea Mall** Ⓒ, with huge franchises of chains like the **Hard Rock Café**.

Outside, crowds stand in line every night outside the giant multi-space nightclubs – some of the world's biggest – like **The City** and the **Coco Bongo**, offering a choice of music, awe-inspiring light shows and live acts, non-stop energy, and fantastically efficient air conditioning. The lines are longest when all the US and Canadian college kids descend on Cancún for Spring Break, and every bar seems to have a wet T-shirt contest.

SHOPPING PLAZAS

Most shopping malls are called plazas in Cancún. Some are upscale, such as **Flamingo Plaza**, with its Maya flavor (Km 11.5; tel: 998 883 2855; www.flamingo.com.mx), and the huge, 350-shop **Kukulcán Plaza** (Km 13; tel: 998 193 0160; www.kukulcanplaza.mx). The classiest shopping venue of all is probably **La Isla Shopping Village** (Km 12.5; tel: 998 883 5025; www.laislacancun.mx), which rather than just a mall is actually a little web of pedestrian "streets" on an artificial island part-open to the skies, and which hosts international fashion brands as well as upscale restaurants, a less expensive food court, a "river walk," souvenir shops, and an aquarium. Other, older malls are frankly tacky, such as **Plaza La Fiesta**, opposite the Centro de Convenciones, where tuneless mariachi bands play outside all-purpose stores selling overpriced souvenirs and garish T-shirts.

Well down the boulevard at Km 15.2 is the very popular **AquaWorld** Ⓓ center (tel: 998 689 1013; daily

Concrete and turquoise waters at Cancún.

Tip

Passenger ferries to Isla Mujeres run from Puerto Juárez just north of Cancún, and from three locations in the Hotel Zone (El Embarcadero Pier, El Caracol, and La Tortuga beaches), operated by Ultramar; there are daily boats running usually between 6am–11.30pm (from Puerto Juárez) or 9.30am–8.30pm (Hotel Zone). The trip takes 20 minutes. Car ferries run from Punta Sam, about 8km (5 miles) north of Cancún, with seven boats a day (Mon–Sat) 7.15am–8.15pm (from Isla, 6.15am–7.15pm) and three on Sunday. Check www.ultramarferry.com and www.maritimaislamujeres.com for details.

7am–8pm; charges vary; https://aquaworld.com.mx), where you can try out some snorkeling, diving, and fishing, or take tours on or under the enticing waters of Laguna de Nichupté by wave-runner, kayak, paddlewheeler, or miniature submarine.

DOWNTOWN CANCÚN

Travelers less addicted to glitz, or maybe on a budget, stay in Ciudad Cancún (downtown), in one of the inexpensive hotels near reliable Sanborns and the bus station where Avenida Uxmal meets the main drag, tree-shaded Avenida Tulum. Explore the side streets for authentic restaurants. Between the **Monumento a la Historia de México** (Mexican History Monument) at the bus station end and the **Monumento Diálogo Norte–Sur** (dedicated to North–South dialog) is everything a visitor might need: markets, shops, money-changers, hotels, bars, and tourist offices. Buses on the R-1 route, conveniently marked Hotel Zone or Downtown, run continually from downtown all the way along the wide boulevard, turning back at the southern end. Taxis are everywhere, and because of the distances in Cancún are often indispensable. Depending on the company, rates may be fixed (site taxis) or negotiable (usually hailed on the street).; tariffs are worked out on a zonal system, with rates around downtown about US$3, while downtown to Km 9.5 (for nightlife) is around US$10.

La Isla Shopping Village.

ISLA MUJERES

A very different atmosphere can still be found on **Isla Mujeres** ⓯, about 8km (5 miles) long, with only two main roads and nowhere more than 1km (0.5 miles) wide. Some have suggested the name "Island of Women" derives from 17th-century pirates who kept their women sequestered here, but it was actually given by some of the first Spaniards who arrived on the island because of the many female idols they saw honoring Ixchel, the Maya goddess of fertility. At the island's southern tip are the tiny ruins of the Temple of Ixchel. Usually identified as the benefactor of weavers and healers as well as women, her male counterpart was Itzamná, the sun god who was patron of the arts and sciences. Like many Maya gods Ixchel had an unfavorable side, and was often depicted as an evil old lady.

Many of today's Isla visitors spend their time on the compact town beach, **Playa Norte**, where the water is very shallow, or snorkeling a couple of miles south in **El Garrafón Reef Park** (winter daily 9am–5.30pm; www.garrafon.com), a natural rock pool. However, this is often teeming with people and now has little coral left, and there's better easy snorkeling around the reefs just offshore. Taxis run all around the island, but the most popular way to get around on Isla is by renting a golf cart. There are rental shops all around Isla town. You can drive around by cart or take a boat trip to visit the **Tortugranja** turtle sanctuary (tel: 998 888 0705; daily 9am–5pm) at Sac Bajo on the west side of the island, or continue down to **Punta Sur** at the southern tip of Isla for great views.

In the center of the island is what remains of **Hacienda Mundaca** (charge), the former mansion of Fermín Mundaca, a 19th-century slave trader who is said to have been spurned by a local *señorita* and left the house he had built for her unattended to fall into disrepair. Mundaca's unoccupied tomb in the island cemetery is decorated with a skull and crossbones and bears the enigmatic inscription: *Como eres, yo fui. Como soy, tú serás* (What you are, I was. What I am, you will be).

Isla Mujeres is the best scuba-diving and snorkeling center close to Cancún. At **Los Manchones**, a reef off the southern tip, crystal-clear waters flow around a 3-meter (10ft) bronze crucifix, placed there in 1994 to mark the 140th anniversary of the island becoming a township. It was sponsored by ecologists hoping to inspire conservation. "In other words," wryly notes writer Pancho Shiell, "they don't want tourists to batter and ruin Los Manchones like they did El Garrafón." The **Cave of the Sleeping Sharks**, in deep waters off the southeast coast, is so called because sharks lie there immobile for hours at a time, a rare phenomenon explained by the fact that an underground river emerges into the sea there, and the sharks "enjoy" the mix of salt and fresh water. Nurse sharks are harmless, and you can dive and snorkel above them.

And there is more to admire underwater than sea creatures: a series of sculptures fixed to the seabed form part of the Museo Subacuatico de Arte or MUSA (Underwater Museum of Art; http://musamexico.org). Created in 2009 in the waters surrounding Cancún, Isla de Mujeres, and Punta Nizuc it comprises 500 life-sized and monumental sculptures by several artists including Jason DeCaires Taylor, Karen Salinas Martinez, and Salvador Quiroz Ennis. The sculptures are made of special materials used to promote coral life and can be seen on pre-booked glass-bottom boat trips or diving/snorkeling excursions.

For a change of scene from the beach, head to **Women's Beading**

Souvenirs at Playa del Carmen, the Yucatán Riviera's second major hub after Cancún.

Isla Mujeres.

Cooperative (La Gloria MZA. 160 Lote 5http://islamujeresbeadingco-op.com) where Maya women make excellent hand-crafted jewelry.

OUTER ISLANDS

Isla Mujeres is the main departure point for day trips by boat to **Isla Contoy** ⓰ 19 miles (30km) to the north, a sanctuary for pelicans, egrets, boobies, cormorants, and sea turtles that is now a protected reserve. Tours (around US$100 per person) last a full day, including a 1.5-hour journey each way to get to the island, with time to walk through the bird reserve and swim in Contoy's lagoons. A list of operators who run properly monitored boat trips can be found on the website of the Amigos de Isla Contoy organization, www.islacontoy.org. It is not permitted to stay on Contoy overnight.

Just around Cabo Catoche, the meeting point of the Caribbean and the Gulf of Mexico, is another inhabited island, **Isla Holbox** ⓱. A narrow strip of mangrove and beach, Holbox has just one village, with sand streets and very few motor vehicles – golf carts and bicycles are the main traffic. Along the beach there are several laid-back, palm-roofed hotels, from simple to luxurious. Idyllically relaxing, Holbox is also a wonderful place for fly-fishing, birdwatching, or snorkeling, especially around **Isla de Pájaros** in Laguna de Yalaháo, between Holbox and the mainland. Holbox also has a special attraction: the gathering off Cabo Catoche, every year from May to September, of large numbers of whale sharks, the world's largest fish, which mass to feed on a rich soup of tunny fish spawn and plankton that the sea serves up at that time of year. All tour operators have to operate according to strict regulations so the sharks are not too disturbed, and snorkelers are not allowed to attempt to touch these silent giants. Trips can also be arranged from Isla Mujeres.

To get to Holbox you must first get to the little port of Chiquilá, 160km (110 miles) or a 2.5-hour drive from Cancún, from where passenger ferries leave about every two hours. If you have a car, there are parking lots at

Plaza del Sol in San Miguel de Cozumel.

Chiquilá where you can leave it safely for a few dollars a day. Buses run a few times a day to Chiquilá and back from Cancún, and once a day from Mérida (at 10.30pm from TAME bus station).

COZUMEL

South of Isla Mujeres is the much larger island of **Cozumel** ⓲, 47km (30 miles) long with a lighthouse at each end, and 16km (10 miles) wide. Cozumel was another island that was a place of pilgrimage for Maya Yucatán in the Postclassic era, with several shrines dedicated to Ixchel. Bishop Landa recorded that everyone in the Yucatán hoped to visit the island at least once in their lives, and that – since Ixchel was the principal goddess of fertility – it was particularly common for women to come here before the birth of their first child. According to legend, Ixchel acknowledged the shrines and temples built in her honor by sending her favorite bird, a swallow. Thus the island was named "Land of the Swallows."

The principal relic of Maya Cozumel is the site of **San Gervasio** (daily Sept–May 8am–3.45pm), in the middle of the island. Similar in style to Tulum and other Postclassic Maya sites, it is quite widely spread out, so exploring involves an enjoyable walk through the woods, often full of flowers and birds. Among the principal structures is the **Chichan Nah** complex, probably the residence of the chief lord of Cozumel.

Cozumel was actually discovered for tourism before Cancún even existed, particularly by divers and fishermen drawn by the riches of its reefs. Things remained fairly low-key, however, until Cancún took off: today Cozumel welcomes around 4 million visitors a year, especially from cruise ships. Frequent passenger ferries run back and forth between the island and **Playa del Carmen**, and there is a less frequent car ferry service from **Puerto Calica**, just to the south.

It was predicted in Maya legends that bearded conquerors would come from the east, and thus early 16th-century locals were perhaps little surprised when Hernán Cortés and his fellow conquistadors landed on Cozumel,

Tip

Tours of the Cozumel reefs near Chankanaab in a 48-passenger submarine are operated by Atlantis Adventures (tel: 987 872 5671; www.atlantissubmarines.travel), on the waterfront boulevard just south of San Miguel; if you reserve in advance online, an adult ticket costs around US$90.

COZUMEL REEFS

Cozumel's modern rediscovery gained momentum in the 1960s when it was brought to the world's attention by the famous French oceanographer Jacques Cousteau, who came to film here. He declared that the Cozumel reefs were one of the richest undersea environments in the world, second only to the Great Barrier Reef in Australia. More and more divers came in his wake, and other tourists soon followed. Its fabulous, colorful coral reefs and vibrant marine life are still Cozumel's biggest attraction.

The increase in cruise-ship traffic and hurricanes have caused serious damage in some areas – particularly the inshore reefs closest to San Miguel town – but the seas are still full of fish and other creatures, and elsewhere the coral is still largely intact.

Cozumel reef life.

Tip

Cozumel has the region's most family-oriented beaches on its sheltered southwest coast, especially Playa San Francisco, with beach clubs that offer facilities for different ages such as snorkeling, kayaks, and banana boats.

before heading up the coast of Mexico. In the century that followed, however, most of its inhabitants succumbed to disease, or simply left once the island's role as a pilgrimage center was ended by Christianity. Hence there was hardly anyone here by the time Henry Morgan and other Caribbean pirates began to hole up in Cozumel's coves and lagoons in the 1670s, replenishing their water supplies between raids on Spanish treasure galleons. Cozumel was again abandoned by the middle of the 19th century, but underwent a slight revival with the newfound popularity of chewing gum from the sap of the zapote tree, *chicle*.

There are over 20 reefs along Cozumel's west coast, providing dives of every degree of difficulty. In many places you can also see a great deal just with a snorkel, or you can observe the underwater wonderland from the comfort of glass-bottomed boats. **Laguna Chankanaab**, 9km (6 miles) south of San Miguel, is a natural lagoon open to the sea, which has been made into a family-friendly "snorkel park," surrounded by a botanical garden (tel: 987 872 0833, www.cozumelparks.com/eng/chankanaab.cfm; Mon–Sat 8am–4pm). It is undeniably touristy, but you can still see plenty of brightly colored fish dart among the yellow sponges and dangling sea anemones. For a larger sum, you can also swim with dolphins. Nearby are some of Cozumel's best beaches, such as popular **Playa San Francisco**, which stretches for 3km (2 miles). Scuba-divers favor reefs a little farther offshore, such as the famous **Palancar Reef**, often filmed by Cousteau, **San Francisco**, or **Santa Rosa**, known for its spectacular wall dives.

The island's only town, **San Miguel de Cozumel** on the west coast, is spread alongside the 14-block waterfront Avenida Rafael Melgar. Local musicians perform on Sunday evenings in the central Plaza del Sol, surrounded by restaurant terraces. The **Museo de la Isla de Cozumel** (Mon–Sat 9am–4pm; www.cozumelparks.com/esp/museo_isla.cfm), on the waterfront in a former hotel, is a charming little museum with exhibits on Maya

Playa del Carmen.

Cozumel, pirates, hurricanes, the local flora and fauna with information in Spanish and English; there's a lovely cafe on its roof terrace too.

The east side of the island is deserted apart from beaches and, at the southern tip, the **Faro Celarain** lighthouse, surrounded by a nature reserve. Birdwatching is popular, especially near Faro Celarain and along the scenic road on the east shore. There the beaches are often hammered by treacherous surf, and the waters are subject to riptides and undertow. The northeast side of Cozumel is virtually empty, with only a dirt road to the Molas lighthouse at the island's tip.

ALONG THE RIVIERA MAYA

On the mainland, Highway 307, the "spine" of the Riviera, runs south from Cancún behind the coast, usually about 2–3km (1–2 miles) inland. At many points elaborate gateways announce the entrances to all-inclusive resort complexes, while at others side roads turn off to more open communities. **Puerto Morelos** ⑲, 36km (22 miles) from Cancún, was the only village on this coast before tourism started up, and is a remarkable survivor: big resorts are gathering around it, but at the center of the town there is still a placid, small-town plaza right on the beach, with kids playing and fishermen. This is in large part due to an alliance of local people and expat residents wishing to keep their bit of paradise, who have opposed large-scale building – so far – and ensured that the Puerto Morelos reefs have been made into a marine national park. It also still has a small working harbor and a couple of good seafood restaurants. Puerto Morelos's unfussy atmosphere makes it a favorite with those seeking a different, less hectic side to the Riviera, and as well as small-scale hotels there are often homes available to rent, as visitors here settle in for months at a time.

Back on the highway, more side roads turn off to white-sand beaches, nearly all of which now have some building on them. The exquisite **Playa del Secreto** is backed by opulent beach houses. The beaches around the "bend" in the coast at **Punta Bete** were until a few years ago only reachable by very bad dirt tracks, but most have now been paved and occupied by upscale hotels. A little to the south are perhaps the two most luxurious resort complexes on the Riviera, the giant **Maya Koba (**www.mayakobagolf.com**)**, with seven hotels and a PGA-standard golf course within the same carefully landscaped area, and the **Hacienda Tres Ríos**.

PLAYA DEL CARMEN

About 68km (42 miles) south of Cancún, **Playa del Carmen** ⑳ is an even more astonishing phenomenon than the capital of the Riviera itself. In 1980 it had about 1,000 people; now it has more than 215,000 residents. Then it had only one sand street, parallel to the beach; this is now the Avenida Quinta (5th Avenue), the pedestrianized

Snorkeling off Cozumel.

Drink

Sit at the colorful Fah Bar (www.siestafiestahotelplaya.com) in Playa del Carmen, on Avenida 5 near Calle 10, and watch the crowds go by. There's live music every night until midnight and the bar stays open until 2am.

main thoroughfare that links up the many new areas of Playa and provides tourists with a day and night promenade, lined with restaurants, bars, shops, and hotels.

The second hub of the Riviera, Playa del Carmen still has a different style from Cancún. Since it began as a real town by a beach, most of its attractions and services are within walking distance of each other – although distances are getting longer – rather than strung out over kilometers like the Cancún Hotel Zone. Its streets are conducive to strolling, whether you enjoy the crowds on the Quinta or wandering along the more tranquil avenues elsewhere, picking out a restaurant that looks attractive. Playa has a more interesting range of restaurants than Cancún, and its nightlife has a more hip, international style.

New in 2017 is the excellent Museo Frida Kahlo (Calle Quinta Avenida corner with 8th street; daily 9am–11pm; http://museofridakahlorivieramaya.org), dedicated to the famous Mexican painter. Interactive displays tell the fascinating story of Kahlo's life, her artistic career, political views and, physical suffering.

Playa's hotels cover a complete range, from backpacker favorites through charming small lodges to chic boutique hotels and resorts. There are also several excellent dive and snorkel operators based in the town. Cozumel ferries run frequently from a dock right on the town plaza.

The biggest resort hotels are in the Playacar development on the south side of the town, which also has an 18-hole golf course, condos, and even some Maya ruins, relics of what was once a departure point for pilgrimages to Cozumel. The Xaman-Ha Aviary (daily 9am–5pm) is also here, home to 200 birds. Just down the coast is **Xcaret** (tel: 984 206 0038; www.xcaret.com; 8.30am–10.30pm), one of the Riviera's most popular attractions, where a natural lagoon – once a Maya harbor – has been made into a "snorkel park" with an artificial underground river, and surrounded by an ecological reserve with a zoo of local wildlife, an orchid farm, a

Exploring Dos Ojos cavern system.

dazzling butterfly garden, aquarium, bat cave, flamingos, an open-air theater, and several restaurants. You can also ride horses, swim with dolphins, snorkel, or just lie on the beach. It may be a little manufactured but is nevertheless a good introduction to many aspects of a tropical environment, and very popular with families. Buses are also provided direct from Cancún (call for times, tel: 998 883 3143) and Playa del Carmen, and most visitors stay until night, when there's a traditional music and dance show in Xcaret's "Maya Village" and open-air theater.

PUERTO CALICA TO AKUMAL

Continuing south along the coast, past the little port of **Puerto Calica** with car ferries to Cozumel, **Paamul** is a fine beach with a reef close to the shore and a scuba school, which also has the best camping and RV site on the Riviera. **Puerto Aventuras**, 20km (12 miles) from Playa del Carmen, is a purpose-built, Mediterranean-style resort village of hotels and villas created around a lavish marina and another beautiful beach. Just beyond is the series of seven bays known as **Xpu-Ha**, which are among the Riviera coast's greatest beauties. However, resort hotels have now taken over most of them, and for non-guests traveling independently access is more difficult.

On the inland side of the highway near Xpu-Ha there are several *cenotes* (natural sinkholes) that are open to visitors for snorkeling and swimming. **Cenote Kantun-Chi** (daily 9am–5pm; www.kantunchi.com) is a low-key "eco-park" with four gorgeous *cenotes*, a forest walk, and a little zoo. Farther down, **Cenote Cristalino** and **Cenote Azul** are less developed, but still attractive for swimming in cool, fresh water.

The clear waters of the Yal-Ku lagoon (where the Spanish ship *Matancero* sank in 1741) flow into the sea at the northern end of the resort town of **Akumal** ㉑, set around some of the most beautiful bays on the coast, above all the arching **Media Luna** ("Half Moon") bay on the north side. While mostly as new as Puerto Aventuras, Akumal also has a real village at its center, and has a more relaxed feel, with hotels, villas, and condos spread along the long beaches. Akumal is Maya for "place of the turtles", and the beaches here and at Xcacel just to the south are among the region's most important turtle-breeding beaches, where from around May to August, green, hawksbill, and loggerhead turtles crawl up onto the sands to lay their eggs. In Akumal village there is the **Centro Ecológico Akumal** (tel: 984 875 9095; www.ceakumal.org), a conservation and research center that organizes "turtle watch" trips at night in the summer season, and is a good source of information. Akumal is also an excellent diving center, with several diving and windsurfing schools.

XEL-HÁ SNORKEL PARK

Easy snorkeling is the biggest attraction at **Xel-Há** ㉒ (tel: 998 883 3143;

Quote

"Besides the deep and exciting interest of the ruins (of Tulum) themselves, we had around us what we wanted at all the other places, the magnificence of nature."

John Lloyd Stephens, from *Incidents of Travel in Central America, Chiapas and the Yucatán*

Sombreros jostle for space with tourist tat.

www.xelha.com; daily 8.30am–6.30pm), just beyond Akumal, where freshwater underground rivers mingle with the ocean in a natural lagoon at the center of an ecological park run by the same organization as Xcaret. An expensive daily admission ticket includes snorkel rental, and swimming with dolphins and bicycle rides through the surrounding forest are other options on the menu. Multicolored fish dart among sprawling mangrove roots in the lagoon, and a colorful variety of birds can be seen around the *cenote*.

The southern Riviera is the most important area in the world for cave diving, with the *cenote* entrances to several spectacular cavern systems such as the celebrated **Dos Ojos (daily 8am–5pm)**, 2km (1.5 miles) south of Xel-Há, which stretches for at least 61km (38 miles) under the ground – though it may well be longer. If you do not have diving certification, you can still see awe-inspiring sights in these caves on a snorkel tour. Other cave-diving operations are based in Akumal and Tulum.

The underground world underneath the Yucatán Peninsula.

TULUM

Some 27km (17 miles) south of Akumal is the clifftop site of **Tulum** ㉓. Originally called Zama, which means "dawn", due to its location watching the sunrise, Tulum was the largest of the communities that grew up along the coastal trade route in the Postclassic era, between about 1300 and the Spanish Conquest. "Long-distance trade provided the nobility with products of great variety, quality or rarity," observes one museum curator, "all symbols of rank."

Around the time of the Spanish Conquest, Tulum is estimated to have had a population of only about 600. The priestly and noble classes perhaps resided within the stone walls which still surround the 6.5-hectare (16-acre) core of the site on three sides, with the rest of the population outside. A supreme lord or *Halach Uinich* headed a council of the leading families, which collected taxes, raised armies, and negotiated alliances with neighboring communities.

Tulum's fortress, if such it was, sits on dramatic limestone cliffs above powdery white beaches, giving it the most

THE MAZE BENEATH

The whole Yucatán Peninsula is riddled with cave systems, most either completely or partly underwater, but it is only since the 1980s that teams of divers have been investigating these dark, complex labyrinths. The figures are astonishing: across the Yucatán there are over 7,000 *cenotes* leading into underground rivers, and in the Riviera Maya area alone more than 100 different cave systems have been mapped. These include seven of the ten longest underground rivers in the world, among them the longest of them all, the Ox-Bel-Ha system around Tulum, which so far has been explored to a distance of 270km (168 miles). Moreover, explorations have also shown that most cave systems are connected at some point, so that anything that enters one filters through to the others.

spectacular location of any Maya ruin. The perimeter wall has five entrances and the remains of what may have been watchtowers. The **Temple of the Frescos**, a two-story structure with columns on the bottom level and a much smaller room on top, has a fresco of human figures in a style that suggests central Mexican influence, and masks of the rain god Chac around the corners of the facade. To the left of the platform in front of El Castillo is the **Temple of the Diving God**, which has a relief of this strange personage – thought, logically, to be related to fishing – in a relatively good state of preservation over the door. The carvings above doorways are protected with *palapa* (thatched) canopies.

Tulum's most imposing building is naturally **El Castillo** (The Castle), fronted by serpent columns, which was built on top of two earlier pyramids, and probably served as a watchtower and lighthouse as well as a temple. When Grijalva's Spanish expedition first saw it in 1518, they recorded that a flame was kept burning here day and night. Sadly – as is now the case with most structures at Tulum – you can no longer climb up the Castillo to enjoy the view, but must admire it from behind wire cordons.

John Lloyd Stephens and Frederick Catherwood spent one night in the Castillo in 1841, at first lamenting the lack of a sea view but then concluding that the experience had "wrought a great change in our feelings. An easterly storm came on, and the rain beat heavily against the sea wall. We were obliged to stop up the oblong openings, and congratulated ourselves upon the wisdom of the ancient builders. The darkness, the howling of the winds, the cracking of branches in the forest, and the dashing of angry waves against the cliff, gave a romantic interest, almost a sublimity to our occupation of this desolate building, but we were rather too hackneyed travellers to enjoy it, and were much annoyed by *moschetoes*."

TULUM BEACH AND SIAN KA'AN

Tulum nowadays is known not only for its Maya ruins but for one of the finest of all the Riviera's beaches, stretching 11km (7 miles) from the ruins

Tip

There is no bus service between Tulum beach and the town, about 2km (1.5 miles) inland. Taxis are plentiful, but be aware that many drivers try to avoid taking passengers to hotels that do not pay them commission. There are also scooter and bike rental shops, and some hotels provide bicycles for their guests.

Maya ruins at Tulum.

down to the entrance gate to the Sian Ka'an reserve. Tulum beach has been the laid-back, bohemian destination on the Riviera, the foremost home of the palm-roofed beach cabaña or hut. However, since its beauties have been recognized by a much broader range of people there is now a wide choice of "grades" of cabaña, including some that are distinctly luxurious, and prices have gone up across the board, even for the most basic backpacker-type. Nevertheless, it is still possible to find wonderfully mellow spots along the beach for some thoroughgoing relaxation. "Beach clubs" dotted along the shore provide snacks and drinks and sunbeds and chairs for waveside lounging. Some local "traditions" are maintained, such as that Tulum beach has no permanent electricity, but most hotels now have solar power or their own generators functioning at least part of the day.

Tulum village, just inland, was until the 1990s one of the most traditional Maya communities in northern Quintana Roo, but is now developing fast to service the burgeoning tourist trade.

Climbing the walls of the Nohoch Mul, the tallest pyramid in the northern Yucatán.

South of Tulum, the beach road continues south to enter the 500,000-hectare (1.25 million-acre) **Reserva de la Biosfera de Sian Ka'an** ㉔, a vast, scarcely inhabited expanse of tropical forest, mangrove swamps, reef, and wetland lagoons, which nurtures 300 species of bird and an abundance of such animals as jaguars, pumas, white tail deer, crocodiles, tapirs, and monkeys. Day tours, including boat trips through the lagoons, are run from Tulum. The access road is unpaved from partway down Tulum beach and in the reserve, and often has basin-sized potholes, particularly after rain. It runs south beside the ocean for 44km (27 miles) to the lobster-fishing village of **Punta Allen** (population 1,500), where you can fish, snorkel, take kayak tours, and stay in a couple of very mellow, off-track hotels. The village had to be evacuated in 2017 ahead of hurricane Franklin. Ascension Bay, beside it, is regarded as one of the world's finest fly-fishing grounds, and there are also a few upscale fishing lodges nearby.

COBÁ

From the main crossroads in Tulum, an almost straight, monotonous road leads to Cobá, 45km (28 miles) to the northwest, toward Valladolid. There are a few villages and several *cenotes* on the way. Many examples of Maya homes can still be seen, constructed in the traditional way on a base of stone with upright poles (Y-shaped at the top) supporting branches covered with palm leaves. These roofs shift and shake during hurricanes but, unlike some more solid structures, usually stay in place. Maya houses stay cool, too, aided by always-open front and back doorways and a breeze blowing between the poles.

The pyramids and temples at **Cobá** ㉕ (daily 8am–5pm) are widely dispersed around the forest, so exploring the site involves a fairly long walk, surrounded by greenery and the sounds of tropical birds (bicycles and tricycle-taxis can be rented at the entrance to make things a little easier). En route you might be able to admire the delicate flights of butterflies and orioles. Toucans and snakes are rarely encountered here, but crocodiles are quite easy to spot in the lakes – so resist the urge for a dip.

The first modern explorer to visit Cobá was the Austrian Teobert Maler, who photographed the 42-meter (138ft) high pyramid (called the **Nohoch Mul** or "Big Hill") – the tallest pyramid in the north of the Yucatán Peninsula – in 1891. In the 1920s the Maya expert Sylvanus Morley persuaded the Carnegie Institute to investigate Cobá, and assigned the British archeologist J. Eric Thompson to lead an expedition. On that first trip, Thompson and his three companions took the train from Mérida to Valladolid, from where they rode on horseback for eight hours.

About the same time, work began on uncovering the 100km (62 miles) of *sacbé*, limestone causeway, linking Cobá to the smaller Maya ruins at Yaxuná. It is now thought Yaxuná was a subordinate community of Cobá, and that this *sacbé* was built in the early 9th century to make it easier to reinforce Yaxuná as a stronghold in Cobá's long wars with its great enemy, Chichén Itzá. However, Cobá lost this struggle around 860, and entered a rapid decline.

Today, Cobá still seems isolated, and relatively unvisited compared to Tulum or Chichén. The main structures are spread out between lakes, which provided the water so rare in the Yucatán and which allowed the community to thrive for a 1,000 years. Over 34 huge stelae have been found at the site, with dates from the Classic era. The soaring heights of Cobá's pyramids, along with their narrow proportions, resemble the architectural style of Tikal in Guatemala, but it is thought Cobá was more closely connected politically with Tikal's enemy Calakmul. There are other buildings at the site in the square, plainer style of Tulum or San Gervasio on Cozumel, for Cobá was "reoccupied" in the Postclassic era, around 1300–1500.

THE TALKING CROSS AND COSTA MAYA

The Riviera Maya ends at Tulum, but Highway 307 continues southward

Tip

Bring plenty of mosquito repellent when you are visiting Cobá, and wear comfortable shoes. The site is surrounded by jungle and the ruins are very spread out, so you are likely to spend a lot of time on foot.

Nohoch Mul (Big Hill) at Cobá.

Tip

The Maya village of Punta Laguna, 20km (12 miles) northeast of Cobá, is one of the best places in the Yucatán to see spider monkeys, with its own reserve around a lake. Local guides provide excellent tours and kayak trips.

as a narrower road with few villages, and no special reason to stop until the unique little town of **Felipe Carrillo Puerto**. Originally called Chan Santa Cruz ("Little Holy Cross"), this was the "capital" of the rebel Maya who defied the authority of the Yucatán and Mexico and maintained their own "mini-state" here from 1850 to 1901. In a small park on one side of the town you can still see the shrine of the "talking cross," around which José María Barrera rallied the remaining rebels after their defeat in the War of the Castes (see page 279). For years the cross gave its *Cruzob* followers instructions, though it is assumed that Barrera and other leaders acted as ventriloquists.

Another 69km (43 miles) south, a good road signposted *Mahahual–Xcalak* turns east toward the coast south of Sian Ka'an, which has been opened up to tourism by this road and officially labeled the **Costa Maya**. The main center is **Mahahual** ㉖, where the road meets the sea, and where a pier was built to receive cruise ships in 2002. This pier was destroyed, and Mahahual devastated, by Hurricane Dean in 2007, but it has since been rebuilt on a larger scale, and Mahahual is gradually taking shape on the familiar road from sand-street fishing village to tourist center. A new malecón (promenade) has been constructed, and the fine offshore reefs and good fishing are drawing ever-increasing numbers of tourists.

South of Mahahual the road carries on 59km (37 miles) to end at easygoing **Xcalak**, on an island right by the border with Belize. It still has only sand streets, and along the beach there are some of the Yucatán's most delightful small get-away-from-it-all hotels. A laid-back atmosphere pervades, but isolated Xcalak is rapidly getting a reputation as one of the Yucatán's key adventure sports centers, with kayaking, diving, snorkeling, and world-class fly-fishing all on offer. Time will tell, but the lack of local beaches in **Xcalak** will probably contain tourist explosion. Around 20km (12 miles) offshore is the diving paradise of **Banco Chinchorro**, a separate atoll within the Great Maya

GUERRERO'S CHOICE

A dramatic statue stands at the western entrance to Chetumal, portraying a Maya warrior with his wife and children, and declaring the city to be the *Cuna del Mestizaje* or "cradle of racial mixing," the birthplace of the blending of races that created modern Mexico. The Maya warrior actually represents Gonzalo Guerrero, a Spanish soldier who was shipwrecked somewhere on the coast of Yucatán with 12 companions in 1511. Most were soon killed, but two survived, Guerrero and a priest, Jerónimo de Aguilar. Aguilar was kept as a slave, but Guerrero made himself useful to his new master, Nachan Kán, Lord of Chetumal, teaching him European techniques of war and joining in battles against other Maya lordships. He became one of Nachan Kán's leading warriors, and married into the lord's family.

When Aguilar heard that Spanish ships had appeared off the coast in 1519, he pleaded with Guerrero to escape with him, but Guerrero answered that he had a wife and three children, and that "I have tattoos on my face and holes in my ears" – like any Maya warrior – "what will the Spaniards say of me when they see me like this?" He stayed behind, and was condemned to death by Cortés. The Spaniards later heard many times of a white man leading warriors against them, and Guerrero is believed to have died in battle in 1536, somewhere in modern Honduras.

Statue of Guerrero with his family.

Reef, with a wealth of coral, marine life, and shipwrecks, and yet still scarcely visited. Dive operators and some hotels provide diving and snorkel tours.

BACALAR AND CHETUMAL

Back on Highway 307, some 50km (31 miles) south of the Mahahual turn you will come to **Bacalar** ㉗, known for the long *laguna* of the same name. On a hilltop in Bacalar town is the **Fuerte de San Felipe**, built by the Spaniards in 1729 to protect the region from British pirates operating from what is now Belize. There is a lovely lakeshore road with a few small hotels and unfussy restaurants; at the southern end a restaurant sits beside the **Cenote Azul**, 90 meters (300ft) deep and separated from the lake by a thin strip of forest.

At the southern end of the Yucatán coast, bordering Belize, is Quintana Roo's state capital, **Chetumal** ㉘, a tranquil, modern city with wide avenues and a very tropical bayside boulevard – the Bulevard de la Bahía – which winds attractively along the seafront all the way north to the fishing village of Calderitas, near a small Maya site at **Oxtankah**. Many of Chetumal's most enjoyable restaurants are spread along the boulevard, ideal places for catching the evening breeze off the bay.

Chetumal also has a (slightly neglected) **Museo de la Cultura Maya** (tel: 983 832 6838; Tue–Sat 9am–7pm, Sun 9am–2pm), on the corner of Avenida Héroes and Avenida Mahatma Gandhi. It does not have many original Maya relics, but seeks to explain ancient Maya culture through modern interactive exhibits, such as reconstructed Maya cities in miniature set under a glass floor. A diagram illustrates the skull-deforming devices employed by the ancient Maya to create a distinct, high, sloping brow – considered a feature of nobility – and a fascinating device enables visitors to move a series of balls and bars to add up Maya numbers.

Highway 186 runs west from Chetumal toward Campeche, passing some spectacular Maya sites. Around 55km (34 miles) west a road turns off north to Dzibanché and Kinichná, two adjacent sites that are believed to have been parts of the same Classic-era city. The phenomenal three-level pyramid of Kinichná is one of the largest in the Maya world. Another 5km (3 miles) west a road turns off south to one of the most beautiful Maya sites, at **Kohunlich**. Its location is stunning, surrounded by lush tropical vegetation and giant fan palms. Kohunlich contains one of the most intricately laid-out Maya palace complexes, but its greatest treasure is the **Palace of the Masks**, with an imposing staircase lined by six beautifully carved, serene *mascarones* (masks), sculptures of giant heads believed to represent rulers of the city. Returning to Highway 186, a turn west takes you on to the Río Bec area of Campeche, and the **Reserva de la Biosfera de Calakmul** (see page 347).

Bacalar Lake, also known as the "Lake of Seven Colors" thanks to its brilliantly colored waters.

Campeche street scene.

CAMPECHE AND CHIAPAS

Most visitors pass through Campeche en route to better-known destinations, but this state has its gems, too, and the jungles of neighboring Chiapas reveal yet more Maya ruins.

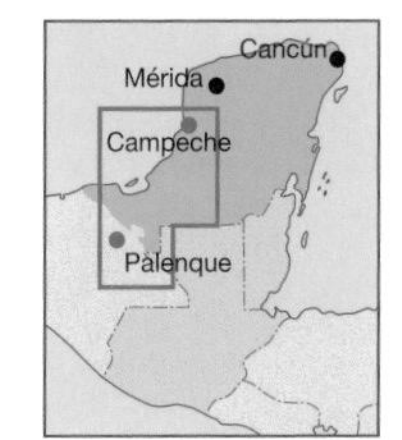

Filling the southwestern corner of the Yucatán, the state of Campeche is the least-known part of the peninsula, and still devotes as much energy to its fishing and oil industries as to tourism. The main draws here are the magnificent Maya sites, some still only partly uncovered, and the highly atmospheric walled city of Campeche. Champotón marks the site of the Spaniards' first landing on Mexican soil (after their brief landing on Isla Mujeres), under Francisco Hernández de Córdoba, on March 20, 1517.

The adjacent state of Chiapas to the south does not lie within the Yucatán Peninsula at all, but is a huge lure thanks to its superb Maya sites: Bonampak, Yaxchilán and, above all, Palenque, with graceful temple pyramids in a jungle setting. In contrast to the pancake-flat Yucatán, much of Chiapas is covered in forested mountains, with crystalline rivers and sparkling waterfalls gushing down steep gorges.

With its rugged landscape, Chiapas is home to over a million Maya, from eight different main groups, each retaining its own culture and language. The Tzotzil and Tzeltal Maya (each numbering over 400,000) are the most numerous of these, inhabiting the mountain highlands around San Cristóbal de las Casas. There are estimated to be just 1,000 or so surviving Lacandón Maya (who refer to themselves as the *Hach Winik*, "True People"), in the forests near Bonampak, some of whom still follow traditional customs, wearing their hair long and dressing in long white smocks.

Leftist Zapatista rebels have challenged the authorities' control in Chiapas since 1994, leading to sporadic confrontations and violent incidents, but in recent years the situation has generally been one of a peaceful standoff, and rarely affects travelers to the region. That said, Mexican military checkpoints are quite common on roads in Chiapas, where your passport may be inspected.

Main Attractions

Calakmul
Campeche
Edzná
Palenque
Bonampak
Yaxchilán

Maps on pages 304, 348, 352

Plaza Principal and Catedral, Campeche.

Getting around Campeche.

ON THE HIGHWAY INTO CAMPECHE

Heading west into Campeche from Chetumal, Highway 186 traverses the base of the Yucatán Peninsula. This hot, humid region has been partly repopulated around the Highway, which is now an important link between central Mexico and the *Riviera Maya*; around 1,500 years ago, this area was one of the heartlands of ancient Maya civilization. Some of the sites, such as **Xpuhil** and **Becán**, are just off the road, while the giant city of **Calakmul** lies hidden in the forest far to the south.

Roads have been built to the most important sites, and much of southern Campeche state is within the **Reserva de la Biosfera de Calakmul**, extending north and south of the Highway and the largest rainforest reserve in Mexico. This forest is home to monkeys, armadillos, tapirs, jaguars, and many other kinds of wild cat, so as you visit the ruins – especially Calakmul itself – you are likely to see plenty of animals as well. The reserve's jungles merge with Guatemala's Maya Biosphere Reserve and Belize's Río Bravo Conservation Area to form a huge, vitally important subtropical forest. There are also more than 60 archeological sites within the Calakmul reserve, although only a few are regularly accessible. Local guides can be found in **Xpuhil** town, and in some hotels.

THE RÍO BEC SITES

The Río Bec style of Maya architecture is characterized by peculiarly tall, steep, thin pyramids, covered in elaborate relief carvings. As in the Chenes style from central Campeche, temple entrances are often in the form of "monster-mouths," making them still more awe-inspiring. This is one of the most theatrical of Maya styles, since the staircases were often so steep they were never actually meant to be climbed, and the temples had other, easier entrances at the back.

The first of the Río Bec sites you will come to from the east is **Xpuhil**, some 118km (73 miles) west of Chetumal, by the roadside just outside the region's shabby little main town of the same name. The main attraction at these

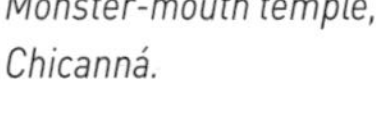
Monster-mouth temple, Chicanná.

small ruins are its three, almost vertical towers with decorated stairways, classics of the Río Bec style.

Becán, another 7km (4.5 miles) to the west, is far more impressive, and was the most significant town in the region. It was occupied for an enormously long period of time, from the Preclassic era around 400 BC until after AD 1200, and has a unique shape: it is the only extensively excavated walled Classic Maya city, its compact core ringed by a solid defensive wall. Within this wall is a spectacular maze of imposing structures, including a unique, dark "alleyway" between two temples, multi-roomed palace complexes and a beautiful, subtly carved stucco mask of a still unidentified figure, built into the south facade of the giant Structure X, one of the most intricate Maya buildings.

Chicanná, on the south side of the Highway 2km (1.5 miles) west of Becán, is smaller, but has some of the most dramatic monster-mouth temples, representing the spirits of the earth. The site actually known as **Río Bec** is down a poor road southeast of Xpuhil town, and often closed to visitors while excavations are in progress. Check in hotels or in Xpuhil before trying to visit.

CALAKMUL

The most important site in the region – not actually part of the Río Bec area, but reached from it, is **Calakmul** ㉙, in the southern portion of the Calakmul Biosphere Reserve, 60km (37 miles) down a winding, but mostly paved, road that turns south off Highway 186 52km (32 miles) west of Xpuhil. At the turnoff you must pay an admission fee to the biosphere reserve, and there is a separate entry charge to the ruins. The way there is a lonely drive – keep a look out for flocks of wild turkeys and toucans in the treetops – and bring drinking water and insect repellent.

The immense site of Calakmul (daily 8am–5pm) is the largest known city in the Maya world, comprising over 6,000 structures, including Structures 1 and 2, vast Maya pyramids, both around 50 meters (165ft) high. The city dates back to the 5th century BC, but its prosperity really took off in the early Classic era,

Quote

"If the number, grandeur, and beauty of its buildings were to count towards the attainment of renown and reputation in the same way as gold, silver, and riches have done for other parts of the Indies, Yucatán would have become as famous as Peru and New Spain have become."

Fr. Diego de Landa

Calakmul stelae.

from AD 350. Intriguingly, many links have been established between Calakmul and El Mirador (see page 176), and archeologists now believe that following the collapse of the original Preclassic Maya superpower, El Mirador, that city's ruling Kaan dynasty upped sticks and founded a second great city 40km (25 miles) or so to the north.

Later in the power politics of the Classic period the dominant powers of Calakmul and Tikal were locked in deadly rivalry. Through networks of alliances and vassal states these giants wielded influence over an area stretching from Palenque in the west to Copán in the southeast, in present-day Honduras. Eventually, Tikal defeated Calakmul in AD 695, almost certainly reinforcing the triumph by sacrificing Calakmul's king, Jaguar Paw.

Visitors have a choice of three different walking routes around the ruins, which are so large that even the short route takes around 90 minutes to complete. Between the 5th and 9th centuries the Lords of Calakmul erected more than 150 great stelae. Many still bear dates, one corresponding to 810, and another to the year 410. Structure VI is part of an astronomical complex. Extensive as the site is, if you climb to the top of the massive **Structure II** pyramid, past its two giant stucco masks, you can see other mounds above the jungle in every direction.

Returning to the main road, about 5km (3 miles) west of the Calakmul turning is yet another site, **Balamkú**, which is small but has in one, now protected structure one of the largest surviving Maya stucco friezes, an astonishing mass of strange monsters, toads, monkeys, and other creatures, still with a good deal of its original color. Beyond there, the Highway rolls on to **Francisco Escárcega**, a giant road junction with an equally huge gas station. From here, Highway 261 heads north to Champotón, Campeche, and Mérida; Highway186 winds southward into the state of Chiapas (see page 352).

CAMPECHE

Traveling north 150km (93 miles) from Escárcega brings you to Campeche's

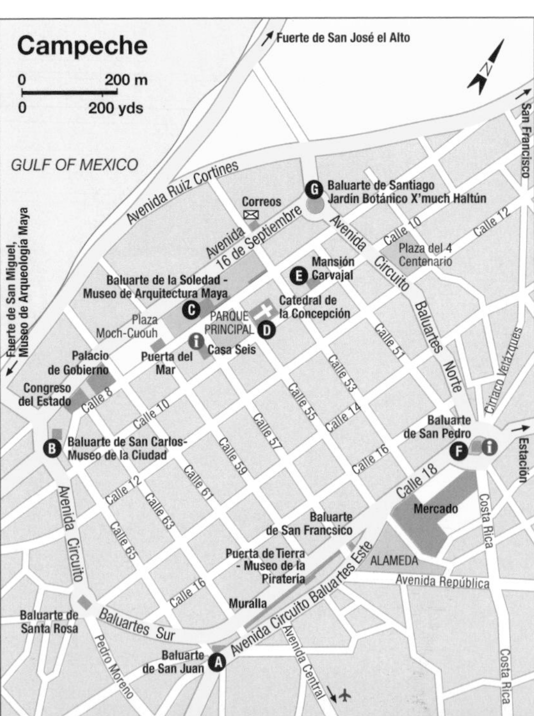

Chamber at Calakmul.

state capital. Founded in 1540 by Francisco de Montejo on the site of a Maya chiefdom called Ah Kin Pech, **Campeche** ㉚ suffered for 200 years from attacks from pirates attracted by the wealthy galleons that set sail from here for Spain. The beleaguered people of Campeche suffered one of the worst assaults in 1663, when buccaneers from several nations launched a ferocious onslaught, raping women, slaughtering the populace, destroying buildings, and seizing treasure.

This finally led the Spanish crown to encircle the city with massive fortifications, between 1685 and 1704. Nearly 3.5 meters (8ft) thick in places, the walls were originally 2,536 meters (8,320ft) long and stretched along today's Avenida Circuito de los Baluartes, making Campeche one of the few fortress cities in the Americas, a hexagonal stronghold guarded by eight towers. Faced with the now impregnable port, the pirates redirected their energies elsewhere.

In the 1960s, official policy was to demolish Campeche's walls, but local planners made a U-turn in the 1990s when they realized the tourist potential of the Old City. Old Campeche's walls were carefully repaired, and the old colonial houses inside them beautifully restored to their former glory and repainted in colors of pastel greens, blues, ochre, and terracotta. The old city of Campeche has a particular charm, and in 1999 was declared a Unesco World Heritage Site.

The **Puerta del Mar** (Sea Gate) is a natural beginning to an exploration of the Old City. Calle 59 runs right through the Old City from there to the **Puerta de Tierra** (Land Gate), which holds a light and sound show called "El Lugar del Sol" (Place of the Sun) about the colonial history of the town (Thu–Sun at 8pm). From the top of the gate you can also walk along the ramparts to the bastion of **Baluarte de San Juan** Ⓐ. The old bastions, or *baluartes*, seven of which still define the shape of the Old Town, have been adapted in various ways. In the northwest corner, **Baluarte de San Carlos** Ⓑ contains the **Museo de la Ciudad** (daily 8am–9pm), where you

Tip

Free shows of traditional music and dancing are performed throughout the year in Campeche, notably in the Casa Seis and outside in the Plaza Principal.

Campeche's Old City.

The careful restoration of the Old City of Campeche has helped it to achieve Unesco World Heritage status.

can visit the dungeons as well as exhibits on Campeche's history. Nearby, the 1960s Plaza Moch-Cuouh contains the State Congress, a squat concrete building known locally as the Flying Saucer.

THE PLAZA PRINCIPAL

The hub of Old Campeche is its **Plaza Principal**. **Baluarte de la Soledad** Ⓒ, on the seaside near the Puerta del Mar, hosts the **Museo de Arquitectura Maya** (Tue–Sun 8am–5pm), with fine carved stelae and other relics from Maya sites around Campeche state. On the west side of the square, **Casa Seis** (daily 9am–9pm; free) is a 19th-century merchant's house with lovely shaded patios that has been beautifully restored, and now houses the main tourist office. Nearby, on Calle 8, is the **Centro Cultural "El Palacio"** (Tue–Sun 10am–7pm) – in fact a historical museum. Every night at 8pm the palace is the venue of an excellent light and sound show about the fascinating history of Campeche.

On the opposite side of the plaza, the **Catedral de la Concepción** Ⓓ is topped with twin towers, flying buttresses, and dome. Campeche's other interesting architecture includes the 1540 church of **San Francisco**, some 20 minutes' walk from the center northeast along the seafront; and the **Mansión Carvajal** Ⓔ, on calles 10 and 53, once the home of a wealthy *hacienda* owner, which has undulating Moorish arches, checkered floors, and a sweeping staircase.

The lively market at calles 18 and 51, where Avenida Gobernadores begins, is near the **Baluarte de San Pedro** Ⓕ, which houses a small crafts museum (10am–5pm). The **mercado** is a rambling bazaar, with women hovering in dimly lit doorways amidst stores and stalls so close to each other that one's pile of gilt sandals overflows into her neighbor's canned hams and cheeses. Not far away, the rebuilt **Baluarte de Santiago** Ⓖ encircles the **Jardín Botánico X'much Haltún** (daily 8am–9pm), filled with tropical plants.

THE FORTRESS MUSEUMS

Campeche's two biggest museums occupy two dramatic Spanish forts

The Museo de Arquitectura Maya, Campeche.

on hills north and south of the city, built from 1779 to 1801. The **Museo de Arqueología Maya** (Tue–Sun 8am–5pm; Sun free) in the **Fuerte de San Miguel**, above the coastal avenue south of the city, is one of the most important collections of Maya artifacts in Mexico, its greatest treasures the jade funeral masks discovered at Calakmul in the 1990s (although these are often on loan to other museums). Also on show is a spectacular array of Maya ceramics, especially the charming little figurines left as tomb offerings on the mysterious island of Jaina, north of Campeche, as well as scale models of the cities of Sayil and Yaxchilán. Plus, as part of the visit, you get a panoramic view from the battlements. The best way to get to the museum is by taxi.

One of Campeche's main attractions, the **Fuerte de San José el Alto**, north of the city, is equally imposing on its massive hill, but the museum it contains, the **Museo de Barcos y Armas** (Tue–Sun 8am–5pm) is less exciting, with exhibits on colonial and maritime history. A tourist bus runs there a few times each day.

BEYOND CAMPECHE

Some 61km (38 miles) southeast of Campeche, **Edzná** 31 was an important Preclassic city. It was already thriving by AD 100, thanks to its location on major trading routes between the highlands and the coast, and continued to evolve for over 1,000 years, until it was finally abandoned around 1300.

Carved stelae with Maya glyphs stand by the ruins' entrance. Beside the expansive main plaza is Edzná's emblematic structure, the **Temple of the Five Stories**, a stepped palace-pyramid almost 30 meters (100ft) high on a huge base, from which a central staircase (65 steps) rises through five levels to a three-roomed temple. Arranged around this central area are several other buildings. The **Temple of the Masks** has fine stuccoed masks representing the sun god; the **Great Tribune**, a giant ramp of steps – or seats – facing the Five Stories, could

Tip

Edzná is reachable by public bus from Campeche, but you can also join a tour for convenience. Xtampak Tours (tel: 981 811 6473) run good-value excursions on most days of the week. You can choose a half-day, transport-only option, or go for a longer trip that includes lunch and a knowledgeable guide.

The Temple of the Five Stories, Edzná.

STEPHENS AND CATHERWOOD

John L. Stephens, North American explorer and travel writer, and his colleague, the English artist and architect Frederick Catherwood, came to Central America in 1839, inspired by an edition they had found of Captain del Río's expedition to Palenque in 1786. This, in Stephens's blunt prose, had "roused our curiosity."

Over the next three years, the two men traveled throughout the region, overcoming illnesses and the threats posed by ongoing civil wars. They visited dozens of Maya cities, including Chichén Itzá, Palenque, Quiriguá, and Copán, and described many places never seen before by outsiders, such as Kabah, Sayil, and Tulum. Stephens and Catherwood were captivated by these fabulous sites, and were among the first to recognize that their creators had to have been the region's indigenous Maya inhabitants, and not some Egyptians or Greeks who had somehow wandered across the Atlantic. In 1841, Stephens published *Incidents of Travel in Central America, Chiapas and Yucatán*, beautifully illustrated with Catherwood's finely detailed lithographs, and after a second trip the pair produced *Incidents of Travel in Yucatán* in 1843. Both are still in print today, as true travel "classics." They never did manage to decipher the glyphs, but they did bring the culture to the attention of the outside world, attracting further study that continues unabated today.

Edzná was an important Preclassic city, abandoned around 1300.

have seated 5,000 people. The **Palace of the Knives** (in which many offertory knives were found) is divided into rooms that may have served as residences for the local elite.

There are many other small Maya sites in the Chenes region, in the middle of Campeche state around the little town of **Hopelchén**: **Hochob**, a three-room temple covered with carved snakes and masks; **Dzibilnocac**, a temple-pyramid near Iturbide, and, far the largest, **Santa Rosa Xtampak**, a dramatic site on steep hills deep in the forest down an often bumpy road 45km (28 miles) northeast of Hopelchén.

CHIAPAS

Leaving the Yucatán Peninsula proper, the state of Chiapas to the south provides an adventurous extension to many visitors' itineraries, to explore some fascinating Maya settlements and ancient ruins deep in the forest.

PALENQUE

Looming out of the dense tropical undergrowth of Chiapas, 355km (220 miles) from Campeche, the Maya ruins at **Palenque** ㉜ are for many visitors the highlight of their trip to Mexico (daily 8am–5pm). The complex site inspires awe, and yet what one sees today represents a fraction of the incredible complex of chambers, terraces, staircases, temples, and palaces and other structures that graced Palenque at its peak in the 7th century AD. At this time, the stucco and limestone relief panels would have been polychromed, and the effect of the colors and the white plaster – set off against the dark-green backdrop – must have been dazzling.

The name Palenque simply means palisade in Spanish; its original name was perhaps Lakam-ha or "Big Water," although it was also known just as Bak or "the Bone Kingdom." It was the largest and most powerful Maya city in the Río Usumacinta region from around AD 400, but went into a precipitate decline around 800, when its ruling dynasty soon collapsed. It was the first Maya site to be investigated in the modern era, when Spanish priests began

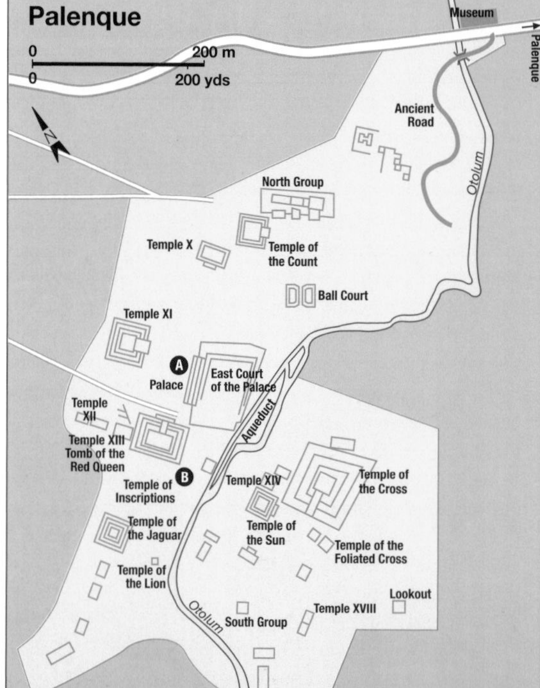

Statue at the Maya site of Tonina, south of Palenque.

to explore it in the 1770s. In 1786, an army captain called Antonio del Río was sent to examine it, and was sufficiently impressed to conclude that other cultures must have helped in their construction. "I do not take upon myself to assert that [the Romans] did actually land in this country, but there is reasonable ground [for suspecting that] some inhabitants of that polished nation did visit these regions."

THE RUINS

Concealing its treasures almost until you stumble into them, the wall of jungle divides beyond the entrance to reveal the two most important and magnificent structures of the site: the pagoda-like tower complex of the **Palace** Ⓐ and, to its right, the **Temple of Inscriptions** Ⓑ, a superb example of Classic Maya architecture, crowned with the characteristic roof comb.

The temple is in fact a pyramid with a temple on top, which, at 26 meters (85ft) high, dominates the whole site. The hieroglyphic inscriptions on the walls, giving a detailed list of the kings of Palenque with their dates, give the temple its name. In 1952, Mexican archeologist Alberto Ruz Lhuillier discovered a sealed stone passageway that led to a burial chamber 25 meters (82ft) down, at the center of the pyramid. It contained the tomb of King Pakal (ruled AD 615–83), greatest of all Palenque's rulers, wearing a mosaic jade death mask with shell and obsidian eye insets, and his body richly adorned with jade jewelry. Closing the tomb was an extraordinary sarcophagus lid carved with an image showing Pakal descending into the underworld of the dead, Xibalba.

In order to preserve them, Pakal's tomb and the rest of the Temple of Inscriptions are no longer open to visitors. However, in the site museum (by the entry road to the site, and included in the ticket) there is a full-size reconstruction of the tomb, the **Sala Tumba de Pakal**, which is the next best thing.

Nearby, in the smaller **Temple XIII**, one can now visit the **Tomb of the Red Queen**, a three-chamber tomb where a sarcophogus of a woman was discovered in 1994, stained with unusually large amounts of the red cinnabar pigment that was used by the Maya to symbolize rebirth. She is believed to have been Pakal's queen, Lady Tzakbu Ajaw.

Almost directly opposite the pyramid is the **Palace**, a complex of buildings with courtyards, passages, and tunnels, arranged around a unique, four-story, square-sided tower. The tower has been reconstructed and its function has attracted much speculation; once thought to have been an astronomical observatory, it probably also served as a watchtower. The walls of the palace are embellished with finely detailed stucco panels, and its grassy courtyards have low walls decorated with hieroglyphics and impressive sculptures of giant human figures carved on huge stone slabs.

There is a **ball court** and another group of lesser temples in a grassy clearing to the north of the Palace,

Fact

When John L. Stephens first came to Palenque in 1840, the local prefect offered to sell him the ruins for $1,500. However, at that time only Mexican citizens or their spouses could own land in Mexico, and he was unable to find a local woman whom he was prepared to marry.

The Maya ruins at Palenque are a highlight of a visit to southern Mexico.

The Sumidero Canyon deep in the Chiapas rainforest.

called the **North Group**. To the east, across the stream, are the three important temples known as the **Cross Group**. All were built in the 690s during the rule of Pakal's son Kan B'alam II (684–702), in order to glorify himself, his father, and their dynasty, and make clear their links to the gods. The imposing Temple of the Cross is the largest of the three, with a frieze inside its main temple showing Kan B'alam II receiving the attributes of kingship from his father.

Opposite, the Temple of the Sun shows Kan Balam II obtaining the power to wage war, while the Temple of the Foliated Cross stresses the role of Palenque's kings in sustaining the cycle of nature. Sadly, these temples are also now often closed to visitors, so you may only be able to see the carvings in copies in the site museum.

Many spectacular discoveries have been made within the last 25 years in the group of buildings just south of the Cross Plaza, known as the **South Group**. However, work is often still going on, and so they are frequently closed to visitors.

The site itself lies about 8km (5 miles) from the town of Palenque, from where there are regular *combi* minibuses to the ruins. The museum is about 1km (0.6 miles) back from the site on the entry road, but you can also walk there from the main site, down a beautiful jungle path. The forest around Palenque is a national park, so visitors must pay a small park entry fee as well as the ruins admission charge.

BONAMPAK AND YAXCHILÁN

The other two most important Maya sites in Chiapas, Bonampak and Yaxchilán, are located deep in the former rainforest near the Río Usumacinta, which marks the international border with Guatemala.

Bonampak 33, 140km (87 miles) to the southwest, is reached from Palenque via a now good paved road parallel to the Usumacinta valley. Take the turning at San Javier for Bonampak (13km/8 miles), stopping at the Lacandón village of Lacanjá after 9km (5.5 miles). Bonampak is in a Lacandón-run reserve, and only their

Selling textiles in San Cristóbal de las Casas.

vehicles are allowed to take you to the site. Lacanjá is also the best place to stay in the area, with several small *campamentos* of cabañas near the sparkling Lacanjá River.

Bonampak was only "discovered" by outsiders in 1946, and its vividly colored murals are the only large Maya paintings that have survived. They startled archeologists by giving them a completely new vision of ancient Maya life. The frescoes cover the walls and ceilings of the Temple of the Frescoes, presenting a historical narrative around a bloody battle between Bonampak's lord Chan-Muaan and an unknown enemy, together with ceremonies, rituals, celebrations, and dances, depicted in tiny, fascinating detail.

An essential part of the same trip – which can be easily combined, especially if you take time to stay over at Lacanjá – is the journey to the larger Maya site of **Yaxchilán** ㉞, spectacularly located on lofty slopes above the Usumacinta. There is no access by road: to get there you must continue 20km (12.5 miles) past San Javier and then turn down a 19km (12-mile) road to the river village of Frontera Corozal, where local *lanchero* (boatmen's) co-operatives offer boat trips to the ruins, which take about an hour each way. Agencies in Palenque also offer tours to both sites.

One of Mexico's most enjoyable and picturesque colonial towns, **San Cristóbal de las Casas** is located at an altitude of over 2,100 meters (7,000ft) and enjoys a beautifully temperate climate. It is highly popular with visitors, and has a cosmopolitan array of restaurants, cafes, and boutiques, as well as some wonderful historic hotels. San Cristóbal is especially atmospheric around the central plaza, which is framed by elegant buildings, including a stately Baroque cathedral. **Na Bolom** (Mon–Fri 9am–7pm; www.nabolom.org), a beautiful 19th-century house with surrounding gardens 500 meters/yds east of the plaza, is another prime attraction. Several tour operators organize trips to the region's indigenous villages, such as Chamula, and natural places of interest.

Tip

From Lacanjá, as well as visiting the Maya sites Bonampak and Yaxchilán, you can also explore the forest with Lacandón guides and go rafting on the Lacanjá River, especially from Campamento Río Lacanjá (www.ecochiapas.com/lacanja.html).

Cathedral on the central plaza in San Cristóbal de las Casas.

Ripening bananas in Santa Cruz La Laguna.

GUATEMALA, BELIZE & THE YUCATÁN

TRAVEL TIPS

TRANSPORTATION

A – Z

LANGUAGE

FURTHER READING

TRANSPORTATION

GETTING THERE

Guatemala

By Air from the US and Canada

Most flights to Guatemala are routed through a few US hub cities: Atlanta, Dallas, Fort Lauderdale, Houston, Los Angeles, Miami, and Newark. You'll also find several non-direct options via San Salvador (with Avianca El Salvador) and Mexico City (Aeroméxico and Interjet). Flying from Canada, you'll have to travel via one of the US gateway cities. All international flights land at **La Aurora International Airport** (tel: 502-2321 5000) 4 miles (6km) south of Guatemala City, except for a few regional flights from Belize and Cancún which land at **Mundo Maya Airport** in Flores (near Tikal).

By Air from Europe

The only direct air itinerary linking Europe to Guatemala is from Madrid, flying with Spanish airline Iberia or the new low-cost operator Wamos Air. Travelers from the UK and Ireland can also choose to fly via one of the US gateway cities, via Panama or via Cuba. Another option is to fly to Mexico, where connections to Guatemala are available with local airlines.

By Road

Bus is the most common way to enter Guatemala. Several bus services run from Mexico, Honduras, Belize, and El Salvador into Guatemala with the San Salvador–Guatemala City connection among the most frequent. There is also a route linking San José (in Costa Rica) with Guatemala City, which involves an overnight stopover.

Belize

By Air from the US and Canada

There are many flights from the US to Belize, and now there are also direct connections from several cities in Canada (Westjet). All international flights into Belize land at the Philip S.W. Goldson International Airport (www.pgiabelize.com), which is located 10 miles (16km) northwest of Belize City on the Northern Highway. American Airlines operates direct flights from Dallas/Fort Worth and Miami, Delta Airlines from Atlanta, and United Airlines (and Southwest) from Houston.

By Air from Europe

To fly to Belize from the UK or Europe you change planes at one of the US gateways. This can be very inconvenient, as most flight times do not match up and can result in long stopovers in the States. An alternative option is to fly directly to Cancún and take a bus or drive from there into Belize. Unfortunately there are no direct flights from Mexico to Belize.

By Road

Several companies run regular buses from Chetumal and Cancún in Mexico to Belize City; the best are run by ADO, whose website is in Spanish only (www.ado.com.mx). If you want to bring your own car into Belize you may incur significant customs charges, so it is worth checking before traveling.

The Yucatán

By Air from the US and Canada

Frequent flights, scheduled and charter, run to Cancún from every part of the US and Canada. There are also scheduled flights to Mérida from Miami and Houston, and to Cozumel from Atlanta, Dallas, Charlotte, Houston, Newark, and Toronto. Both airports also have additional charter and seasonal services. Tropic Air flies from Belize City to Cancún.

Flight information

Aeromexico: https://world.aeromexico.com
American Airlines: www.aa.com
British Airways: www.britishairways.com
Copa Airlines: www.copaair.com
Delta: www.delta.com
Iberia: www.iberia.com
Interjet: www.interjet.com
Spirit: www.spirit.com
United Airlines: www.united.com
US Airways: www.usairways.com
Westjet: www.westjet.com

The bus station at Punta Gorda, Belize.

Riding to market at Solalá, Guatemala.

By Air from Europe

There are many direct flights to Cancún from Europe, notably by Iberia from Madrid, British Airways from London, and Air Berlin from Düsseldorf, and there are also many charter flights. Note that some of these flights are seasonal.

By Road

The distance from the nearest main US border crossing (Brownsville, Texas) to Cancún is about 1,850km (1,150 miles). This amounts to about 30 hours' driving, but most people take at least four days. To bring a US- or Canadian-registered car into Mexico beyond the border area you must obtain a temporary import permit and a Mexican insurance policy, as US and Canadian policies are not valid in Mexico. The AAA offices and insurance services such as www.mexinsure.com advise on current procedures.

GETTING AROUND

Guatemala

Though Guatemala is a small country, the mountainous terrain and ancient buses mean that travel can be time-consuming and uncomfortable. Stick to the main highways and things move reasonably well, but many of the minor routes are unpaved, and the going can be tediously slow. Thankfully, the scenery is usually spectacular.

From the Airport

Public service buses depart from outside **Aurora International Airport** heading for Guatemala City's historic centre, Zona 1, although this method is not recommended; the easiest, and far safer, way of getting to and from the airport is by taxi. Inside the Arrivals hall, a taxi desk enables you to prepay for your journey (expect to pay around US$12 to travel into Zona 1). Reliable companies include Taxi Amarillo Express (tel: 1766; www.amarilloexpress.com/m.html) and Checker Taxis (tel: 5033 3308; www.checkertaxigt.com). Note that practically all of the city's top-end hotels and a few of the guesthouses will lay on a free pickup service if you book ahead.

Travelers to Antigua can catch one of the shuttle buses (US$10–12 per person) leaving at fairly regular intervals. Alternatively, a taxi will set you back around US$40–50.

By Air

The only scheduled internal flights currently in operation are the 50-minute Guatemala City–Flores flight (to visit Tikal), which saves an 8–10-hour trip by road, and to Retalhuleau (around $130) – although you can expect to pay a fairly steep US$140 for a return ticket. Flights are operated by TAG airlines, but you'll probably get a better deal by booking your ticket via a travel agent, rather than the airline. Try to make reservations well in advance for all flights.

Domestic Airlines
TAG
Tel: 2380 9494
www.tag.com.gt

By Bus

The regular Guatemalan bus, called a *camioneta*, is an old North American school bus. It's three to a seat, and as many as possible standing in the aisle. Progress is always pretty slow, but never dull, as *ranchero* and merengue music blares from tinny speakers, children wail, and chickens cluck. Traveling on a "chicken" bus is one of the quintessential Guatemalan experiences; just make sure you get a more comfortable bus for long journeys. A *camioneta* will stop just about anywhere, and, as the joke goes, a "chicken" bus can never be full. Expect to pay about Q8 an hour.

There are also first-class buses *(pullmanes)* that connect the major towns along the main highways and into Mexico and the other Central American countries. They are much quicker, don't stop so frequently, and you'll have a seat reservation.

Shuttle buses, usually modern Japanese minibuses, provide a useful, fast, and comfortable alternative. They mainly cover the prime tourist destinations, such as Antigua–Chichicastenango–Panajachel, but are increasingly common throughout the country. If your destination does not happen to be on a regular route, it is even possible to organise a custom-made, *especial* service – although this comes at a higher cost. Operators include Adrenalina Tours (www.adrenalinatours.com) and Linea Dorada (www.lineadorada.info). Even the longest trip within Guatemala should only cost around US$30.

Another method of transport now common in Guatemala is non-tourist minibuses (*microbuses*) which have replaced the old chicken buses on many paved-road routes.

By Boat

Boats connect the villages around Lago de Atitlán, Puerto Barrios, and Lívingston, and Lívingston and Río Dulce town. These routes all have daily services, and it's not possible or necessary to book in advance.

By Car

Driving in Guatemala can be a hair-raising experience due to a combination of local practices – such as overtaking on blind corners – and the rough, unpaved condition of many roads bar the main ones. Traffic congestion is high in the capital, and the Interamericana and the highway to Puerto Barrios tend to be busy. Security is also an issue you will need to bear in mind: always choose a guarded car park in which to leave your vehicle. However, driving in Guatemala will undoubtedly open up the country to you.

Renting a car here costs from US$150 per week. Many companies

Island ferry from San Pedro on Ambergris Caye, Belize.

will ask you to sign a clause accepting your responsibility for the first US$1,000 of expenses in the event of an accident, theft, or damage – so ensure you take out full-cover insurance.

By Train

There are currently no passenger train services at all in Guatemala.

Belize

The main roads in Belize are paved, and there are frequent, cheap buses to most destinations. There is also an excellent network of internal flights – the quickest, but certainly not the greenest, way to get around. Boat transfers to the *cayes* are easy to come by and relatively cheap.

From the Airport

At **Phillip Goldson International Airport** (www.pgiabelize.com) immigration can be entertaining or infuriating, depending on your attitude. There is a currency-exchange window near the exit (if this is closed, you can get by on US dollars without a problem), as well as an ATM machine and a tourist information booth.

Most tour operators put visitors straight on to connecting flights or provide a minibus service to out-of-town hotels or jungle lodges.

There is a taxi rank outside the airport. Rates into Belize City are fixed and are fairly hefty for the 20-minute ride (B$50/US$25). Rates to other parts of Belize can be negotiated (confirm the price before you get in). You can pay for your taxi at the Airport Taxi Counter, conveniently located next to the arrivals hall exit.

By Air

Small propeller plane services cover most of Belize. This is by far the most convenient way to get around. Most of the flights run on time and few take longer than half an hour. The most popular destinations are from the International Municipal airports to San Pedro on Ambergris Caye (which takes 20 minutes, and gives you spectacular views of the coral reef), and to Placencia and Dangriga, both in the south. If leaving from Belize City, make sure you know whether the flight you are taking will be departing from the International Airport, or the smaller but more commonly used (and cheaper) Municipal Airport in the northern suburbs of Belize City.

National Operators
Maya Island Air
Tel: 671 2190/672 2220
www.mayaislandair.com
Tropic Air
Tel: 226 2626
www.tropicair.com

By Boat

The alternative to flying to Caye Caulker or Ambergris Caye is to take a boat service from Belize City's Marine Terminal next to the Swing Bridge, or from Courthouse Wharf on the other side of the creek. Some services will stop off at St George's Caye on request. Transport to and from other *cayes* by boat is mostly arranged by hotels. Alternatively, you can book your own boat at the docks.

By Bus

Buses run at least hourly between Belize City and the major towns to the north and the west, and hourly to Punta Gorda in the south. Most are the non-air-conditioned US school bus variety. The main bus station in Belize City is just west of the center, and is used by all companies serving all the towns and main roads in Belize; smaller bus lines serving some villages depart from nearby streets. Expect to pay BZ$2–25 depending on the length of the journey. Most buses will stop whenever requested, but Express buses, which cost a little more, only stop in the main towns.

By Car

One way to start your trip is to pick up a rental car (or preferably 4x4) from the airport. Your own transportation comes in very handy in the interior of Belize. Lodges tend to be in isolated areas, and having your own transportation allows you to come and go as you please; you are free to visit wildlife reserves and archeological sites at your own pace, and make trips into town whenever you wish.

Driving is on the right-hand side of the road. Speeds and distances are measured in miles, and although signposting is rare, surprisingly you don't get lost.

Renting a car in Belize is expensive (from around US$80 per day) and a large damage deposit, taken by credit card, is required; insurance is about US$15 a day. The other drawback is the bad condition of some roads. Both the companies below have offices at the International Airport and in Belize City.

Budget
2.5 Miles Northern Highway, Belize City, tel: 223 2435; www.budget-belize.com
Crystal Auto Rental
5 Miles Northern Highway, Belize City, tel: 223 1600; www.crystal-belize.com
This is the largest rental fleet in Belize, excellent value, and the only company which allows you to take its vehicles to Tikal.

By Taxi

Downtown Belize is small enough to handle on foot, and during the cool of the day this is the best way to get around. At night, you should travel by private car or taxi, even for short distances; expect to pay US$3.50–5 for a ride. Hotels and restaurants are used to calling for taxis, which arrive almost immediately; always remember to confirm the price with the driver before setting off.

Transfers between hotels are often pre-arranged for tourists by their tour operator. It is also possible to hire taxis to travel between towns or to explore the countryside.

The Yucatán

The Yucatán is easy to get to and to get around. There are abundant international flights into Cancún, and to some other airports. Unless you have a car, buses provide the main means of getting around, but Mexico's domestic flight network can be useful for making short hops quickly. Aeroméxico and Interjet are the main domestic airlines.

From the Airports

Cancún Airport (www.cancun-airport.net) is 15km (9 miles) south of the city and has two main terminals. Most US and European airlines use Terminal 3; most Mexican airlines, Air Canada, and some others use Terminal 2. A free shuttle bus runs between them. ADO airport buses run every 30 minutes from Terminal 2 to the bus station in downtown Cancún, and once or twice an hour to Playa del Carmen. The fare to Cancún is about US$3. Alternatively, you can take a *colectivo* minibus from either terminal direct to the beach hotels in Cancún for about US$15 per person. Taxis cost from US$35 to the Cancún hotel zone (check rates at https://es.cancun-airport.net/transportation.php).

At Mérida Airport (www.asur.com.mx), ADO buses to the center leave from across the car park, running about every 45 minutes until 7pm. A public bus no 79 (Ruta Aviación, US$0.4) runs along Calle 23. Taxis charge about US$13. At Cozumel Airport there's no bus service, so use *colectivos* (US$7) or taxis (around US$14) to reach your hotel.

Island Runabouts

As **Isla de Mujeres** and **Holbox** are so small, the favorite way to get around is by golf cart. There are plenty of rental shops on each island, and rates are around US$30 a day on both. On Isla de Mujeres the same shops usually rent out motor scooters (from around US$20), and both islands also have bicycle rental facilities. **Cozumel** is that much bigger, so rental cars or scooters are popular.

Ferries to the Islands

Cozumel

Passenger ferries run from **Playa del Carmen**. The two companies, Mexico (www.mexicowaterjets.com.mx) and Ultramar (www.ultramarferry.com), run ferries almost every hour, daily 6am–11pm. A single fare is about US$14. Car ferries are operated by Transbordadores del Caribe (www.transcaribe.net) and run from **Puerto Calica**, south of Playa, 3 times daily (fares start from US$50).

Holbox

The ferry port is tiny **Chiquilá**, a 2–3-hour drive from Cancún. Boats make the crossing every 1–2 hours between 6am–9pm; the fare is about US$5. Second-class buses run to Chiquilá and back from Cancún and Mérida. Drivers can leave cars in safe parking lots in Chiquilá for about US$3–4 a day. For details, go to www.holboxisland.com/transportation/ferries.

Isla de Mujeres

There are passenger ferries from **Puerto Juárez** and **Cancún's Hotel Zone (Embarcadero, Playa Caracol, and Playa Tortugas)**, north of Cancún, run by Ultramar (www.ultramarferry.com) company. From Puerto **Juárez/Isla de Mujeres** there are ferries every 30 minutes in each direction between 5am and 11.30pm and the ticket costs around US$9. Ferries from the hotel zone are less frequent and are more expensive (around US$14 one-way); see website for more details. Buses run to Puerto Juárez from Av Tulum in Cancún. Car ferries run from **Punta Sam and are operated by Maritima Isla Mujeres** (www.maritimaislamujeres.com), seven times each way daily (Mon–Sat) and three times on Sunday.

By Bus

The bus is a basic Mexican institution: every village has a bus or *combi* service of some sort, so there really is nowhere that cannot be reached by public transportation. **First-class** buses are air-conditioned, modern, and very comfortable. All luggage is checked in, and buses are usually very punctual. The main first-class company in the Yucatán is ADO (www.ado.com.mx), while ADO-GL and Platino offer extra-luxury services, with more leg-room, AC air purifier and on-board entertainment and cafeteria. **Second-class** buses provide local services. They are cheaper, less comfortable, and naturally slower than first-class. There are also *intermedio* services, which stop often but have first-class comfort. The most important are the **Riviera** shuttle buses that run every 15 minutes between Cancún and Playa del Carmen, and Mayab buses (one or more each hour) which run the length of the Riviera between Cancún and Tulum. First-class tickets can be bought online or from **Ticketbus** shops (tel: 5784 4652; www.miescape.mx) in many cities. **Terminal CAME** (Calle 70, between calles 69 and 71; tel: 999-924 8391) is the main long-distance, first-class bus terminal in Mérida.

Car Rental

All the main international chains have franchises in Mexico, especially around Cancún, and you can now get very good rates by booking online. If you decide to rent a car once you're in Mexico, you will often get better deals from small local agencies, particularly in Mérida. To rent a car in Mexico you must be over 21 and have your driving licence, passport, and a credit card.

Taxis

Most Mexican taxis do not have meters; instead there are fixed rates for each area which are posted at taxi stands. In Cancún taxi rates are higher in the Hotel Zone than in the city. The general rules are: get an idea of what the correct rates should be, and always agree a fare before getting into a cab. Mérida now has meters in many of its cabs.

Speed bumps ahead.

A

Accommodations

Guatemala

Accommodations in Guatemala range from luxury colonial hotels to backpackers' hostels. There are plenty of budget hotels to choose from and an increasing number of boutique places. *Pensiones* or *hospedajes* have very basic rooms, and these guesthouses are usually run by local families.

Room rates are at their highest and harder to find during Semana Santa (the week leading up to Easter Sunday), Christmas to New Year, and July and August.

Belize

Belize offers a brilliant choice of accommodation ranging from comfortable budget hotels to luxurious beach resorts, country cottages to jungle lodges.

There are a few large internationally owned chain hotels and plenty of small private lodges, hotels, and guesthouses. Travelers with special interests are well catered for – there are remote dive resorts on the outer *cayes*, lodges catering for the eco-tourist and the bird-watcher, and jungle health resorts for those in need of serious pampering. Styles and atmospheres differ wildly: the environment makes a difference, as does the personality of the owners. Many of these places have American and European owners, who make their marks on the feel of the places.

Hotel prices vary greatly depending on the season. The price categories are high-season rates, usually charged between November 15 and May 15 (but may vary between hotels). Prices may drop dramatically in the low season.

The Yucatán

The Yucatán can cater for pretty much all tastes: options run from glittering beach palaces to small town hotels with whirring roof fans. For extra graciousness, there are elegant hotels in restored colonial *haciendas*, and there's a growing number of charming, individually run small hotels and B&Bs, especially in Mérida and Campeche. As alternatives to big resorts, the coasts and islands offer a seductive variety of romantic palm-roofed cabins by the beach – from basic to luxury-standard – and some of the most enjoyable places to stay are in the most apparently remote locations.

Hotel prices are higher overall – often a lot higher – in Cancún, Isla Mujeres, Cozumel, and the Riviera Maya than in the rest of the Yucatán. Hotel rates, especially in resort areas, rise about 10 or 15 percent in the peak season, with additional price hikes for Christmas, New Year, and Easter.

Admission Charges

In Belize admission fees for museums, attractions, Maya sites, and wildlife sanctuaries range from B$8–30. Admission fees for snorkeling and diving at protected marine areas range from B$20–80. Guatemalan Maya ruins cost $4–8, except Tikal which is US$21. Minor Guatemalan museums are US$2–4, important ones US$6–8.

Virtually all archeological sites and major museums in Mexico are administered by the Instituto Nacional de Antropología e Historia (INAH). There are a few variations, but sites are nearly all open daily, 8am–5pm; museums are usually open the same hours, but are closed on Mondays. INAH has a standard set of charges and entry fees: at the time of writing Chichén Itzá and Palenque cost about US$4 and Uxmal $12 (due to the extra fee imposed by the state authorities); smaller sites may charge even less (this is mostly due to the falling value of the Mexican peso).

B

Budgeting for Your Trip

Guatemala is cheap country to travel in, but Belize and Mexico, while still reasonable by North American standards, are about 30 percent more expensive. In Guatemala, backpackers can budget US$25 per day or less (for a hotel stay, food from a *comedor*/market stall and travel); "mid-range" travelers perhaps US$40–50 per person a day; and for those looking to travel in real comfort, US$80–120 per person a day. If you have a taste for exclusive jungle lodges and dive resorts in Belize, rates can run up to US$2,000 a week. In Mexico, costs vary a lot according to where you are: the Riviera Maya has become increasingly expensive, but Yucatán state is cheaper, and costs fall radically in Campeche and Chiapas. To be comfortable, expect to spend around US$80 a day per person, although not traveling solo will obviously cut costs.

C

Children

Guatemala, Belize, and Mexico are superb countries for children to visit. Critically, the locals love kids, and you will find that by traveling with children cultural barriers are immediately broken and everyone will spoil your kids rotten. In general you will find that hotels and restaurants are far more accommodating toward children than their counterparts in Northern Europe or North America, and will go out of their way to provide an extra bed or a child's portion.

Health

Health concerns are obviously paramount (see page 366); contact your doctor before you go. You will have to weigh up whether you and your kids take malaria pills. Getting young children to swallow malaria tablets is troublesome, so you might have to grind the pills up and add the powder to a drink or food. Breast-feeding babies will be protected through their mother's milk. A baby mosquito net is a sound investment.

Where to Go

With young children, you will have to choose your destination carefully. The highland market towns of Guatemala may be culturally fascinating, but trying to keep an eye on your children among the crowds and commotion could be a nightmare. The Museo de los Niños and the Parque Zoológico La Aurora in Guatemala City, as well as the Chapín Safari Park, are safe bets; otherwise, anywhere by the sea, or a hotel with a pool, will quickly cool capricious young tempers. Do bear in mind, however, that the Pacific coast beaches claim several lives each year due to the strong undertow of their waters.

As a well-developed tourist area, the Riviera Maya naturally has extensive, purpose-built facilities for families that are not found elsewhere in the region, and every hotel over a certain size has a pool. However commercial they may feel to more hardened travelers, centers such as AquaWorld in Cancún and "eco-parks" like Xcaret and Xel-Ha provide a very safe, well-organized introduction to tropical nature, as well as activities such as snorkeling, and are likely to appeal to kids.

Touring

If you plan to travel independently with your children, don't set an ambitious itinerary or the heat and hours on the road will exhaust you and your kids. Think about how you plan to travel around: it's far easier to stop and change a diaper or go to the restroom if you're in a rental car than if you're packed on a chicken bus. Remember to order a baby seat from the rental company for kids too young to wear a seatbelt. The occasional bus journey in Mexico, where the buses are much more comfortable and air-conditioned, should be tolerable, but in Belize (and especially Guatemala) it can be a different story.

Flying

Airplanes can also be problematic with very young children, some of whom find the experience uncomfortable and even painful (on their ears). You will need a bassinet (hanging cradle) for your baby – order one from the airline in advance and confirm before you fly.

Entertainment

Relieving boredom is another crucial consideration. One small tip for whiling away hot afternoons is to take a small selection of Lego or Duplo pieces. Unfortunately most children are going to suffer in the lowland humidity and heat of the jungle (where many of the best ruins are). They may not be too impressed by the stones anyway. If you are going to Tikal, and your hotel has child-minding facilities, it might be a good idea to visit on a day-trip excursion.

What to Bring

Disposable diapers are available throughout the region, but bring your own changing mat. You may want to invest in a child-carrying backpack – this will save a lot of grief as most of the roads are far too bumpy for a pushchair.

The local food is rarely very spicy and most children find it delicious. Tummy troubles are another concern, so bring children's diarrhea pills with you. Powdered milk is everywhere. The other main hazards are the sun (hats and waterproof sunblock are essential), dogs (keep them away), and traffic.

Climate

The Maya region is subtropical, and temperatures are governed far less by the seasons than by altitude.

The Rainy Season

The rainy season is from May to October, but it very rarely rains all day. Often mornings are clear, followed by an afternoon downpour. In most of the region, maximum temperatures are kept to a moderate level (25–30°C/75–85°F), because of cloud cover, and nights are warm.

The Dry Season

November to April is the dry season, when the skies are usually clear. At this time of year it can get quite chilly at night anywhere in the region, but especially in the Guatemalan and Chiapas highlands, where frosts are

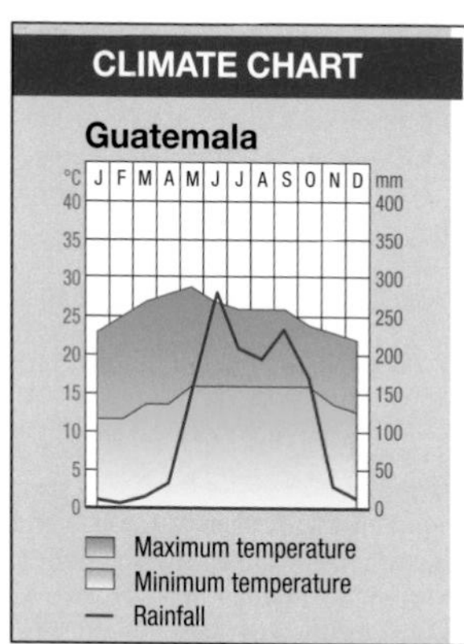

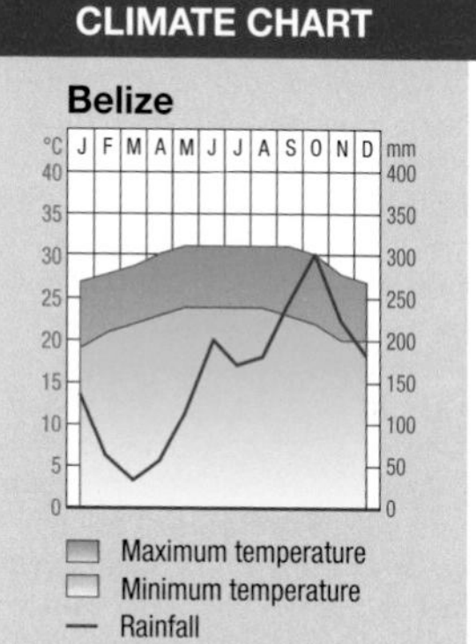

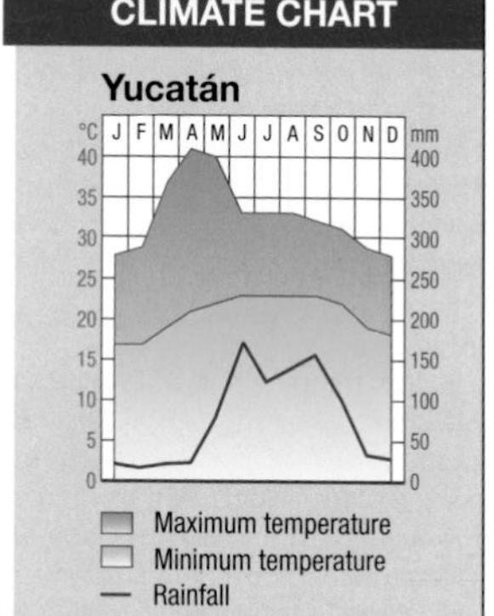

not unknown in high-altitude towns such as Quezaltenango and San Cristóbal de las Casas.

Altitude

Altitude is the most important climatic factor. Much of Guatemala enjoys a delightful climate (the tourist board like to call it "Land of the Eternal Spring"), especially Guatemala City, Antigua, and Lago de Atitlán which are all around 1,500 meters (5,000ft) above sea level. Above this altitude at Quezaltanango and in the Cuchumatanes mountains, nights can get very cool between December and February.

In Belize, the Maya mountains have the most pleasant temperatures, while the low-altitude forests are the most uncomfortable, with humid conditions most of the year. The Yucatán is very flat and low-lying, so it's nearly always hot but rarely too humid inland around the major ruins.

The central lowland forests in the southern Yucatán and northern Guatemala are hot and pretty humid all year round, but most manageable in the dry season, which starts a little later, in December.

By the Coasts

There is normally a pleasant breeze off the ocean to cool things down a little by the Pacific and Caribbean coasts; the Belizean *cayes* are never too sticky. Severe storms can strike during hurricane season (June to October), but warnings are usually excellent locally, and Mexico in particular has very high-standard hurricane precautions. If you hear of a storm, hotel owners will be able to pass on instructions. In 2005, Hurricane Wilma was the worst hurricane ever recorded in the region and hit Cancún very hard, yet with minimal loss of life and injuries – far less than when comparable hurricanes have hit the US. Fortunately, hurricane Irma (the strongest ever recorded in the Atlantic), which ravished many Caribbean islands and Florida in 2017, spared the Yucatán and the Belize coast.

When to Visit

There's no bad time to visit the Maya world, but perhaps the very best season is between November and March, when temperatures are never oppressive, the skies are clear, and the humidity low. It is worth bearing in mind that at the height of the rainy season, visiting Petén's more remote ruins can land you in mud thigh-deep.

Crime and Safety

It's important to take some basic precautions when visiting the Maya countries, but not to adopt a paranoid attitude – crime against tourists is still relatively rare, and the majority of visitors will not experience trouble of any kind. Having said that, general crime levels in Guatemala are among the highest in Latin America, and tourists have been targeted by (occasionally armed) criminals on the roads (including the notorious Carretera Salvador linking the capital with the El Salvador border) and on buses. It's a good idea to register with your embassy on arrival and to keep abreast of what's going on – Inguat (http://www.inguat.gob.gt), the Guatemalan tourist institute, provides up-to-date security information via their Asistur line which can be reached on tel: 1500. The US State Department (https://travel.state.gov/content/travel/en.html) and the UK Foreign and Commonwealth Office's travel advice pages for Guatemala also give a solid overview of the current security situation (www.gov.uk/foreign-travel-advice).

Probably the two cities with the worst reputations are Belize City and Guatemala City, especially the downtown areas. Both are considered safe during the day, but after dark it's best to take taxis to get around. There are hustlers in Belize City who will try to intimidate you into parting with a dollar, but the threats are seldom serious. Walk on, or speak to the tourist police if you are persistently harassed. Be particularly vigilant in the areas around George Street and Kraal Road.

The Yucatán Peninsula, particularly Yucatán state and Campeche, has a much lower level of crime of any kind than other parts of Mexico. There's little or no threat from drug traffickers in this part of Mexico, but there is some petty crime such as bag thefts and pickpocketing in parts of the Riviera Maya, notably Cancún, Playa del Carmen, and Tulum. The north side of downtown Cancún is an area where it pays to be careful (and tourists can easily avoid it). Elsewhere, be particularly careful not to leave anything valuable on the beach while swimming, and do not leave valuables in budget hotel rooms or basic beach cabañas that are easily broken into. If in doubt, ask hotels to lock up your bag when you go out.

Hikers will feel safe in most parts of the Maya world. In Guatemala, although the mountain areas of the Western Highlands are remote, the indigenous communities are very insular and attacks are extremely rare. However, there have been cases of armed robbery, such as on the trails around Lago de Atitlán. The Pacaya and San Pedro volcanoes are now well guarded and considered safe to climb without the security of a guided tour, but take a tour if you are climbing other volcanoes, including Agua.

Marijuana (called *ganja* in Belize) is illegal throughout the region, as are other drugs. If you get into any trouble with the police, the first thing to do is to contact your embassy.

Customs Regulations

Guatemala

Duty Free: 80 cigarettes or 3.5 ounces of tobacco; 1.5l of alcohol; cameras for personal use; no restriction on perfume.
Restricted Items: fresh food.

Belize

Free imports: 200 cigarettes or 50 cigars or 250 grams of tobacco, 1 liter of wine or spirits. Removal, sale, and exportation of the following are prohibited by law in Belize: any kind of coral without a license, archeological artifacts, orchids, shells, fish, crustaceans, turtles and materials from turtles.

The Yucatán

Free imports: 200 cigarettes or 50 cigars or 200 grams of pipe tobacco, 3 liters of wine or liquor, goods up to a value of $300. There are severe penalties for carrying drugs, weapons, or (when leaving) any item from any archeological site.

D

Disabled Travelers

Disabled travelers will have a hard time in the Maya region, except in Cancún where the sidewalks are smooth and the hotels have elevators. Access for wheelchair users is usually non-existent everywhere else, and mobility is compounded by potholed sidewalks and roads, cobblestones, and an almost complete absence of elevators outside the five-star city-center hotels.

Travel by public transportation is another challenge. In **Mexico**, traveling by first-class long-distance bus need not be too much of a problem, since wheelchairs can be stored in the luggage compartment, there's a conductor at hand to assist passengers, and you will be assigned your own seat. Traveling by "chicken bus" in **Guatemala** is not worth thinking about, though there are a number of privately run shuttles that ply the main tourism towns and whose driver will assist passengers with their luggage Thankfully, many Guatemalan hotels are low-rise, so even outside the more upscale hotels with their lifts and ramps, you shouldn't have too much of a problem finding accessible sleeping quarters. In **Belize**, travel is also difficult, though again shuttle services present a more accessible alternative to taking public buses.

If you can travel with an able-bodied friend to help you get around, these difficulties will be reduced.

There are organizations that will direct you to tour operators that are well set up for disabled travelers. Try **Twin Peaks** (County Road 36, 80645 La Salle, Colorado); tel: 303 678 7080; www.twinpeakstravel.com) or consult the website Sath (http://sath.org/home) for excellent travel advice for the disabled.

E

Embassies and Consulates

Guatemala

Canada: 8th floor, Edificio Edyma Plaza, 13a Calle 8-44, Zona 10; tel: 2363 4348; www.canadainternational.gc.ca

UK: 11th floor, Torre Internacional, 16a Calle 00-55, Zona 10; tel: 502 2380 7300; www.gov.uk/world/organisations/british-embassy-guatemala

US: Av La Reforma 7-01, Zona 10; tel: 2326 4000; https://gt.usembassy.gov

Belize

Canada: Consulate of Canada, 80 Princess Margaret Drive, Belize City; tel: 223 1060; http://www.embassy-canada.com/belize.html

UK: North Ring Road/Melhado Parade, Belmopan; tel: 822 2146/2147/2717/2981; www.gov.uk/world/organisations/british-high-commission-belmopan

US: Floral Park Road, Belmopan; tel: 822 4011; https://bz.usembassy.gov/

The Yucatán

Canada: Calle Schiller 529, Col. Bosque de Chapultepec, Mexico City; tel: 5724 7900; www.canadainternational.gc.ca/mexico-mexique

UK: Calle Río Lerma 71, Col. Cuauhtémoc, Mexico City; tel: 55 1670 3200; www.gov.uk/world/organisations/british-embassy-mexico-city

US: Paseo de la Reforma 305, Col. Cuauhtémoc, Mexico City; tel: 5080 2000; https://mx.usembassy.gov

Canadian Consulate in Cancún: Centro Empresarial, Oficina E7, Blvd Kukulcán Km 12; tel: 998 883 3360

British Consulate General in Cancún: Torre Europea, Blvd Kukulcán Km 12.5; tel: 551670 3200

US Consulates

Cancún: Blvd Kukulcán Km 13, Torre La Europea; tel: 998 883 0272

Mérida: Calle 60, 338K and calles 29 and 31, Col. Alcalá Martin; tel: 999 942 5700

Playa del Carmen: Calle 1 Sur, between Av 15 and Av 20; tel: 984 873 0303

Emergencies

Guatemala

Police **100**
Fire **123/122**
Ambulance **125**
Tourist Police **110**
Inguat (Guatemala tourist board)-backed Tourist Assistance 2421 2800 or **1500** (24-hour help line)

Belize

Police **911**
Fire/Ambulance **90** (Belize City only)

The Yucatán
National Emergency Number 911

Mérida

In **Mérida** the Tourist Police (tel: 999 924 400) wear brown-and-white uniforms and patrol on foot or motorcycles. They are there to help, so don't be afraid to ask for assistance if you need it.

Police 999 924 400/930 3200

Cancún
Police 060
Tourist Police 998 885 2277
Red Cross 998 884 1616

Campeche
General emergency number (police, fire brigade, ambulance) – **911**

Electricity

Guatemala: 110 volts, flat North American-style two-pronged plugs.
Belize: 110 volts, flat two-pronged plugs.
Yucatán: 110 volts, flat two-pronged plugs.

Etiquette

Politeness, a smile, and an effort to speak a little Spanish will help you get more out of the Maya countries. Avoid being openly critical of the region's problems, including corruption, inefficiency and poverty – Mexicans, Guatemalans, and Belizeans recognize their countries' difficulties, but some are sensitive to criticism.

If you have an appointment, get there on time, but don't be too surprised if you have to wait around a while – punctuality is not generally considered a great virtue. Try not to talk too loudly, as the Maya in particular find Westerners overbearingly loud. If you visit one of the smaller highland markets in Guatemala (not Chichicastenango or San Francisco El Alto), one of the most interesting aspects is how quiet the whole affair is, with business being conducted *sotto voce*.

If you add some flexibility to your travel plans, and expect the odd delay, you will have a far less frustrating time if you get held up. Perhaps the biggest mistake inexperienced travelers make is to try to see too much in too short a time. With the inevitable delays, by setting a punishing itinerary you will spend most of your time on buses and in bus stations. Sometimes less is more.

Public nudity is offensive in most of the region, but topless and nude bathing are now accepted in trendier parts of the Riviera Maya (Playa del Carmen, away from the main town beach, and Tulum). It's also advisable to cover your legs and shoulders when you visit churches – short shorts are usually frowned upon.

F

Festivals and Events

Guatemala

January 15 The greatest pilgrimage in Central America, as thousands of pilgrims descend on the Basilica of the Black Christ at Esquipulas.

February 20 Día de la Marimba. The celebration of the instrument declared the country's national symbol in 1955. Concerts in cities and towns.

March Huge pilgrimage to remote Chajul in the Ixil region on the second Friday of Lent.

Semana Santa (Easter Week) The most spectacular place in the world to witness Easter is Antigua, Guatemala. There are four days of huge processions, colored sawdust carpets fill the streets, and the whole town seems to dress up and re-enact the last days of Christ.

Good Friday In Guatemala City, this day is marked with political satire from the city's students in Zona 1, an event called Huelga de Dolores. There is also a famous confrontation between Maximón and Christ in Santiago Atitlán.

June 30 Army Day.

August 15 Spectacular fiesta in Joyabaj, Western Highlands, with ceremonies that include the *palo volador* – men swinging upside down attached to a pole.

September 15 Independence Day.

October 12 Discovery of Americas anniversary. A controversial bank holiday, celebrated by many *ladinos*, but many of the politically active indigenous population use "Columbus Day" to protest against racial discrimination.

October 20 Revolution Day.

November 1–2 All Saints' Day and Day of the Dead. Wild alcohol-charged horse race in Todos Santos Cuchumatán on the 1st. Flying of giant kites in Santiago Sacatépequez and Comalapa. "Day of the Dead" on the 1st, when families head to cemeteries to remember their dead.

November 25–28 A huge Garifuna Festival in Livingstone celebrating the Afro-Caribbean culture of the Garifuna people from Guatemala, Belize, and Honduras.

December 7 La Quema del Diablo (Burning of the Devil). Effigies of the Devil made of paper are burnt at 6pm sharp in order to cleanse homes of devils. Best observed in Guatemala City and Antigua.

December 21 Culmination of the Chichicastenango fiesta with firecrackers and the *palo volador*.

December 25 Christmas Day.

Belize

February Carnaval. It culminates a week before Lent when boisterous celebrations are held in San Pedro.

March Baron Bliss Day. A celebration in honor of Sir Henry Edward Ernest Victor Bliss with sailboat race, horse races and kiting competitions.

March/April Easter. A weeklong religious celebrations take place across the country.

June/July Lobster festivals in San Pedro and Placencia.

August Costa Maya Festival in San Pedro. A five-day celebration of Maya music, dance, cuisine and art with artists from five Maya countries: Belize, El Salvador, Guatemala, Honduras and Mexico. Deer Dance Festival in San Antonio with dancers emulating the hunting of a deer and competitors trying to climb a greased pole.

September 21 Independence Day. Celebrations include colourful parades, processions, and parties across the country.

November 19 Garifuna Settlement Day. A week-long festival of Garifuna culture celebrating the arrival of Garinagu people in Dangriga in 1832. Music and dance galore.

The Yucatán

January Los Reyes Magos festival in Tizimín. This is a celebration of the three wise men, images of whom are displayed in front of the church in Tizimín. Here the faithful pay their respects with fresh green branches. Mérida celebrates its foundation (January 6) with a 20 day-long celebrations featuring concerts, colourful processions and numerous cultural activities.

January–February Cozumel, Campeche, Cancún, and several other towns celebrate Carnival, a week-long pre-lenten celebration with parades, floats, and dances.

January 26–February 3 La Candelaria festival, in Valladolid and Chicxulub, is a Christian festival celebrating the presentation of Jesus at the Temple.

March 19–21 Equinox and Descent of Kukulcán celebrated in Chichén Itzá.

March–April Ticul, Acanceh, and many other towns hold Easter celebrations.

May Cedral Fair with cattle shows, races, rides, and bullfights is held in Cozumel. Celestún, Chumayel, and other towns hold a fiesta in honor of Santa Cruz, around May 3.Marine Day fishing tournament in Cozumel.

June Some towns hold a fiesta in honor of San Pedro and San Pablo.

August Traditional fiesta in Oxkutzcab. San Felipe holds festival of Santo Domingo de Guzmán.

September San Román, a week-long fiesta, is held in Campeche. Mérida holds the Cristo de las Ampollas (Christ of the Blisters) festival until October.

October San Francisco de Asis fiesta held in Telchac Puerto.

October 31–November 2 Day of the Dead *(Hanal Pixan)*, marked across the region.

November–December Xmatkuil, south of Mérida, hosts the Yucatán State Fair.

December 12 and preceding days: Virgin of Guadalupe, processions all over Mexico.

H

Health and Medical Care

Hygiene standards are much better than in many other parts of the developing world, but diarrhea may still strike no matter how careful you are. Stomach upsets are likely to be your main concern, but you should also be inoculated against polio, cholera, tetanus, typhoid, and hepatitis. None of these diseases is at all common in the Maya countries, immunization is not a mandatory requirement, and the risk is very low, but every year there are cases. Getting bitten by a rabid animal is also statistically extremely unlikely, but if you are bitten you should begin immunization shots immediately.

Mosquitoes are likely to be much more of a concern, and it's imperative to minimize the chances of being bitten, especially in remote, lowland areas. Diligently apply repellent *(repelente)* to all exposed areas of skin, especially around your ankles. You may want to buy your own mosquito net, though they are often provided by hotels in lowland areas. Burn mosquito coils (available locally) and leave a fan on at night while you sleep.

Malaria is present in rainforest (and some lowland) areas but is not at all common across the region, and virtually unknown in most of the Yucatán Peninsula. There have been no reports of chloroquine-resistant strains of mosquito in the region, but for the latest information check with a specialized travel health clinic before you go. There's no malaria above 1,500 meters (5,000ft) in the region, so if you are restricting your visit to highland Guatemala or Chiapas, you may choose not to take the course.

Dengue fever, carried by a daytime mosquito, is on the increase worldwide, and there have been a few outbreaks in the Maya region. It's normally caught by being bitten near pools or puddles of dirty, stagnant water. The symptoms are fever, severe headache, complete loss of energy, and usually a skin rash. There is one rare strain, **dengue hemorrhagic**, that can be very serious but is rarely fatal in adults: in most cases the body heals itself within a few days. There's no vaccine for any strain of dengue, so you should take great precaution against being bitten; the only remedy is to take complete rest until the dengue clears, which seriously interrupts your holiday.

Recently, the **Zika virus** has been reprorted in Guatemala, the lowlands of Mexico and Belize, so pregnant women should either avoid these areas altogether or take extra precautions to avoid being bitten by mosquitoes. Check this website for more information about the virus and precautions to be taken: https://wwwnc.cdc.gov/travel/page/zika-information.

Take high-factor sunscreen, a hat for protection against the sun, and drink plenty of (bottled) water to avoid dehydration, especially at high altitudes.

Dos and Don'ts

A few sensible measures will help you enjoy your stay:

Don't drive or take buses after dark.

Avoid fanny packs (bum bags) and use a concealed money belt instead.

Adopt an air of confidence: this is excellent protection.

When sitting at an outdoor restaurant table, never leave a bag on the back of a chair or on the floor where you can't see it.

When downtown in big cities, enter a cafe or restaurant to check your map rather than looking lost on the street.

Avoid wearing jewelry or an expensive-looking watch.

Conceal cameras, smart phones, and iPads in a daypack when you're not using them.

Don't walk down quiet streets after dark.

Drinking Water

Don't drink tap water and don't brush your teeth with it – contaminated water can transmit the hepatitis A virus and is a major cause of sickness in Guatemala. In the cities, drinking water is heavily chlorinated but should still be avoided. It's sometimes difficult to avoid, but you are unlikely to catch anything by, for example, accidentally swallowing some water in the shower. In Mexico, most restaurants, even cheap ones, use purified water to make ice and diluted fruit juices (*aguas*). If in doubt, ask that drinks are served without ice *(sin hielo)*. As a general rule, only eat fruits and vegetables that you have washed in clean water or peeled yourself.

Clean water is called *agua purificada* (which is just guaranteed clean, not mineral, water) and you should always drink this rather than tap water. Use this to brush your teeth as well. Many hotels provide bottles of purified water in each room. *Agua mineral* (mineral water) is quite rare and expensive. Bottled drinks like colas, beer, and so on are a safe bet, as are fresh juices. *Licuados* (shakes) are normally made with milk or purified water in Mexico, but you need to be more wary of them in Guatemala.

If you plan to spend much time camping, either buy a water filter and purification tablets or boil water for 20 minutes to be safe.

Guatemala

You must have medical insurance before coming to Guatemala. Public hospitals are not good and should be avoided if at all possible; the private sector is generally much more efficient and better equipped. Your embassy will have a list of English-speaking doctors and dentists. In remote areas, it may be best to get to a city as soon as possible if you can travel. Keep all receipts and contact your insurance company immediately if you do need medical treatment.

Alerta Médica (http://alertamedica.com.gt/) is a private medical emergency assistance service. Contact them by phoning **1711**.

Hospitals

Centro Médico, 6 Av 3-22, Zona 10, Guatemala City; tel: 2279 4949; www.centromedico.com.gt

Casa de Salud Santa Lucía, Calzada Santa Lucía Sur 7, Antigua; tel: 7832 3122

Centro Médico Galeno, 2 Calle 3-08, Zona 3, Cobán; tel: 7951 3175

Dentists

Central de Dentistas Especialistas, 20C 11-17, Zona 10, Guatemala City; tel: 2285 6767

Belize

No **vaccinations** are required if traveling to Belize, except a yellow fever certificate if you are arriving within six days of visiting an infected area. However, typhoid, polio, and hepatitis A jabs are recommended by most doctors.

There is **malaria** in some parts of Belize, so if you are planning to spend extended stays in jungle areas it is advisable to take a course of anti-malaria tablets. Belize has also be affected by the Zica virus epidemic.

It is important to be extremely careful in the strong sun and to drink plenty of water, especially on walking trips. Avoid too much activity between 11am and 4pm on hot days, and pack sunscreen and strong insect repellent (twice as much as you think you'll need) as it is often not that easy to purchase outside tourist areas.

If you are going diving or snorkeling be very careful to avoid touching the coral, both to protect the reef and yourself. Disturbances to live outcroppings can destroy the coral's fragile ecosystem, while cuts and abrasions from the reef often become painfully infected and take a long time to heal.

The quality of food preparation is generally good, so there is not a great risk of stomach problems. Although tap water is potable in most towns and resort areas, it is recommended that you drink bottled or sterilized water, especially on the *cayes* or in the south. Tap water on Caye Caulker is unfit to drink.

Medical Services

It is uncommon for visitors to contract any serious health problems, but should you require a doctor your hotel should be able to recommend one. There are modern hospitals in Belize City, Belmopan, and all the district towns, with health centers in San Pedro, Caye Caulker, Placencia, and some villages. In an emergency in Belize City, contact one of the following doctors or hospitals.

Belize Medical Associates, 5791 St Thomas Street, Belize City; tel: 223 0303; www.belizemedical.com

Karl Heusner Memorial Hospital, Princess Margaret Drive, Belize City; tel: 223 1548; www.khmh.bz

The Yucatán

It is essential to have a comprehensive travel insurance policy, with full medical cover including the option of repatriation by air in an emergency, when traveling in Mexico. There are no special precautions required, but it is advisable to be inoculated against tetanus, typhoid, and hepatitis A. Note that here is a moderate Zica virus risk in the region.

In the main cities and tourist areas there are well-equipped private hospitals with English-speaking staff that are the best places to head to if you need any kind of treatment. In rural areas, there are public health centers (Centros de Salud), which are more basic but can still deal with emergencies. In most of Mexico there is a common phone number to call for all emergency services: 911.

Private Clinics

Cancún: Amerimed Hospital, Av Tulum Sur Mza, 260; tel: 998 881 3400; www.amerimed.com.mx

Mérida: Centro Médico de las Américas, Calle 54, 365, off Av Pérez Ponce; tel: 999 926 1111; www.centromedicodelasamericas.com.mx

I

Internet

Guatemala

Most of Guatemala offers some type of internet access. Free wi-fi is widely available in larger cities' restaurants (including the popular Pollo Camperos branches), cafés, and some public spaces. Even the smallest towns tend to have internet cafés. You can check the free wi-fi hotspots map at https://wifispc.com/guatemala.

Belize

Internet is widely available across the country, but rather expensive. Internet cafés are found in all major towns and some villages. Wi-fi is also available in many hotels and resorts while cafés only offer free wi-fi once you something to eat or drink.

The Yucatán

Even the smallest town seems to have at least one internet café. For those traveling with laptops and smart phones, a remarkable number of cheap hotels now offer wi-fi connections, often for no extra charge, or computer terminals for guests.

L

LGBTQ Travelers

The Maya world presents no serious difficulties for gay travelers, but the scene in all three countries is very underground, with very few gay bars and almost no meeting places for lesbians. Though Mexico's reputation as an overtly macho society is well deserved, the Maya states are among the least homophobic in the country. Indigenous Mexicans are much less concerned with crude machista postures than the *mestizos* of the cities and desert states in the north.

Guatemala

Guatemala has a small gay scene, centered in the capital where there are a few gay clubs and bars. While it's best to be discreet (holding hands in public is unwise), most gays and lesbians find little local hostility. Exercise some common sense and avoid the more macho men-only cantinas. For more information contact Gay Guatemala (www.gayguatemala.com).

Belize

Homosexuality has been legal in Belize since 2016 and the first Pride Week was held in 2017. Generally, gay travelers shouldn't have any trouble, but discretion is of the essence. Caribbean attitudes towards gay people can be homophobic, so holding hands is not an option.

Mexico

Homosexuality is legal in Mexico, since there are no federal laws forbidding it, but cruising zones are occasionally targeted by police in campaigns to protect "public morality", making discretion wise. Cancún is the exception, as it's much more in tune with US resorts than rural Mexico. There is a smallish but visible gay scene in Cancún and Playa del Carmen, with several small, buzzy nightclubs, and a fairly well recognized "gay beach" north of Playa

M

Maps

All of the region's tourist offices can provide you with a basic map of their country, which are fine for general use, but tend to be outdated and inadequate if you plan to venture off the beaten track. Local, free English-language magazines such as Mérida's *Yucatán Today* or the Riviera's *Cancún Tips* contain useful basic maps.

The best maps of the Maya countries are published by **International Travel Maps and Books** (12300 Bridgeport Road, Richmond, BC, Canada V6V 1J5; tel: 604-273 1400; www.itmb.com). The company produces maps of Guatemala, Belize, the Yucatán, and southeastern Mexico. Purchase before you travel, since they are not that widely available in the region. In Mexico, the Guía Rojí (www.guiaroji.com.mx) maps are good for drivers.

Hikers will need larger-scale maps. Ordnance Survey maps (1:50,000) of Belize cover most of the country; you can buy them at **Stanfords** (12–14 Long Acre, London WC2; tel: 020-7836 1321; www.stanfords.co.uk) or online. The best large-scale maps of Mexico are produced by the state cartographers INEGI (www.inegi.org.mx), but are hard to find. Mérida is the only place in the region where you can find bookshops with a decent map selection.

Media

Newspapers and Magazines

Guatemala: The main daily newspapers are *Prensa Libre*, *Siglo XXI*, *El Periódico*, and *La Hora*. All are published in Spanish. The *Guatemala Times* (www.guatemala-times.com) is a good online source of news. There is also the free, monthly English-language magazine *The Revue* (www.revuemag.com), produced in Antigua.

Public Holidays

Guatemala

January 1 New Year's Day
Semana Santa Holy Week, the four days preceding Easter
May 1 Labor Day
June 30 Army Day, anniversary of the 1871 revolution
August 15 Guatemala City fiesta
September 15 Independence Day
October 20 Revolution Day
November 1 All Saints' Day
December 24 Christmas Eve
December 25 Christmas Day
December 31 New Year's Eve

Belize

January 1 New Year's Day
March 5 National Heroes and Benefactors Holiday
March/April Easter weekend
May 1 Labor Day
May 21 Sovereign's Day Holiday
September 10 St George's Caye Day
September 21 Independence Day
October 8 Pan-American Day
November 19 Garífuna Settlement Day
December 25 Christmas Day
December 26 Boxing Day

The Yucatán

January 1 New Year's Day
February 5 Constitution Day
February 24 Day of the Flag
March 21 Benito Juárez's birthday
March/April Good Friday and Easter Sunday
May 1 Labor Day
May 5 Victory Day
September 16 Independence Day
October 12 Día de la Raza
November 2 Day of the Dead
November 20 Revolution Day
December 12 Day of Our Lady of Guadelupe
December 25 Christmas Day

The Revue deals with tourism and cultural issues of interest to an expat and tourist readership, and is worth consulting for its informative features and listings. There's a page or two devoted to different regions in Guatemala, and also Belize.

Belize: Newspapers in Belize are all weekly and are either owned by, or connected to, political parties, and thus often dwell on bad-mouthing the opposition. The main mastheads are *Amandala*, the *Belize Times*, the *Guardian*, and the *Reporter*.

The Yucatán: *Yucatán Today (*http://yucatantoday.com*)*, a free monthly, is widely available and is very informative about activities and tourist facilities in Yucatán state. *The News (*http://www.thenews.mx/*)*, an English-language daily produced in Mexico City, is available at some newsstands, and a special local Cancún edition of the *Miami Herald* is widely distributed, and often free in hotels. There are also innumerable free booklets and brochures including maps and information about the region. The All About Cancún website (http://allaboutcancun.com) offers essential information for travelers visiting Yucatán while the *Inside Mexico* (www.inside-mexico.com) monthly magazine publishes articles on Mexican culture, history and society, and provides tourist information too.

Radio and Television

Guatemala: There are hundreds of radio stations, devoted to everything from merengue to Evangelical worship. La Marca (94.1 FM) is a popular reggaetón station, while Atmosfera (96.5 FM) plays rock and indie.

There are dozens of television stations in Guatemala, and several foreign channels (including CNN) are broadcast on cable, which is available in most of the main towns.

Belize: There are a couple of local channels, but the most popular TV is from cable (mostly pirated from satellite) and is all American soaps, sport, and chat. Channel 5 broadcasts the best television, producing a daily news program and good documentaries. Radio is a big favorite in Belize. Love FM at 95.1 FM has English and Spanish programs – tune in for a mix of local and BBC World news, weather reports interspersed with chat shows, and a selection of rock and reggae. The other popular channel is KREM FM at 91.1 FM.

The Yucatán: Even budget hotels in Mexico often have satellite or cable TV, with a variety of US channels (CNN, ESPN) as well as Mexican ones, and sometimes BBC World and other international channels too. Movies on Mexican TV are often shown in English with Spanish subtitles, and the Spanish-language Sports Channels (Fox Sports Americas, ESPN en Español) regularly show English, Spanish, and other league soccer games.

Money

Debit cards are the most popular way to access money, and credit cards are useful in upmarket hotels, restaurants, and stores. Visa and MasterCard are widely recognized. Most towns will have an ATM machine or two for 24-hour withdrawals, but banks often charge a commission and a slightly lower exchange rate. For safety reasons it is always advisable to use ATMs in shopping centers and banks.

US dollar bills are accepted almost everywhere in Belize, where the Belize dollar is pegged to the US dollar at a rate of B$2 to US$1. Some prices are quoted in US dollars, so it is important to check which currency a price is in before agreeing to it. Elsewhere, dollars are not widely accepted, and if you do pay for things in dollars you will usually pay a little more. It's worth having a few bills for emergencies, however, since some shopkeepers and hotels will change dollars (usually for a poor rate) if the banks are closed.

Currency

Guatemala: the quetzal comes in notes of Q0.50, Q1, Q5, Q10, Q20, Q50, Q100, and Q200. It is divided into 100 centavos.

Belize: Belizean dollars, with notes from $2 to $100, are divided into 100 cents.

The Yucatán: At the time of writing, the Mexican peso stood around 18 pesos to the dollar. *Casas de Cambio* change money, although the exchange rate is often better at a bank. ATMs (cash machines) are easy to find in most towns, but not in the more remote beach and rural areas, so be sure to take enough cash (in pesos) for your stay.

O

Opening Hours

Guatemala

Businesses and offices are generally open between 9am and 5pm, but they often close for an hour or two between 12 noon and 2pm. Many banks stay open until 7pm (and even 8pm), especially in tourism-orientated towns, some open on Saturday mornings. Archeological sites are usually open daily from 8am to 5pm (Tikal from 6am to 5pm), and nature reserves are also usually open daily, such as the Quetzal Reserve (6am–4pm) and Cerro Cahui (7am–4pm).

Belize

Most stores and offices open Mon–Fri 8am–noon, with afternoon hours varying from 1–5pm to 3–8pm. Most banks open Mon–Fri 8am–3 or 4pm; some are also open on Saturdays. Almost everything is closed on public holidays.

The Yucatán

Banking hours are usually from 9am to any time between 3 and 7pm. Many shops close at lunchtime for a lengthy break, reopening around 4 or 5pm and remaining open until late evening. Larger shops and malls stay open all day.

Outdoor Activities

Guatemala

Volcano Climbing
Volcano climbing is a very popular activity, and there are over 37 volcanic peaks in Guatemala to choose from.

Adrenalina Tours
Several offices in the country
Tel: 5308 1489
www.adrenalinatours.com
Volcano climbs including Santa María, hiking and tours around the Xela region and Western Highlands.

Old Town Outfitters
5 Av Sur 12, Antigua
Tel: 7832 9170
www.adventureguatemala.com
Terrific volcano and rock-climbing trips.

Ox Expeditions
7th Calle Poniente #17 (7th Street W. #17), AntiguaTel: 7832 0468
www.oxexpeditions.com
Easy-to-difficult volcano climbing, including bespoke hikes up Pacaya. They also offer a five-day extreme tour of all the active volcanoes in Guatemala.

Quetzaltrekkers
Casa Argentina, 12 Diagonal 8-43, Zona 1, Quezaltenango
Tel: 7765 5895
www.quetzaltrekkers.com
A superb organization that arranges trips to Volcán Tajumulco, the highest peak in Central America, as well as amazing hikes between Todos Santos and Nebaj. All the profits benefit a local charity for street children.

Bird-watching
There are over 700 species of birds found in Guatemala, making it a bird-watchers' paradise. Contact **Cayaya Birding** (tel: 5308 5160; www.cayaya-birding.com) for the best locations for birdwatching and trip details.
National parks offer many bird-watching opportunities.

Belize

Diving
Belize is one of the world's top scuba-diving and snorkeling destinations. Introductory courses are available with qualified dive instructors. The most popular dive sites are the atolls, the Blue Hole, Shark Ray Alley, and Hol Chan Marine Reserve.

Amigos Del Mar
San Pedro, Ambergris Caye
Tel: 226 2706
www.amigosdivebelize.com
Very experienced dive operators, offering full PADI instruction and trips to the reef and outer atolls.

Frenchies Diving Services
Caye Caulker
Tel: 501 226 0234
www.frenchiesdivingbelize.com
Frenchies is *the* dive company on Caye Caulker. Trips to Hol Chan and the Blue Hole, as well as to locations on the reef around Caye Caulker.

Garbutt's
Joe Taylor Creek
Punta Gorda
Tel: 813 0616
www.garbuttsfishinglodge.com/
For diving trips to the far southern *cayes* of Belize, including the Sapodillas.

Cavemans Snorkeling Tours
Caye Caulker (Front Street, Playa Asunción)
Tel: 501 605 0345www.cavemansnorkelingtours.com
Best dive operators in this region, offering trips to the Belizean Barrier Reef, Hol Chan Marine Reserve, Shark Ray Alley.

Horseback Riding

Banana Bank Lodge
Mile 49, Western Highway, just outside Belmopan
Tel: 832 2020
www.bananabank.com
Belize's largest equestrian centre, with 100 well-trained horses. Picnic facilities are also available, and you can swim in the Belize River.

Hanna Stables
San Lorenzo Farm, nr San Ignacio
Tel: 661 1536
www.hannastables.com
Horse riding along the Mopan River and to Maya ruins.

Mountain Equestrian Trails
Mile 8 Mountain Pine Ridge Road, Cayo district
Tel: 1-800-838 3918 or 669 1124
www.metbelize.com
This is Belize's top horseback-riding holiday center, with fantastic forest trails.

The Yucatán

Diving

The Islands

Isla Mujeres
This is the best diving center near Cancún, with sites for every level of expertise, and small operators offering personal service at decent rates. The shallow **Manchones** reef is great for snorkelers and scuba novices, while further out there are more testing sites such as **Sleeping Sharks** cave, where (harmless) reef sharks bask in the current. Most dive shops also offer fishing trips.

Carey Dive Center
Avenida Matamoros 13A; tel: 998 877 0763; www.careydivecenter.com. One of the biggest dive shops in Isla, with professional staff and reliable service.

Cozumel
The most famous dive area of all, Cozumel has the region's most comprehensive diving infrastructure, with several specialist dive hotels. Many other hotels also offer good-value diving packages.

Deep Blue, Calle Adolfo Rosado Salas 200, corner of Avenida 10; tel: 987 872 5653; www.deepbluecozumel.com. Top of the line in dive shops: first-rate staff and equipment, and offers every option right up to advanced specialist courses.

Dive Cozumel, Calle Adolfo Rosado Salas 85, between Av. Melgar and Av. 5 Norte; tel: 987 872 4567; www.divecozumel.net. One of the best-equipped operators, with special facilities for advanced and technical diving.

Studio Blue, Calle Adolfo Rosado Salas, between avenidas 5 and 10; tel: 987 872 4414; www.cozumel-diving.net/studio-blue. Good-value operator offering basic dives and low-cost instruction.

Playa del Carmen
The base for some of the most experienced dive operators, who run trips to many parts of the coast.
Phocea Riviera Maya, Calle 10 between 1 and 5 Av.; tel: 984 873 1210; www.phoceamexico.com. High-quality French-run company with an exciting range of dive packages, including *cenote* and reef dives.
Yucatek Divers, Avenida 15, between calles 2 and 4 Norte; tel: 984 803 2836; www.yucatek-divers.com

Akumal and Tulum
Divers are most drawn by the *cenotes* and caves, but there's good offshore diving as well.
Aquatech-Villas De Rosa, Aventuras Akumal, Akumal; tel: 984 875 9020; www.cenotes.com. Cave diving specialists, but with a full range of open-water diving as well. Has a very attractive hotel for dive-accommodation packages.
Cenote Dive Center, Andromeda Ote and Centauro Sur; tel: 984 871 2232; www.cenotedive.com. Cavern and cave specialists, who also provide excellent *cenote* snorkeling trips.

Mahahual and Xcalak
The big attraction in the deep south is the Banco Chinchorro offshore.
Dreamtime Dive Resort, Km2.7 beach road; tel: 983 124 0235; www.dreamtimediving.com. Offers small groups (a maximum of 12 divers per boat) and trips to the Banco Chinchorro. Also caters for snorkelers.
XTC, KM54 Camino Costero, Xcalak; tel: 983 831 0461; www.xtcdivecenter.com. Has a license to dive Banco Chinchorro and offers a full range of courses and training, including technical diving .

Fishing
Fishermen discovered these coasts before divers did. Offshore, there is fine deep-sea fishing for barracuda, snapper, sierra, and (from April to June) marlin, sailfish, and dorado. Onshore, the flats around **Ascension Bay** south of Tulum, and further south behind **Xcalak**, contain some of the world's best fly-fishing grounds, above all for permit, tarpon, and bonefish. Also excellent for fly-fishing is the lagoon around **Holbox**, particularly for tarpon and snook.

Most dive shops will also arrange fishing trips with expert local boat captains.
3 Hermanos, Cozumel; tel: 987 107 2030; www.cozumelfishing.com. Well-equipped deep-sea and fly-fishing trips from Cozumel. In the south, **XTC** (KM54 Camino Costero, Xcalak; tel: 983 831 0461; www.xtcdivecenter.com) offers fly-fishing for bonefish and tarpon, and trolling for jacks, tuna, barracuda, grouper, and snapper.
Holbox Tarpon Club, Holbox; tel: 984 875 2144; www.holboxtarponclub.com. Alejandro "Mr Sandflea" Vega is a superb fishing guide, with many return customers.

Sailing and Kayaks
The best place to rent sailboats is **Puerto Aventuras**. Windsurfing is best between December and April, and boards are available on Isla Mujeres, Holbox, Playa del Carmen, Puerto Aventuras, and Tulum.

Kayaks can be rented on many beaches, but some of the most enjoyable places to explore are the lake at Bacalar, Xcalak, and Sian Ka'an, where the tour operator CESiaK (see page 371) offers unforgettable kayak tours.

Baseball
One characteristic feature of the Yucatán Peninsula is that its favorite sport is not soccer – as in most of Mexico – but baseball. The Mexican Baseball League (MLB) has minor league status, and the season runs from March to August. Mérida's **Leones de Yucatán** (tel: 999 926 3022; www.leones.mx) is one of the most successful teams in the league. They play in Parque Kukulcán, in the southwest of the city. Other local teams, the **Piratas de Campeche** (www.piratasdecampeche.mx) and Cancún's **Tigres de Quintana Roo** (http://tigresqr.mx/), are also worth watching.

Soccer/Fútbol
A great proportion of Cancún's population comes from other, football-crazy parts of Mexico, and in 2007 the city finally acquired its own team – when a local businessmen went out and bought one. **Atlante** (www.atlantefc.mx) is an old Mexico City club founded in 1916, when Cancún consisted of only a few huts. Since moving to Cancún, Atlante has been surprisingly successful. Games are played in the Estadio Andrés Quintana Roo, on the west side of downtown Cancún.

Golf
The Camaleón golf course at the lavish Maya Koba resort north of Playa del Carmen is the first PGA-standard course in Mexico, and hosts Mexico's only PGA tour event, the Maya Koba Golf Classic in late February each year (tel: 984 206 4653; www.mayakobagolf.com).

Conservation in Belize

Green Reef 100 Coconut Drive, Ambergris Caye (tel: 226 3254 ext. 243; www.ambergriscaye.com/greenreef). Dedicated to the conservation of Belize's marine environment. It implements management plans for bird sanctuaries and educational programs for schools in Belize.
Monkey Bay (tel: 533 3029; www.monkeyriverbelize.net). Environmental field study center in central Belize offering courses in tropical ecology. Involved in watershed protection, biological corridors, and advocacy. Offers dorm and cabin accommodation and library with wireless internet. Open to groups and individuals. Internships available.
Programme for Belize (PFB), 1 Eyre Street, PO Box 749, Belize City (tel: 227 5616; www.pfbelize.org). Manages a huge swathe of land in the Río Bravo Conservation Area, which is open to visitors by prior appointment. Cabaña and dorm accommodation available.
The Belize Coalition to Save Our Heritage (https://belizecoalition.wordpress.com. It is a coalition of environmental, industry and social organizations whose goal is to introduce a ban on oil exploration and offshore drilling in all protected areas in Belize. The organisation is collecting signatures to organise a referendum on the issue.

P

Photography

The Maya world is an extremely exciting photographic destination – the scenery, ruins, buildings, and people are all astoundingly picturesque, and the fiestas and markets unleash a riot of color.

Equipment

Memory cards for digital cameras are fairly easy to find.

What to Photograph

Be sensitive about photographing Maya people (and anyone else, for that matter). Many people object to intrusive camera-toting, so it's best to ask permission before you start snapping. Be especially sensitive if you visit highland Chiapas – the Maya there object strongly to being photographed without being asked – and always ask the permission of a parent before taking pictures of children. Children go missing every year in Guatemala, and the fear of child kidnaping for Western adoption can trigger violent reactions.

Occasionally, some locals may ask for money in exchange for a photograph, so agree on a moderate sum before you take any pictures. Similarly, be very careful not to offend local customs in religious or spiritual places including churches (photography inside the Santo Tomás church in Chichicastenango and village churches in Chiapas is completely taboo). Markets and fiestas are often ideal places to photograph people from a distance.

The lowland jungle ruins (especially Tikal) can be difficult to capture well. The acute humidity that cloaks the temples in thick mist at all times of the year can steam up your lenses. Normally, professional photographers love the "golden hours" just after sunrise and before sunset when the harsh tropical sun is tempered by longer shadows, but in the rainforest you will often have to wait for the morning sun to burn off the mist. Conversely, if you plan to climb a volcano, it's best to start as early as possible, even before dawn, in order to reach the summit before the clouds sweep in.

Underwater Photography

If you plan to snorkel, consider buying a disposable camera that's waterproof to 3 meters (10ft) or so, or bring your own waterproof case. The larger scuba schools will often have underwater cameras available for rent, and some will even video your dive for a price.

Postal Services

Guatemala

There are post offices *(correos)* in every town. Air mail takes between three days and a week to reach North America, but between one and two weeks to get to Europe. The postal service is quite reliable, but many people choose to use a courier company to send anything important overseas.

Both DHL (http://www.dhl.com.gt) and FedEx (www.fedex.com) operate in the country.

Belize

Belize City Post Office is on the north side of the Swing Bridge (near the intersection of Queen and North Front streets). Belizean stamps are beautiful, with depictions of native flora and fauna, and are highly prized by collectors. Belize provides one of the most economical and reliable postal systems in Central America. Allow around 4–7 days (for International Express Mail, longer for regular airmail) for mail to arrive in the US and around two weeks (often less) to Europe, Asia, or Australia. The post office is open weekdays 8am–noon and 1–4.30pm. For detailed information, see www.belizepostalservice.gov.bz.

The Yucatán

Post offices usually stay open all day (only mornings on Saturdays) but mail deliveries are very slow, and when receiving mail it is safest to have it sent to your hotel. Mail sent to post offices to be picked up (within 10 days) should be addressed to Lista de Correos. The Mexican post office also has a reliable courier service, Mexpost, and you should use this rather than standard mail when sending anything home.

R

Religious Services

Guatemala

Almost 40 percent of Guatemala's population are members of one of the US-based, Evangelical Protestant churches that have proliferated here in the last few decades – making Guatemala the least Catholic country in Latin America. In Guatemala City, services in English are held at (among other places) Saint James Episcopal (Avenida Castellana 4-46, Zone 8) and at Union Church (12 Calle 7-37, Zone 9). There are Catholic services in English in the private chapel at 10 Avenida A, 11-65, Las Conchas, Zone 14, and you will find the Centro Hebreo synagogue located at 7 Avenida 13-51, Zone 9. Mezquita de Aldawaa Islámica (4 Calle 7-77, Zone 9; www.aldawa.org) is one of the two mosques in Guatemala City.

Belize

Belize has a wide variety of religious denominations, including Anglican, Episcopalian, and Methodist, with the majority being Catholic. The two main places of worship in Belize City are St John's Cathedral (Albert Street; tel: 501 227 3029) and Holy Redeemer Catholic Church (North Front Street; tel: 501 227 2122). There are mosques in Belize City, Belmopan, and San Pedro.

The Yucatán

A large majority of people in the Yucatán are Catholic – with local "variations" in Maya communities – although the chapels of Protestant sects are also numerous. Catholic services in English are held at the Cristo Resucitado church (Blvd Kukulcán Km 4, Cancún; www.cristoresucitadocancun.org) and at Merida's Cathedral every Sunday at 9am. There are also several English-speaking church groups of different denominations, which often announce activities in local English-language magazines. There is a tiny but growing Muslim population in Chiapas, and a mosque (Al-Kausar Mosque) in San Cristóbal de las Casas.

S

Shopping

Guatemala

Coffee

Guatemalan coffee is said to be one of the tastiest in the world. In Guatemala City, you can buy it at specialist cafes such as El Injerto Café (www.fincaelinjerto.com), Café Divino (www.facebook.com/cafedivinoguatemala), or Rojo Cerezo (www.rojocerezo.coffee).

Jade

Guatemala is one of the world's most important producers of jade (pronounced "ha-day" in Spanish). Antigua has the best selection of stores: try **Jades S.A.** (4 Calle Oriente 34; www.jademaya.com) or **Casa del Jade** (4 Calle Oriente 10; www.lacasadeljade.com).

Jewelry

There are several smart stores in Antigua selling silver and gold. Try **Pablo's Silver Shop** (5 Calle

Poniente 12; ww.facebook.com/Platería-Pablos-Silver-Shop-235005536794/), owned by the family who founded **La Antigüeña** silver factory.

Textiles

Guatemala's unique weavings are justifiably world-famous, and are the country's premier handicrafts. The most authentic weavings are *huipiles* (women's blouses), but in recent years a massive textile industry geared to Western tastes has developed. Called *típica*, these weavings encompass everything from trousers and waistcoats to tablecloths, napkins, purses, wallets, and bedspreads made from colorful Guatemalan fabric. The *típica* industry is an important part of the Guatemala economy, which exports all over the world, and is a vital income source for many indigenous women.

To get an idea of the quality and variety of Guatemalan weavings, there's no better place than **Museo Ixchel** (https://museoixchel.org/home) in Guatemala City *(see page 116)*. You'll find another amazing collection of textiles at **Nim Po't** in Antigua (5 Av Norte 29; www.nimpotexport.com); here the weavings are for sale. Weaving co-operatives can be found throughout the country; the best ones are in the villages of Todos Santos Cuchumatán, Nebaj, Zunil, San Antonio Palopó, San Juan La Laguna, and San Antonio Aguas Calientes. One of the best places to find weavings is **Panajachel**, where there are an amazing number of stalls and weavers. Other markets include Chichicastenango, San Francisco El Alto, Antigua, and Sololá. There is also a good selection in the market in Zona 1, Guatemala City.

Wooden Masks

Ceremonial wooden masks, called *máscaras*, are another superb Guatemalan craft and have been used since Preclassic Maya times. They are still used in fiestas throughout the highlands, especially in Maya dances. You'll find mask-makers (*mascareros*) in **Chichicastenango**; there are two stores on the path to the hilltop site of Pascual Abaj. There are also some interesting pieces in the **Chichicastenango Regional Museum** and in Guatemala City in the **Popol Vuh Museum** (http://popolvuh.ufm.edu/index.php/P%C3%A1gina_Principal).

Wool

By far the best place to buy woolen blankets is the highland Maya village of **Momostenango**; ideally you should try to make it for the Sunday market.

Belize

Unlike Mexico and Guatemala, Belize has not developed such a strong souvenir industry, although it is improving. A couple of small operations around San Ignacio are teaching old skills such as Maya pottery and slate carving.

Many hotels near **San Ignacio** stock Guatemalan handicrafts. They are of course much cheaper if bought on the other side of the border.

In Belize City, gourmets would be thrilled to visit to the Caribbean Spice Belize (https://caribbeanspicebelize.com/) specialist shop offering original Belizean spices, sauces, marinades and salts which all are excellent ideas for a present. For souvenirs head to Belize Tourism Village (Fort St. no.8) with dozens of shops. Bargain hard as many items are overpriced. Some of the best handicrafts and handmade jewelry as well as countless books on Belize can be bought at the Image Factory Shop (91 North Front Street)

In **Belmopan**, there is an excellent Art Box center offering Belizean handicraft, coffee, souvenirs, woven clothes and beautiful wood furniture as well as handmade Maya baskets, bowls, vases and other ceramics. There are a few places in **San Pedro** worth glancing at, including 12 Belize (www.12belize.com) that offers only Belizean made products such as Maya bags, jewelry, leather purses as well as food, beauty products and home accessories. Another place to look for original Maya and Garifuna handicrafts and handmade products is the Garimaya Gift Shop (South Road) in Hopkins.

Specialty items are always a good bet, with many visitors taking home habanero pepper sauce, cashew nuts, coconut rum, berry or cashew wine, or Gallon Jug coffee. Local preserves (chutney and jam) made from mangoes, bananas, papayas, and other tropical fruits also make good gifts. Herbal remedies or bush medicines are sold by individual herbalists.

Look out for the delicate baskets woven from jipijapa plant fibers by Maya women, who also continue the traditions of their grandmothers making beautiful blouses with Maya animal motifs around the neck and sleeves. Groups of Maya women and their daughters set up stalls at the entrance to the archeological sites in the Maya mountains of Toledo district. You can also find a good selection of decent-quality handicrafts produced by an artisans' co-operative at the **Fajina Craft Center**, opposite the market in Punta Gorda. Keep an eye out for cloth dolls in ethnic costumes made by Garífuna women.

Hammocks made in Guatemala, both the nylon string and cotton cord variety, are sold in the better gift shops, but are much more reasonable from street vendors. Be wary of the nylon type – if poorly made, they readily come apart.

Mexican jewelry is sold at better shops, but never purchase black coral or turtle shell souvenirs: it encourages their depletion and is illegal.

The Yucatán

Mérida

Two blocks southeast of Plaza Mayor is Mérida's giant **Mercado** (market), which actually has two main buildings, Mercado Luis de Gálvez and Mercado San Benito, and spreads over a whole district, covering several blocks between calles 65, 71, 54, and 58. Its maze of stalls and shops is the best place to find every kind of traditional Yucatecan product: hammocks, baskets, belts, *huipiles* (embroidered smocks), Panama hats, *guayaberas* (loose shirts with large pockets), and many other kinds of craftwork. A special section is set aside as the **Bazar de Artesanías** (Handicrafts Bazaar; on the upper level, reached via a ramp from Calle 67, also known as 'García Rejón' among locals), but you can actually find similar things in the main market. Another place worth a visit is Alma Mexicana shop (Calle 54 No. 476) featuring vintage Mexican pictures, retro beach bags, silver jewelry, handmade bread spreads and much more.

The streets around the market are also great for finding unusual local products. Calle 65 is especially good for hammock shops. A shop that specializes in fine *guayaberas* is **Jack** (Calle 59, 507; www.guayaberasjack.com.mx).

Away from the market area, there are plenty more handicrafts shops of varying quality: **Hamacas Aguacate** (Calle 58 no. 604; http://hamacaselaguacate.com.mx) or Hammocks RADA (Calle 60 between 65 and 67; http://hammocksrada.com) have a huge choice of good hammocks. The official state **Casa de las Artesanías** (Calle 63, between calles 64 and 66) displays Yucatecan handicrafts and foodstuffs in a more tranquil setting, though at higher prices. The 100 percent Mexico shop, in the Hotel Casa San Angel (Paseo Montejo, corner of Calle 49; www.hotelcasasanangel.com), has beautiful original craftwork from all over Mexico.

Cancún

The Hotel Zone's giant shopping malls, or plazas, are Cancún landmarks. **La Isla Shopping Village** (Blvd Kukulcán Km 12.5; tel: 998 883 5025; www.laislacancun.mx) is the most attractive, with a promenade by the Nichupté lagoon, and offers the greatest variety. Not far away on the other side of the boulevard, **Kukulcán Plaza** (Blvd Kukulcán Km 13; tel: 998 885 2200; www.kukulcanplaza.mx) is the biggest mall, with a wide choice of fashion stores.

For buying tequila, the best place is the shop at **La Destilería** restaurant (Blvd Kukulcán Km 13; tel: 998 885 1087/6; www.ladestileria.com.mx). Downtown shopping is much more downmarket, with countless T-shirt shops.

Cozumel

The island has some duty-free privileges, and San Miguel has any number of shops catering to cruise-ship passengers by selling jewelry, silverware, watches, and bags, as well as handicrafts. **Los Cinco Soles** (Av Melgar, corner Calle 8; tel: 987 872 9004; www.loscincosoles.com) has Cozumel's best handicrafts range, while **Sergio's Silver** (Av. Benito Juarez 117; www.sergiosilver.com) sells beautiful Taxco silver jewelry.

Campeche

Casa de Artesanías Tukulná (Calle 10, between calles 59 and 61; tel: 981 816 9088; www.tukulna.com) is a charming, spacious shop selling a variety of Campechano craftwork.

Specialist Tours

Guatemala

Antigua Tours, Casa Santo Domingo Hotel, 3 Calle Oriente, 22, Antigua; tel: 7832 5821; www.antiguatours.net. Elizabeth Bell leads exceptional guided tours of the old capital, focusing on the history and colonial architecture.

Clark Tours, 7 Av 14-76, Zona 9, Plaza Clark, Guatemala City; tel: 2412 4700; www.clarktours.com.gt. For tours of Guatemala City and beyond.

Explore, 4 Calle and 7 Av, Zona 1, Santa Elena; tel: 7926 2375; www.exploreguate.com. Tours to Ceibal, Aguateca, and Lago de Petexbatún.

Martsam Travel, Antigua; tel: 7832 2742; www.martsam.com. Trips to Maya ruins and tailored cultural trips.

Maya Expeditions, 13 Av. 14-70, Zona 10, Guatemala City; tel: 2366 9950; www.mayaexpeditions.com. Take visitors to explore the isolated ruins of Petén, or on white-water rafting trips.

Posada Belén, 13 Calle A 10-30, zona 1, Guatemala City; tel: 2232 6178; https://posadabelenmuseoinn.com. Offer guided walking tours of the historic capital, and museum day tours.

Belize

Sun Creek Tours Front Street, Punta Gorda; tel: 501 607 6363; www.suncreeklodge.de. Superb personalized tours to Maya sites, nature reserves, and *cayes* throughout Belize, specializing in Toledo district. Also offers car rental and accommodations in comfortable, economical cabañas in attractive gardens.

Toledo Ecotourism Association PO Box 157, Punta Gorda; tel: 702 2119; www.southernbelize.com/tea.html. Tours to the Maya villages, waterfalls, and archeological sites in the lush hills of the Maya mountains.

The Yucatán

Mérida

Open-sided buses with multilingual commentary leave from Plaza Grande (in front of the cathedral) every half an hour from 9am Mon–Sat and from noon on Sun (for details, see http://turibusmerida.com/). *Calesas* (horse-drawn buggies) can be hired at Calle 61 between 58 and 60; arrange the route and price with the driver before setting out.

Iluminado/Casa K'in Tours, Calle 66, 588A, by Calle 73; tel: 999 924 3176; http://casakin.org/. Small-group tours giving a special insight into Maya culture today, with visits to villages around the city.

Mérida House and Garden Tours, from Mérida English Library, Calle 53, 524, between calles 66 and 68; tel: 999 924 8401; www.meridaenglishlibrary.com. Interesting walks in English around some of Mérida's lovely, but often closed, patios and gardens. Available on Tuesdays from Nov to March (start at 10am).

The tourist information office also offers a free walking tour of the city daily (except Sunday) at 9.30am – reserve your place in advance.

Caribbean Coast

Akumal Guide, Hotel Club Akumal Caribe, Akumal Village; tel: 984 875 9115; www.akumalguide.com. Tours to Maya ruins and natural attractions, from Akumal.

Yukatreks, 10th Avenue between 10th St. and 12th St, Playa del Carmen; tel: 984 803 1265; www.yucatreks.com. Offers a wide range of shared and private tours.

Monica Rendón Rivas, Playa del Carmen; tel: 9841 644 487. A highly personalized tours offered by Monica, a knowledgeable driver and guide.

XTC, KM 54 Camino Costero, Xcalak; tel: 983 831 0461; www.xtcdivecenter.com. Great tours, including bird-watching trips.

Campeche

Xtampak Tours, Calle 57, 14, between calles 10 and 12; tel: 981 811 6473;. Frequent tours to Edzná, adventure tours, and other trips around Campeche state.

Chiapas

Alex y Raúl, San Cristóbal de las Casas; tel: 967 678 3741; www.alexyraultours.wordpress.com. Friendly, expert guides taking daily tours to the Maya villages of Chamula and Zinacantán, and other destinations by arrangement. They can be found every day in the main plaza, in front of the cathedral, at 9.30am.

Explora Ecoturismo y Aventura, Calle 1 de Marzo 30, San Cristóbal de las Casas; tel: 967 631 7498; www.ecochiapas.com. Exciting tours to remote areas of Chiapas. Also handles bookings for the best cabaña site at Lacanjá, near Bonampak.

Kukulcán Travel, Av Juárez, near bus station, Palenque; tel: 916 345 1506; www.kukulcantravel.com. Tours to Palenque ruins, Yaxchilán, Bonampak, Agua Azul waterfalls, and other destinations in Chiapas.

T

Telephones

Guatemala

Guatemala's telecommunications network has improved greatly in recent years and can be considered reliable and efficient. Cellular coverage is extensive across most of the country, and compatible with many North American cellphones.

Due to the widespread development of the mobile network, pay phones are hard to come by these days. The cheapest way of calling abroad is to visit an internet café. Pay-as-you-go cellphones come cheap, and many visitors now buy one. Inserting a local SIM card into your own handset is also a possibility if your phone is unlocked; roaming agreements exist with some international companies. The main mobile phone providers in Guatemala are Movistar, Tigo and Claro (the latter two offering the best coverage). Please note that there are no area codes in Guatemala (to call just mark the eight-digit number). Guatemala's international dialling code is 502.

To make a collect-call (reverse charge call) to the US, Canada, and Mexico from Guatemala, tel: 147120 from a Telgua phone.

Calling Cards

These are becoming rare as mobile phones get popular. You can buy a local prepaid phone card, such as a Telgua one, which you insert in street telephones to make calls. Using an international phone charge card is another option.

Belize

Although public telephones are still available throughout Belize, they are being quickly replaced by mobiles. International phone cards are the cheapest way to make international calls when using a public telephone. Your hotel will also have fixed rates for national and international calls. Check the rate before you make the call and watch out for the service charge some hotels may add to your bill.

The country's main telephone and cellphone provider is **Belize Telemedia Ltd** (www.belizetelemedia.net), its main competitor being Smart! (www.smart-bz.com). Cellphone coverage is best in towns and cities. Most North American cellphones should work in Belize, but only tri-band or multi-band European phones will pick up a signal.

The Yucatán

By using Skype or another internet call system you can cut costs considerably. Alternatively, buy a **Ladatel** phone card to use **in** pay phones. Beware of telephones promoting easy access to worldwide destinations – they often charge exorbitant rates. Internet cafes are abundant throughout Mexico, and wi-fi networks are getting increasingly popular in hotels and restaurants in tourist resorts as well as large cities.

Cell (mobile) phone coverage is now good in most of the Yucatán Peninsula and in towns in Chiapas, but charges may be high if you use a foreign cellphone here. The main Mexican mobile phone operators are: Telcel, Movistar, and AT&T Mexico.

International Dialing Codes

Guatemala: tel: 502
Belize: tel: 501
Yucatán: tel: 52

Time zone

US Central standard time; GMT minus 6 hours.

Tourist Information

Guatemala

Inguat (www.visitguatemala.com), the Guatemalan tourist board, has offices in 13 locations. The staff are generally very helpful and will provide you with myriad glossy color brochures, which tend to be visual rather than useful. All the offices will try to point you in the right direction and solve any difficulties, but the Guatemala City, Antigua, and Quezaltenango offices are probably the most efficient.

Guatemala City: 7 Av 1-17, Zona 4, Centro Cívico; tel: (502) 2421 2854; email: info-lobby@inguat.gob.gt. Also has a kiosk at the airport

Antigua: 2 Calle Oriente No. 11 Casa del Turista; tel: (502) 2290 2800; email: info-antigua@inguat.gob.gt

Quezaltenango: 7 Calle 11-35, Zona 1, Edificio Casa de la Cultura; tel: (502) 7761 4931; email: info-xela@inguat.gob.gt

Panajachel: Calle Principal 0-87, Zona 2 Panajachel, Solola; tel: (502) 2421 2953; email: info-panajachel@inguat.gob.gt

Isla de Flores: Playa Sur, Flores, Petén; tel: (502) 4210 9992; email: info-ciudadflores@inguat.gob.gt. Also has a kiosk at Petén's airport (email: info-mundomaya@inguat.gob.gt).

Antigua has tourist police (corner of 4 Av Norte and the plaza), who can help with security problems.

Belize

Belize Tourism Board, 64 Regent Street, Belize City; tel: (501) 227 2420 (toll-free: 1-800-624 0686); www.travelbelize.org; email: info@travelbelize.org. Open 8am–noon and 1–5pm.

For further information on Belize's ecology and protected areas, contact:

Belize Audubon Society, 16 North Park Street, Belize City; tel: (501) 223 5004; www.belizeaudubon.org; email: base@btl.net. Open Mon–Fri 8am–5pm. Belize's oldest conservation organization.

The Belize Zoo and Tropical Education Center, Ladyville GPO, Belize City; tel: (501) 822 8000; email: info@belizezoo.org; www.belizezoo.org

For more detailed information about Maya archeological sites, or for permission to visit certain sites in the region, contact:

Belize Institute of Archaeology, Museum Building, Culvert Road, Belmopan; tel: (501) 822 2106; email: ia@nichbelize.org; www.nichbelize.org

The Yucatán

The **State of Yucatán** has a useful tourism website (www.yucatan.travel/). You will find offices in downtown **Mérida** (Teatro Peón Contreras, Calle 60; tel: 999 930 3760) and in **Campeche** (Casa Seis, Calle 57 no. 6 between 8 and 10, Centro Histórico; tel: 981 816 1782). The **State of Campeche** also has a comprehensive tourist website: www.campeche.travel. In other towns there are local offices that do not give information by phone but can be useful for getting maps and leaflets on local tours, such as those in **Chetumal** (Calzada del Centenario No. 622 Col. del Bosque) and **San Cristóbal de Las Casas** (Teatro Zebadua, Calle 1o de Marzo 2).

Tour operators

Guatemala

Antigua Tours, Casa Santo Domingo Hotel, 3 Calle Oriente, 22, Antigua; tel: 7832 5821; www.antiguatours.net. Elizabeth Bell leads exceptional guided tours of the old capital, focusing on the history and colonial architecture.

Clark Tours, 7 Av 14-76, Zona 9, Plaza Clark, Guatemala City; tel: 2412 4700; www.clarktours.com.gt. For tours of Guatemala City and beyond.

Explore, 4 Calle and 7 Av, Zona 1, Santa Elena; tel: 7926 2375; www.exploreguate.com. Tours to Ceibal, Aguateca, and Lago de Petexbatún.

Martsam Travel, Antigua; tel: 7832 2742; www.martsam.com. Trips to Maya ruins and tailored cultural trips.

Maya Expeditions, 13 Av. 14-70, Zona 10, Guatemala City; tel: 2366 9950; www.mayaexpeditions.com. Take visitors to explore the isolated ruins of Petén, or on white-water rafting trips.

Posada Belén, 13 Calle A 10-30, zona 1, Guatemala City; tel: 2232 6178; https://posadabelenmuseoinn.com. Offer guided walking tours of the historic capital, and museum day tours.

Belize

Sun Creek Tours Front Street, Punta Gorda; tel: 501 607 6363; www.suncreeklodge.de. Superb personalized tours to Maya sites, nature reserves, and *cayes* throughout Belize, specializing in Toledo district. Also offers car rental and accommodations in comfortable, economical cabañas in attractive gardens.

Toledo Ecotourism Association PO Box 157, Punta Gorda; tel: 702 2119; www.southernbelize.com/tea.html. Tours to the Maya villages, waterfalls, and archeological sites in the lush hills of the Maya mountains.

The Yucatán

Mérida

Open-sided buses with multilingual commentary leave from Plaza Grande (in front of the cathedral) every half an hour from 9am Mon–Sat and from noon on Sun (for details, see http://turibus-merida.com/). *Calesas* (horse-drawn buggies) can be hired at Calle 61 between 58 and 60; arrange the route and price with the driver before setting out.

Iluminado/Casa K'in Tours, Calle 66, 588A, by Calle 73; tel: 999 924 3176; http://casakin.org/. Small-group tours giving a special insight into Maya culture today, with visits to villages around the city.

Mérida House and Garden Tours, from Mérida English Library, Calle 53, 524, between calles 66 and 68; tel: 999 924 8401; www.meridaenglishlibrary.com. Interesting walks in English around some of Mérida's lovely, but often closed, patios and gardens. Available on Tuesdays from November to March (start at 10am).

The tourist information office also offers a free walking tour of the city daily (except Sunday) at 9.30am – reserve your place in advance.

Caribbean Coast

Akumal Guide, Hotel Club Akumal Caribe, Akumal Village; tel: 984 875 9115; www.akumalguide.com. Tours to Maya ruins and natural attractions, from Akumal.

Yukatreks, 10th Avenue between 10th St. and 12th St, Playa del Carmen; tel: 984 803 1265; www.yucatreks.com. Offers a wide range of shared and private tours.

Monica Rendón Rivas, Playa del Carmen; tel: 9841 644 487. A highly personalized tours offered by Monica, a knowledgeable driver and guide.

XTC, KM 54 Camino Costero, Xcalak; tel: 983 831 0461; www.xtcdivecenter.com. Great tours, including bird-watching trips.

Campeche

Xtampak Tours, Calle 57, 14, between calles 10 and 12; tel: 981 811 6473;. Frequent tours to Edzná, adventure tours, and other trips around the state of Campeche.

Chiapas

Alex y Raúl, San Cristóbal de las Casas; tel: 967 678 3741; www.alexy-raultours.wordpress.com. Friendly, expert guides taking daily tours to the Maya villages of Chamula and Zinacantán, and other destinations by arrangement. They can be found every day in the main plaza, in front of the cathedral, at 9.30am.

Explora Ecoturismo y Aventura, Calle 1 de Marzo 30, San Cristóbal de las Casas; tel: 967 631 7498; www.ecochiapas.com. Exciting tours to remote areas of Chiapas. Also handles bookings for the best cabaña site at Lacanjá, near Bonampak.

Kukulcán Travel, Av Juárez, near bus station, Palenque; tel: 916 345 1506; www.kukulcantravel.com. Tours to Palenque ruins, Yaxchilán, Bonampak, Agua Azul waterfalls, and other destinations in Chiapas

Websites

The "information revolution" is now fully activated in the Maya countries, and there are plenty of websites and online services, some of which are US-based, to add to the tourist offices and publications.

The following organisations and websites provide a useful range of travel information and news.

US

Mesoamerican Tourism Alliance, 4076 Crystal Court, Boulder, CO 80304; tel: 1-800-682 0584; www.travelwithmea.org. A good channel for discovering local eco-tourism schemes throughout the region.

UK

Canning House Library, 14/15 Belgrave Square, London SW1X 8PJ; tel: 020- 7811 5600; www.canninghouse.org/library/.The UK's largest public collection focused on Latin America; they also hold business and cultural events, courses and concerts related to the Hispanic- and Portuguese-speaking world.

Latin American Bureau, Institute of Latin American Studies, University of London Malet Street, London WC1E 7HU; tel: 020-7278 2829; www.lab.org.uk. Have an excellent library.

The Guatemalan Maya Centre, 94 Wandsworth Bridge Rd, London SW6 2TF; tel: 020-7371 5291; www.maya.org.uk. A library of over 2,000 books on the Maya.

Maya World

Defensores de la Naturaleza, 4 Av 23-01, Zona 14, Guatemala City, tel: 2310 2929; www.defensores.org.gt. Help to manage the Sierra de las Minas and other reserves.

Pronatura Península de Yucatán, Aspérgulas 22 (Antes Pino), colonia San Clemente, Delegación Álvaro Obregón, Mexico DF; tel: 5635 5054; www.pronatura.org.mx. Non-profit organisation promoting local eco-tourism projects.

ProPetén, Calle Central, Flores, Petén, Guatemala, tel: 7867 5143; www.propeten.org. Conservation

Weights and Measures

Guatemala: Generally metric, though some quirky endemic measures are still used, including *legua* (about 6.5km/ 4 miles) and *manzana* (about 0.7 hectares/2 acres).
Belize: The British Imperial system is generally used, with speed and road signs in miles. However, fuel is sold by the American gallon, and some imported goods are weighed using the metric system.
Yucatán: Metric. There are 2.2 pounds to the kilogram, 2.5cm to the inch, and 0.62km to the mile.

group fighting to protect the Petén environment. Also organizes trips into the forest.

Guatemala

www.aroundantigua.com
www.atitlan.com
www.lanic.utexas.edu
www.revuemag.com (in Spanish)
www.revuemag.com
www.visitguatemala.com

Belize

www.travelbelize.org
www.belizeit.com
www.belizefirst.com
www.belizeforum.com/belize/
www.belizenet.com
www.belizetimes.bz
www.guardian.bz

Mexico (The Yucatán)

www.cancun.travel/en/
http://mundomaya.travel/
http://mesoweb.com/
www.inside-mexico.com
www.mexonline.com
www.yucatantoday.com

Tour Operators

There are a number of excellent specialist companies that offer tours to the Maya region, often specializing in archeology, eco-tourism, adventure activities, and scuba-diving. Many will allow you to create your own bespoke trip and arrange flights and hotel reservations for you.

US

Far Horizons, tel: (415) 482 8400; www.farhorizons.com. Specialize in archeological expeditions throughout the Maya region, with expert guides.
Global Exchange, tel: 415-255 7296; www.globalexchange.org. Off-the-tourist-trail trips to Guatemala and Mexico that concentrate on increasing travelers' knowledge about the region.
International Expeditions, tel: 866 905 4259; www.ietravel.com. Archeological and eco-tourism tours throughout the Maya countries.
The Mayan Traveler, tel: 1-888-843-6292; www.themayantraveler.com. Offer a very wide range of options, from cultural tours to adventure travel.
Mayatours, tel: 1-888-349-MAYA; www.mayatour.com. Look at archeology and heritage in every part of the Maya region.
Slickrock Adventures, tel: 1-800-390 5715; www.slickrock.com. Organize sea-kayaking, rafting, snorkeling, and caving trips to Belize.
Tread Lightly Limited, tel: 800 966 9900; www.treadlightly.org. Cultural and natural history tours of the Maya region.

Canada

Adventures Abroad, tel: 1-800-665 3998; www.adventures-abroad.com. Quality low-impact tours of the main ruins and natural sites.
G Adventures, tel: +44 207 243 9878; www.gadventures.com. Good variety of trips, with camping and kayaking options, in all countries of the region.
Island Expeditions, tel: 1-800-667 1630; 1 800 667 1630. Arrange excellent diving, river- and sea- kayaking trips to Belize and the Yucatán.

UK

Cathy Matos Mexican Tours, tel: 020-8492 0000; www.mextours.co.uk. Archeological and cultural trips with a personal touch.
Imaginative Traveller, tel: 1728 862 230; www.imaginative-traveller.com. Affordable tours to Mexico and Guatemala.
Journey Latin America, tel: 020 3131 7959; www.journeylatinamerica.co.uk. Long-established company offering bespoke trips plus the Quetzal escorted tour.
Reef and Rainforest Tours, tel: 01803-866 965; www.reefandrainforest.co.uk. Nature- and scuba-diving-orientated trips to Belize. Affordable tours to Mexico and Guatemala.

V

Visas and Passports

Guatemala

All visitors require a valid passport to enter Guatemala for stays of up to 90 days; citizens other than those of the USA, UK, EU states, Canada, Australia, and New Zealand will also need a Guatemalan visa, which they can obtain from a Guatemalan embassy or consulate. The initial 90-day period can be extended by a further 90 days by visiting Migración in Guatemala City (6 Avenida 3-11, Zona 4; tel: 2411 2411).. There is no charge if you enter or leave overland at one of the more remote border crossings, though officials often demand a small fee.
Other requirements: immigration officials can also ask for proof of sufficient finances to fund your stay, though this is rare. A credit card should be adequate.

Belize

Visas are not required by most nationalities, including citizens of the United States, United Kingdom, Canada, Australia, New Zealand, South Africa, and CARICOM (Caribbean Community) countries, as well as members of the European Union. It is advisable to check with your nearest consulate or embassy before travel as requirements do change. All people from the above countries still need an international passport which is valid for at least six months, as well as an onward or round-trip air ticket.

All visitors are permitted to stay up to 90 days. To apply for an extension visit any **Immigration Office**. A moderate fee is charged, and applicants must demonstrate sufficient funds ($75 per day) for the remainder of their stay, as well as an onward ticket. Note that there's a departure tax of US$15 to leave the country, by land or sea (payable even if you're on a day trip to Tikal).

The Yucatán

All visitors, including Canadian and US citizens, require a valid passport to enter Mexico. Visitors will be issued with a tourist card upon arrival, which will be marked with the permitted length of stay (usually 180 days). The card must be retained during a stay and surrendered on leaving the country. If you lose it, you can apply for a duplicate (for a cost of around $17).

LANGUAGE

PRONUNCIATION TIPS

Although many Mexicans speak some English, it is good to have basic Spanish phrases at your disposal; in remote areas, it is essential. Most Guatemalans do not speak English, except in tourist regions. In general, locals are delighted with foreigners who try to speak the language, and they'll be patient – if sometimes amused. Pronunciation is not difficult. The following is a simplified mini-lesson:

Vowels
a as in *father*
e as in *bed*
i as in *police*
o as in *hole*
u as in *rude*

Consonants are approximately like those in English, the main exceptions being:
c is hard before **a**, **o**, or **u** (as in English), and is soft before **e** or **i**, when it sounds like **s**. Thus, *censo* (census) sounds like *senso*.
g is hard before **a**, **o**, or **u** (as in English), but before **e** or **i** a Spanish **g** sounds like a guttural **h**. **G** before **ua** is often soft or silent, so that *agua* sounds more like *awa*, and Guadalajara like *Wadalajara*.
h is silent.
j sounds like the English h.
ll sounds like y.
ñ sounds like ny, as in *señor*.
q is followed by **u** as in English, but the combination sounds like **k** instead of like **kw**. *¿Qué quiere usted?* is pronounced: Keh kee-er-eh oosted?
r is often rolled.
x between vowels sounds like a guttural **h**, eg in México or Oaxaca.
y alone, as the word meaning "and," is pronounced **ee**.
Note that **ch** and **ll** are separate letters of the Spanish alphabet; if looking in a phone book or dictionary for a word beginning with **ch**, you will find it after the final **c** entry. A name or word beginning with **ll** will be listed after the **l** entry (**ñ** and **rr** are also counted as separate letters.)

SPANISH WORDS/PHRASES

please *por favor*
thank you *gracias*
you're welcome *de nada* (literally, for nothing)
I'm sorry *lo siento*
excuse me *con permiso* (if, for example, you would like to pass) *perdón* (if, for example, you have stepped on someone's foot)
yes *sí*
no *no*
Can you speak English? *¿habla (usted) inglés?*
Do you understand me? *¿me comprende?/¿me entiende?*
this is good *(esto) está bueno*
this is bad *(esto) está malo*
good morning *buenos días*
good night/evening *buenas noches*
goodbye *adiós*
Where is...? *¿dónde está...?*
exit *la salida*
entrance *la entrada*
money *dinero*
credit card *la tarjeta de crédito*
tax *impuesto*

At the Bar/Restaurant

In Spanish, *el menú* is not the main menu, but a fixed menu offered each day (usually for lunch) at a lower price. The main menu is *la carta*.
restaurant *un restaurante*
cafe or coffee shop *un café*
Please bring me some coffee *un café, por favor*
Please bring me... *tráigame por favor...*
beer *una cerveza*
cold water *agua fría*
hot water *agua caliente*
soft drink *un refresco*
daily special *el plato del día/el especial del día*
breakfast *desayuno*
lunch *almuerzo/comida*
dinner *cena*
first course *primer plato*
second course *plato principal*
May I have more beer please? *¿más cerveza, por favor?*
May I have the bill please? *¿me da la cuenta, por favor?*
Waiter! (waitress!) *¡Señor! (¡Señorita! ¡Señora!)*

At the Hotel

Where is there an inexpensive/cheap hotel? *¿dónde hay un hotel económico/barato?*
Do you have an air-conditioned room? *¿tiene un cuarto con aire acondicionado?*
Do you have a room with bath? *¿tiene un cuarto con baño?*
Where is... *¿dónde está...*
the dining room? *el comedor?*
key *la llave*
manager *el gerente*
owner (male) *el dueño*
owner (female) *la dueña*
Can you cash a traveler's check? *¿puede cambiar un cheque de viajero?*

Shopping

department store *el departamento*
market, marketplace *el mercado*
souvenir shop *la tienda de recuerditos*
What is the price? *¿cuánto cuesta?*
It's very expensive *es muy caro*
Can you give me a discount? *¿me puede dar un descuento?*
Do you have...? *¿tiene usted...?*
I will buy this *voy a comprar esto*
Please show me another *muéstreme otro (otra) por favor*
Just a moment, please *un momento, por favor*

Transport

airplane *el avión*
airport *el aeropuerto*

ferry boat *el barco*
train station *la estación del ferrocarril*
train *el tren*
first class *primera clase*
second class *segunda clase*

Useful Phrases when Traveling

How much is a ticket to...? *¿cuánto cuesta un boleto a...?*
I want a ticket to... *quiero un boleto a...*
Please stop here *pare aquí, por favor*
Please go straight *recto, por favor*
How many kilometers is it from here to...? *¿cuántos kilómetros hay de aquí a...?*
How long does it take to go there? *¿cuánto se tarda en llegar?*
left *a la izquierda*
right *a la derecha*
What is this place called? *¿cómo se llama este lugar?*
I'm going to... *Voy a...*

On the Road

car *el carro/el automóvil*
Where is a petrol station? *¿dónde hay una gasolinera?*
a repair garage *un taller mecánico*
auto parts store *almacén de repuestos*
Fill it up, please *lleno, por favor*
Please check the oil *cheque el aceite, por favor*
radiator *el radiador*
battery *el acumulador*
I need... *necesito...*
tire *una llanta*
spare wheel *la llanta de repuesto*
towtruck *una grúa*
mechanic *un mecánico*
tune-up *una afinación*
it's broken *está roto/a*
they're broken *están rotos/as*

Taxis

taxi *el taxi*
taxi stand *el sitio de taxis*
Please call me a taxi *pídame un taxi, por favor*
What will you charge to take me to...? *¿cuánto me cobra para llevarme a...?*

Months of the Year

January enero
February febrero
March marzo
April abril
May mayo
June junio
July julio
August agosto
September septiembre
October octubre
November noviembre
December diciembre

Days of the Week

Monday *lunes*
Tuesday *martes*
Wednesday *miércoles*
Thursday *jueves*
Friday *viernes*
Saturday *sábado*
Sunday *domingo*

Numbers

1 *uno*
2 *dos*
3 *tres*
4 *cuatro*
5 *cinco*
6 *seis*
7 *siete*
8 *ocho*
9 *nueve*
10 *diez*
11 *once*
12 *doce*
13 *trece*
14 *catorce*
15 *quince*
16 *dieciséis*
17 *diecisiete*
18 *dieciocho*
19 *diecinueve*
20 *veinte*
21 *veintiuno*
25 *veinticinco*
30 *treinta*
40 *cuarenta*
50 *cincuenta*
60 *sesenta*
70 *setenta*
80 *ochenta*
90 *noventa*
100 *cien*

UNDERSTANDING CREOLE

English is the official language of Belize, but the reality on the streets is somewhat different. There are dozens of Creole languages in the Caribbean; Belize Creole (spoken by about 150,000 people) is a hybrid of English and the diverse language groups of West Africa with a smattering of words derived from Spanish and Nicaraguan Miskito. Essentially vernacular (see examples below), Creole isn't taught, written, or read, so there are no definitive spellings. As is the case with many folk languages, Creole is particularly rich in proverbs. (See the book *Creole Proverbs of Belize* for further information.)

Fowl caca white an tink e lay egg A chicken defecates white and thinks she's laid an egg. (Used in relation to a self-important person)
Dis-ya time no tan like befo time It was different in the old days.
Da weh da lee bwai mi di nyam? What was the little boy eating?

GUATEMALAN AND YUCATECAN GLOSSARY

Aguadas – seasonal water holes in lowland Maya region
Atol – drink made from maize dough or sometimes rice
Ayuntamiento – town hall
Brujo – Maya priest
Cacique – political leader (originally "native chief" in Carib)
Ceiba – sacred kapok (silk-cotton) tree
Cenote – natural well in the Yucatán
Chapín – colloquial term for a Guatemalan
Chicle – tree sap (from which chewing gum is derived)
Cofrade – *cofradía* member
Cofradía – religious group common among Maya in the Guatemalan highlands
Creole – the people and language of Afro-Caribbean Belize
Criollo – native of Spanish descent
Finca – large farm estate (Guatemalan)
Guayabera – loose shirt with large pockets
Huipil – Maya women's blouse
Indio – pejorative term for native Indian
Ladino – Meaning "Latin," used for any non-Indians, or for those Indians who have adopted Hispanic culture
Long Count – Maya calendar from late Preclassic and early Classic period
Marimba – Guatemalan musical instrument similar to a xylophone
Mestizo – person of mixed Indian and Spanish heritage, who is generally part of Hispanic or *ladino* society; common term in Mexico
Milpa – traditional maize field
Sacbe – "white road" between ancient cities or leading to a temple, especially in the Yucatán
Típica – traditional handmade Guatemalan clothes and weavings produced for tourists
Traje – traditional Guatemalan clothing
Yaxche – Yucatec Maya word for the sacred *ceiba* tree

FURTHER READING

There's a recommended book list to the region below, but useful supplementary guidebooks include Joyce Kelly's ***An Archaeological Guide to Northern Central America*** (1996) and ***An Archaeological Guide to the Yucatán*** (1993). William C. Coe's ***Tikal: A Handbook of the Ancient Maya Ruins*** (1988) is essential for in-depth exploration. In the Yucatán, Richard Perry's ***Maya Missions*** covers colonial Mexico superbly well. There are few bookshops in the Maya region that stock a good selection of the titles below, with Antigua, in Guatemala, being the exception.

MAYA CIVILIZATION

The Ancient Maya by Robert Sharer. Authoritative, formidable study of the Maya.

The Blood of Kings by Linda Schele and Mary Ellen Miller. The late Linda Schele was one of the greatest Mayanists of the late 20th century, who proved the Maya did not live a peaceful existence governed by priests and astronomers, but were warlike and obsessed with bloodletting and sacrifice. Read with ***A Forest of Kings***, written by Schele and David Freidel.

Chronicle of the Maya Kings and Queens by Simon Martin and Nikolai Grube. Based on epigraphic studies, this book reveals the historical records of several key Maya cities – including Palenque, Tikal, and Caracol – and provides biographies of many Maya kings and queens.

The Fall of the Ancient Maya by David L. Webster. Fascinating survey of what happened to the Classic Maya based on an imaginative analysis of just what Maya civilization was.

The First Maya Civilization by Francisco Estrada-Belli. Devoted to the culture and importance of the Preclassic Maya, based on research in Petén.

The Lost Chronicles of the Maya Kings by David Drew. Very readable overview of Maya history.

The Maya by Michael D. Coe. A good general introduction to the subject, and well illustrated with maps, drawings, and photographs, the ninth edition (2015) incorporates the latest findings about the Maya civilisation. Coe also wrote the influential ***Breaking the Maya Code***, which confirmed that Mayan gylphs were a written language.

Maya Civilization by T. Patrick Culbert. Concise, well-structured summary written by a leading archeologist.

Maya Civilization, editors Schmitt, de la Garza, and Nalda. Encyclopedic volume, outstandingly illustrated with lavish color plates. The subject is addressed as a series of essays, all written by notable Mayanists, covering everything from vegetation and ancient trade routes to ceramics and dynastic history. Includes discussions on the power politics of the Classic Maya and the importance of Calakmul.

Maya: The Riddle and Rediscovery of a Lost Civilization by Charles Gallenkamp. Serious but approachable analysis of Maya archeology, life, and culture including the civilization's collapse.

Mythology of the Americas by Cottie Burland, Irene Nicholson, and Harold Osborne.

Popol Vuh translated by Dennis Tedlock. The K'iche' "bible," the masterful book of creation that is both one of the most important pre-Columbian texts in the Americas and also an incredibly rich and imaginative read.

The Rise and Fall of the Maya Civilization by J. Eric S. Thompson. Another excellent introduction to the Maya, and, though many of Thompson's more utopian theories have now been overturned, much of the text still reads well. Thompson's ***Maya History and Religion*** is another useful study.

Silent Cities by Norman F. Carver.

Tales and Legends of Ancient Yucatán by Ermilio Abreu Gómez.

Yucatán Before and After the Conquest by Diego de Landa, translated by William Gates. On-the-spot reporting of Maya culture from a friar who witnessed the advance of the conquistadors.

Jungle of Stone: The Extraordinary Journey of John L. Stephens and Frederick Catherwood, and the Discovery of the Lost Civilization of the Maya by William Carlsen. A thrilling tale about the discovery of the ancient Maya cities.

TRAVEL

Beyond the Mexique Bay by Aldous Huxley. Vintage Huxley, full of purple prose, brilliant one-liners and quirky observations; the book covers Guatemala and southern Mexico.

Incidents of Travel in Central America, Chiapas and Yucatán by John L. Stephens. One of the finest travel books ever written, the book sold in its thousands when originally published and remains in print today. Stephens and artist Catherwood traveled through the region during the Central American War but still managed to rediscover many ruins (including Copán) that were unknown in the West.

Sweet Waist of America by Anthony Daniels. Mainly concerned with Guatemala, the book was written toward the end of the civil war. Daniels interviews a cross-section of Central American society including Guatemalan soldiers, priests, schoolchildren, and two military dictators.

Time Among the Maya by Ronald Wright. The finest contemporary travel account of the region, both erudite and entertaining. Wright completes the Ruta Maya "loop" between the Yucatán, Belize, Guatemala, and Chiapas, and meets an incredible assortment of characters. Combines dense study with incisive comment.

Visit Guatemala 2017: The Essential Guide to Visiting the Land of Eternal Spring by David Anicetti. The ultimate guide to Guatemala: its culture, people, traditions, and natural wonders.

HISTORY, POLITICS, AND SOCIETY

Caste Wars of the Yucatán by Nelson Reed. Fascinating account of the revolt of the Maya in the Yucatán in 1847.

Gift of the Devil by Jim Handy. Excellent opinionated history of Guatemala. An essential text, but written before the end of the civil war, so the peace accords are not covered.

Inside Guatemala; Inside Mexico; Inside Belize all by Tom Barry. Concise and reliable summaries of the Maya countries, with sections on government and politics, religious issues, society, economics, and the environment.

Rites: a Guatemalan Boyhood by Víctor Perera. An autobiography of Perera's early years in Guatemala City's tiny Jewish community. Perera's ***Last Lords of Palenque*** is a brilliant study of Mexico's Lacandón Maya.

MODERN MAYA CULTURE

Deciding to be Legal: a Maya Community in Houston by Jacqueline Maria Hagan. Interesting account of the struggles and successes of Maya immigrants as they adjust to life in El Norte.

I, Rigoberta Menchú – an Indian Woman in Guatemala by Rigoberta Menchú. Extremely harrowing autobiography of the K'iche' Maya Nobel Prize winner, who lost her mother, father, and brothers in the civil war. The second volume, ***Crossing Borders***, is a much lighter, more optimistic read, dealing with her life in exile and her return to Guatemala.

The Maya Atlas. An insightful collaboration between academics and villagers, the atlas documents the history and everyday experiences of the Toledo Maya of Belize.

The Maya of Guatemala by Philip Wearne. Concise study of the history and culture of the Guatemalan Maya.

Son of Tecún Umán; Campesino: The Diary of a Guatemalan Indian; Ignacio; Joseño by James D. Sexton. Superb four-part autobiography of a Tz'utujil Maya from Lago de Atitlán told over a 20-year period during the civil war.

Zapatistas: Making Another World Possible by John Ross. Written by a well-connected journalist, this book deals with the ongoing Maya rebellion in Chiapas.

A Journal from the End of Times: On the Trail of the Modern Maya by Grant J. Riley. A fascinating tale documenting daily struggles of the Central American indigenous people.

LITERATURE

Beka Lamb by Zee Edgell. Fascinating story of life in 1950s Belize.

Belize 1798, The Road to Glory by Emory King. Bombastic account of the Battle of St George's Key, written by one of Belize's larger-than-life American settlers. King is also the author of **Hey Dad, This is Belize**.

The Bridge in the Jungle by B. Traven. Compelling tale of death in a Maya village in Chiapas, written in the 1920s.

Long Night of White Chickens by Francisco Goldman. Brilliant debut novel by the Guatemalan-American Goldman. It's an incredibly intricate tale of illegal baby adoptions, murder, and death squads that's set in Guatemala City and Boston.

On Heroes, Lizards and Passion by Zoila Ellis. Insightful tales of life in Belize, written by a local.

Return of the Maya by Gaspar Pedro González. The fascinating tale of a Q'anjob' al Maya, and his crisis of identity in *ladino*-dominated Guatemala, following his return from exile in Mexico. This book claims to be the first novel by a Maya writer.

ENVIRONMENT

A Guide to the Birds of Mexico and Northern Central America by Steve N.G. Howell. The definitive reference book of the region's birds.

OTHER INSIGHT GUIDES

Insight Guide Belize. The definitive guide to Belize. Superb features, breathtaking photography, and indispensable travel information.

Insight Guide Mexico. In-depth coverage of the entire country from Baja California to Chetumal, with stunning photography and maps, and revealing analysis.

Insight Guide Central America. An overview of all Central American countries, with stunning photography and maps, and indispensable travel information.

Send Us Your Thoughts

We do our best to ensure the information in our books is as accurate and up-to-date as possible. The books are updated on a regular basis using local contacts, who painstakingly add, amend and correct as required. However, some details (such as telephone numbers and opening times) are liable to change, and we are ultimately reliant on our readers to put us in the picture.

We welcome your feedback, especially your experience of using the book "on the road". Maybe you came across a great bar or new attraction we missed.

We will acknowledge all contributions, and we'll offer an Insight Guide to the best letters received.

Please write to us at:
Insight Guides
PO Box 7910
London SE1 1WE

Or email us at:
hello@insightguides.com

CREDITS

PHOTO CREDITS

akg images 43, 45
Alamy 8B, 158, 159B, 160T, 175, 231, 232T, 233, 249, 251, 340
Alex Havret/Apa Publications 6ML, 6MR, 7TL, 10/11, 18B, 48, 50, 52, 56, 58, 59, 61, 96, 98, 262, 263T, 263B, 264B, 264T, 265, 268, 269, 270, 271, 272, 273, 274/275, 276, 277, 280, 281, 282, 283, 284, 285, 286, 287, 288/289T, 289BL, 289TR, 290, 291, 292, 293, 300, 301T, 301B, 304, 305, 308B, 308T, 311, 312, 313, 316, 317, 318, 319, 320, 321T, 321B, 322, 323, 324, 325, 326, 327, 328, 329T, 329B, 332, 333, 334, 335, 336, 337, 338, 339, 341, 342, 343, 344T, 344B, 345, 346, 347, 348T, 348B, 349, 350T, 351, 359, 360, 376
Andreas M. Gross 42, 47TR
AP/Press Association Images 85, 193
AWL Images 154, 222, 223, 228, 232B, 253B, 309
Bigstock 41
Corbis 33B, 38, 63, 92, 194, 266/267, 278, 306, 307, 310
Corrie Wingate/Apa Publications 6BL, 6BR, 7TR, 7BL, 7BR, 7ML, 7MR, 8T, 9TR, 9BR, 9TL, 12/13, 14/15, 16, 17T, 17B, 18T, 19, 21, 22, 23, 24, 25, 26, 27, 30T, 30B, 33T, 35, 37, 39, 46/47T, 46BR, 47ML, 47BR, 47BL, 49, 51, 53, 54, 55, 57, 60, 64/65, 66/67, 72, 73T, 73B, 74B, 74T, 75, 76/77, 82, 84, 86, 87, 88, 89, 90, 91, 94, 95, 97, 100/101, 106, 107T, 107B, 111, 114T, 114B, 115T, 116, 118, 119, 120, 121, 123, 124, 125, 126T, 126B, 127, 128, 129, 131, 132, 133, 134, 135, 136, 137B, 137T, 138B, 138T, 139, 140, 141, 142, 143, 144/145T, 144BR, 144BL, 145ML, 145BR, 145BL, 145TR, 146, 147, 151, 152, 153, 156, 157, 159T, 160B, 161T, 161B, 162, 164, 165, 166, 168, 169T, 169B, 171T, 171B, 172L, 173, 174, 176/177T, 176BL, 177ML, 177BR, 177BL, 177TR, 178/179, 180/181, 184, 185T, 185B, 186B, 186T, 187, 188/189, 195, 201, 202/203T, 202BR, 202BL, 203BL, 210, 211, 220, 221T, 221B, 224, 226T, 226B, 227B, 227T, 229, 234BL, 234TL, 237, 238, 239, 241, 242, 243, 244, 245, 246, 247, 248B, 248T, 250B, 250T, 252, 253T, 254, 354, 356B, 356T, 357, 358
Darrell Jones 46BL
Dreamstime 200
Fotolia 204, 207, 289BR
Fotoseeker 203BR, 203TR, 230, 234BR
Getty Images 4, 62, 68/69, 102/103, 104/105, 110, 115B, 176BR, 182/183, 199, 209, 212/213, 214/215, 235, 294/295, 296/297, 314
iStock 9BL, 34, 40, 93, 113, 117, 196, 197, 203ML, 208, 236, 240, 255, 256/257, 258/259, 260/261, 279, 289ML, 298/299, 315, 330, 331, 352B, 353, 378
Jamie Marshall/Guatemalan Maya Centre 20, 79, 81, 83
Mary Evans Picture Library 44, 78, 80, 190
McPHOTO 206
Mexico Tourism 288BR
Mockford & Bonetti/Apa Publications 288BL
Public domain 28/29
Rex Features 31T
Robert Harding 0/1, 150B
Shutterstock 36, 216/217
TIPS Images 99, 198, 205, 350B, 352T
TopFoto 31B, 32, 172R

COVER CREDITS

Front cover: Ruins of Palenque, Mexico *Shutterstock*
Back cover: Ambergris Caye, Belize, *Corrie Wingate/Apa Publications*
Front flap: (from top) Iguana, Guatemala *Corrie Wingate/Apa Publications*; Wall of Skulls, Chichen Itza *Shutterstock*; Market in Chiapas *iStock*; Tobacco Caye, Belize *orrie Wingate/Apa Publications*
Back flap: Tulum beach *Alex Havret/ Apa Publications*

INSIGHT GUIDE CREDITS

Distribution
UK, Ireland and Europe
Apa Publications (UK) Ltd;
sales@insightguides.com
United States and Canada
Ingram Publisher Services;
ips@ingramcontent.com
Australia and New Zealand
Woodslane; info@woodslane.com.au
Southeast Asia
Apa Publications (SN) Pte;
singaporeoffice@insightguides.com
Worldwide
Apa Publications (UK) Ltd;
sales@insightguides.com
Special Sales, Content Licensing and CoPublishing
Insight Guides can be purchased in bulk quantities at discounted prices. We can create special editions, personalised jackets and corporate imprints tailored to your needs.
sales@insightguides.com
www.insightguides.biz

Printed in China by CTPS

First Edition 2000
Fourth Edition 2018

www.insightguides.com

Editor: Carine Tracanelli
Author: Iain Stewart
Head of Production: Rebeka Davies
Update Production: Apa Digital
Picture Editor: Tomasz Schmidt
Cartography: original cartography Cosmographics, updated by Carte

CONTRIBUTORS

Iain Stewart is an expert travel writer on Central America and has authored many books on the region.

This edition builds on foundations laid by an impressive team of experts: **Nick Caistor**, **Krystyna Deuss**, **Phil Gunson**, **Ellen McRae**, **Barbara MacKinnon**, **Neil Rogers**, **Simone Clifford-Jaeger**, **Ian Peedle**, **Jo Clarkson**, **Tony Perrottet**, **Karla Heusner**, **Tony Rath**, **John Wilcock**, and **Chloe Sayer**.

ABOUT INSIGHT GUIDES

Insight Guides have more than 45 years' experience of publishing high-quality, visual travel guides. We produce 400 full-colour titles, in both print and digital form, covering more than 200 destinations across the globe, in a variety of formats to meet your different needs.

Insight Guides are written by local authors, whose expertise is evident in the extensive historical and cultural background features. Each destination is carefully researched by regional experts to ensure our guides provide the very latest information. All the reviews in **Insight Guides** are independent; we strive to maintain an impartial view. Our reviews are carefully selected to guide you to the best places to eat, go out and shop, so you can be confident that when we say a place is special, we really mean it.

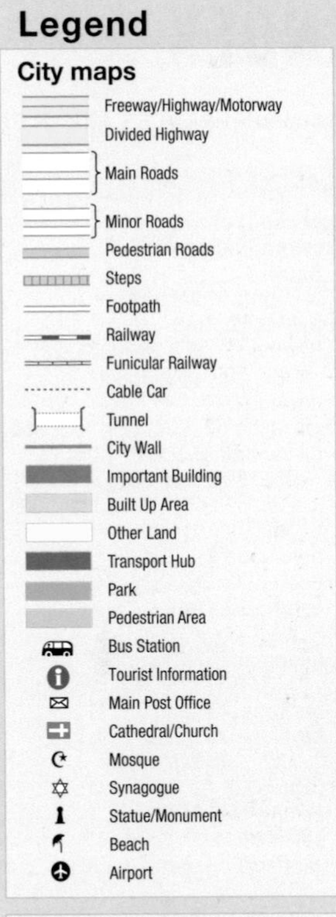

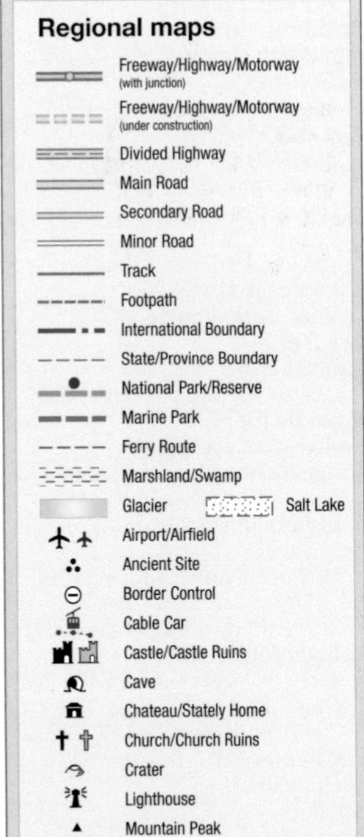

INDEX

MAIN REFERENCES ARE IN BOLD TYPE

D

E

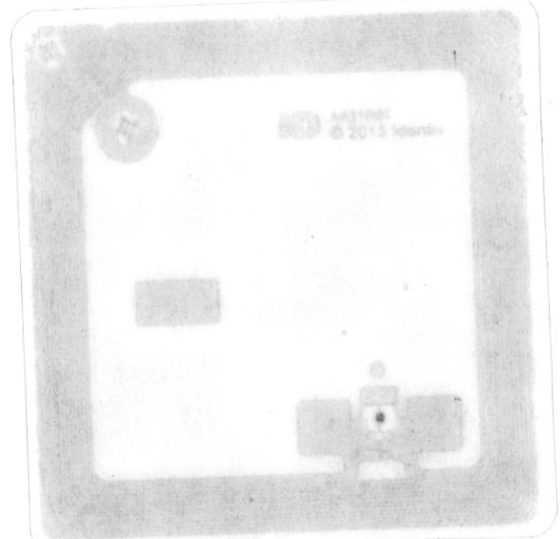

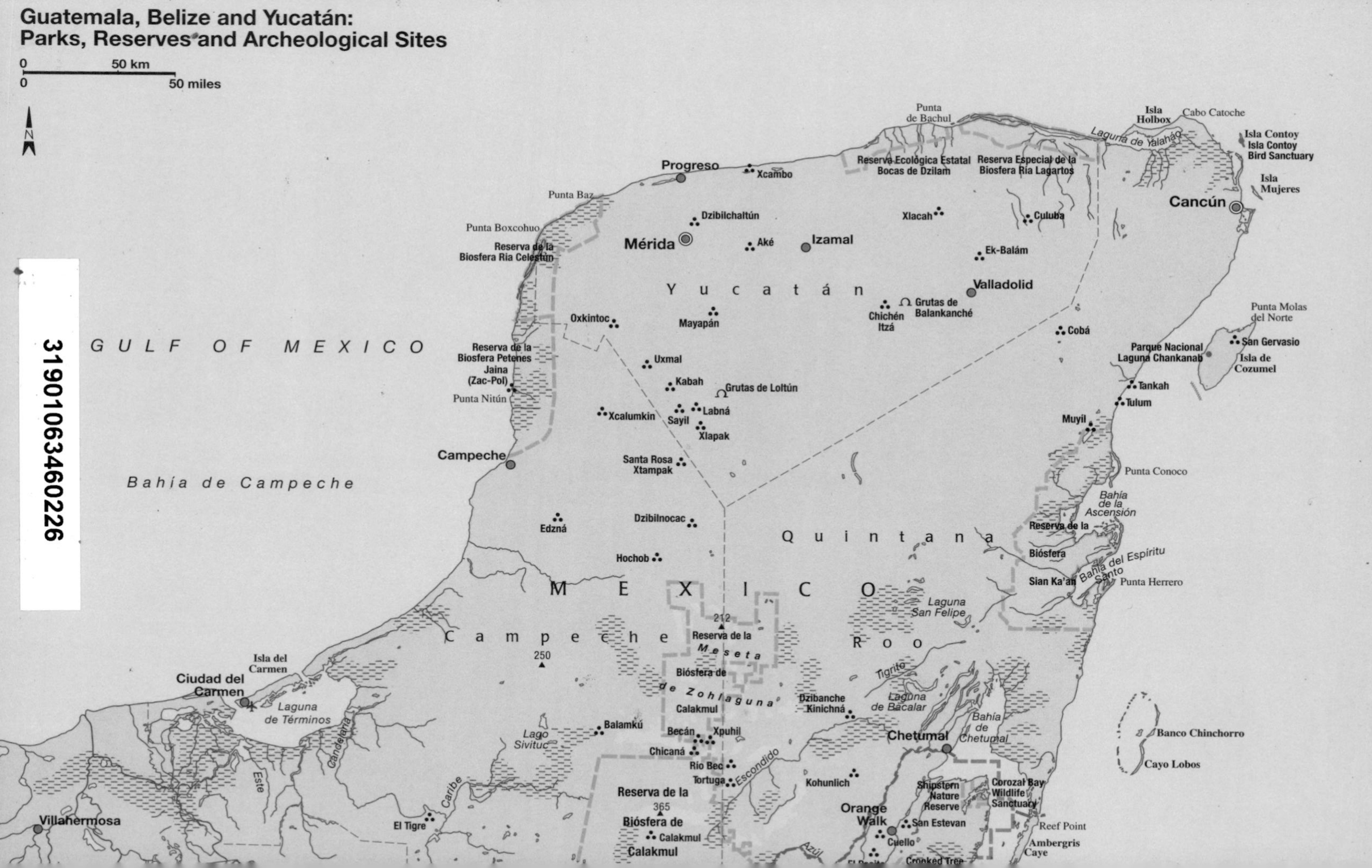
Guatemala, Belize and Yucatán:
Parks, Reserves and Archeological Sites
0 50 km
0 50 miles
N
GULF OF MEXICO
Bahía de Campeche
Punta de Bachul
Isla Holbox
Cabo Catoche
Laguna de Yalahao
Isla Contoy
Isla Contoy Bird Sanctuary
Isla Mujeres
Cancún
Progreso
Xcambo
Reserva Ecológica Estatal Bocas de Dzilam
Reserva Especial de la Biosfera Ría Lagartos
Punta Baz
Punta Boxcohuo
Reserva de la Biosfera Ría Celestún
Dzibilchaltún
Mérida
Aké
Izamal
Xlacah
Culuba
Ek-Balám
Valladolid
Yucatán
Chichén Itzá
Grutas de Balankanché
Oxkintoc
Mayapán
Punta Molas del Norte
San Gervasio
Isla de Cozumel
Parque Nacional Laguna Chankanab
Cobá
Reserva de la Biosfera Petenes
Jaina (Zac-Pol)
Punta Nitún
Uxmal
Kabah
Grutas de Loltún
Xcalumkin
Sayil
Labná
Xlapak
Tankah
Tulum
Muyil
Campeche
Santa Rosa Xtampak
Punta Conoco
Bahía de la Ascensión
Edzná
Dzibilnocac
Reserva de la Biósfera Sian Ka'an
Quintana Roo
Bahía del Espíritu Santo
Punta Herrero
Hochob
MEXICO
Laguna San Felipe
212
Campeche
Reserva de la Biósfera de Calakmul
Meseta de Zohlaguna
250
Isla del Carmen
Ciudad del Carmen
Laguna de Términos
Tigrito
Laguna de Bacalar
Bahía de Chetumal
Dzibanche Kinichná
Chetumal
Banco Chinchorro
Cayo Lobos
Balamkú
Lago Sivituc
Becán
Xpuhil
Chicaná
Río Bec
Tortuga
Escondido
Kohunlich
Candelaria
Este
Caribe
Shipstern Nature Reserve
Corozal Bay Wildlife Sanctuary
Reserva de la Biósfera de Calakmul
365
Calakmul
Orange Walk
San Estevan
Reef Point
Ambergris Caye
Villahermosa
El Tigre
Cuello
Crooked Tree
Azúl